Neither Hee
Nor Any of His Companie
Did Return Againe

Neither Hee Nor Any of His Companie Did Return Againe

Failed Colonies *in the* Caribbean *and* Latin America 1492–1865

David MacDonald *and* Raine Waters

WESTHOLME
Yardley

Facing title page: *Americae sive qvartae orbis partis nova et exactissima descriptio* ("A new and most exact description of America, or the fourth part of the world"), detail, Antwerp, c. 1562. (*Library of Congress*)

Westholme Publishing, LLC
904 Edgewood Road
Yardley, Pennsylvania 19067
Visit our Web site at www.westholmepublishing.com

ISBN: 978-1-59416-399-9
Also available as an eBook.

Printed in the United States of America.

When any group sees itself as the bearer of civilization this very belief will betray it into behaving barbarously.

—Simone Weil

Juan Corteso arrived at the river of Amazones or Orellana with three hundred men. He marched up into the country, but neither hee nor any of his companie did return againe.

—Laurence Keymis, 1596

Contents

Illustrations

ILLUSTRATIONS

Introduction

Colonies made Spain rich through gold and silver looted from the Native cultures of Mexico and Peru, silver mines in Bolivia and Mexico, emeralds from Colombia, pearls from Venezuela, rare and exotic products such as tobacco, sugar, and dyewood, and even humble products such as hides. Other European monarchies and merchants sent out colonizing expeditions in the hope of garnering a share of the resources of the New World. The primary age of colonization in the Caribbean and South America was the sixteenth and seventeenth centuries. All European settlements founded in the New World faced a variety of challenges: food supply, inconsistent support from Europe, leadership, ignorance of the area colonized, irrational expectations, religious discord, the multinational population of many colonies, relations with Native peoples, slave revolts, pirates, and frequent violent national rivalries. The colonies that succeeded and those that failed faced the same challenges, although in differing degrees and circumstances. The margin between survival and disaster was always small, and there were few chances to succeed and always the risk of failure.

The supply of food was the primary concern of almost all colonies. In the age of colonization, Europeans could not reliably preserve and transport large quantities of wholesome food. Shipments were often delayed, insufficient in quantity, and poorer in quality than the colonists needed. Food was preserved by a variety of imperfect techniques, such as drying, salting, and larding, sometimes in combination. Such provisions often lacked important nutrients, contained unhealthy levels of salt and other preservatives, and deteriorated during transit in the leaky, ill-ventilated holds of ships. Colonists often arrived at the wrong season to plant crops, and when they could plant, they often attempted to grow familiar European crops in new and different climates with poor success. Colonists also frequently had food prejudices that delayed their adoption of native crops until compelled by necessity.

As we described in our previous volume on failed North American colonies*, the age of colonization was also an age of European economic expansion, but the resources of governments were seldom equal to the demands on them, particularly the frequent wars that characterized the era. Usually short of money, national monarchies were frequently unwilling or unable to bear the full costs of colonization, but members of the aristocracy, gentry, and wealthy merchants participated in these ventures in the expectation of profits. They usually anticipated gains immediately or in a very short time, but even the most successful colonies usually took several years to become self-sustainable and longer to become profitable. Investors were quick to become discouraged and withdraw support.

Colonial leaders were often selected according to influence at the royal court, exercised either personally or through family, friends, and allies. Military experience was also an important consideration, as conflicts with Native Americans or other Europeans were frequent. Other personal qualities or lack thereof were often ignored. The distance and the slow communications with the homelands ensured that colonial commanders had a great degree of independence, and that too often provided the opportunity for commanders to behave autocratically and even atrociously. Usually, commanders proved more interested in acquiring personal wealth by looting Indians and raiding for slaves than in pursuing reasonable plans to promote a colony's self-sufficiency and economic development.

The age of colonization was also an age of religious conflict in Europe and in its colonies. The primary friction was, of course, between Catholicism and Protestantism, but deep divisions existed within each

---

* *We Could Perceive No Sign of Them: Failed Colonies in North America, 1526–1689* (Yardley, PA: Westholme Publishing, 2020)

of these groups. Particularly in France, moderate Catholics contended with conservative Catholics, and even in conservative Spain, Catholic orders such as the Capuchins and Jesuits squandered opportunities and resources in bitter opposition to one another. In England, differences between conservative elements in the Church of England and the Puritans contributed to the circumstances that led to civil war and the death of a king, even while the Puritan movement itself was notoriously riven by theological divisions. Radical Dutch Calvinists contended with moderate, pragmatic Dutch Calvinists. Jews played important roles in the age of colonization, but everywhere they suffered from discrimination and achieved a modicum of tolerance only where and when they were deemed useful. The Inquisition and other religious authorities in Spain and Portugal and in their colonies fiercely persecuted Jews and *conversos*, those who had been forcibly converted to Catholic Christianity. During the age of colonization, religion often reflected not only contrasting theologies but also economic, social, and national differences.

Colonists frequently embarked with little understanding of the conditions they would encounter. Those who described conditions and who organized colonizing expeditions consistently underestimated the challenges and overestimated anticipated benefits. Disappointment often led to desertion, as colonists returned to their homeland or fled to other colonies, and, more importantly, lack of appropriate preparation led to deaths and failure. Colonists were frequently recruited from diverse sources, and the combination of nationalities, social classes, and religious sects contributed to unrest and conflict. The frequent infusion of refugees of diverse origins from other colonies also contributed to tensions.

The age of colonization in the Caribbean and South America was a period of numerous wars fought in Europe by the emerging national monarchies. These conflicts were also fought in the New World, as European powers issued letters of marque licensing privateers to prey on the ships of hostile nations and to use ports to market their loot and reequip their vessels. Privateers often acted much like pirates. Only a scrupulous privateer, a rare creature, would pass on acquiring a rich prize, especially if even a questionable pretext could be found, such as maintaining that a consignment aboard a captured ship belonged to a merchant from a hostile nation. Privateering was a source of great potential profit, but with consequentially great risk, as privateers were actively hunted by opposing forces and seldom granted quarter. Even when peace was made in Europe, attacks on shipping often continued in the Caribbean as "no peace beyond the line," a phrase indicating that despite treaties that were observed in Europe, the Caribbean was still an area of conflict. Piracy, without any pretense of loyalty to any country, was also common, particularly during intervals of peace when armies and navies frequently disbanded soldiers and mariners, leaving them without means of honest employment and sometimes stranded in colonial ports. Privateers and pirates not only captured ships but also raided colonies. Fellow Europeans proved as dangerous to colonists as hostile Natives.

The Native peoples of the Caribbean and South America often re-sisted predatory European colonization vigorously until their numbers were severely reduced by warfare, slave raids, and European diseases. Indian cultures that survived were those that most effectively opposed domination by colonists. All nationalities practiced slavery, and regret-tably few condemned abuses inherent to slavery; opposition to all slav-ery was even rarer and of deplorably little influence. Initially, colonists enslaved Indians, but as Indian populations declined, colonists im-ported African slaves in large numbers, used primarily to farm crops of tobacco, indigo, cotton, and particularly sugar. The specter of slave revolts haunted colonists and led to repressive and brutal treatment of slaves, which failed to lessen but rather increased the likelihood of re-volts. Slaves often escaped and sometimes were able to create their own settlements that existed in a state of endemic warfare with Euro-pean colonists.

Although the sixteenth and seventeenth centuries were the period of primary colonization, settlements were founded still later, even well into the nineteenth century. These later colonies were of a different sort. They were founded on territories already securely claimed by es-tablished powers, and they often had no overt intentions of establish-ing themselves as independent political units or remaining politically connected to their homeland. Rather, they intended to establish reli-gious or cultural enclaves. Confederates sought to recreate a defeated and disappearing culture, and British colonists hoped to find in Poy-ais—a rare example claiming independence—an idealized version of their homeland offering greater opportunities. In their failure, these later attempts are in some ways even sadder than the earlier attempts.

A Note about Names

In recent years, attempts to find an acceptable term of general reference for the indigenous people of the Americas have produced no good resolution. Native people, of course, are best designated as members of a specific tribe, band, or community. Many familiar names for tribes, however, are not those used by members themselves, but rather imposed by other, frequently hostile groups, while the proper names often remain unrecognizable to modern readers.

The term "Indian" is, of course, an absurdity, based on Columbus's mistaken belief that he had reached the Far East, but it remains in general use, even among Native people who generally do not find it pejorative. Russell Means, who became a prominent member of the American Indian Movement, accepted and used "Indian" in preference to "Native American." Both, however, obscure basic differences among groups. Nevertheless, "Native American" has gained some currency, as opposed to "Amerindian," which enjoyed brief popularity but has faded, as have a number of other usages. The terms "Native" and "indigenous person" are useful in cases of ambiguity, uncertainty, or to avoid repetition. We capitalize Native in respect, as in Paul Kelton, *Epidemics and Enslavement: Biological Catastrophe in the Native Southeast, 1492–1715.*

Most Indian tribal, band, and community names are mass nouns, and as such, one form serves as singular and plural. So, for example, we write "Guale" rather than "Guales" and "Etchemin" rather than "Etchemins."

Similar problems arise in referring to people of African origin or descent. Here we have conformed to the general current consensus, "Black."

ONE

Columbus's Failures:
La Navidad *and* La Isabela
(1492–1497)

The First Voyage and the Establishment of La Navidad

Christopher Columbus first landed in the Americas on an island in the Bahamas that he named San Salvador. Most scholars have concluded that the location of Columbus's landfall was Watling Island, renamed San Salvador in the twentieth century. For some, however, the site of Columbus's first landfall in 1492 remains a matter of dispute, and advocates of alternate sites often press their claims with vehemence that tolerates no dialogue.

Columbus met the Taino people on San Salvador and elsewhere in the Caribbean. They spoke a language of the Arawakan group, but they were far different from the fierce Arawak people of northern South America. Columbus praised the Taino as kind and gentle, but he added ominously that they were unarmed, fled confrontation, and could be easily enslaved. Columbus kidnapped Native people to exhibit in Spain and train as translators, the first of many explorers and colonists who routinely did so. The sources do not reveal exactly how many he captured, but the number was certainly more than twelve and most likely more than twenty. A few escaped, some died on the return to Spain, and more died there. Columbus was a man of his age, and the only model he had of interaction with non-Christian people involved subjugation. Christians enslaved Muslims captured during Mediterranean wars, and Muslims similarly enslaved Christians. Europeans purchased and captured slaves in Africa even before the discovery of America and enslaved the natives of the Canary Islands, the Guanches. The Roman Church condoned such slavery, which seemed to be supported biblically. The European sense of cultural and religious superiority and enthusiasm for exploiting the Native peoples of the New World was evident from the beginning.

After investigating several smaller islands, Columbus came to Cuba. There, on November 22, Martín Alonso Pinzón, commander of the *Pinta*, one of Columbus's ships, set sail to the east without permission. Pinzón was apparently pursuing tales of abundant gold on the isle of Babeque, modern Great Inagua, second largest of the Bahamas Islands. The riches of Babeque ultimately proved to be imaginary, and Pinzón did not rejoin Columbus until the second week of January. After sailing along the coast of Cuba, Columbus steered for what has become modern Haiti, where he arrived in the evening of December 5, 1492. Seeing a resemblance to Spain, Columbus named it *La Isla Española*. Pietro Martire d'Anghiera, an Italian writer active in Spain in the late fifteenth and early sixteenth centuries, rendered the name in Latin as *Hispaniola*.

Columbus was greeted enthusiastically by the Natives, and Guacanagarí, the primary *cacique* (leader) in northwestern Haiti, exchanged messengers with Columbus. The Spanish had acquired a few words of the Taino language, and the Indians that Columbus had abducted had acquired a little Spanish, but communication was still deficient, made more so by differences in dialect. Guacanagarí sent presents to Columbus, including gold that excited the Spanish cupidity, and invited Columbus to visit his village farther up the coast.

For two days and nights, curious Indians swarmed over the ships before Columbus sailed along the coast toward the rendezvous with Guacanagarí, battling adverse current and wind. After a tiring day, the *Santa María* and the *Niña*, Columbus's other two ships, anchored on Christmas Eve in calm water and light air in a bay on the northern coast of Haiti. After Columbus turned in for the evening, Juan de la Cosa, officer of the watch and part owner of the *Santa María*, also retired for the night, foolishly leaving only a boy at the tiller. Late in the night, the *Santa María* drifted onto a coral reef and panic ensued,

Area of the *Santa María* shipwreck and La Navidad on the northern coast of Hispaniola, in modern Haiti.

squandering any opportunity to save the ship. Swells battered the hull until seams opened, and the *Santa María* remained impaled on the reef. Efforts turned to recovering the cargo and much of the wood of the ship itself. Guacanagarí sent men and canoes to help salvage all that could be saved. The loss of the flagship presented a major problem. The *Pinta* was missing, and it was not known whether it would ever be seen again. The *Niña*, much smaller than the *Santa María*, could not accommodate forty additional men stranded by the loss of the *Santa María* and the provisions necessary to feed them on the return to Spain. Columbus had no intention of founding a settlement on his first voyage, but the shipwreck made that imperative.

Near the site of the shipwreck and a little inland, Columbus had the men construct a fort and habitations largely out of the timbers and planks of the *Santa María*. He named the settlement La Navidad in memory of the Christmas shipwreck, and there thirty-nine men remained until Columbus returned on his second voyage. Men eagerly volunteered to remain at La Navidad undoubtedly attracted by gold and the friendly Taino women. Columbus left the men well equipped with weapons, tools, and food, including seeds to be planted in the spring, and he also left the *Santa María*'s boat and instructed the colonists to use it to explore the coast to find the source of the Indians' gold and to locate a better harbor where a permanent colony could be planted.

On January 4, 1493, Columbus set sail, and two days later he fell in with the *Pinta*, whose captain, Pinzón, tried to excuse his absence. Columbus was unimpressed, and animosity existed between the two. After a little more exploration along the northern coast of Española, Columbus set sail for Spain on January 16.

The Second Voyage: Disaster at La Navidad

Well received in Spain, Columbus set forth on this second voyage with an armada of seventeen ships on September 25, 1493, with the goals of establishing a permanent settlement, converting the Natives, and finding gold, though events would show these were not the order of their priority. The flagship of the fleet was named *Santa María*, like the lost flagship of the first voyage. The new *Santa María*, nicknamed *Mariagalante* (Bold Maria) by sailors, was much larger than the older ship. Many of the other ships, however, were small and of shallow draft, suitable for exploring in shoal waters and among coral reefs. The expedition consisted of about twelve hundred men, although a few sources suggest as many as fifteen hundred. In addition to the sailors, there were colonists to establish a permanent settlement, bureaucrats to govern it, ecclesiastics to minister to the members of the expedition and convert the Natives, and some two hundred gentlemen volunteers who possessed status but few skills.

On November 3, after a rapid and almost trouble-free crossing, Columbus's fleet sighted land, the island of Dominica. Proceeding along the chain of islands to the north and west, Columbus came at length to the large island he called San Juan Bautista, modern Puerto Rico, and from there he proceeded to Hispaniola. When men went ashore about thirty-five miles from La Navidad to scout for a site for a permanent location, they found four unburied bodies, much decomposed. One of the dead seemed to have the remnant of a beard, an indication he was Spanish. Farther along the coast a group of Indians appeared, led by Guacanagarí's cousin, who claimed that other than a few who died of disease and a couple of men killed in disputes, the others were alive and well. He also indicated that Guacanagarí had not greeted Columbus because he had been wounded in a confrontation with another cacique, but he eagerly awaited him at his village. The interpreter, however, reported that the other Indians said the men left at La Navidad were all dead. Columbus was incredulous, but when he arrived at La Navidad the next day, he found the fort and the habitations burned and no sign of life. Guacanagarí's cousin came aboard again, and this time he admitted that all the men were dead, killed, he claimed, by the cacique Caonabó and his men. While Columbus and others investigated the area around the fort, Indians pointed out the moldering corpses of eleven Spanish. A small Indian village in the vicinity contained material taken from the fort and an anchor salvaged from the wreck of the *Santa María*.

At Guacanagarí's village, Columbus found the cacique in bed, his leg heavily bandaged. He reported that after Columbus had sailed for home, the men abandoned all sense of discipline and decency and took women from the Taino, three or four for each man. Finally, Caonabó and his ally Mayreni killed the Spanish and burned the fort. Guacanagarí maintained that he had been wounded fighting Caonabó, but when Columbus had Guacanagarí's leg bandage removed there was no trace of an injury. Guacanagarí's story received only slightly more credence when he exhibited one of his villagers who had a spear wound.

In the following days, more details emerged about the end of La Navidad. After Columbus's departure, the men began to kidnap Native women and quarrel over them and gold. After several murders, they divided into gangs, some traveling inland searching for more women and gold. Caonabó destroyed one group and then attacked and destroyed La Navidad, killing a few there and driving others into the sea where they drowned. Other groups that had been scouring the interior for gold were also attacked and obliterated. Whether Guacanagarí's people played a role in the destruction cannot be resolved.

Many of Columbus's men felt the cacique's faked wound indicated his culpability in the massacre and urged Columbus to seize and kill him, but Columbus chose to believe Guacanagarí—or at least claim he did. In any case, the men were dead, and it was now apparent that the Taino, whom Columbus had thought so timid and cowardly, could rise in anger when sufficiently provoked. Columbus also realized that if the stories of his men's' behavior were true, as seemed likely, then they brought their destruction upon themselves. Moreover, Columbus was also conscious that he and his companions were outnumbered, that he needed Native allies, and that a conflict with Caonabó, whose territory was supposedly a source of gold, was inevitable in the foreseeable future. Guacanagarí, apparently aware of Spanish suspicions, quietly left the area along with his attendants and continued to avoid the Spanish for some time, although he eventually aided Columbus against other caciques.

The Second Voyage: The Founding and Abandonment of La Isabela

Once the sad fate of La Navidad had been resolved, Columbus faced the pressing need to find a site for the proposed permanent settlement. The area around La Navidad was low lying, subject to flooding, ill omened, and—perhaps most importantly—not close to the area of inland Hispaniola reputed to be the source of gold. Columbus set sail along the northern coast of the island only to encounter the seasonal trade winds that made movement in sailing ships maddeningly slow and tiresome. Alternately waiting vainly for favorable winds and repeatedly and exhaustingly tacking into the contrary trade winds, the ships progressed little in twenty-five days. By the end of December, the sailors were exhausted, illness was spreading among the colonists, and animals on board were dying. Columbus had to establish his colony quickly or abandon all plans and report utter failure to Ferdinand and Isabella, king and queen of Spain.

On January 2, 1494, Columbus announced they had reached the site for the new settlement, now in the modern Dominican Republic. The town was named La Isabela in honor of the queen and officially founded on January 6, the day of the Feast of the Epiphany. The primary settlement was to be located by the shore on a slight promontory. The site was not ideal, but it offered some advantages. It was well drained and above any chance of flooding, and there was abundant agricultural land on an adjacent plain. There were nearby sources of good stone, lumber, and firewood. What passed for a harbor was poor but provided at least some shelter from trade winds. There was no immediate source of fresh water, but Columbus anticipated that a simple canal could be constructed from a river about a mile away. Perhaps most importantly, Indians indicated that the site was near the inland source of gold. Columbus disembarked the colonists, who began to plant crops and build a settlement consisting of a church, a storehouse, dwellings—including one larger than average for Columbus—and a surrounding wall. Shallow wells were to provide water until the anticipated canal could be constructed, but the wells proved inadequate and probably soon became contaminated. That was, of course, not recognized at the time, but was likely a source of illnesses that continually afflicted the colonists of La Isabela. Archaeology has revealed

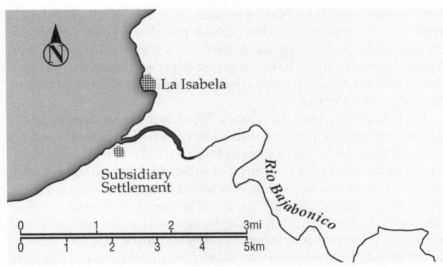

La Isabela on the northern coast of Hispaniola, in modern Dominican Republic.

that a secondary settlement was also established a short distance to the south near good sources of clay and adjacent to a river where a grain mill could be built. This establishment may have been named Marta, perhaps Santa Marta, mentioned by the expedition's doctor, Diego Alvarez Chanca.

Gold was always a major—perhaps *the* major—object of the voyage, and so within a few days of landing, Columbus also dispatched a scouting party to search inland in hope of locating gold deposits. The main body was stopped by a flooding river, but a small group pressed on. The explorers returned with some gold nuggets obtained from the Indians and reports of much more in the mountainous interior. Throughout the age of exploration and colonization, great wealth was always reported to be just beyond the current reach but accessible soon. In reality, it was seldom found and seldom met expectations.

Columbus wished to organize a mining expedition, but before he could do so, disease broke out among the colonists, spreading to more than three hundred. The expedition's doctor, Chanca, attributed it to the long confinement on the voyage followed by exposure to unfamiliar water, food, and hard labor. The contemporary Spanish writers Gonzalo Fernández de Oviedo y Valdés and Father Bartolomé de las Casas, seeking a moral lesson, attributed the illness to syphilis, the result of cohabiting with Native women. The relation of New World syphilis to an apparently milder version previously known in Europe remains a much-discussed and imperfectly understood phenomenon. Modern commentators have suggested that the disease that ravaged the colonists was more likely dysentery resulting from water-borne pathogens or influenza.

On February 2, 1494, Columbus dispatched twelve ships to Spain, bearing the gold he had obtained—less than he had hoped—and his report of discoveries, the massacre of the men at La Navidad, the foundation of La Isabela, and promises of substantial quantities of gold to come in the future. Columbus also sent a long, detailed request for goods and provisions, praise for some of his men and complaints about the conduct of others, as well as the proposal of an absurdly odd scheme of transporting numbers of cannibal Caribs to Spain, there to be civilized and converted to Christianity. Ferdinand and Isabella were unenthused at the prospect and suggested that Columbus see to their conversion on their own islands.

During February, Columbus faced a challenge from his own men. He insisted that every man not disabled by illness work to build and fortify the town and plant crops. This was bitterly resented by the gentlemen volunteers, who regarded such manual labor as beneath their dignity, and particularly by the *hidalgos*, the horsemen, who equally disdained such labor for themselves and their horses. This led to a short-lived agitation supported by the aristocratic Fray Buil, the leading ecclesiastic in the colony, and a royal accountant, Bernal Díaz de Pisa. Columbus jailed De Pisa and hanged several others of lesser social standing, but this event marked the beginning of enmity between Columbus and members of the gentry that pursued him the rest of his life.

In mid-March, Columbus led a major *entrada*, an expedition into the interior of the island in force. Only the ill and a garrison force were left behind at La Isabela. The rest, military and civilian, marched forth under flowing banners and accompanied by blaring trumpets. After leaving the coast plain, they crossed the Cordillera Setentrional, a rugged range of hills and low mountains, into the Vega Real, a broad, fertile, well-watered valley. There Indians greeted them with presents of food and little packets of gold. After crossing the Vega Real to the foothills of the high and rugged Cordillera Central, Columbus established a small fort, named Santo Tomás, where he left a garrison of fifty men. The return to La Isabela was slow and difficult, frequent rain swelled streams and rivers, and the men ran short of provisions. No sooner had Columbus returned than a message arrived from Santo Tomás that Caonabó, the cacique reputed to have destroyed La Navidad, was rumored to be planning an attack on Santo Tomás. Columbus dispatched seventy men to the fort as reinforcements.

At La Isabela, Columbus renewed his demand that everyone, even the hidalgos, engage in manual labor, including digging a canal from the river. The gentry felt themselves above such menial toil, and yet another grievance was shared by gentlemen and commoners alike: they came from Spain for gold, not to dig ditches. The months on sea and land had produced no riches, and men now clamored to return to Spain. To stifle dissent, Columbus sent a force of four hundred men, including the most dissatisfied, to Santo Tomás. On the way, the able but volatile commander Alonso de Ojeda overreacted to the report that some Indians had stolen clothes from three Spanish men and that the local cacique had subsequently appropriated the clothing. Ojeda cut the ears off one Indian and sent the cacique and his nephew in chains to La Isabela, where they were first sentenced to death but then reprieved when other chiefs appealed to Columbus. Bartolomé de las Casas, the famed Dominican friar and advocate for Indians, wrote that this incident was the beginning of enmity between the Spanish and Native peoples, but many of the Spanish had been suspicious and resentful since the discovery of the massacre at La Navidad and the cacique Guacanagarí's sham injury.

Toward the end of April, Columbus left La Isabela with the *Niña* and two smaller ships in search of Japan and the coast of China that he still thought must be in the vicinity. He left his brother, don Diego Columbus, as president of a ruling council, but Diego, a mild-mannered individual, lacked the personality to maintain firm control over discontented and disillusioned colonists and high-spirited Spanish gentlemen whose expectations of quick and easy fortunes in gold had been badly disappointed.

Columbus investigated the southern coast of Cuba, which he believed was a peninsula of the Asian mainland; much of the coast of Jamaica; and the southern coast of Hispaniola. He contemplated a slave raid against the Caribs who terrified the Taino, but fell dangerously ill, so the small fleet returned to La Isabela, arriving on September 29. During his long voyage from late April until the end of September,

Columbus failed to acquire or even see any gold, and the situation at La Isabela had deteriorated significantly.

At Santo Tomás, Ojeda assumed command of the garrison, and Mosén Pedro Margarit, the previous commander there, led 376 Spanish into the interior to search for gold. Columbus had instructed Margarit and the others to respect the Indians, although Columbus also ordered him to seize Caonabó by any means necessary, including false promises of safe conduct. The expedition carried few provisions, expecting to live on food provided by the Indians, but the Indians had little surplus. The Spanish soon alienated the Natives by seizing food, kidnapping and raping women, taking young boys as servants, extorting gold, and generally abusing the Indians. The members of the expedition had learned nothing from the destruction of La Navidad.

Margarit and his men extracted only a disappointingly small amount gold from the Indians. Notwithstanding early exaggerated Spanish reports, there was only a modest amount of gold in Hispaniola, and the Taino had extracted most that could be easily found before the arrival of Columbus. The Taino regarded gold as a pretty and malleable material, but it did not hold great importance for them, and they had already given and traded most of what they had to Columbus and the Spanish. Little gold remained in the Indians' possession, and more could be obtained only by the slow and hard work of mining and panning.

At La Isabela, Bartolomé Columbus, brother of Christopher, arrived in midsummer from Spain with three ships bearing provisions and equipment. When reports of Margarit's activities reached La Isabela, the mild-mannered don Diego wrote to remind the commander of his orders to treat the Indians kindly and equitably. Margarit felt the reprimand besmirched his honor and encroached on his commission. Outraged, he returned to La Isabela, joined with other dissatisfied colonists, seized the three ships that Bartolomé had brought, and sailed for Spain along with the aristocratic Fray Buil and other dissidents. In Spain they spread defamatory reports about Columbus at court and in public.

Margarit left his men in the interior without any firm leadership, and they soon broke up into wandering bands preying brutally on the Taino. Some Taino naturally fought back and killed some Spanish. The cacique Caonabó, accused of the destruction of La Navidad, was prominent among those who opposed Margarit's men. Christopher Columbus, who had returned after Margarit's desertion, had the

Foundations of the church at La Isabela. (*Atomische/Creative Commons*)

choice of siding with the rogue Spanish troops or the victimized Indians. He chose his countrymen, perhaps fearing reaction in Spain if he
sided with pagans against Christians, or perhaps he feared that if he
condoned the killing of any Spanish, he would invite a Native uprising
against the colony. An even-less-honorable motive may be suspected.
Columbus had failed to find the gold he had promised his sovereigns.
Slaves were another source of revenue. Indians could only be enslaved
legally if captured during war, and the death of some of the marauding
Spanish would be judged a cause of war and sufficient excuse to take
slaves.

Columbus organized a force of foot soldiers, cavalry, and war dogs
that rounded up about 1,600 Indians, young and old, men, women,
and children, and drove them to La Isabela. The last hope of peaceful
relations between the Spanish and the Taino now died. In winter 1494,
four ships arrived from Spain bearing provisions and equipment. Early
in 1495, Columbus's men loaded 550 of the Taino judged "the best"
on these ships, which set sail for Spain, there to sell the Taino as slaves.
About 200 died during the crossing, most of the rest arrived in poor
health, and many soon succumbed. Indian slaves gained the reputation

in Spain as being worth little because they were short lived. An additional 750 were retained as slaves at La Isabela, and the remnant, about 400 judged useless, were simply turned loose. They fled in panic, even abandoning infants, only to face a grim future as their communities had been depopulated and destroyed.

While Bartolomé commanded at La Isabela, Christopher Columbus led soldiers who subjugated the Taino of Hispaniola. He imposed tribute on the conquered Indians: each Taino over fourteen had to produce a set amount of gold or cotton annually, but war, slavery, disease, and severe famine led to such profound social disruption of Taino society that within two years the tribute system failed. Large groups of Taino were reduced to such misery that they committed mass suicide. At the time of first contact in 1492, around three hundred thousand Taino lived on Hispaniola. Ferdinand Colón, Christopher Columbus's son and historian, wrote that in the short interval of 1495–1496, a third of the Taino perished, and the Spanish writer Oviedo estimated that by 1548, no more than five hundred remained alive.

Famine also affected the Spanish at La Isabela. The colony failed to become self-sufficient agriculturally, and the Spanish found themselves living mainly on provisions shipped from Spain, never sufficient in quantity and often lacking in quality. Hunger exacerbated diseases among the colonists, and deaths increased. At least part of the chronic food shortage at La Isabela is often blamed on Columbus's selection of the site, which today seems arid and unproductive, but contemporary accounts describe the area as rich and fertile. Michele da Cuneo, a childhood friend of Columbus's who took part in the second voyage, wrote that the colonists simply did not take the time and effort to sow and cultivate crops because they had no desire to settle permanently in the colony. They anticipated finding gold and returning triumphantly to Spain. As hunger became more acute at La Isabela, the stronger and healthier men formed bands that roamed the countryside to extort food from the Indians, but the Indians had little, and the Spanish mainly succeeded in provoking more unrest and social disintegration.

In June 1495, a hurricane struck La Isabela, sinking three ships in the harbor. In October, Juan de Aguado arrived from Spain with four ships of provisions and a royal commission to investigate Columbus's actions. Columbus, now aware that his critics in Spain were spreading damaging accounts, decided to return to Spain with De Aguado to de-

Earliest Spanish settlements on Hispaniola.

fend himself, but before they could leave, a second hurricane sank De Aguado's ships. The two had to wait until new ships were built.

Before departing for Spain in March 1496, Columbus dispatched an expedition commanded by Bartolomé to investigate southern Hispaniola where gold mines were reputed to be located. He found worthwhile deposits there and was able to send samples back to Columbus before he sailed. The gold, however, could only be recovered by laborious mining and was far from the bonanza envisioned by the Spanish when they first departed for Hispaniola. Even before he left for Spain, Columbus anticipated moving the population of La Isabela to a more salubrious and prosperous location, and when Bartolomé located an excellent harbor near a gold-mining area, the decision was made to abandon La Isabela for a new settlement to be named Santo Domingo. Bartolomé first moved the healthy men from La Isabela to commence building at the new site.

Conditions continued to deteriorate at La Isabela as the chronic illness that beset the colony from its beginning was exacerbated by the continuing food shortage, and about three hundred colonists died in a short time. Rumors indicated that the surviving Taino were planning a potentially dangerous general insurrection against the Spanish. Spanish forces were divided between La Isabela and Santo Domingo, and the Taino had lost their fear of Spanish firearms and understood how to combat them. Bartolomé moved against the Taino before they could act, capturing several important caciques in a nighttime raid, and the anticipated uprising collapsed.

In May 1497, a new threat arose in the person of Francisco Roldán, whom Columbus had appointed *alcalde mayor*, chief justice, of La Isabela. Roldán played on the continuing frustration of the people remaining at La Isabela and fears that Bartolomé had abandoned them to die there. Roldán's men looted the royal storehouse at La Isabela and slaughtered breeding cattle belonging to the king before departing for the interior of the island where he and his men repeated the now-familiar scenario of extorting the Taino for gold and kidnapping women. Roldán then took his men to the long peninsula in southwestern Hispaniola where food was less scarce, and there he maintained a separate regime. By the end of 1497, La Isabela was abandoned. The last of the inhabitants had either joined Bartolomé at Santo Domingo or followed Roldán.

Columbus's Third and Fourth Voyages

Columbus went on a third voyage of discovery in 1498, still convinced he was near Japan and China. He touched on Trinidad Island and the northern coast of South America before sailing to Santo Domingo, where he was greeted by dissatisfied and rebellious colonists. Ill with crippling rheumatoid arthritis and weak, he accepted humiliating conditions to make peace with Roldán. In the royal Spanish court, faith in Columbus and his brothers collapsed because of the failure to produce significant treasure despite oft-repeated promises, the increasing chorus of complaints and accusations of mismanagement, and even cruel and bloody repression of dissenting voices on Hispaniola. Ferdinand and Isabella sent Francisco de Bobadilla to Hispaniola with extraordinary powers to inquire into matters, and there Bobadilla received lists of grievances and charges so serious he sent all three of the Columbus brothers to Spain in chains. There Christopher Columbus pleaded that the charges against him were made maliciously by those who wanted to usurp control of the colony. The sovereigns heard him with sympathy and dismissed the charges, but they did not place him in charge of the colonial government again. Instead, they appointed don Nicolás de Ovando as governor and supreme justice of the Indies, effectively suspending Columbus's rights and privileges.

While Columbus remained in Spain, others undertook voyages that greatly expanded geographic knowledge and brought back abundant pearls from Margarita Island. On his third voyage, Columbus had sited Margarita Island but failed to investigate it, further discrediting him in the eyes of Ferdinand and Isabella. Finally, the sovereigns authorized Columbus to undertake another voyage, but it was poorly equipped in comparison with earlier efforts.

In April 1502, Columbus departed Spain on his fourth voyage to the New World with just four small caravels—a great contrast to the fleet of thirty ships of various owners that had sailed to Hispaniola two months previously. Royal instructions ordered Columbus to search for a passage to the east, a quest that would long futilely occupy Europeans. Despite orders that he was not to visit Hispaniola, Columbus approached Santo Domingo to warn of an approaching hurricane and request shelter in the harbor. Governor Ovando, no friend of Columbus's, denied him entry and disregarded the warning as the fleet of thirty ships departed to return to Spain. Columbus's caravels managed to survive the storm, but most of the larger fleet were destroyed by the storm with tremendous loss of gold and lives, including Bobadilla, Roldán, and most of the leaders of the rebellion against Columbus. A few ships, badly damaged, crawled back to Santo Domingo, and only one ship, one of the smallest of the entire fleet, reached Spain. That ship carried Columbus's personal wealth. His enemies muttered that he had employed witchcraft.

Columbus then sailed along the shores of modern Honduras, Nicaragua, and Costa Rica without discovering the fabled strait to the East or anything else of great interest. On the coast of Panama, he met Indians who had ornaments of fine gold and could be persuaded, sometimes reluctantly, to trade. As Columbus ranged along the coast seeking the source of the gold, he was beset by heavy winter storms that left the ships barely seaworthy, provisions consumed, and men exhausted. Columbus attempted to establish a settlement, Santa María de Belén, but warfare broke out with the Indians, some Spanish were killed, and the attempt was quickly abandoned. By this time the vessels were riddled with shipworms and leaking badly. Columbus abandoned one caravel by the failed settlement and another a little later; the remaining two could only be kept afloat by constant bailing. As the condition of the ships deteriorated, so did Columbus's health. He suffered from malaria in addition to arthritis, and his eyesight was failing, all aggravated by winter weather, storms, poor diet, and the stresses of the voyage.

The two remaining ships managed to make it to Jamaica, where Columbus beached the sinking vessels. The Indians in the area initially proved peaceful and eager to trade, providing the stranded Spanish with food. Diego Méndez de Segura, chief clerk and crown representative on the expedition, agreed to lead a dangerous voyage in two canoes with about a dozen other Spanish and some Indians across about 124 miles of open water to Hispaniola. Méndez encountered Ovando in western Hispaniola, but it was evident that the governor, long hostile to Columbus, was in no hurry to send aid. Méndez proceeded to Santo Domingo on foot and there bought and equipped a ship to rescue Columbus and his crew.

Meanwhile, on Jamaica, Columbus faced a mutiny that damaged relations with the Indians, who almost ceased bringing provisions until Columbus frightened them with his prediction of a lunar eclipse. Finally, in March, a caravel arrived, sent by Ovando. The ship was too small to rescue Columbus's men, and it departed quickly, leaving only a barrel of wine and some salt pork. The Spanish on Jamaica remained divided between Columbus's loyalists and mutineers until the loyalists defeated the rebels in a violent confrontation.

Finally, Méndez's ship arrived, and Columbus and the others were rescued at the end of June 1504 after having been stranded on Jamaica for over a year. Columbus returned to Spain shortly before the death of Queen Isabella, who had been his chief supporter. He sought to have the king restore his entitlements and honors and even dreamed of a new voyage of discovery, but his health deteriorated, and he died on May 20, 1506, believing to the last that he had been to the edge of the Orient.

Aftermath

There have been many attempts to evaluate Columbus in his own cultural context, and far too many to judge him by values inapplicable to his age. He was a complex person, acted on by influences now for the most part so foreign to us that it is doubtful we can achieve more than an incomplete understanding of the man. Columbus was a skilled, pragmatic navigator and a religious mystic who was convinced that he served a divine purpose. He sought wealth to make the Spanish monarchy powerful so it might conquer the Holy Land and return Jerusalem to Christianity. He also expected that his role as the manifestation of divine will would naturally be recognized and honored. Like many others convinced that they serve a higher purpose, Columbus could commit and excuse repulsively brutal acts, as the Taino and even the Spanish colonists discovered to their mortal cost. Yet he remains a figure of importance to the development of Western civilization.

The exact location of La Navidad has not been discovered, although it is certainly in the vicinity of the modern villages of Limonade Bord-de-Mer and En Bas Saline. Archaeologists have found scattered material particularly at En Bas Saline that almost certainly came from La Navidad, but no indisputable remains of the fortress have been identified. In the eighteenth century, an anchor from the late fifteenth or early sixteenth century was discovered about a mile and a half to the east. This may be the anchor from the *Santa María* that the Taino brought to shore and that was seen by Columbus's men on the second voyage. It is exhibited as such in the Musée du Panthéon National Haïtien, the National Haitian Museum of the Pantheon.

The location of La Isabela has never been forgotten. The misery experienced there and the many deaths led to the belief that the site was haunted, and people long avoided it. This proved ideal for smugglers who later utilized the site. Lightly built structures decayed, leaving little trace, and the more substantial buildings were robbed for their material during the nineteenth century. Misguided efforts to make the overgrown site more presentable in the mid-twentieth century thoughtlessly destroyed many of the surviving traces of the colony. Since the 1980s, archaeologists Kathleen Deagan, José Maria Cuxent, and others have recovered the foundations of buildings and evidence illuminating life and death at La Isabela during its brief existence.

Sources

The fundamental sources for Columbus, La Navidad, and La Isabela are the writings of Columbus himself, the early accounts by Pietro Martire d'Anghiera, and the works of Fray Bartolomé de las Casas, Fernando Columbus, and Gonzalo Fernández de Oviedo y Valdés, known generally as Oviedo.

Columbus wrote a report of his first voyage in the form of a letter sent to Luís de Santángel, the Spanish royal treasurer, but obviously intended to be conveyed by Santángel to Ferdinand and Isabella. It would have been presumptuous of Columbus at this stage of this career to address the sovereigns directly. The letter was quickly published, appearing as Christopher Columbus, *Epistola Christofori Colom, cui [a]etas nostra multu[m] debet, de insulis Indi[a]e supra*

Gangem nuper inuentis: ad quas perquirendas octauo antea mense auspicijs [et] [a]ere inuictissimi Fernandi Hispaniarum Regis missus fuerat: ad magnificum d[omi]n[u]m Raphaelem Sanxis eiusdem serenissimi regis tesaurariu[m] missa (Rome: Stephan Plannck, after April 29, 1493). The publication was widely copied, and seventeen reprints appeared in various countries by 1497.

Pietro Martire d'Anghiera, often referred to as Peter Martyr in English, was born in Italy in 1457. He migrated to Spain in 1487, where, along with other Italian scholars, he introduced Renaissance concepts to Spain. In 1511, he became the chronicler of the council that evolved into the Real y Supremo Consejo de las Indias, the Royal and Supreme Council of the Indies. He continued in that office until his death in 1526, and thus had excellent access to primary source material. Pietro Martire's most important historical work is *De Orbe Novo Petri Marturis Mediolanensis Protonotarij Senatoris Decades* (Compluti [i.e., Alcalá de Henares, Spain]: Apud Nichaele[m] d[e] Eguia, 1530). The standard English translation is Francis Augustus, ed., intro., and notes, *De Orbe Novo: The Eight Decades of Peter Martyr D'Anghera*, 2 vols. (New York: G. P. Putnam's Sons, 1912). They were composed and published over many years, from as early as 1493 until 1525, shortly before the author's death. They did not appear together until 1530. They take the form of letters addressed to eminent people describing Spanish discoveries and activities as well as the customs of the Native peoples throughout Spanish America. Most of the material relevant to Columbus is in the first and second *Decades* of Pietro Martire's work. *Decades* in this case refers to chapters, not periods of ten years.

Bartolomé de las Casas was born in 1484. In 1502, he and his father joined Nicolás de Ovando y Cáceres's expedition to Hispaniola, where Las Casas became the owner of an estate worked by Indian slaves. He took part in warfare and slave raids against the Native population on Hispaniola, but he also showed a religious inclination and was ordained as a priest in 1510. He nevertheless participated in the bloody conquest of Cuba in 1513. Sickened by the atrocities he witnessed there, he gave up his land holdings and slaves and began preaching against the enslavement of Indians. Father Bartolomé de las Casas knew Columbus. He admired some of the explorer's qualities, but he was extremely critical of much of his behavior toward Indians. In the Indies and later in Spain, Las Casas found only limited success amid opposition by those who profited from the exploitation of the Natives. After a failed attempt to establish an idealistic colony at Cumaná, he become a Dominican friar.

Las Casas spent the rest of his life working to abolish the abuses the Spanish inflicted on the Indians, particularly the *encomienda* system, by which a Spanish settler, the *ecomendero*, was granted the labor of a group of Indians living in a particular area. The Indians might be required to work on land granted to the settler, or the settler might usurp control of the land on which the Indians resided. The *encomienda* system supposedly required the *ecomendero* to protect the Indians and instruct them in the Christian religion, but in fact it quickly degenerated into simple slavery and was responsible for the destruction of Indian communities, cultural loss, and widespread mortality.

Las Casas wrote abundantly. His most important work is the massive *Historia de las Indias*, which covers the period from Columbus's first voyage in 1492 until 1520, much of which Las Casas witnessed. He also utilized material from other eyewitnesses. The work reached its final form in 1561, with the instruction that it was not to be published for forty years after his death, which occurred in 1566. Manuscript copies circulated soon after his death, but the work remained unpublished until 1875. (Fray Bartolomé de las Casas, *Historia de las Indias,* 3 vols., ed. El Marqués de la Fuensanta and José Sancho Rayon [Madrid: Miguel Ginesta, 1875]). The work is now available in many modern Spanish editions. It has never been translated entirely into English, but portions are available in translation in Andrée Collard, *History of the Indies* (New York: Harper and Row, 1971), some copies of which have misnumbered and misbound pages, and in *Repertorium Columbianum* (Berkeley: University of California Press, 1993–), vol. 6: *A Synoptic Edition of the Log of Columbus's First Voyage,* ed. Francesca Lardicci, trans. Cynthia L. Chamberlin and Blair Sullivan; vol. 7: *Las Casas on Columbus: The Second and Fourth Voyages,* ed. Anthony Pagden, trans. Nigel Griffin; and vol. 11: *Las Casas on Columbus: The Third Voyage,* ed. Geoffrey Symcox, trans. Michael Hammer.

Las Casas was a controversial figure during his lifetime and subsequently. In recent decades, the tendency has been to idealize him. He truly worked heroically to minimize the often cruel behavior of his contemporaries, but at the same time he was absolutist in his convictions, intolerant of other views—even those that differed only in small degree—and not above using private influence to suppress the publication of writers with whom he disagreed. His shorter work, *Brevisima relacion de la destruccion de las Indias* (Seville: Sebastian Trugillo, 1552) was important in alerting Europe to the abusive Spanish behavior in the New World, but it could have been more so if it had been published earlier and named specific wrongdoers, which Las Casas carefully avoided. For much of his life, Las Casas advocated replacing Indian slavery with the importation of Black slaves from Africa, only late in his life concluding Black slavery was also unjust. While he argued against Indian slavery and eventually against Black slavery, he did not oppose slavery, adhering to the traditional view that pagans captured in a just war could legitimately be enslaved. He had no tolerance for those he and contemporary Spanish Catholics regarded as heretics, Muslims, or Jews, the latter particularly ironic since some have argued that Las Casas's own claim to be descended from a French aristocratic family is false and his antecedents were actually Jewish.

Las Casas's claims about the initial size of Indian populations and number of deaths caused by the Spanish are usually expressed in suspiciously round numbers and often do not bear modern scrutiny. He also failed to notice that much of the destruction of the Indian populations was the result of epidemic diseases rather than atrocities and massacres. Las Casas's works, particularly his *Brevisima relacion de la destruccion de las Indias*, figured large in the creation of the Black Legend, the concept that the Spanish were particularly brutal and self-righteous. In fact, many Spanish were brutal and self-righteous, but no more so than many Dutch, French, and English. Despite all, Bartolomé de las Casas's denunciation of the abuses of the Indians remains powerful and a source of great importance for virtually all aspects of early Spanish colonialism and particularly for Columbus's actions.

Fernando Columbus was the natural son of Christopher Columbus and his mistress, Beatriz Enríquez de Arana. His name is also rendered as Ferdinand and Hernando. Columbus recognized him as his son, and Fernando accompanied his father on his fourth voyage to the Americas. Fernando later returned to Spain, where he became a scholar and collected an important library. He wrote a biography of his father in Spanish, but it was first published in Italian as *Historie del S. D. Fernando Colombo; nelle quali s'ha particolare, & vera relatione della vita, & de fatti dell'Ammiraglio D. Cristoforo Colombo, suo padre:*

Et dello scoprimento ch'egli fece dell'Indie Occidentali, dette Mondo Nuovo (Venice: De' Franceschi Sanese, 1571). The work, predictably favorable to Columbus, is one of the most important sources. It is readily available in English translation: Ferdinand Columbus, *The Life of the Admiral Christopher Columbus by his Son Ferdinand*, trans. and annot. Benjamin Keen (London: Folio Society, 1960).

Gonzalo Fernández de Oviedo y Valdés, known generally as Oviedo, was born in Spain in 1478. A member of an aristocratic family and well connected at court, he served in a variety of posts, going to Santo Domingo in 1514 as the royal controller of gold mining and smelting, a post he held almost twenty years. Oviedo's greatest work is *La historia general y natural de las Indias*, in which politics play a major role. The first part of that work appeared in 1535 as *Primera parte de la historia natural y general y de las indias yslas y tierra firme de mar oceano* (Sevilla: Juan Cromberger, 1535). Oviedo made an enemy of Father Bartolomé de las Casas, a man who tolerated no disagreement. Las Casas maintained that the indigenous people of America were inherently mild and friendly and could be won over to Christianity by kindness, but Oviedo argued that some Native peoples were aggressive cannibals too corrupt and debased for conversion. Las Casas harshly denounced Oviedo's writings and probably hindered publication of the second part of Oviedo's *Historia natural y general*. It finally appeared shortly after Oviedo's death in 1557 as Gonzalo Fernández de Oviedo y Valdés, *Libro XX. De la segunda parte de la general historia de las Indias* (Valladolid, Spain: Francisco Fernandez de Cordoba, 1557). The entire work, consisting of fifty-five books (i.e., chapters), was first published in its entirety as Gonzalo Fernández de Oviedo y Valdés, *Historia General y Natural de las Indias, Islas y Tierra Firme del Mar Oceano*, 4 vols., ed. José Amador de los Rios (Madrid: Imprenta de la Real Academia de la Historia, 1851–1855).

Samuel Eliot Morison. *Admiral of the Ocean Sea, a Life of Christopher Columbus*, 2 vols. (Boston: Little, Brown, 1942), remains of great importance for understanding Columbus and the course of his voyages. Some have challenged Morison's identifications of locations, but Morison sailed along the coasts and amid the islands, observing currents and the appearance of landfalls as Columbus described them. Few of his critics have done so. For a more modern treatment of Columbus's career and travels, see Laurence Bergreen, *Columbus: Four Voyages 1492–1504* (New York: Penguin, 2011).

Archaeology has recovered materials from La Navidad and established at least the general vicinity of the settlement. See Kristy M. Capobianco, "Excavation Site Prediction Using High Resolution Satellite Imagery and GIS Data Development of Archaeological Deposits for En Bas Saline, Haiti" (MA thesis, University of Central Florida, 2005), purl.fcla.edu/fcla/etd/UFE0011762; John Noble Wilford, "Columbus's Lost Town: New Evidence Found," *New York Times*, August 27, 1985, sec. C, p. 1; and Frances Maclean, "The Lost Fort of Columbus," *Smithsonian Magazine*, January 2008, 72-76, https://www.smithsonianmag.com/history/the-lost-fort-of-columbus-8026921/.

Extensive work at La Isabela has clarified the physical organization of the town and details of the lives of the colonists. See Kathleen Deagan and José M. Cruxent, *La Isabela: Columbus's Outpost among the Tainos, 1493–1498* (New Haven: Yale University Press, 2002); Kathleen Deagan and José M. Cruxent, *Archaeology at La Isabela: America's First European Town, 1493–1498* (New Haven: Yale University Press, 2002); Marcio Veloz Maggiolo, *Nuova raccolta colombiana, 20, Archeologia della scoperta colombiana* (Roma: Istituto poligrafico e Zecca dello Stato, 1994).

TWO

The Follies *of* Alonso de Ojeda *and* Diego de Nicuesa: San Sebastian de Uraba (1510) *and* Santa María la Antigua del Darién (1510–1524)

Alonso de Ojeda

The foundation and fate of the colonies of San Sebastián de Urabá and Santa María la Antigua del Darién are closely tied to two rivals: Alonso de Ojeda (also spelled Hojeda) and Diego de Nicuesa. Ojeda was born in 1466 or 1468 in northern Spain into a family that was aristocratic but far from wealthy. The family, however, still had significant social connections that benefitted the young man, particularly his uncle, Juan Rodríques de Fonseca, bishop of Burgos, then archbishop of Rossano, chaplain to Queen Isabella, and vested with a major role in colonial administration as early as 1493. Ojeda took part in the conquest of Granada, winning a good reputation and the support of his uncle, who recommended him to Columbus. Ojeda took part in Columbus's second voyage to the New World.

Ojeda was a small man but exceptionally athletic, well coordinated, skillful with a variety of weapons, and noted for his bravery. He was also quick witted, hot headed, violent, vindictive, and deeply, even superstitiously, religious. Columbus saw in Ojeda an able military leader and entrusted him with expeditions into the interior of Hispaniola seeking gold. Ojeda overreacted, however, to a minor incident in which Indians stole clothing from several Spanish. Ojeda cut off one Indian's ears and sent an important cacique and his advisers to Columbus at La Isabela, where he initially condemned them to death, though later Columbus pardoned the Indians when other caciques begged for leniency.

By 1499, Ferdinand and Isabella, having grown discouraged with Columbus's failure to produce the riches he kept promising, decided to support voyages to the newly discovered lands by others who might prove more successful. Among those was Alonso de Ojeda, who sailed in that year with a royal commission, much to the irritation of Columbus. Ojeda made landfall on the northern coast of South America near the mouth of the Essequibo River, from where he sailed northwest along the coast, also visiting the Trinidad, Margarita, and Aruba islands. He discovered the entrance to Lake Maracaibo, and, after touching briefly at the nearby Cabo de la Vela, sailed to Hispaniola, where he ended the exploratory voyage. During the expedition, Ojeda visited Native villages built on stilts in the water, and some claim he named the area Venezuela from a fancied resemblance to Venice, while others maintain that the name of a local tribe, the Veneciuela, gave rise to the name. The voyage mapped much of the northern coast of South America and obtained some pearls, a little gold, and a few slaves, but it was not an economic success. Columbus and his supporters regarded Ojeda's exploration, despite his royal commission, as an illegitimate infringement on Columbus's privileges and discoveries. Fights between Ojeda's crew and Columbus's supporters on Hispaniola left men dead and injured.

In 1501, Ojeda received another royal commission. For the voyage he partnered with two Spanish merchants, Juan de Vergara and García de Campos, who were able to provide resources he could not otherwise afford. Ojeda and his partners set sail in January 1502 on four ships following the course of his first voyage, intending to obtain pearls and gold from the Natives and to found a colony on the South American mainland. Columbus had sighted the island of Margarita, but Ojeda discovered it was a rich source of pearls. Subsequently, the Spanish ruined the Margarita pearl beds by excessive exploitation.

When the expedition's food supply proved inadequate, Ojeda sent Vergara to Jamaica for supplies. While Vergara was gone, Ojeda established a settlement that he called Santa Cruz on the Guajira Peninsula in modern Colombia near the border with Venezuela. The settlement consisted of little more than a fort and lasted only three months. Ojeda's men attacked neighboring Native villages in the search for pearls and gold, underestimating the resilience of the Indians, who fought back using the terrain and tropical growth to their advantage. The Spanish, practically confined to their fort and facing starvation, blamed Ojeda. When Vergara returned, the two merchants charged Ojeda with malfeasance, removed him from command, and sent him to Hispaniola as a prisoner. This led to complicated legal procedures during which Ojeda was imprisoned for over a year. He was finally freed through the influence of Archbishop Fonseca, but Ojeda had to pay a large settlement that left him nearly impoverished. Yet he managed to find support for a third voyage.

Diego de Nicuesa

Diego de Nicuesa was born in 1464 at Baeza in the Andalucía region of Spain to a moderately wealthy family and raised in the house of don Enrique Enríquez, uncle of King Ferdinand and high official at the royal court. Nicuesa, too, became a member of the Spanish court, holding the office of royal carver, serving meat to the sovereigns. By all accounts he was a polished speaker, talented musician, famous horseman, and fashionable dresser. His friends also praised him for his integrity and chivalric sense of honor; enemies found him arrogant and pretentious.

Diego de Nicuesa first traveled to Hispaniola in 1502 along with Nicolás de Ovando y Cáceres, who was appointed the third governor of the Indies. Ovando sailed from Spain with a fleet of thirty ships and 2,500 colonists, among whom were people who would play important roles in Latin America, including Bartolomé de las Casas, Francisco Pizarro, and Lucas Vazquez de Ayllón, who founded the first colony—unsuccessful—in what is now the United States. Hernán Cortés was also supposed to take part in the expedition but could not because of an injury. Nicuesa served under Ovando, whose treatment of the Indians on Hispaniola was notoriously brutal, causing the death of tens of thousands. Nicuesa took an active part in warfare against the Natives and in the exploitation of Native labor on land granted to him, growing wealthy.

By 1508, the Spanish royal government wished to establish colonies on the mainland. Both Ojeda and Nicuesa sought the royal authorization, and both received it. Each had desired a sole commission, and from the beginning the two were rivals, competing for scarce resources and seeking to control as much territory as possible. Ojeda was to colonize and govern the area known as Urabá, which he renamed Nueva Andalucía. Ojeda, who had not profited significantly from his earlier voyages, had little to invest in the new enterprise, but he enlisted the support of a wealthy lawyer, Martín Fernández d'Enciso, whom he appointed as *alcalde*, an office combining the functions of judge and administrator. Ojeda also enjoyed the support of Juan de la Cosa, a famed pilot and leading cartographer of the Caribbean. De la Cosa's participation undoubtedly made it easier for Ojeda to recruit men for the expedition. Ojeda's initial force consisted of four small ships, about three hundred men, and twelve horses. Enciso was to follow later with another ship carrying provisions.

Nicuesa's assigned area of Veragua was adjacent and to the west of Ojeda's concession. This new province was retitled Castilla del Oro (Golden Castile), the name derived from Columbus's wishful accounts of the area. Nicuesa had more money than Ojeda and was able to hire more ships and recruit more men, 785 according to the best source, and many horses, carried in seven ships. Despite his wealth, he exceeded his resources and fell into debt.

Ojeda and the Colony of San Sebastian de Uraba

At Santo Domingo on Hispaniola, Ojeda and Nicuesa immediately began to argue about the territory included in their respective grants. At one point, Ojeda wanted to settle matters in a duel with Nicuesa, but the calmer wisdom of Juan de la Cosa prevailed, and the two agreed that the Darien River, today the Atrato River, would form the border between their provinces. In addition to mutual resentment, both faced the hostility of Diego Colon, the son of Christopher Columbus. Ferdinand and Isabella granted extensive hereditary rights and privileges to Columbus, leaving Diego Colon to believe that commissions awarded to Ojeda and Nicuesa usurped his rights. Colon did everything he could to hinder recruitment on Hispaniola and denied the two control of Jamaica despite royal orders that they were to have the island as a source for provisions. The Spanish royal government was not an absolute monarchy, but rather a web of institutions and entitlements, many dating from the Middle Ages, tied together by a maze of courts and legal procedures. A governor such as Diego Colon could challenge royal orders for a while, especially if buffered from royal power by distance and slow communications. Diego Colon could not, however, defy royal power with impunity, and in 1514, royal officials recalled Diego to Spain. In 1520, King Carlos I restored Diego to his position, but apparently Diego had learned nothing about obedience, and the king recalled him again three years later.

In November 1509, Ojeda managed to depart from Santo Domingo on Hispaniola to Spain slightly in advance of Nicuesa, who was delayed when jailed briefly for failure to pay debts. Ojeda first sailed to the bay where Cartagena would be founded in 1531. Ojeda decided to undertake some slave raiding in the area before sailing to his province, despite the advice of Juan de la Cosa who pointed out that the Indians in the area were already hostile and used poisoned arrows. Although it was seventeen years after Columbus's first voyage, the reputation of the Spanish as violent slave raiders had spread widely among the Indians. Ojeda initially attacked a small Indian village, capturing seventy Natives whom he sent under guard to his ships. He then moved to a larger village called Turbaco from which the inhabitants fled before he arrived. He and his men foolishly spread out seeking the fugitives, only to be attacked vigorously by the Indians. The Spanish fell back to an improvised fort, but the Indians continued their counterattack until only a few Spanish remained alive. Just Ojeda and one other managed to fight their way free and get to the coast, where men from Ojeda's ships rescued them. Ojeda's losses are reported as seventy or one hundred dead, including Juan de la Cosa. Ojeda had hardly been rescued when Nicuesa's fleet appeared. Contrary to Ojeda's fears, Nicuesa treated Ojeda with utmost courtesy and chivalry. The two joined forces and with four hundred men fell upon Turbaco, to which the Indians had returned. They massacred everyone—men, women, and children—and burned the village.

Ojeda then proceeded to his province, on the eastern side of the Gulf of Darien, where he founded a colony he named San Sebastian de Uraba. After dispatching the slaves he had captured to Santo Domingo on Hispaniola to be exchanged for provisions, Ojeda led an expedition inland against Indians reputed to have much gold. The Spanish were quickly driven back to San Sebastian, where Ojeda and the colonists found themselves virtually under siege and running short of provisions. Ojeda hoped that the lawyer Enciso would soon arrive with a ship full of food, but when relief appeared, it was from an unexpected source: the pirate Bernardino de Talavera, now captain of a ship once owned by Genoese merchants. He now appeared at San Sebastian, where Ojeda was glad to purchase the cargo of food, cassava, and bacon, despite its stolen origins. Talavera's purloined supplies, however, were only sufficient to sustain the colony for a short time.

During an Indian attack, Ojeda was wounded for the first time in his life when a poisoned arrow passed entirely through his thigh. Wounds from such arrows almost always proved fatal, but Ojeda insisted that the full depth of the wound be cauterized, and he survived. It is uncertain whether the cauterization was effective or if the arrow simply did not shed much poison in passing through his leg.

The food provided by Talavera was rapidly consumed, and Enciso still had not appeared with provisions, so Ojeda decided to return to Hispaniola to obtain supplies for the colony. He left Francisco Pizarro, destined to achieve fame and infamy as the conqueror of the Inca Empire, in command with instructions that if Ojeda did not return in fifty days, the colonists were to abandon the settlement, take the ships, and sail wherever they thought best. Ojeda sailed with Talavera, but the two soon quarreled. Ojeda demanded to go to Hispaniola, but Talavera, in possession of a stolen ship, could hardly appear there without facing justice. The ship did not reach Hispaniola or any other port but rather wrecked on the coast of Cuba. Talavera initially confined Ojeda in chains, but when confronted by hostile Indians, Talavera and his companions quickly realized they needed Ojeda's fighting prowess. As they sought to make their way to a Spanish settlement, the shipwrecked men repeatedly fought off Indian attacks and then blundered into a swamp through which they struggled for a full month. During this period, Ojeda's religiosity was much on display. He always carried an image of the Virgin Mary that Bishop Fonseca had presented to him, and whenever the men paused in their march, Ojeda would hang the image on a convenient branch and pray, promising to install the image wherever they found rescue. Indians and the swamp killed half the men before they found their way to dry land and an Indian town called Cueyba. Ironically, considering Ojeda's prior conduct, the Indians there took pity on the Spanish, feeding and healing them. Ojeda built an oratory there for the image and instructed the Indians to adore it. With the aid of the Natives, the shipwrecked Spanish sent one of their number by canoe to Jamaica, and the governor of Jamaica sent a ship that rescued Ojeda and transported him to Hispaniola. Virtually without funds, Ojeda could not send aid to San Sebastian, which in any event was abandoned by the time Ojeda was rescued. Talavera came to a bad end, arrested in Jamaica for piracy and hanged in 1511.

Without resources, Ojeda remained in Santo Domingo. Shortly before his death in 1515, he assumed the dress of a monk, a common practice at the time, and arranged to be buried just beyond the threshold of the monastic church of St. Francisco as an act of humility. Some wrote that Ojeda died of the lingering effects of the poisoned arrow, but Bartolomé de las Casas wrote that was not true. He had seen Ojeda at Santo Domingo, and Ojeda had completely recovered from his wound. Las Casas also wrote that before Ojeda's death, God may have given him a consciousness of the sinfulness of his deeds toward the Indians.

Nearly out of provisions, the surviving colonists left San Sebastian in the two small ships. During the voyage, one ship suffered some catastrophe and sank suddenly. The other, captained by Pizarro, arrived at the harbor where Cartagena would be founded years later, there to find Enciso with a ship carrying provisions and 150 reinforcements for the colony at San Sebastian. Aboard was also a stowaway, Vasco Nuñez de Balboa, who had escaped Hispaniola because of debts. Enciso was suspicious of Pizarro's account of events and suspected that the survivors of the colony were deserters. He insisted on proceeding to San Sebastian, accompanied by Pizarro and the others. Approaching the colony, Enciso's ship struck a hidden rock and sank. The men clambered ashore, but almost all provisions were lost, and they found that the Indians, who remained implacably hostile, had burned San Sebastian.

Santa María la Antigua del Darién

The situation was desperate, but Balboa had been on an earlier expedition in the region, and he guided Enciso with one hundred men to a rich Indian town on the other side of the Gulf of Darien in the territory reserved for Nicuesa. Balboa assured Enciso and the others that these Indians did not use poison arrows. There are conflicting reports of what happened next. Either the reputation of the Spanish had preceded them and five hundred angry warriors confronted them, or they were initially received peacefully, but when the Spanish tortured the cacique to find the source of gold ornaments worn by the Indians, matters turned hostile. Before the ensuing battle, the Spanish vowed that if they won they would name a colony after Santa María de la Antigua, build a church in her name, and send dedications to her shrine in Seville. The Indians lacked poison arrows, and the Spanish routed them easily. After looting the Indian town, Enciso and the others founded a colony they accordingly named Santa María de la Antigua del Darién and transported there those who had remained behind near ruined San Sebastian.

At Santa María, problems soon arose. The lawyer Enciso initially retained command, but he proved an unpopular leader. He prohibited individuals from trading with Indians for gold and threatened the death penalty for anyone caught doing so. Men soon began to feel that in this and other matters he acted out of personal interest rather than the general good. He also seems to have been a rather remote, arid personality, in contrast to Balboa, who was gregarious and charismatic. The unhappy men argued that since they were no longer in Ojeda's concession, Ojeda's lieutenant Enciso had no authority. They forced an election, choosing Balboa and a man named Zamudio as *alcaldes*, but that did not settle matters. Three factions emerged: those who continued to support Enciso, Balboa's supporters, and a group who regarded Nicuesa as the legitimate commander. No one knew, however, where Nicuesa might be. At this point, Rodrigo Enrique de Colmenares arrived at Santa María seeking Nicuesa. Nicuesa had arranged for Colmenares to sail after him bringing provisions for the colony he intended to establish in his territory. The provisions were most welcome and strengthened the position of those who supported Nicuesa as the legitimate commander.

There are several conflicting accounts of Nicuesa's adventures. According to one, soon after Nicuesa sailed from Hispaniola with his fleet, he encountered a storm that separated him from the other ships. As he searched for his ships along what is now the coast of Panama, Nicuesa sailed up an unnamed river, but the rapid recession of the tide stranded his ship on a sandbar, where it listed far to one side and rapidly came apart in the tidal flow. The men were able to salvage little other than the ship's small boat. The tale is suspiciously similar to an event that Columbus experienced in the same area years earlier and probably represents a historical doublet, a story copied from one source and applied to a different situation by an unscrupulous or naïve

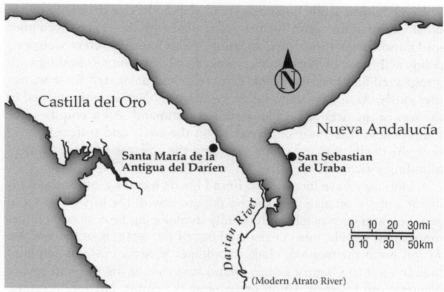

Gulf of Darien and location of the colonies of San Sebastian de Uraba and Santa María de la Antigua del Daríen.

writer or his source. Whatever the circumstances, Nicuesa lost his ship, and as a result he and his stranded crew moved along the coast on foot. They had a small boat, but it could only accommodate a few men. Coming to a large bay, Nicuesa sought to save time and effort by having the men conveyed by the small boat a few at a time from one headland to the other. Once the men had been transferred, they realized that what they had believed to be the headland on the other side of the bay was actually a barren island with no source of fresh water other than several small swamps. At this juncture, the men in charge of the boat absconded and left Nicuesa and the others on the island. Meanwhile, the scattered ships of Nicuesa's fleet regrouped after the storm, but they suffered damage, and many of the provisions on board spoiled. Shipworms, common in the area, further ravaged the vessels, and the crews readily agreed with Nicuesa's lieutenant, Lope de Olano, that Nicuesa must have perished in the storm and that he, Olano, should assume command.

An alternate account maintains that despite a storm, Nicuesa reached the mainland together with five ships, three of which he left in a safe harbor while he in one small ship and Lope de Olano in another explored the coast. Nicuesa quarreled with the experienced pilot on Olano's ship about their location. Olano and his crew were evidently estranged by Nicuesa's ignorance and arrogance in dealing with a respected and knowledgeable pilot who had navigated these waters previously. At night, Olano sailed away from Nicuesa and returned to the rest of the fleet, where he assumed command. All accounts agree that Nicuesa was soon shipwrecked on the coast and suffered privation, the death of many of his men, and the collapse of his dreams of founding a rich colony.

Olano may have intended to found his own colony, but instead his major ships soon also wrecked on the coast with the loss of men and supplies, and he was left with rapidly diminishing provisions and just three small vessels, one constructed out of the remains of the wrecks. At this point the men who had abandoned Nicuesa in the stolen boat blundered into Olano's camp. Olano sent one of his ships to rescue Nicuesa and his men. Upon arriving at the camp, Nicuesa resumed command and, rather than expressing gratitude at his rescue, ordered Olano's arrest and reprimanded the other officers harshly for their failure to search for him. Perhaps Nicuesa had begun to break down mentally. The once-elegant courtier degenerated to a harsh, vindictive, arbitrary, petulant tyrant, estranged from those he commanded. He took the three small ships and sailed east along the coast until he came to the harbor called Nombre de Dios, where he built a fort and brought together the sad remnant of his command, only about 100 men of the 785 who had left Hispaniola with him. The survivors were so short of provisions that they attacked Indians in the area to steal food, but they gained little, and men died of combat, starvation, and sickness.

Meanwhile, the faithful Rodrigo Enrique de Colmenares left Santa María with others to search for Nicuesa. By the time Colemenares found him, only Nicuesa and seventy of his men remained alive. Rather than greet this rescue with enthusiasm, Nicuesa raged against the remnant of Ojeda's men who had presumed to enter his province and swore he would take from them what loot they had accumulated. Lope de Olano, whom Nicuesa held in chains, and others reported Nicuesa's disturbed behavior to the rescuers, who returned directly to Santa María la Antigua del Darién. Nicuesa followed more slowly, taking time to conduct a slave raid on nearby Indians. At Santa María,

Balboa carefully nurtured the negative reports about Nicuesa and turned the colony against him, so when Nicuesa finally arrived, the colonists refused to accept him as commandant. They provided him with a small ship in poor condition with which he set sail for Hispaniola in early March 1511 with only seventeen companions who remained loyal to him. Nicuesa and his little crew were never seen again.

Those remaining at Santa María la Antigua del Darién consisted of a mixed group of survivors from the expeditions of Ojeda, Nicuesa, Enciso, and Colmenares. They agreed that Balboa should lead them, and the royal government, recognizing reality, appointed him governor for the time being. Balboa proved a competent leader, popular with his men and able to repair relations with the Indians in the area to some degree. Balboa did not hesitate to use violence against Indians or take slaves, but he was also open to forming alliances and promoting trade. Through a combination of violence, intimidation, and trade, the colonists accumulated significant amounts of gold and pearls from the Natives, and news of their success attracted more people to Santa María. Balboa also explored the region, and in response to reports of a great Southern Ocean, he set out in 1513 with 190 Spanish and a few native guides. They crossed the jungle isthmus with difficulty, sometimes fighting Indians, sometimes exchanging presents with friendly chieftains. Finally, Balboa and a much-reduced group, including Francisco Pizarro, reached the Pacific Ocean, which he called the "South Sea," and claimed it in the name of Spain.

Enciso returned to Spain, where he criticized Balboa before King Ferdinand, who decided to send a new governor. His choice was Pedro Arias de Ávila, usually referred to as Pedrarias Dávila or simply Pedrarias. It is not known when he was born, but in 1514, when he set out from Spain, he was over seventy years old, ancient by the standards of the age but still vigorous. Pedrarias had won a reputation as an able military leader fighting against the Moors in Granada and in North Africa, and now he commanded a fleet of 19 ships carrying 1,500 men.

Pedrarias had scarcely landed at Santa María before matters began to go wrong. His expedition was, like so many others, undersupplied, and the food he carried was soon consumed. The settlers already at Santa María had barely enough for themselves and could do little for the new arrivals. Soon illness compounded hunger, and reportedly seven hundred of Pedrarias's settlers were dead within a month. Pedrarias radically changed Balboa's policy of reconciliation with the Indians. He sent out expeditions to raid their villages for gold, pearls, and anything else of value, and to capture Indians for slaves. Las Casas, who criticized Ojeda and Nicuesa for their behavior toward Indians, reserved his harshest criticism for Pedrarias, whom he blamed for the death of thousands of Indians over a large portion of Central America. Pascual de Andagoya, a member of Pedrarias's expedition and less critical of his behavior than Las Casas, nevertheless wrote of many ill deeds done over an area of a hundred leagues around Santa María resulting in the enslavement and depopulation of Native peoples.

Pedrarias regarded Balboa as a rival, resenting his popularity and suspicious of his every action. At one point he seemed to seek an alliance, arranging a marriage between Balboa and one of his daughters, María de Peñalosa. As Pedrarias's daughter was in a convent in Spain, the ceremony had to be performed with Pedrarias himself standing for his daughter. The marriage remained more theoretical than real; Balboa never saw his bride. Pedrarias and Balboa made plans to explore and exploit the Pacific, beginning with an expedition to the Pearl Islands off the coast of Panama. To prepare for the voyage, Balboa went as commander to the new town of Acla on the Caribbean coast of Panama north of Santa María. There he had parts of ships prefabricated to be carried across the isthmus at great labor and loss of life for assembly on the Pacific coast. While Balboa was so occupied, the paranoid Pedrarias decided to rid himself of his potential rival. He had Balboa arrested on the specious grounds that he plotted to set himself up as an independent ruler. Despite Balboa's insistence that he was a loyal servant of the Spanish king, Pedrarias's allies convicted him and his supporters in a manifestly unjust trial and had Balboa and four of his chief allies beheaded.

In 1519, the same year as Balboa's execution, Pedrarias founded a new colony on the Pacific coast, Panama City. To populate the new settlement, Pedrarias moved the population from Santa María la Antigua del Darién across the isthmus to Panama City. The transfer took some time, but as soon as Santa María was completely abandoned in 1524, the surviving Indians exultantly burned the colony, destroying it so thoroughly that its location was long forgotten. Acla also failed. The location was unhealthy, and the population drifted away to Panama City or Nombre de Dios, the town founded at the harbor of that name. By the early 1530s, Acla was deserted.

Aftermath

Alonso de Ojeda and Diego de Nicuesa lacked the personal character-istics necessary to found and lead colonies successfully. Both were more interested in gold and pearls than projecting Spanish royal power by establishing colonies on the mainland. Ojeda was too much a man of action and too little a man of thought and planning. Even before he founded his colony, he foolishly attacked Indians, underestimating their capacity for resistance, and as many as a hundred of his men died, including his able adviser Juan de la Cosa. Ojeda apparently learned nothing from the experience. Scarcely had he founded San Sebastian before he attacked Indians again, and in retaliation the Indians virtu-ally besieged San Sebastian, and it soon had to be abandoned.

Nicuesa, described in the years before he left Spain as arrogant, proved to be a poor leader of men, and as the pressure of unfortunate events mounted, his personality seems to have further deteriorated until the colonists at Santa María la Antigua del Darién rejected his leadership, and he sailed off to oblivion.

Vasco Nuñez de Balboa, charismatic and popular, was an able leader, although he too did not hesitate on occasion to abuse Indians. He rose to leadership at Santa María initially without royal sanction and was never able to overcome royal misgivings on that account. Even when officially named governor, he was intended as an interim appointment, serving until the suspicious and unscrupulous Pedrarias replaced him and then arranged Balboa's judicial murder. Santa María la Antigua del Darién was founded out of necessity by refugees without long-range planning. Ultimately, its location proved inadequate as the region developed, and Pedrarias abandoned the town.

Pedrarias was never punished for the death of Balboa or his numer-ous barbarous depredations on Indians. He was finally replaced as governor of Panama in 1526, when he became governor of Nicaragua, a post he held until he died in 1531 at more than ninety years old.

The location of Santa María la Antigua del Darién, lost for cen-turies, has been recovered by archaeologists, whose investigations have revealed new information about the colony. The town consisted of two communities, Spanish and Native Indian, living side by side. There was considerable mutual cultural exchange. For example, the Spanish lived in homes architecturally adapted from Indian prototypes and uti-lized earthenware of both Spanish and Indian types, while Indian ce-ramics sometimes adopted and adapted Spanish motifs. Despite evidence of mutual influences, the relations between the communities were unequal. The Spanish, clearly dominant, referred to the Native population as *naborías,* servants, and after the Spanish abandoned the colony, the Indians joyously burned it. Exemplary archaeological work on the site has led the government of Colombia to establish an archaeological park at the site.

Sources

Bartolomé de las Casas's most important work directly relevant to the San Sebastian de Uraba and Santa María la Antigua del Darién colonies is *Historia de las Indias,* which remained unpublished until 1875 (Fray Bartolomé de las Casas, *Historia de las Indias,* 3 vols., ed. El Marqués de la Fuensanta and José Sancho Rayon [Madrid: Miguel Ginesta, 1875]). The work is now available in many modern Spanish editions, but it has never been translated entirely into English, and La Casas's Spanish is tortuous to read. Portions are available in translation in Andrée Collard, *History of the Indies* (New York, Harper and Row, 1971), and in *Repertorium Columbianum* (Berkeley: University of California Press, 1993–), vol. 6: *A Synoptic Edition of the Log of Columbus's First Voyage,* ed. Francesca Lardicci, trans. Cynthia L. Chamberlin and Blair Sullivan; vol. 7: *Las Casas on Columbus: The Second and Fourth Voyages,* ed. Anthony Pagden, trans. Nigel Griffin; and vol. 11: *Las Casas on Columbus: The Third Voyage,* ed. Geoffrey Symcox, trans. Michael Hammer. For a fuller discussion of Las Casas, see chapter 1 above.

Gonzalo Fernández de Oviedo y Valdés, known generally as Oviedo, was born in Spain in 1478. He came to Hispaniola in 1514 as the royal controller of gold mining and smelting, a post he held for almost twenty years, during which time he simultaneously held a number of other significant government posts and published works of great importance. His most significant work is *La historia general y natural de las Indias,* in which he records observations on the culture of the Indians and the plants and animals of the Indies, as well as an able history of the course of Spanish exploration, colonization, and politics. The first part appeared in 1535 as *Primera parte de la historia natural y general y de las indias yslas y tierra firme de mar oceano.* (Sevilla: Juan Cromberger, 1535). Publication of the second part was apparently delayed by Las Casas and did not appear until shortly after Oviedo's death as *Libro XX, De la segunda parte de la general historia de las Indias* (Valladolid: Francisco Fernandez de Cordoba, 1557). The entire work, consisting of fifty-five books (i.e., chapters), was first published in its entirety as Gonzalo Fernández de Oviedo y Valdés, *Historia General y Natural de las Indias, Islas y Tierra Firme del Mar Océcano*, 4 vols., ed. José Amador de los Rios (Madrid: Imprenta de la Real Academia de la Historia, 1851–1855). He provides important information about Ojeda and Nicuesa from a somewhat different aspect than Las Casas.

Pietro Martire D'Anghera, often called Peter Martyr in English, was born in Italy in 1457. In 1487, he moved to Spain, where he became the official chronicler of the royal council for the Indies. Pietro Martire's most important historical work is *De Orbe Novo Petri Marturis Mediolanensis Protonotarij Senatoris Decades*, composed and published over many years, from as early as 1493 until 1525, shortly before the author's death, although the eight *Decades*, the term Martire used for chapters, did not appear together until 1530 (Compluti [i.e., Alcalde de Henares, Spain]: Apud Nichaele[m] d[e] Eguia, 1530). The standard English translation is Francis Augustus, ed., intro, and notes, *De Orbe Novo: The Eight Decades of Peter Martyr D'Anghera*, 2 vols. (New York: G. P. Putnam's Sons, 1912). In the second decade, he provides a narrative account of the misadventures of Ojeda and Nicuesa, enlivened by anecdotes. He was not a firsthand witness, but he had excellent access to official reports and information from officials who had returned to Spain. While not adverse to criticizing actions, he was more concerned with providing a coherent narrative that in places ignores conflicting versions of events.

Pascual de Andagoya was born in Spain in 1495. He traveled to America in 1514 as part of the expedition commanded by Pedrarias. He took part in Pedrarias's administration, including the founding of Panama City, and later became governor of San Juan in Colombia. He received early intelligence of the existence of the Inca Empire, but he fell ill and took no part in the conquest. Had he rather than Pizarro taken the lead, the conquest of Peru might have taken a much more humane course. Andagoya wrote an account dealing with the governorship of Pedrarias and subsequent events through Pizarro's conquest of Peru. The work remained unpublished and ignored in the archive of the Naval Museum in Madrid until Martín Fernández de Navarrete discovered and published it in *Coleccion de los viages y descrubrimientos, que lvicieron por mar los Espanoles, desde fines de siglo xv*

(Madrid: Imprenta Real, 1825–[1837]), Seccion iii, Establicimientos de los Espanoles en el Darien, Tom. iii, No. vii, p. 393, entitling it *Relación de los sucesos de Pedrarias Dávila en las provincias de Tierra Firme y Castilla del Oro.* An excellent translation into English is readily available as Pascual de Andagoya, *Narrative of the proceedings of Pedrarias Davila in the provinces of Tierra Firme or Castilla del Oro, and of the discovery of the South Sea and the coasts of Peru and Nicaragua,* trans. and ed. Clements Robert Markham (London: Hakluyt Society, 1865). Andagoya's account of Pedrarias is curiously neutral, even when describing terrible depredations against Indians or Balboa's judicial murder.

Francisco López de Gómara, *Historia General de las Indias* (Medina: n.p., 1553) adds little. He never traveled to the Americas and derived his information from other writers. His chief focus was Hernán Cortés and the conquest of Mexico, and he was sometimes far from accurate even regarding Cortés.

Antonio de Herrera y Tordesillas (1549–1626 or 1627) was a prolific Spanish writer of the second half of the sixteenth and early seventeenth centuries. His most relevant work is *Historia general de los hechos de los castellanos en las Islas y Tierra Firme del mar Océano que llaman Indias Occidentales* [General History of the Deeds of the Castilians on the Islands and Mainland of the Ocean Sea Known As the West Indies] (Madrid: en la Emplenta Real, 1601), which contains an account of the activities of Ojeda and Nicuesa. Initially well regarded, Herrera's work is now generally discounted as of little worth. Herrera, too, never traveled to the Americas and had no interest in Native American people. He derived all he wrote from others, seldom acknowledging their work even when incorporating large sections of others' text with little or no modification. He wrote to promote the royal bureaucracy's official views, and as a courtier he was described as a greedy, scheming opportunist.

Archaeologists have provided insight into life and death at Santa María la Antigua del Darién: Alberto Sarcina, "Santa María la Antigua del Darién, la primera ciudad Española en Tierra Firme: una prospección arqueológica sistemática," *Revista Colombiana de Antropología* 53, 1 (Enera-Junio 2017), 269-300; Luis Fernando González Escobar, *El Darién: Ocupación, poblamienta y transformación Ambiental, Una revision histórica, parte I* (Medellín: Instituto Tecnológico Metropolitano, 2011); Marilena Cozzolino, Julian Andres Gallego, Vincenzo

Gentile, and Alberto Sarcina, "Santa María de la Antigua del Darién (Colombia), the First Spanish City in Tierra Firme: A Systematic Archaeological and Geophysical Prospection," first International Conference on Metrology for Archaeology, Benevento, Italy, October 22–23, 2015, https://www.researchgate.net/publication/284027969. The Colombian government has now established an archaeological park at the site.

THREE

German Bankers *in the* Jungles: Venezuela (1528–1556)

Background

As Holy Roman emperor and king of Spain, Charles V controlled vast resources, but he also faced profound crises. In 1519, he paid enormous bribes to the seven electors to the Holy Roman Empire to secure his election as emperor. He required even more money to finance conflicts with France and the Ottoman Empire, to deal with disruptions associated with the early years of the Reformation, and to maintain his elaborate court. Charles V borrowed heavily from German and Italian banking and merchant houses, particularly the German Fuggers and Welsers, who continued to loan money to the emperor over the course of years. Although the Fuggers lent more to the emperor, the Welsers were more intimately connected to Spain. They had agents operating on the island of Madeira, in the Atlantic by the northern African coast, as early as 1490; in 1524, they established a branch in Seville, the Spanish port for trade with the Americas. In 1526, the Welsers had a representative at Santo Domingo on the island of Hispaniola dealing mainly with the pearl trade. The Caribbean representative of the Welsers, far separated from the company administration in Germany, necessarily exercised considerable independence. In the future that would become a problem.

The Welser Grant

To service his debts, in 1525, Charles V granted the Fuggers control of the silver mines of Tyrol and the royal revenues from the Spanish orders of knighthood, and in 1528, he conferred on the Welsers a large portion of the northern coast of South America, today Venezuela. The area remained, of course, under Spanish sovereignty, but the Welsers gained the right to colonize, explore, and exploit the territory in accordance with the terms of the grant. The concept of a corporation as a legal entity similar in law to an individual was not entirely formed at the time, so rather than a representative signing the agreement in the name of the House of Welser, two members of the House, Heinrich Ehinger and Hieronymous Sailer, signed as individuals. Later the contract was transferred to Anton and Bartholomäus V. Welser, head of the Welser family and business.

The Spanish found it difficult to deal with German names, and Heinrich Ehinger's first name appears as Ambrosio or Ambrosius in Spanish documents, and his last name most often as Alfinger, but it was also rendered as Einguer, Inger, Inguer, Ynger, Einger, Ynguer, Eynguer, Lespringer, and Dalfinger. The Spanish had less trouble with Sailer, whose name appears as Saylor, Sayler, Seyler, and Seiler. Welser appears in Spanish documents as Belezer and Belzare.

Charles V's grant to the Welsers was like other grants awarded to those who endeavored to colonize and settle in Spanish America. The representatives of the Welsers were charged with establishing two new towns of at least three hundred settlers within two years, to establish three forts, and to bring fifty German miners as colonists. Colonists were to receive exemption from taxes for eight years, free lots for houses in the new towns, and agricultural land that would become their private property after having cultivated it for four years. The Welsers would only have to remit to the crown a tenth of gold or silver acquired during the first three years and then an annually increasing amount over the next five years until the crown received the normal fifth. The Welsers were instructed to treat the Indians fairly, but the crown permitted them to enslave Indians who resisted Spanish rule. The Welsers were also permitted to import up to four thousand African slaves during the first four years.

In 1528, little was known about the geography of South America, and much of what had been learned had not yet been widely shared and fully integrated. It was not yet even apparent that South America was a single continuous land mass. The northern part of South America was thought by some to be an island separated from land farther south by a strait yet to be discovered but believed to provide a short route to the Pacific. Spanish slave raiders alienated many of the Native peoples who lived near the northern coast even before Charles V granted the area to the Welsers. Unlike the relatively centralized Aztec and Inca Empires, there was no tradition of central authority that once conquered served to reduce an entire area to obedience. Loosely organized Native villages normally acted independently, coming together only when some force from outside threatened them collectively. The Native people resisted Spanish intrusion fiercely, and their use of deadly poison arrows was justly feared.

The Spanish knew little of the area beyond the coast and had established few settlements in northern South America by the mid-1520s. To the east of the Welser grant, there was a Spanish settlement at Cumaná. In 1515, the Franciscans established a small monastery there, and the Dominicans built another small monastery nearby on the bank of the Chiribichi River, today the Manzanares River. Slave raiders from the pearl fishery on the isle of Cubagua near Margarita preyed on the Carib Indians in the area, alienating them from the Spanish and placing the friars in danger. The missionary Pedro de Córdoba suggested to Bartolomé de las Casas, the famous advocate for the Indians, that he establish a settlement at Cumaná to proselytize the Indians peacefully and protect them from abuse. Las Casas petitioned the king, but he was opposed by powerful factions in court. In 1520, Las Casas received a concession from the crown, but it was much less than he requested. Late that year, he sailed from Spain with a small group of poor Spanish farmers whom he hoped would become the core of his planned settlement, but when he arrived at Puerto Rico, he received the news that the Indians, outraged at continued slave raiding, had destroyed the Dominican monastery and killed two friars. The Spanish launched a retributive campaign that was no more than another slave raid.

Although the Spanish farmers deserted Las Casas to remain in Puerto Rico, he continued to Cumaná with a small group of missionaries. He labored for months to establish peaceful relations with the Indians and build the nucleus of a colony, but the continued activity of slavers negated his efforts. In 1522, Las Casas left Cumaná for Hispaniola to lodge complaints with the royal authorities, but while he was gone the Indians burned Cumaná and killed four of Las Casas's companions. Las Casas abandoned his hopes for Cumaná and joined the Dominican order. Henceforth he devoted his efforts to writing, recording abuses visited upon Indians, and hoping to move the conscience of his readers. The Spanish sent yet another campaign against the Natives and refounded the town, officially named Nuevo Toledo although it remained Cumaná in common use.

To the west of the Welser grant lay the Spanish colony of Santa Marta, a small settlement founded by Rodrigo de Bastidas. Bastidas had a long career in the New World, beginning when he sailed with Columbus on his second voyage in 1493. He first visited the future site of Santa Marta in 1501 and noted its suitability for a colony, although he was not able to establish a settlement there until 1525. In 1527, Bastidas led a trading expedition into the interior, acquiring a considerable quantity of gold. He refused to distribute any to his troops, claiming he required all for the expenses of the colony, and he was soon assassinated. García de Lerma replaced Bastidas. Lerma was a banker and merchant who aided in the negotiations between Carlos V and the Welsers that resulted in the Venezuela grant.

The territory granted to the Welsers extended from the small harbor of Maracapana, near Cumana in the east, to Capo de la Vela in the west, over 650 miles in a direct line and about twice that following the coast. Along this expanse there was only one settlement, Santa Anna de Coro, generally called Coro, established in 1527 by Juan Martín de Ampiés, who was acting on orders from royal officials at Santo Domingo. Ampiés, whose name also appears as Juan Martínez de Ampeús, established peaceful relations with the Indians, who traded food in exchange for Spanish goods.

Ehinger

In 1528, four ships set sail for Santo Domingo on the island of Hispaniola. On board were García de Lerma, the new governor of Santa Marta, and about 280 troops. Lerma bore documents appointing Ambrosius Ehinger, at that time the Welsers' representative at Santo Domingo, as the governor of Venezuela. Ehinger was eager to get to his new post, while Lerma wished to remain for a while in Santo Domingo. By agreement, Lerma remained behind with one ship, about fifty men, and a sixth of the supplies, while Ehinger sailed to Coro with the remaining ships, the rest of the men, and some additional troops he raised on Hispaniola, for a total of about three hundred. The great majority were Spanish soldiers, but there were also Portuguese and some African slaves. Ehinger announced that he, by royal order, was replacing Ampiés, who disliked the order but could do nothing to resist it. Ehinger shipped Ampiés off to Santo Domingo initially, but the Spanish crown eventually appointed him governor of the three islands of Aruba, Curaçao, and Bonaire, poor recompense for loss of the settlement he founded.

Ehinger named the Welser colony Klein Venedig (Little Venice). There are conflicting theories about the names "Venezuela" and "Klein Venedig." Some claim "Venezuela" is derived from the name of an Indian tribe, and any connection to Venice stems from the coincidental similarity of the names. Others hold that Indians, especially those around Lake Maracaibo and in the coastal region, built their villages on the water, driving posts into the lake bottom on which to erect their shelters, and this led to a fancied resemblance to Venice.

The removal of Ampiés was one early manifestation of a recurring problem: ill feelings between Spanish and Germans. Charles V, as Holy Roman emperor and king of Spain, decreed that the Welsers commanded in Venezuela, and loyal Spanish subjects obeyed, but there was resentment nonetheless at the elevation of foreigners over Spanish. The Germans, moreover, openly preferred their countrymen even to the extent of replacing experienced and respected Spanish military men with untested, inexperienced youths fresh from Germany.

The Welsers administered the Venezuela colony differently than the usual Spanish pattern. The Spanish government provided basic provisions and equipment until colonies were established and self-sufficient, but from the beginning the Welsers, in an exhibition of early corporate capitalism, charged their colonists for everything except the house lots and agricultural land specifically allowed to the colonists in the Spanish grant. The common colonists, poor farmers, miners, and soldiers had few resources with which to pay, so the Welsers extended credit at a significant rate of interest. As a result, almost all colonists were soon deeply in debt, discontent, and with no way out of their predicament unless they found a sudden source of wealth. There seemed to be such an opportunity.

Ehinger and others soon heard tales from Indians about a spectacular ceremony enacted at a sacred lake. The chief would be ceremonially covered in gold dust, and then El Dorado, the Gilded Man, would

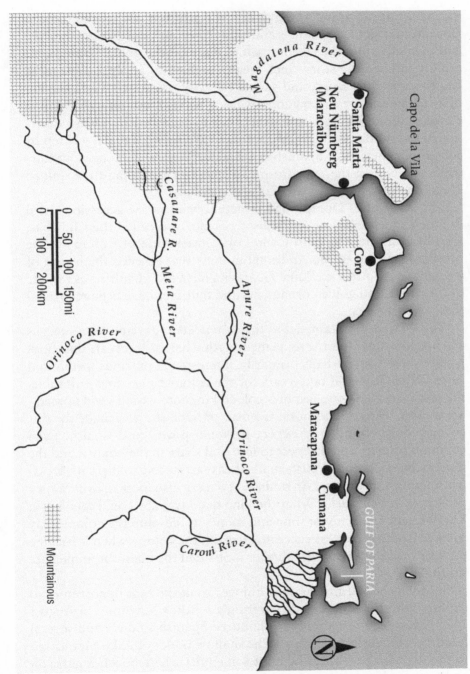

German Venezuela and surrounding areas with indication of mountainous regions.

mount a raft along with attendants who paddled out on the lake. El Dorado cast gold, emeralds, and other precious stones into the lake and then dove into the lake himself to wash off the gold. Assumptions rapidly inflated the story. Such wealth seemed to imply a substantial city that the chief ruled, and such a rich city could only be the center of a substantially rich kingdom, waiting to be discovered by German conquistadors. Ehinger and others who succeeded him were determined to find this bonanza. Accounts of Welser Venezuela, written by contemporaries, later Spanish colonial authors, and modern authors tend to focus on the expeditions to find El Dorado and the golden kingdom, ignoring other aspects of the colony.

The story of El Dorado had a factual basis in the accession ritual of a new chief (*zipa*) of the Muisca people, also called the Chibchas, who lived in the Altiplano Cundiboyacense region of Colombia, the northern portion of the Andes mountains that extends the length of western South America. Lake Guatavita has been identified as the site of the ritual, and golden ornaments and figurines have been recovered there over the years.

The Welsers maintained that they intended to develop Venezuela as a center of trade, but the agreement with Charles V reveals that both parties were also, perhaps primarily, interested in precious metals and gems. While it would take years for the colony to become profitable, the discovery and conquest of a golden kingdom would yield immediate wealth. The conquistador, German or Spanish, who made the discovery could confidently expect personal power and wealth. Even common soldiers could expect to loot and share in the bounty, and the indebtedness of the colonists made it easy to recruit soldiers for treasure hunting expeditions. An ominous concern also loomed over Welser prospects in Venezuela. What the king had given, he could take back. The Welsers might invest time and money to develop the colony only to have Charles V or his successor reclaim the colony when it became prosperous. This possibility further motivated the quest for immediate profit.

So it was not surprising that Ehinger took the first opportunity to explore with the object of discovering a wealthy kingdom. In August 1529, he sailed with about two hundred Spanish soldiers and several hundred Indian slave porters to the shallow outlet of Lake Maracaibo to the sea, and near there he built some huts where he left a garrison and some of his men who were ill with tropical fevers. He named the

Muisca gold depiction of El Dorado on a raft with attendants. The relic was found in 1969 and is now housed in the Gold Museum, Bogotá, Colombia. (*Pedro Szekely/Creative Commons*)

little settlement Neu Nürnberg, and while the settlement survived, the name did not. The Spanish called the town by the name of the lake: Maracaibo. Ehinger explored the shores of Lake Maracaibo, the extent of which was then not known. He soon discovered that it did not offer a waterway to the Pacific and there was no golden kingdom there, but Ehinger ravished many Indian villages around the lake, taking slaves and leaving behind devastated communities. The expedition ended when Ehinger fell ill and returned to Coro.

Ehinger and Federmann

At Coro, no word had been heard of Ehinger for about a year, and he was widely believed to be dead. During that year, a Welser associate, Nikolaus Federmann, arrived from Spain with settlers and miners. Shortly thereafter another Welser official, Hans Seissenhofer, also arrived. Seissenhofer, who was senior to Federmann, assumed control of the colony and appointed Federmann his second in command. Seissenhofer died shortly before Ehinger emerged from the wilderness to resume command at Coro, but Ehinger soon departed to Santo Domingo to recuperate after his expedition, leaving Federmann in command. The slaves Ehinger had captured around Lake Maracaibo

were also sent to Santo Domingo and there sold to work on plantations and mines.

Federmann soon grew bored in Coro and departed in September
1530 on an unauthorized expedition along with 16 mounted soldiers,
110 foot soldiers, and about 100 Native bearers. He nominally sought
to find the Pacific coast, still believing it to be not far to the south, but
he was at least as much interested in gold and discovering the rumored
golden kingdom of El Dorado. He even spent some time searching for
a reported tribe of pygmies. Federmann traveled a modest distance to
the south, but he was soon discouraged by local Indians and returned
to Coro in March 1531, bearing new reports of a rich kingdom to the
west and a couple thousand ounces of gold acquired by trade and looting Indian villages.

Ehinger dispatched Federmann to Spain to answer for his unautho-
rized expedition, the complications of which occupied several years.
During this time, Federmann wrote about his expedition, although it
would not be published until over two decades later: *Indianische His-
toria: Eine shone kurtzweilige Historia Niclaus Federmanns de
Jüngern von Vlm erster Raise* [Indian History: A beautiful entertaining
History of Nicolaus Federmann the Younger of Ulm's First Expedition]
(Hagenaw: Sigmund Bund, 1557).

Ehinger's first expedition lasted a year and produced little profit,
most of that from captives sold as slaves. He was, however, far from
discouraged, and soon after he returned to Coro from Santo Domingo,
he organized a new expedition comprising 40 mounted men, 130 foot
soldiers, and several hundred Indian bearers. Ehinger first proceeded
to Maracaibo by sea and from there by land to the southwest, crossing
from Welser territory into that of Santa Marta and going as far as the
Magdalena River. He must have known he was trespassing, but it did
not bother him. If he found the golden kingdom all would undoubtedly
be forgiven, and if he did not, the Spanish at Santa Marta might never
discover his actions. No one had yet traveled down the Magdalena
River from Santa Marta to the area where Ehinger reached the river.

It is virtually impossible to trace with certainty the later parts of
Ehinger's course, and that is also true of other Welser expeditions deep
into the jungles and plains of northern South America. Writers have
come to contrasting conclusions about their paths. It is apparent, however, that Ehinger moved south along and paralleling the path of the
Magdalena River.

Ehinger and his troops committed atrocities that astounded even the Spanish chroniclers. Early in the march tribes greeted Ehinger peacefully, bearing gifts, only to be attacked violently, their villages looted, and chiefs tortured to reveal the location of the golden kingdom, which they could not reveal because they did not know. Indians quickly realized that the best way to rid themselves of the Germans and Spanish was to make up a location. So the Indians told them their goal was to the south, and the conquistadors marched on. They left behind a swath of destruction, chiefs slaughtered, entire villages massacred to intimidate tribes, men kidnapped to serve as bearers, who, when they collapsed from fatigue and abuse, were casually killed and their bodies abandoned along the trail. Word of Ehinger's cruelty quickly spread to other tribes, who resisted fiercely, but the Europeans possessed steel weapons, armor, firearms, and mounted troops. Casualties among the Indians were horrendous, but the conquistadors also lost men to warfare, fevers, and other illnesses. Ehinger still pressed on.

It may be suspected that some of the gaudy accounts of Ehinger's atrocities are exaggerated, perhaps to show that the much-publicized cruelty of the Spanish was exceeded by others. Even Bartolomé de las Casas, however, describes Ehinger's depredations as crueler than any other, calling them unnatural and fiercer than the most vicious wild animals. Las Casas, the great advocate for the Indians, was never hesitant to condemn Spanish behavior and even threaten ever-lasting damnation for owning Indian slaves. It is unbelievable that he would obliquely attempt to defend the Spanish by slandering Ehinger. Moreover, the greatest number of Ehinger's troops were Spanish, with some Portuguese and a few of other origins. Ehinger certainly permitted and encouraged atrocities, but there is no record of any objection from the officers or common soldiers.

At the village of Tamalmeque on the Magdalena River, Ehinger began to run short of provisions despite all despoiled from the Indians. He detached thirty-five men under the command of Iñigo de Vascuña and ordered them to return to Coro carrying a significant portion of the gold looted from the Indians and there to use the wealth to recruit reinforcements and secure equipment and provisions. Vascuña and his men could not return along the route where Ehinger had left only devastation and implacable enemies, so they headed to the northeast, passing south of Lake Maracaibo into an area not yet explored by

Europeans. They found themselves in thick jungle and trackless swamps, and beset by Indians. As men fell by the wayside from exhaustion, fever, and ambush, the load of gold became too heavy to carry, and they buried it beneath a prominent tree. Despite later searches, there is no indication the treasure was ever recovered, and it may still be there. The survivors soon quarreled about how to proceed and split into separate groups, only to perish before reaching Coro. Just one man, Francisco Martín, survived. Captured by Indians, he soon showed talent as a healer, adopted the Native culture, and married an Indian wife.

Ehinger waited in vain for Vascuña to bring relief before concluding that he had been betrayed and left to die, yet he would not turn back. Indian reports claimed the land of El Dorado lay in the mountains, and the Magdalena River ran in a tropical valley between two mountain ranges. A scouting party reported that to the southeast there seemed to be access to cooler uplands and the mountain chain. The uplands provided relief from the fetid jungle, but as Ehinger and his men attempted to penetrate the high mountains, they encountered icy cold. Almost all the bearers, Indians from the hot lowlands, died of exhaustion, hunger, and the cold. Troops, similarly malnourished and wracked by tropical fevers, also perished. Of the 170 troops that began the march, Ehinger now had only about 40 remaining, but still they had not found El Dorado. Ehinger finally admitted defeat and began to return toward Coro, avoiding the areas he had ravaged. Word soon spread of Ehinger's return, and during one of the confrontations with Indians, he was struck in the neck by a poisoned arrow and died three days later. A Spanish officer, Pedro de San Martin, took command, and the remnant of Ehinger's force pressed on. They chanced to encounter the sole survivor of Vascuña's ill-fated detachment, Francisco Martín, who persuaded the Indians to allow the troops to pass peacefully. The survivors reached Maracaibo and then returned to Coro over two years after their departure. Each soldier received a share of the gold that Ehinger had accumulated, but the sum was paltry compared to the number of Indians slaughtered, the comrades killed, and sufferings endured.

George Hohemut/Jorge de Spira and Federmann

At the time the survivors arrived, Coro was in chaos. Relations with neighboring Indians had broken down. From the founding of the set-

Drawing by Hieronymus Köler the Elder, ca. 1560, based on a description written in 1537 of George Hohemut (Jorge de Spira) and Philipp von Hutten proceeding to the inspection of Welser forces in Spain before their dispatch to Venezuela. Hohemut is depicted top right preceded by two mounted drummers and Von Hutten below, followed by a footman. (*Kolorierte Zeichnung von Hieronymus Köler d. Ä. [um 1560]*)

tlement, the colonists had traded for food and labor from a friendly tribe and consequently neglected to establish their own farms. The colonists grew careless about their relations with the Indians and began to abuse them, and the tribe abandoned the area. Colonists attempted to coerce other tribes to provide food but only provoked hostility, and now it was unsafe for colonists to leave the immediate area of the settlement. Food was in short supply and dependent on imports from Santo Domingo and other Spanish ports.

Before Ehinger departed on this fatal expedition, he appointed Bartolomé de Santillana to act in his absence at Coro. Santillana feuded with the royal treasurer and other royal officials, who drew up charges against him that they sent to the royal *audiencia* at Santo Domingo. The audiencia was a court to administer justice in cases involving royal prerogative and to oversee the administration of royal officials. While waiting for the audiencia to act, Santillana's enemies at Coro imprisoned him and transferred the government to Pedro de San Martín. The audiencia finally officially deposed Santillana and appointed Bishop Rodrigo de Bastidas as interim governor until the government in Spain provided further guidance. The Welsers objected that the audiencia was usurping its authority, but the Welsers and the Spanish crown both agreed to the appointment of Nikolaus Federmann as the new governor. Spanish officers, however, complained of Federmann's earlier appointment over more-experienced men and his unauthorized and failed expedition, and so the appointment was rescinded even before he could reach Venezuela. Instead, George Hohemut, a German knight from the city of Speyer on the Rhine River, became governor, arriving in 1534, and as a conciliation, Federmann became his assistant with the title of captain general. The Spanish tongue does not easily conform itself to a name like Hohemut, so the new governor became known simply as Jorge de Spira or occasionally de Speyer or de Espira.

New colonists came to Coro at irregular intervals, but it remained a small, ill-developed settlement. Most arrivals went on expeditions to find gold, only to find anonymous graves in the jungle. Some six hundred new colonists arrived with Jorge de Spira, and a decision had to be made whether they would become agriculturalists and develop the land around Coro or serve as soldiers seeking the golden kingdom of El Dorado. The failure of early expeditions and the high rate of deaths did not discourage enthusiasm for treasure hunting. The rumors of El Dorado and a golden kingdom in northern South America were strong, and some gold had been looted from Indians, seeming to promise much more. Word reached Coro of Francisco Pizarro González's conquest of Inca Peru and the vast treasure there. Men could only think that if an illiterate pig herder could find a golden kingdom and become one of the great men of the Spanish Empire, why not us here in Venezuela also? And the Spanish who had settled near the mouth of the Orinoco River also heard and believed in the rumors of a rich kingdom, and they were launching expeditions up that vast river complex seeking the prize. If the Welsers, their agents, and their colonists were to find the golden kingdom, they had to act quickly before others could do so. All far outweighed the dubious attractions of laboring in fields hacked out of the humid jungle and rough hill country to grow crops offering little more than subsistence, all the while wary of possible attacks by Indians. Thus, Jorge de Spira had no difficulty in recruiting troops for yet another expedition in search of the kingdom of El Dorado.

Before departing on his own expedition, De Spira had to deal with the new governor of Santa Marta, who was trying to expand his territory by claiming a valley that was clearly within the Welser grant. De Spira sent Federmann with some troops who quickly asserted control. Federmann was glad of the opportunity, as he was now convinced that the golden kingdom lay to the southwest among the mountains, and he began planning his own expedition.

In May 1535, De Spira sent an advanced contingent south from Coro, apparently not deterred by Federmann's failure to find great wealth in the region. De Spira's advanced troops were repulsed by Indians, but his main force of about three hundred infantry and one hundred mounted troops quickly routed the Natives. Soon, however, a tropical fever devastated the troops. The ill returned to Coro, and De Spira's forces were reduced to about 150 infantry and 50 mounted men. He altered the course of march to the southwest to reach the foothills of the great mountain spine of Colombia and then south along the foothills and plains. Running short of provisions, the conquistadors raided Indian villages for corn and hunted for meat.

De Spira and his men persisted throughout 1635 without finding substantial gold or even encouraging reports about a wealthy kingdom. In early spring 1636, they reached the Casanare River, a tributary of the Meta River, itself a tributary of the Oronoco. Near there friendly Zaquitios Indians entertained him with reports of a tribe living on a plateau to the west across the mountains. They claimed that the tribe was rich in gold, that there was a great temple filled with golden dedications at the chief settlement, and that they raised domesticated animals that Spira and his Spanish troops interpreted as sheep but were probably lamas or alpacas. As Spira and his men sought in vain for a pass, they were attacked by Indians. He moved farther south, searching for a pass through the mountains to the west; he found no pass but more Indians and torrential rains that caused widespread flooding. He retreated north to regroup and then moved south again, overwhelming the tribes. Friendlier Indians again reported a golden kingdom existed in the mountains, and De Spira and his troops, slowly diminishing in numbers, pressed farther south while continuing to search in vain for a pass to the mountain plateau.

By August 1537, De Spira had marched so far south that he was only one degree north of the equator, and here he finally gave up and began the long retreat to Coro. His force was now reduced to only about fifty healthy men, all the rest either dead or invalids barely able to keep up with the main body of troops. He arrived in Coro at the end of May 1538, after a little over three years of marching and fight-ing. De Spira had begun with 400 men, but only 160 survived. Many of them, including De Spira, were in poor health, worn out by their exertions and diseases. De Spira had accumulated less than four thou-sand ounces of gold, not enough to satisfy him, his surviving soldiers, or the Welsers, but enough to reinforce the belief that a fortune re-mained to be found. On the return trip, De Spira heard reports that Federmann had traveled far to the south of his assignment to secure the western border with the Santa Marta colony, and when De Spira arrived at Coro, Federmann was conspicuously absent.

Federmann had gone to the west and warned off the Spanish at Santa Marta who had trespassed on the Welser grant, but after return-ing to Coro, he quickly organized his own expedition to the interior in search of riches, departing in spring 1536. Federmann's effort began like another vain march into the interior, but it would prove quite dif-ferent. With about four hundred men, Federmann set out from Coro to the southeast. This route enabled him to avoid most of the jungle and reach *los llanos*, literally the plains, an enormous tropical grassland to the east of the Andes mountains in Venezuela. Travel there would seem easier and healthier than through the jungles, but the llanos offer their own difficulties. Many waterways feeding into the tributaries of the enormous Orinoco River cut across the plain, flooding large areas after rains. Thick canebrakes and swamps flank these streams and rivers, impeding passage and housing swarms of disease-bearing mos-quitos and other insects. The track to the southeast, however, enabled Federmann to avoid De Spira and continue his independent expedition.

After reaching the confluence of the Apure River with the Orinoco, Federmann turned west by southwest, roughly paralleling the course of the Meta River until he reached the westernmost branch of the Andes. There he too sought a pass that would lead to the fabled land of El Dorado. The search occupied late 1537, all of 1538, and into 1539. Federmann and the troops raided Indians for food and kid-napped bearers, and the troops grew ragged and exhausted before they discovered a route onto the plateau, but it could hardly be called a pass. The troops had to ascend to over thirteen thousand feet, scramble over precipitous bare rock faces, and haul their remaining horses up slopes they could not traverse on their own. They finally arrived at a high savannah, the home of the Muisca, the people of El Dorado, but all was not as they hoped.

The Muisca had a more complex culture than the tribes through whose territory they had passed, but they were in no sense as rich as the Aztec and Inca. The Muisca grew abundant crops of potatoes, but their chief wealth lay in salt and skilled weaving and, to a much lesser degree, in emeralds. Several salt lakes in their territory enabled them to export the mineral in high demand by tribes who lived far from the sea. The Muisca traded salt for cotton, which they could not grow on their high plateau, and their skilled weavers converted the cotton into beautiful clothing that was also a highly valued export. The Muisca also mined emeralds, but the deposit was not particularly rich and was subsequently little exploited. The Muisca imported fruit, grain, and gold, as they had no source of gold in their territory. The metal was too soft to be useful, but its luster and color made it an appropriate sacrifice to the gods, as in the famous El Dorado ceremony. By the time Federmann arrived, the ceremony had not been celebrated for a generation, but the story had spread and persisted. The Muisca were so little like the inflated Spanish and German expectations that they did not recognize them as the object of their quest. Despite the discovery of the Muisca, the search for the fabulously wealthy kingdom of rumor continued.

Federmann and his men faced an even greater disappointment. The Spanish from Santa Marta had beaten them to the plateau and secured the Muisca's limited reserve of gold. Gonzalo Jiménez de Quesada, officer of the governor of Santa Marta, led his men on a hellish journey down the valley of the Magdalena River, hacking their way through jungle and confronting Indians who well remembered Ehinger's earlier brutalities. Finally, they entered the high plateau through a better pass than Federmann's troops had found.

The Muisca culture was organized around two chiefdoms that existed in a sort of perpetual contest for domination. Originally, the *zipa* was the highest chief, and the *zaque* a subordinate, but the two offices evolved into rivals, uniting only to repel attacks by other tribes from beyond the plateau. At the time of Quesada's arrival, the *zaque* and his people had a significant reserve of imported gold, which Quesada looted. Federmann and his troops were left with poor gleanings, and tension grew between the two groups of conquistadors. The situation grew more complex with the arrival of a third group of Spanish, from Peru.

Sebastián de Belalcázar was a companion of Pizarro's, who appointed him commander of the garrison of the important port of San

Miguel on the coast of Peru. Soon after Pizarro marched off to conquer inland Peru, Belalcázar, like Federmann, deserted his post to seek his own fortune. Along with about a hundred Spanish soldiers and many Indian allies, Belalcázar conquered Quito, today the capital of Ecuador, and founded the town and province of Popayán, but he secured little treasure. There, however, he heard the story of El Dorado and set out to find the fabled golden kingdom.

The meeting of the three commanders and their troops might have resulted in bloody conflict as they fought over Quesada's treasure. Quesada, however, proposed a reasonable solution. Quesada, Belalcázar, and Federmann sailed down the Magdalena River to travel together to Spain to lay the discovery before the king. They avoided Santa Marta, fearing the governor there would confiscate the treasure, and made their way to Spain, but there their fortunes miscarried. Rather than remaining together, they separated, each to press his own case, and none of the three prospered.

Federmann sought to be appointed governor of Venezuela, but the Welsers had no use for a man who had twice deserted his post to seek the land of El Dorado and had failed to secure significant treasure. They accused Federmann of disloyalty and stealing wealth that justly belonged to the company and demanded he surrender emeralds worth one hundred thousand gold ducats and fifteen thousand ducats in gold to them. Federmann had no such resources. He contested the Welsers' claims in court in Ghent, Belgium, and before the Council of the Indies in Spain, accusing the Welsers of cheating the king of his share of profits. The case dragged on until 1541, when a settlement was arranged by which the Welsers abandoned their claims against Federmann, and Federmann ceded his lands in Colombia to the Welsers. Bitterness, however, continued between the two parties, and the Welsers may have been responsible for spreading rumors that Federmann was irreligious and perhaps even a Lutheran. The Inquisition took interest, and it is reported that he died in a Spanish prison in 1542 at age thirty-seven.

After a short interval in Spain, Belalcázar returned to South America as the governor of the province of Popayán, where he became involved in a civil war among the Spanish conquistadors during which he hanged a court favorite. The crown tried him in absentia and convicted him of murder. He set out for Spain to appeal the conviction but died of natural causes at Cartagena in 1551.

On the return to Spain, Quesada initially landed in Portugal, where he remained for months, addicted to gambling, while the worthless son of a previous governor of Santa Marta turned the Spanish court against him. Denied office, Quesada left Spain and for nine years drifted through Europe, living as a gambler. During that time, he wrote an autobiography that does not survive. He eventually returned to Spain and sought an office in South America. He was given a largely honorific post with a small stipend in 1550. In 1569, he led an expedition into the llanos, and after three years he returned with pitifully few survivors of his original force, again having found no significant wealth. He lived on into old age, honored but poor and burdened with debt.

Philip von Hutten and Bartholomäus Welser VI

Meanwhile at Coro, the government was in chaos. While De Spira and Federmann were away on their quests for treasure, the audiencia of Santo Domingo again intervened in Venezuela, appointing a royal judge, Antonio Navarro, to inquire into the Welsers' administration. As other officials' powers were suspended during the inquiry, the judge also effectively became the governor. The inquiry, however, achieved nothing. The great majority of the population of Coro were off in the wilderness with De Spira or Federmann, and fewer than a hundred people remained at Coro, mainly invalids in no condition to take part in expeditions and too low in rank to provide significant information to the judge. Navarro simply delayed the inquiry and enjoyed the power and enhanced salary of the position at Coro. The Welsers appealed to Spain, claiming unjust interference in their territory, and in 1538, Navarro was expelled and sent to Santo Domingo for an inquiry into his actions, but he died during the voyage.

De Spira finally returned to Coro in 1539. He had acquired little gold, and over half of his men had died during his long expedition, but he immediately began preparations for a new exploration, still convinced a great golden kingdom existed somewhere amid the jungles and plains of the interior. But he died in mid-1540. The Welsers and the audiencia agreed that Rodrigo de Bastidas y Rodriguez de Romeram, who had been bishop of Coro since 1531, should serve as governor. Although officially a protector of the Indians, Bishop Bastidas sent slave raiders into the region of Maracaibo and began to organize yet another treasure hunt into the interior, appointing Philip von Hutten commander of the new exploration. Hutten was a relative of the Welser family, and he had gained experience as a member of De Spira's long expedition. He was accompanied by young Bartholomäus

Welser VI, son of the head of the House of Welser, newly arrived from Germany, and aided by Pedro de Limpias, who had been on Federmann's second expedition and who exhibited fanatic determination to find the rumored kingdom of gold.

Bastidas's tenure as governor of Coro was short. He returned to Puerto Rico in 1541 and was appointed bishop there, assuming office in 1542. The expedition, however, went ahead, departing in July 1541. It followed a now-familiar pattern. The men wandered around for over two years, changing directions as they followed Indians' tales of distant tribes rich in gold. They found little, Hutten was gravely wounded, and Welser and Limpias quarreled over leadership. Limpias broke away with a small following to make his own way back to Coro, and Bartholomäus Welser returned slowly toward Coro, resting his men for some months at a convenient village and hoping for reinforcements that did not come.

When Bishop Bastidas departed for Puerto Rico, he appointed Diego de Boiça as his representative. Boiça soon had to flee to avoid prosecution for criminal misrule, and he was followed by several other interim governors distinguished for their short tenure and corrupt behavior. At that point, one of the most controversial figures in Spanish colonial history, Juan de Carvajal, took power at Coro.

Juan de Carvajal

Juan de Carvajal first came to Venezuela as a youth of twenty in 1529. He served in several minor but responsible posts: notary public and registrar at Maracaibo, official clerk and attorney general at Coro. In that later post he prosecuted the Welsers for failing to abide by the conditions of their grant from the king. He accused them of cheating the king of a fifth of the precious metals recovered and of selling food and goods to settlers at extortionate prices. He also maintained that the fruitless expeditions into the interior were responsible for the deaths of over six hundred Germans, one thousand Spanish, and around six thousand Indians who served as porters, not to mention the number of free Indians slaughtered. Henceforth Carvajal was an avowed enemy of the Welsers.

The prosecution required Carvajal's presence in Santo Domingo from 1540 through 1543. The Spanish legal system was extremely cumbersome, a heritage of Spain's medieval history as several separate kingdoms imperfectly integrated in the sixteenth century. There were many courts and regulatory organizations with ill-defined and over-lapping jurisdictions, and many opportunities to appeal judgments and rulings. As a result, most legal actions, including Carvajal's, ultimately came to nothing. In early 1544, the audiencia at Santo Domingo sent Juan de Frias to Coro as judge and interim governor, and Carvajal went with him as his assistant with the title interim lieutenant governor. In 1545, Frias left Coro for the island of Margarita, and Carvajal assumed the position of governor. Sources say he falsified documents claiming he had been appointed permanently to the post.

Carvajal had a much different concept of the future of Venezuela than his predecessors. Coro had never developed beyond a small settlement in a not-particularly-fertile region, serving primarily as a center to organize treasure hunting expeditions and market slaves. On his own authority, Carvajal removed most of the population from Coro and led them inland to the south, where the land was more suitable for farming and stock raising. There he founded the town of Nuestra Señora de la Pura y Limpia Concepción de El Tocuyo, generally just called El Tocuyo, and transferred the administration there. Pedro de Limpias returned before Hutten and Welser—whom he now regarded as enemies—warned Carvajal that they would soon appear, and swore allegiance to Carvajal. Word also reached Carvajal that Juan de Frias had returned to Venezuela. Carvajal now faced major confrontations from two directions.

Hutten and Welser encountered Carvajal at El Tocuyo. Hutten expected Carvajal to yield command to him, but that did not happen, and Hutten reproached Carvajal for largely depopulating Coro and establishing El Tocuyo without authorization. Discussion grew heated, and the principals drew swords. Welser, armed with a lance, repeatedly rushed Carvajal and had to be restrained. Calmer heads prevailed, and open warfare was avoided for the moment.

Hutten and Welser along with their troops marched off toward Coro to join Frias, but Carvajal rallied his men, covertly followed, and ambushed and quickly overwhelmed Hutten, Welser, and others. Carvajal held a mock trial and had Hutten, Welser, and three of their highest officers brutally beheaded with a dull machete.

The execution of Philipp von Hutten and Bartholomäus Welser VI effectively marked the end of Welser Venezuela. Word of events quickly reached Spanish authorities, who sent Juan Pérez de Tolosa with troops to Venezuela as governor and captain general. Carvajal's men quickly deserted him, and before the end of 1546, Tolosa hanged Carvajal as a rebel and murderer. The Spanish crown revoked the Welser grant, though with the immovability of the Spanish legal system, matters stretched out until 1556 before the Council of the Indies pronounced the last word.

Aftermath

The Welser attempt to colonize Venezuela failed for many reasons. The diversion of effort and resources to repeated attempts to find a mythical golden kingdom was the most obvious, but not the only cause. Welser apprehension that the Spanish crown might revoke their grant encouraged the search for immediate wealth, and the Welser failure to establish strong control of their agents in Venezuela contributed. Officials who were supposed to be administering the colony were absent for years as they explored jungles and plains in search of El Dorado's kingdom. The Welser system of credit kept colonists in debt, stifled development, and encouraged colonists to follow leaders in the quest for immediate wealth rather than work to develop a viable colony. Many colonists died on fruitless expeditions, leaving behind unpaid depts to the Welsers. As the colony proved an increasing economic drain, the impetus to discover a wealthy kingdom in the interior increased, and the cost in the lives of colonists and Natives was appalling.

Had the Welsers appointed trustworthy administrators, adequately supervised them, and not themselves been readily seduced by the prospect of a golden kingdom, it is possible the Welsers could have built an economically viable colony in Venezuela and established trade links that would have outlasted any formal revocation of their grant.

Sources

Relevant original sources are gathered in Eberhard Schmitt and Friedrich Karl von Hutten, eds., *Das Gold der Neuen Welt: die papiere des Welser-Konquistadors und Generalkapitans von Venezuela, Philipp von Hutten 1534–1541* (Berlin: Berlin Verlag Arno Spitz, 1999), and Enrique Otte, ed., *Cedulas reales relativas a Venezuela 1500–1550* (Caracas: La fundacion John Boulton y la fundacion Eugenio Mendoza, 1963). Nicolaus Federmann, *Indianische Historia: Eine shone kurtzweilige Historia Niclaus Federmanns de Jüngern von Vlm erster Raise* (Hagenaw: Sigmund Bund, 1557) is an important record of events and an insight into the minds of conquistadors, both German and Spanish.

Fray Bartolomé de las Casas's *Brevísima relación de la destrucción de las Indias* (Seville: Sebastian Trugillo, 1552) describes the Welser atrocities against the Indians but does so without mentioning specific names. Las Casas did not publish during his lifetime his much-more-detailed work in which he does provide names and details. It was finally completely published in 1875: Fray Bartolomé de las Casas, *Historia de las Indias*, 3 vols., ed. El Marqués de la Fuensanta and José Sancho Rayon (Madrid: Miguel Ginesta, 1875). In this work, Las Casas's description of Ehinger's expedition is particularly horrendous.

Gonzalo Fernández de Oviedo y Valdés, known generally as Oviedo, was an important royal official who served in Hispaniola for many years. His most important work is *La historia general y natural de las Indias*, the first part of which was published in 1535. He disagreed with Las Casas, who maintained that Indians were inherently peaceful and mild. Oviedo wrote that some were, while others were aggressive cannibals beyond any possibility of conversion or civilization. Las Casas, never tolerant of disagreement, may have been responsible for delaying the appearance of the second part of Oviedo's work. The entire work of three parts did not appear until the middle of the nineteenth century: Gonzalo Fernández de Oviedo y Valdés, *Historia General y Natural de las Indias, Islas y Tierra Firme del Mar Océano*, 4 vols., ed. José Amador de los Rios (Madrid: Real Academia de la Historia, 1851–1855). Oviedo was an interested contemporary of the Welser venture and an important source.

Antonio de Herrera y Tordesillas (1549–1626) was a reprehensible character. Described personally as a devious and conniving courtier, he never visited the Americas yet promoted himself as an expert on the subject. His writings are derivative, and he seldom credited his sources, which he often incorporated with little or no modification. He never evidences interest in or sympathy for Native Americans. His work does retain importance because Herrera always sought to present the official royal interpretation of events. His most important works are *Descripcion de las Indias Ocidentales* (Madrid: Emplenta Real, 1601), which served as an introduction to *Historia general de los hechos de los castellanos en las Islas y Tierra Firme del mar Océano que llaman Indias Occidentales*, 4 vols. (Madrid: Emplenta Real, 1601–1615).

Fray Pedro Simón was born in Spain in 1574. He joined the Franciscan order and went to Cartagena, Colombia, in 1603. In 1623, he was appointed to the office of Custodio de la Provincia Franciscana del Nuevo Reino de Granada (Custodian of the Franciscan Province of the New Kingdom of Granada). Although he lived and wrote nearly a century after the Welsers were active in Venezuela, Simón was a careful and conscientious writer with good access to records. His most notable work was *Noticias historiales de las conquistas de Tierra Firme en las Indias Occidentales* (Cuenca, Ecuador: Domingo de la Yglesia, 1626), a particularly valuable source for the Welser activity and for the subsequent expedition of Pedro de Ursua and Lope de Aguirre.

An even later but nonetheless important writer was José de Oviedo y Baños, whose major work was *Historia de la Conquista, y Poblacion de la Povincia de Venezuela* (Madrid: Gregorio Hernosilla, 1723). Oviedo y Baños had good access to documents and was an insightful writer. He realized El Dorado's golden kingdom was a myth even while others still believed and continued to search. He was one of very few who recognized that Indians created stories to encourage unwelcome conquistadors to depart from their vicinity to search elsewhere. Oviedo y Baños was also a literary stylist who wrote singularly clear and attractive Spanish. Few translations rise to the level of literature, but Jeannette Johnson Varner's *The Conquest and Settlement of Venezuela* (Berkeley: University of California Press, 1987) captures the quality of Oviedo y Baños's work and provides a good introduction to it.

Most modern studies of the Welsers in Venezuela are in Spanish or German. Notable among Spanish studies are Pedro de Aguado and Guillermo Moron, *Recopilación historial de Venezuela, Tomo I* (Caracas: Academia Nacional de la Historia, 1987); Rafael Arráiz Lucca, *Venezuela, 1498–1728: coquista y urbanización* (Caracas: Editorial Alfa, 2013); Juan Friede, *Vida y viajes de Nicolás Féderman, conquistador, poblador y cofundador de Bogotá, 1506–1542* (Bogotá: Ediciones Libreria Buchholz, [1960]); Juan Friede, *Los Welser en la Conquista de la Venezuela* (Caracas: Ediciones Edime, 1961); and Manuel Lucena Salmoral, *Historia general de España y América, El Descubrimiento y la fundación de los reinos ultramarinos, Hasta fines del siglo XVI*, vol. 7 (Madrid: Ed. Rialp, 1982). Important recent German studies include Jörg Denzer, *Die Konquista der Augsburger Welser-Gesellschaft in Sudamerika (1528–1556): historische Rekonstruktion, Historiografie und lokale Erinnerungskultur in Kolumbien und Venezuela* (Munich: C. H. Beck, 2005); Dietmar Felden, *Ber die Kordilleren bis Bogota: Die Reisen der Welser in Venezuela* (Gotha, Germany: Perthes, 1997); Karl Heinrich Panhorst, *Los alemanes en*

Venezuela durante el siglo XVI; Carlos V y la casa Welser (Madrid: Editorial Voluntad, s.a., 1927); and Götz Simmer, *Gold und Sklaven: die provinz Venezuela wahrend der Welser-Verwaltung (1528–1556)* (Berlin: Wissenschaft und Technik, 2000). Most of the popular works focus almost entirely on the expeditions into the interior: Adolph Francis Alphonse Bandelier, *The Gilded Man (El Dorado) and other pictures of the Spanish occupancy of America* (New York: D. Appleton, 1893); John Hemming, *The Search for El Dorado* (New York: Dutton, 1978); and Robert Silverberg, *The Golden Dream: Seekers of El Dorado* (Athens: Ohio University Press, 1996).

Early Spanish historians depict Carvajal as a monstrously cruel tyrant, but modern Venezuelan historians see the founding of El Tocuyo as the first significant development of the country and represent Carvajal as a sympathetic figure despite his subsequent actions: Nieves Avellán de Tamayo, *En la Ciudad de El Tocuyo, 1545–1600,* 2 vols. (Caracas: Academia Nacional de la Historia, 1997); and Ermila Troconis de Veracoechea, *Historia del El Tocuyo colonial: perioro historico, 1545–1810* (Caracas: Universidad Central de Venezuela, 1984).

FOUR

Quarrelsome French in Brazil: France Antarctique (1555–1567)

Two factors complicate the understanding of the French attempt to establish a colony in Brazil: the absence of surviving relevant archival materials and passionate religious beliefs that motivated principal characters and deformed their accounts of events. Both Catholic and Calvinist narratives are harshly partisan, often filled with half-truths and falsehoods. Full understanding of the leading figures seems impossible, but a reasonable account of events can be salvaged from the discord.

Background

In 1494, Spain and Portugal ratified the Treaty of Tordesillas, establishing the border between their respective spheres in the Atlantic along a meridian 370 leagues west of the Cape Verde Islands. At the time, neither party knew much about the geography of the land Columbus had discovered two years earlier, nor did they initially realize that the dividing line granted a significant portion of South America to Portugal. Portuguese interest was directed primarily toward Africa and India. In 1498, Vasco de Gama reached India, and trade with Africa and India made Portugal rich. Even the fisheries and the rich hauls of cod from Newfoundland initially attracted greater attention from the Portuguese than the area of Brazil.

In 1500, Pedro Álvares Cabral, seeking a new route to India, was the first who came to Brazil, although by accident. Contrary winds and unfamiliar currents took him to South America. Amerigo Vespucci may have made early voyages to the coast of Brazil, but his role in early exploration has been obscured by the falsification of letters published under his name. Portuguese explorers quickly recognized a major resource in the new land, *Paubrasilia echinata,* more commonly known as *pau de Pernambuco,* or brazilwood, which was much prized in early modern Europe as a source of dye ranging from bright red to purple. A somewhat similar species of brazilwood had long been obtained from the eastern Mediterranean but only at great expense. The importance of the new, less costly source of dyewood gave the European name to the land, Brazil. In the first decades after the discovery of the new land, the Portuguese also exported parrots, monkeys, and, ominously, slaves.

The Tupí Indians, a collective designation for the Tupinambá, Tupiniquim, and other tribes speaking the same or highly similar languages, lived primarily along the coast and rivers of eastern Brazil. They hunted, gathered wild edible plants, practiced slash-and-burn agriculture, and moved their villages every few years as the soil suffered depletion and prey grew scarce. The Portuguese found them to be gentle within their tribe, but the Tupí lived in a state of endemic warfare with neighboring Tupí tribes and practiced ritual cannibalism of captured enemies. Cannibalism both repulsed and fascinated Europeans and forms a disproportionately large portion of Portuguese and French accounts of the Tupí. Europeans generally had little understanding of the cultural context of the practice: on ceremonial occasions, the Tupí ate captives to absorb their strength and courage. The Tupí, who had little else to trade, soon learned to exchange brazilwood and captives to the Portuguese for prized European goods instead of eating them. The Portuguese collectively called other diverse Indian tribes Tapuias; they lived mainly in the interior, although in one area they occupied a section of the coast, and according to the Portuguese they were even more warlike and cannibalistic than the Tupí.

The Portuguese initially traded with the Tupí at temporary landings and established a few *ferorias,* fortified trading posts of more enduring character. To organize and control Brazil, the Portuguese crown turned to *donatários* (donataries) and *capitães* (captaincies). Donataries were men appointed by the king who were awarded captaincies in which

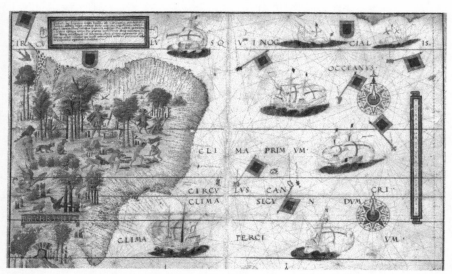

Map of Brazil, 1519, by the Portuguese cartographers Lopo Homen and Pedro Reinel and decorated by the miniaturist António de Holanda, from the Miller Atlas, Bibliothèque Nationale de France. (*Library of Congress*)

they were expected to promote trade and establish settlements at their own expense in exchange for a variety of valuable trade concessions and privileges. After a few isolated experiments, the Portuguese crown divided the coast of Brazil into fifteen captaincies awarded to twelve donataries—several favored individuals were given two captaincies. Theoretically, each captaincy consisted of fifty miles of coastline, but rivers were used to designate the borders of captaincies and the size of each captaincy was only approximate. The scheme did not produce the results hoped. Some donataries quickly became discouraged and never left Portugal, while others made an initial settlement but soon abandoned the effort when they failed to discover substantial sources of immediate profit. A few captaincies prospered and became centers of the Portuguese settlement of Brazil. In addition to exploiting brazilwood, settlers soon began to experiment with growing sugarcane, which flourished in the climate of Brazil. In time, sugar would become the most important Brazilian export.

In a departure from the normal European practice of kidnapping Indians to train as translators, the Portuguese stranded *degradados*, criminals condemned to exile, along the coast. The degradados, a few

Indians harvesting brazilwood. Detail by the miniaturist António de Holanda, from the map of Brazil, 1519, in the Miller Atlas, Bibliothèque Nationale de France. (*Library of Congress*)

Portuguese castaways, and deserters found refuge among the friendly Tupí Indians, where they learned their language and married into the tribes. They and their multilingual offspring served as translators and cultural interpreters as the Portuguese sought to form permanent settlements in Brazil.

Binot Paulmier de Gonneville commanded the first French expedition that came to Brazil. Like Cabral, Gonneville was seeking to travel to India, but the unfamiliar winds and currents of the south Atlantic drove him to Brazil. On the return voyage, Gonneville's ship fell victim to pirates who looted the cargo, and Gonneville had to abandon his sinking ship. He survived to report that Brazil offered great potential for profitable trade, and soon the French joined in the exploitation of brazilwood. The Portuguese sent ships to patrol the coast of Brazil, and they treated intruders they captured savagely, hanging some and torturing others to death. The Portuguese and French crowns exchanged angry accusations and complaints, and at one point the French government did agree to prevent ships from sailing to Portuguese possessions, but the prohibition was ineffective. The Portuguese were able to discourage incursions in areas where they were most heavily settled in southern Brazil, but their ships were few, the coast was long, and the French continued to come in large numbers and even founded trading posts despite Portuguese territorial claims.

Bertand d'Ornesan and the La Pélérine Affair, 1530–1532

In 1530, Bertrand d'Ornesan, Baron de Saint-Blanchard, admiral of France, obtained permission from the French king Francis I to establish a large trading post in Brazil. D'Ornesan dispatched the ship *La Pélérine* (*The Pilgrim*) under the command of Jean Duperet to the coast of Brazil with 120 men. Six Portuguese ships attacked the French shortly after they arrived in Brazil, but the well-armed *La Pélérine* successfully defended itself. The French and Portuguese concluded a truce, and the French built a fort and cabins on an island that the Portuguese called Santo Aleixo and the French Saint-Alexis, near the future site of Recife in central Brazil. The French soon filled their ship with Brazilian goods and set sail for France. Chance and wind took the French ship to Malaga in Spain, where the French encountered a group of six Portuguese ships. The Portuguese greeted the French cordially, offered provisions that the French needed, and suggested that they sail together for safety, which the French captain naively accepted. Becalmed at sea, the Portuguese commander invited the French officers to visit his ship. The French must have anticipated good food and drink, but instead they were seized, and the Portuguese took their ship. The French were outraged by what they saw as treachery, while the Portuguese claimed they had merely captured criminal interlopers.

While diplomatic protests flew back and forth between the French and Portuguese courts, the Portuguese prepared a force of three armed ships to attack the French on Santo Aleixo Island. After a siege of eighteen days, the Portuguese forced the fortified post to surrender and afterward hanged the French commander along with twenty others and turned several other captives over to their Indian allies to be eaten. The rest of the captives were sent to Portugal. The French claimed that the terms of the surrender guaranteed that De la Motte and his men would be conveyed to neutral territory and released, and they further alleged that in Portugal the survivors had been maltreated and forced to sign false confessions. The affair poisoned relations between the two monarchies, and while the French king took no decisive action against the Portuguese, French merchants and pirates (often one and the same) preyed on the Portuguese in Brazil with increased violence.

Almost thirty years later, the French would make a much more substantial effort to establish themselves in Brazil.

The Founders of France Antarctique: Villegagnon and Coligny

The guiding hands behind the major French attempt to found a colony in Brazil were Nicolas Durand, sieur de Villegagnon (also spelled Villegaignon), and Gaspard de Coligny, seigneur de Châtillon. Villegagnon was born in France in 1510 to a privileged and well-connected family. His uncle was the grand master of the *Supremus Militaris Ordo Hospitalarius Sancti Ioannis Hierosolymitani Rhodiensis et Melitensis* (Sovereign Military Hospitaller Order of Saint John of Jerusalem, Rhodes, and Malta), generally known as the Knights of Malta. Villegagnon entered the order at age twenty-one and fought against the Ottoman Empire in North Africa, the Mediterranean, and Hungary, earning fame for his bravery, devotion, and service to the society. In 1548, he commanded a fleet of French galleys that successfully conveyed the young Mary Stuart, Queen of Scots, to France under difficult and dangerous circumstances. According to Claude Haton, a Catholic priest and author of memoirs covering much of the second half of the sixteenth century, Villegagnon set out shortly after this Scottish voyage on an exploratory expedition to Brazil. There is no other information about this voyage. It could have taken place as early as 1550 or as late as 1554. In 1551, Villegagnon was fighting against the Turks on Malta. After a falling out with the head of the Knights of Malta, he returned to France, where he became vice admiral of Brittany in 1553. There he quarreled with the influential commander of the fortifications at Brest. The king supported the commander but retained enough faith in Villegagnon to approve his colonial venture in 1555.

In common with others of similar background and social position, Villegagnon had a highly developed sense of duty and honor. He also possessed a love of adventure and a strong, almost quixotic desire to achieve something great and memorable. Highly intelligent, Villegagnon had broad intellectual interests and a deep concern about the religious controversies of the era. Stern and rigidly moral, he also was supremely confident of his own opinions and had no toleration for anyone who differed.

Gaspard de Coligny was born in 1519 to a noble family; his father was a marshal of France. Coligny took part in France's frequent wars, where he was wounded several times, noted for his bravery, and knighted on the field of battle. As he rose in rank, Coligny distinguished himself as an able commander and military reformer. In 1552, the king appointed him the admiral of French naval forces, and as such he was interested in the possibilities of establishing French colonies in the New World. Like Villegagnon, Coligny was immersed in the current religious controversies, and he famously promoted religious tolerance, an attitude unusual in that era.

In seeking to understand the motivations of Villegagnon and Coligny, it is necessary to distinguish between official and private motivations and between immediate and long-term goals. Failing to make these distinctions, many modern commentators have claimed that the Brazilian colony was created as a refuge for Huguenots, even though the tiny colony initially accommodated only a few hundred men and those both Catholics and Protestants while Huguenots made up about 10 percent of the French population. Some may have hoped privately that the colony might eventually develop into such a refuge, but it certainly could not have been so at the time of its founding or in the near future, and it is apparent that the official goals were much different.

Officially and immediately, Villegagnon sought to found a colony that would increase French trade opportunities in the Americas and thereby enrich France and enhance the prestige of the French crown while at the same time threatening the Iberian kingdoms, France's chief foes. No contemporary account provides anything like a balanced report of his private motivations, and little can be said with certainty. At the time the colony was founded, Villegagnon was apparently interested in the growing Huguenot movement in France, and at least initially he may have shared some measure of Coligny's ideal of religious tolerance. Soon, however, religious conflicts in the colony drove Villegagnon to more-extreme positions, and partisans interpreted his motivations and actions according to their ideology. For Catholics. he was a virtuous man plotted against and lied about by nefarious heretics, while for Huguenots, he was a murderous villain who betrayed righteous Reformers. The assertion of Huguenot writers that Villegagnon had left the Catholic Church and embraced the Reformation by the time the colony was founded or shortly thereafter only to return to Catholicism later is at best highly dubious. He did bring Calvinist clergy to the colony to serve Huguenots among the colonists, and while Villegagnon was in Brazil his theological speculations and arguments certainly moved beyond the boundaries of Catholicism, although he never fully embraced Calvinism and ultimately rejected it.

Gaspard de Coligny was largely responsible for persuading Henri II to support the colonial venture, but the French king was hardly the man to finance a refuge for Huguenots. He actively persecuted the Calvinists, even to the extent of having them mutilated and burned at the stake. Coligny had more realistic intentions than attempting to persuade a hostile king to found a Huguenot refuge. Like Villegagnon, he saw that colonies had made Spain and Portugal rich, and the establishment of a successful French colony could bring some measure of wealth to France, heighten the prestige of the French crown, and proclaim that France too was significant globally. The colony might even develop into a base that could threaten Spanish and Portuguese holdings in South America, strengthening France in its continuing confrontations with the Iberian kingdoms. Never a fanatic, Coligny advocated religious tolerance and may have hoped that a colony including both Huguenots and Catholics could demonstrate that they could coexist in harmony and would work, sacrifice, and encounter danger together to advance French national interests.

Gaspard de Coligny, ca. 1560. Attributed to "l'Anonyme Lécurieux." Bibliothèque nationale de France. There are no authentic portraits of Villegagnon. An engraving often reproduced as his portrait is a later imaginary work. (*Bibliothèque Nationale de France*)

Coligny would eventually leave the Catholic Church and join the Huguenots, but he had not yet done so when the colonists set sail on July 12, 1555, and did not do so until years later. Coligny's first tentative indication of interest in the Calvinists came late in 1555 or early in 1556, but he was still far from committing to the movement. In November 1556, he wrote to Cardinal Carlo Caraffa, the nephew of Pope Paul IV, pledging his service to the papacy in the efforts to oppose the Spanish in Italy, and there is no reason to doubt Coligny's sincerity. A letter from John Calvin to Coligny seems to indicate that in 1558, Coligny was concerned with the Reform movement but not yet dedicated to it. Coligny first appeared as an acknowledged follower of Calvinism in 1560.

France Antarctique: The Colonizing Expedition

Villegagnon's initial proposal to Coligny seems to have envisioned a colony in Spanish territory, but as the plan developed, the focus shifted to Portuguese Brazil, probably as the area offered better prospects of immediate profitability and the Portuguese were less able to offer formidable resistance. King Henri II approved the project and provided three ships, two large vessels of two hundred tons each and a smaller transport of a hundred tons, and money in the amount of ten thousand livres, a relatively small sum for such a project. French merchants also contributed funds. Villegagnon initially recruited soldiers, artisans, and gentlemen adventurers, but the number of volunteers was inadequate, so he conscripted prisoners from the jails of Paris until a total of about six hundred men were ready to sail to Brazil. The colonists consisted of a mixed company of Catholics and Huguenots. The Reform movement was strong and growing in France's Atlantic ports, and any project involving shipping would necessarily include a substantial number of Huguenots. No women were included in the initial contingent. Women and whole families could come once the colony was fortified and well established.

Two notable individuals who took part in the expedition were Nicolas Barré, who served as Villagagnon's secretary, and the Franciscan friar André Thevet, who was the chaplain on Villagagnon's flagship. Both would write accounts of events. Equipment for the expedition included an abundance of artillery and ammunition to repel any attack by the Portuguese or Indians. The expedition sailed on July 12, 1555, but a strong storm struck two days later, and the flagship began to leak so badly that the little fleet returned to France on July 17. Some volunteers disembarked and would have nothing more to do with colonization; the conscripts did not enjoy that option. Repairs and unfavorable winds delayed the final departure until August 14. The ships proceeded to the Canary Islands, but when the French tried to refresh their water casks there, the Spanish fired on them. The three ships sailed on to the coast of Africa, where a deadly fever broke out on the ships and spread among the colonists as they set out across the Atlantic. The crossing was slow and difficult, hampered by contrary winds and unfamiliar currents. By the time they reached Brazil, the crews and colonists had consumed most of the provisions aboard, and much of what remained was decayed and useless. Villegagnon and the colonists had to hope that the Indians and nature would provide for their needs.

Guanabara Bay, Brazil, with the location of Le Ratier and Villegagnon Islands.

The French finally sighted the coast of Brazil on November 3, and on November 10, they entered a spectacular, enormous bay. The Tupinambá called it Guanabara; the Portuguese explorer Pedro Lopez de Souza entered the bay on January 1, 1531, and called it Baía de Janeiro; today it is officially known as Guanabara Bay, the site of the great city of Rio de Janeiro. Earlier the Portuguese left a few degradados there with the hope of establishing trade relations with the local Indians, but the degradados alienated the Indians, who killed them, and the Portuguese subsequently sided in wars with tribes hostile to the local Indians. French merchants, however, traded peacefully with the Natives at the great bay and established friendly relations. Ville-gagnon intended his colony would take possession of the bay, supported by the Indians well disposed toward the French.

The entrance to Rio de Janeiro Bay is relatively narrow. A well-fortified position there could deny safe anchorage to any potential enemy and yet protect friendly ships within the harbor. The French initially built a small wood fortification on a rocky island near the middle of the entrance to the bay, which the French called Le Ratier, but it was too low and flooded during the highest tides, and they soon abandoned it for another island a little farther in the bay, a good defensive site with only one landing area. Villegagnon set the men to work improving the defensive capability with earthworks and artillery positions enforced with stone. There was, however, no source of fresh water on the island, and a constructed cistern could not keep water fresh in the hot and humid climate. The island was also too small to farm, but the colonists must have anticipated that in time, the settlement would expand to the mainland. Villegagnon named the island fortress Fort Coligny, and today it is called Ilha de Villegagnon (Villegagnon Island). Originally well separated from the mainland, the shoreline has been extended over the years, and what was once water is now the site of the Santos Dumont Airport, separated from Ilha de Villegagnon by only a short causeway. Since 1938, the island has been the site of the Brazilian Naval School. The colony was named France Antarctique, the second element of the name indicating it was south of the equator. The name had nothing to do with the continent of Antarctica, not yet discovered at that time.

The First Years of France Antarctique, 1555–1557

European culture in the colonial period was highly hierarchical, and Villegagnon, an aristocrat supremely confident in his own judgement, left no doubt that he was in charge of all aspects of the colony. The presence of soldiers, sailors, and men conscripted from the French jails undoubtedly required firm control, and Villegagnon enforced his commands with harsh physical punishment typical of the age. Fever came ashore with the colonists, continued to claim victims among the French, and spread to the Tupinambá, the local Tupí tribe. The fever created strain between the two peoples, but Villegagnon was respected by the Indians, and he was able to reconcile them. The Indians' name for Villegagnon was Paycolas, a compound of a Brazilian honorific of respect and their understanding of Villegagnon's first name, Nicolas. Colonists engaged in active trade with the Tupinambá, exchanging iron tools, fishing nets, and ornamental trinkets for food, brazilwood, cotton, pepper, parrots, and monkeys. Villegagnon also traded with the Indians to acquire slaves captured from other tribes. Most were put to work on the fortress, though a group of young Indian boys were acquired to send to the king in France, who distributed them among his aristocratic supporters.

During the first two years, Villegagnon also directed the religious life of the colonists, and Catholics and Huguenots worked and coexisted with little sectarian discord. Villegagnon and the most religious Catholics and Calvinists among the colonists insisted that high moral standards be enforced universally in the colony. Villegagnon's strict control of access to alcohol was not popular, but Indian women posed still greater problems. The Brazilian Indians had no use for clothing and routinely lived entirely naked. Villegagnon and others insisted that Indian women employed in the colony wear clothing, but they stripped it off several times a day to refresh themselves in the water of the bay and discarded clothing at the end of the workday. Indians beyond the island continued to live as they were accustomed. Young Indian women were willing to enter into relations with the colonists, but Villegagnon insisted that no such alliances be permitted unless and until the women had received religious instruction, converted to Christianity, and were duly married. These regulations were predictably unpopular among the least religious of the colonists, and there were desertions to live with the Indians, even though they were cannibals, or to go to the Portuguese, even though they were Catholics.

Years earlier, a group of Norman French had been stranded in Brazil and had integrated to the local tribe, learned the language, took wives according to the Native customs, and had children. One of these men now served as an interpreter at the colony. Villegagnon ordered him to have nothing to do with his Indian wife until they entered into Christian marriage. Resenting the interference in his established relationship, the interpreter turned his discontent into a conspiracy with twenty-six soldiers, but when the conspirators tried to enlist Villegagnon's Scottish bodyguards, they loyally reported the plot. The translator escaped to live with the Indians, but Villegagnon seized four other major conspirators. He hanged one of the four, who earlier had been involved in other offenses, and another committed suicide by leaping into the ocean. Villegagnon condemned two others to hard labor in chains but pardoned the rest. His actions were moderate, even generous, given the standards of the age.

On February 4, 1556, Villegagnon dispatched a ship back to France bearing brazilwood, other goods, and several gentlemen discouraged by hard work and poor conditions, André Thevet among them. He had contracted a fever during the voyage to Brazil and now returned to France to recuperate; perhaps he also had had enough of hardships in Brazil. Villegagnon also sent letters to the king and Coligny, and perhaps to the magistrates of Geneva, requesting artisans and missionaries from that center of Calvinism.

The Geneva Calvinists and Religious Discord

The nature and even the existence of Villagagnon's letter to Geneva is a matter of controversy. Jean de Léry, a Calvinist who subsequently went to Brazil and wrote an extremely partisan account of events, published what the Calvinists claimed was a copy of Villegagnon's letter. Villegagnon denied that was what he wrote and defied the Calvinists to produce the original; there is no record that they did so. At this distance it cannot be determined whether the letter De Léry published was an original letter from Villegagnon, an altered version, or even a completely forged text. It is possible that Villegagnon did not write directly to Geneva but rather to Coligny, who wrote to Geneva forwarding perhaps a paraphrase of what Villagagnon had written, explaining what he wanted from the Calvinists who had sought refuge in Switzerland. It is also possible that Villagagnon, who later returned to the Catholic Church, then found it expedient to deny authorship. The interpretation most charitable to both sides suggests that Villagagnon's rhetorical expressions were misunderstood to mean that he had definitely converted to the Reform movement and desired missionaries to assume control of the spiritual life of the colony when actually he just intended to invite the Calvinists to send some artisans and a minister or two to attend to Huguenots among the colonists.

Coligny approached Philippe de Corguilleray, Sieur du Pont, an old acquaintance then living in Geneva and an enthusiastic Calvinist, to organize a group to go to Brazil to provide spiritual guidance to the Huguenots and proselytize among the Indians. Corguilleray recruited two ministers, Pierre Richer, also spelled Richier, about fifty years old, and Guillaume Chartier, about thirty years of age, and eleven artisans, also enthusiastic Calvinists who could both practice their professions and aid in evangelism. Pierre Richer and Jean de Léry, one of the artisans who afterward became a Calvinist minister, later wrote accounts of events in Brazil. A total of 290 colonists, including the Geneva Calvinists, boarded the three ships commanded by Villegagnon's nephew, Sieur Legendre de Boissy, seigneur Bois-le-Comte, at the French port of Honfleur. Among the colonists were five unmarried women accompanied by an older chaperon. Also aboard was Jean de Cointac (whose name was also written as Cointa and Contat). This former Dominican friar was initially attracted to Calvin's movement, but his theological speculations ultimately left him in disagreement with both Calvinism and Catholic doctrines. He had a great influence on Villegagnon and played a major role in disputes in the colony.

The ships set sail on November 19, 1556. The voyage was even more trying than the initial expedition, finally reaching the colony after almost four months on March 7, 1557, food and water exhausted. Initially, Villegagnon greeted the Geneva Calvinists enthusiastically, and both parties were delighted with prospects for the future. About that time, Villegagnon even experimented with creating a ruling council of ten men, supporters that he selected, reserving to himself only the right of pardon, but he subsequently reverted to direct personal rule when the relations between him and the Geneva Calvinists were embittered by theological differences.

After a short period of concord, religious disputes arose pitting Villegagnon, who had a high opinion of his capacities as a theologian, and Jean de Cointac on one side against the Geneva Calvinists on the other. Ostensibly the conflicts were theological, involving the nature of the Eucharist, the correct form of baptism, the use of images, and still other esoteric matters, but a key passage in De Léry's memoir reveals the human struggle that lay behind the religious confrontations. According to De Léry, Villegagnon and De Cointac had a greater desire to debate and dispute than to learn and profit from the Geneva theologians. Although the arguments were conducted in the language of theology, on another level the object of contention was whether Villegagnon or the Geneva Calvinists would be the religious authority in the colony, and in the sixteenth-century religious and secular authority were profoundly intermingled.

In addition to the religious disputes, the Geneva Calvinists later also objected that Villegagnon set them to work building fortifications immediately after they arrived. It would perhaps have been better to allow them a short period of respite after the difficult voyage, but it was also believed at the time that vigorous exercise was the best way to recover from a long passage. The Calvinists also complained about the quality of the water from the island cistern and the foreign food, although it was the same as the other colonists drank and ate. By this point the Geneva Calvinists were so alienated from Villegagnon that they seem to have sought any excuse to criticize him.

Villegagnon sent one of the Calvinist ministers, Guillaume Chartier, back to Geneva to seek the opinion of Calvin himself on disputed points, but as the arguments continued, both sides hardened their positions that grew more extreme. Predictably, there were no satisfactory resolutions. Finally, Villegagnon declared that he had changed his opinion of Calvin, now regarded him as an arch-heretic and apostate, and ordered the Geneva Calvinists off the island. They went willingly, joined by a few other zealous Calvinists, to live on the mainland at La Briqueterie (the Brickyard), where workmen had erected several cabins. There they traded with the Indians for food. André Thevet marked a roughly similar position on an imprecise, impressionistic map of the region, calling it alternately Henriville or Ville Henri in honor of the king. De Léry casts scorn on Thevet for this, maintaining there was no such settlement, but it is possible that Henriville was the name Thevet gave to what he hoped the Brickyard cabins would become.

The Geneva Calvinists and a few others arranged for passage back to France with a merchant captain who had come seeking a cargo of brazilwood and other trade goods. Villegagnon gave the captain a sealed packet of letters, a usual procedure. The Calvinists assumed that among them would be a document attesting that they were honest travelers. Shortly after they set sail, it became apparent that the ship was leaky, worm eaten, and barely seaworthy. Five of the men decided not to risk the voyage, so the captain gave them a boat in which they returned to the colony with great difficulty. Villegagnon admitted them to the colony and for a short time all was well, but then Villegagnon accused three of attempting to subvert his rule and of heresy and had them cast into the sea from a high rock to drown; the other two agreed to a statement of faith that Villagagnon demanded and continued to reside in the colony. De Léry and others interpreted the deaths of the three as religious martyrdom. In Brazil, Villegagnon had a falling out with De Cointac who also left the island to find his own way back to France on a trading vessel.

The return voyage to France for the Geneva Calvinists was a horror. The leaky ship took five months to reach port. The crew and passengers exhausted the provisions and then ate the monkeys and parrots they had brought to trade in France. After that they turned to the ship's rats, leather wherever it could be found, and even boiled and ate the lanterns made of horn. Several of the crew died, and the rest barely survived. When they finally arrived in France, the captain gave the local authorities the sealed packet of letters entrusted to him by Villegagnon. According to De Léry, one of the letters stated that the Geneva Calvinists were heretics and ought to be put to death, but the officials shared the same religious attitudes as the Calvinists, who suffered no harm.

Trading vessels seeking brazilwood and other trade goods came irregularly to Fort Coligny, and they brought little other than just goods for trade with the Tupinambá. The colony waited in vain for regular shipments from France bringing vital supplies to support, expand, and defend it. In 1559, Villagagnon took ship for France. Enemies later claimed that he left France Antarctique because he was disgusted and disillusioned with the religious controversies, but by 1559, Villegagnon had expelled his opponents and quelled dissent in the colony. Villegagnon sailed to France to campaign for support for the colony and to encourage immigration, leaving his nephew Bois-le-Comte in command during his absence.

The Portuguese Reaction: Mem de Sá

Initially the Portuguese watched the French activities in Guanabara Bay and waited for the colony to fail, but matters changed in 1558. By then it was apparent that the French colony was unlikely to collapse by itself, and a new, able, active governor arrived in Portuguese Brazil. In an age when holders of high offices were regularly members of the hereditary nobility, Mem de Sá was a notable exception. Born about 1500, the bastard son of a relatively minor church official, and a canon in the town of Coimbra in Portugal, he had no advantages except his natural intelligence and diligence. He earned a law degree from the University of Salamanca, and over the years, his evident ability led him to rise through the royal bureaucracy. In Brazil, his predecessor had supported planters who enslaved Indians and so created a state of unceasing warfare between the Portuguese and the Tupí tribes. Mem de Sá reversed the policy, supporting the Jesuits who opposed Indian slavery and working to pacify the Indians and gather them together in *aldeias*, missionary villages where the Jesuits instructed and converted the Indians to Christianity. Two Jesuits, Manuel da Nóbrega and José de Anchieta, were particularly effective in this endeavor and proved able allies to Mem de Sá. He also made war against tribes that did not acquiesce to the Jesuits' initiatives, until the coastal area was largely pacified. Mem de Sá also did much more to improve Portuguese Brazil, personally visiting each of the captaincies, improving the efficiency and honesty of the administrative and judicial systems, and taking effective measures to improve the economy.

Mem de Sá gathered his forces to move against the French, and in 1560, he struck with a force of twenty-two ships. He arrived before Guanabara Bay on February 21, 1560, and easily entered, but confronted by the apparent strength of the island fortress, he sent for additional troops. The Portuguese formally requested the French to surrender, and the French refused with equal formality. André Thevet alone claims that Bois-le-Comte and most of the French forces were away from the fort at the time of the Portuguese attack, a falsehood evidently intended to minimize the Portuguese accomplishments. On March 15, Mem de Sá began the bombardment of Fort Coligny, which continued for fifteen, nineteen, or twenty-one days according to conflicting sources. The French in Fort Coligny replied with fervor, damaging ships and causing casualties, but they could not repel the Portuguese. Fifteen years after the event, André Thevet published an engraving of the bombardment. The scene is imaginary, but it captures what it must have felt like for the French. When the French fortifications were battered to a ruin, Mem de Sá made a landing on the island, opposed by the Tupinambá allied with the French. The Indians gave way in the face of gunfire, but they were able to delay the Portuguese sufficiently so they could not assault the ruined fort before nightfall. Realizing the position was no longer defensible, Bois-le-Comte withdrew his men in small boats to the mainland, covering the retreat by blowing up the fort's powder magazine. Amid the dark and confusion, most of the French were able to slip away without any pursuit. Those French not able or willing to join the retreat were taken prisoner by the Portuguese, and the Portuguese killed Indians they encountered on the island. Mem de Sá then burned the remnants of the colony and withdrew.

Many who have written about France Antarctique, impressed by the sound and fury of the theological disputes and the Calvinist polemic literature that depicts Villegagnon in the most negative terms,

The Portuguese bombardment of Fort Coligny, from André Thevet, *Cosmographie universelle* (Paris, Chez Guillaume Chandiere: 1575), Vol. II, Livre XXI, p. 909.

have blamed the fate of the colony on religious disputes within it and on Villegagnon personally. A moment's reflection, however, reveals that the religious quarrels had little to do with the end of the colony. The Geneva Calvinists left Brazil on January 4, 1558; over two years later, Fort Coligny fell to the Portuguese in late March 1560. There is no evidence of significant religious dissent in the interval that contributed to the destruction of the colony.

Villegagnon was dictatorial, quarrelsome, tactless, and intolerant, poor qualities for a leader of a colony, but none of his faults contributed significantly to the destruction of the colony. He utilized all the resources at his command to fortify Fort Coligny and prepared it for an inevitable Portuguese assault. He was not present at the time of the Portuguese attack because he had gone to France to rally support and obtain supplies for the colony. He has been faulted without reason for leaving Bois-le-Comte in control while he was absent, but Bois-le-Comte defended the colony ably against overwhelming force and then capably conducted a strategic withdrawal under difficult circumstances. It is hard to imagine what anyone could have done better.

The fall of France Antarctique was due to two chief factors: the indifference or inability of the French crown to support the colony adequately and Men de Sá's able campaign. France's failure to supply the colony is explicable. When the colony was founded in 1555, France was engaged in the last of the series of wars against Spain and the Holy Roman Empire begun in 1495. Barely had that war ended in 1559 when the French king, Henri II, died after a jousting accident, leaving the throne to his three sons in succession, all young, weak, and short lived. Growing antagonism between Huguenots and Catholics in France led to open violence. The Protestant Conspiracy of Amboise in 1560 failed to destroy the power of the ardently Catholic Guise family, and in 1562, the first of the French religious wars erupted that would ravage France almost to the end of the century.

By the second half of the sixteenth century, the resources and maritime capacities of Portugal were seriously overextended, and Portugal could hardly defend its widespread colonial and trade interests. Despite that, Men de Sá was able to supplement a modest military force sent from Portugal with resources he mustered in Brazil to confront the French colony in a well-conducted campaign that overwhelmed the underdeveloped settlement. Despite all the accusations and allegations made after the destruction of France Antarctique, religious disputes did not play a significant role in the annihilation of the French colony in Brazil.

Continued French Presence at Guanabara Bay

Mem de Sá destroyed France Antarctique, but he did not end the French presence in and around Guanabara Bay. The surviving French took refuge with the local Indians, and together they harassed any Portuguese who ventured into the area. The French traded with ships that came for brazilwood and other forest products until the Portuguese finally initiated a campaign to eliminate the French and pacify the Indians. As the Jesuits Manuel da Nóbrega and José de Anchieta worked to undermine support for the French among the Indians, Mem de Sá's nephew, Estácio de Sá, arrived from Portugal in 1563 with two warships. In March 1565, the Portuguese and Brazilian reinforcements landed near the mouth of Guanabara Bay, where they constructed fortifications and a settlement by Sugar Loaf Mountain that they named São Sebastião do Rio de Janeiro, modern Rio de Janeiro. After receiving still more reinforcements, including allied Indians, the Portuguese began a major offensive in January 1567, destroying the strong palisaded Indian village of Uruçumirim on the mainland. Five French were killed in the capture of Uruçumirim, and the ten taken captive were hanged the next day. During the assault, Estácio de Sá was hit in the eye by an arrow; he died of the wound a month later. The Portuguese went on to destroy the major fortified village of Paranapuã on the large island in Guanabara Bay, today called Ilha do Governador, and they ravaged and burned Indian villages all around the bay. Most of the French managed to escape by ship and establish a small settlement at Cabo Frio to the north, where they continued to prove a problem, raiding along the coast and trading with the Indians whom they agitated against the Portuguese. Finally, in 1575, the Portuguese launched an overwhelming offensive against the French at Cabo Frio and their Indian allies. The survivors initially fled into the hinterlands and then accepted an armistice allowing them to withdraw after surrendering their weapons. This marked the end of the chief French endeavor in Brazil, but not of all French efforts there.

Hundreds of French ships continued to come for brazilwood and increasingly for exotic hardwood lumber, sugar, tobacco, and agave, which the Europeans saw as a form of aloe and thought was a cure for migraine headaches. Today agave is used to make tequila, a cause of headaches. French merchants were even able to establish fortified trading posts. A post at Ibiapaba endured for fourteen years until the Portuguese launched a major campaign to capture and destroy it in 1604. French pirates also preyed on shipments to and from Brazil and raided the Portuguese in Brazil itself. The English and Dutch also traded and raided in Brazil despite the Portuguese efforts to prevent them, and the Dutch would soon threaten Portuguese control of Brazil to a greater extent than the French.

Aftermath

Arguments begun in the colony of France Antarctique continued back in the homeland. Villegagnon, his supporters, and their opponents attacked one another's theological positions and personal character in books and pamphlets, often in the crudest and most extreme terms. Inevitably, the literary confrontations distorted events and motivations of those involved in France Antarctique. The false assertion that the Brazilian colony was initially founded as a Huguenot refuge first emerged in this contentious literature, and accusations alternatively blamed the failure of the colony on Villegagnon and on his Calvinist opponents.

In France, Villegagnon did much more than write. He had barely landed before he joined the Catholic forces as religious warfare broke out in France. He took part in the suppression of the Conspiracy of Amboise in 1560, and soon after he sought to engage Calvin in a theological debate, but Calvin disdained the challenge. At the siege of Rouen in 1562, a round from a cannon killed King Antoine of Navarre and broke Villegagnon's leg so badly that he required two years to recuperate, the injury leaving him lame for life. During 1564, Villegagnon was in the service of the Holy Roman Emperor Maximilian II fighting in Hungary against the Ottoman Turks, and in 1567, he was in French service defending the city of Sens against Huguenot forces. The following year the Knights of Malta appointed Villegagnon as ambassador to France. Villegagnon's health seems to have worsened in late 1570, and he retired to the commandery of Beauvais, an estate awarded by the Knights of Malta to support him, where he died in January 1571.

Jean de Léry returned to France, where he endured the terrible siege at Sancerre, which he described in *Histoire memorable de la Ville de Sancerre* ([La Rochelle]: [ ], 1574). His account of events in Brazil, *Histoire d'un voyage faict en la terre du Brésil* (La Rochelle: A. Chuppin, 1578) has played the chief role in forming opinions about Villegagnon and the fate of the colony. Later in life he became a Calvinist minister, and he died in 1619.

Pierre Richer was initially ordained as a Carmelite friar, but he left that order in 1546 to join Calvin in Geneva. After returning from Brazil, he became the principal minister in the Protestant stronghold of La Rochelle. His pamphle *Réfutation des folles resveries, excecrable blasphèmes, erreurs et mensonges de Nicolas Durand, qui se nomme Villagagnon* (Geneva: 1561) helped shape the negative image of Villegagnon. Richer died at La Rochelle in 1580.

Despite contemporary criticisms of André Thevet as an author, he prospered. His work *Singularités de la France Antarctique* (Paris: Chez les héritiers de Maurice de la Porte, 1557) was a great success although not without controversy. A scribe sued Thevet claiming he had authored significant portions, and Thevet settled the suit as quietly as possible. Despite negative publicity, he rose to become the royal cosmographer, a chaplain to Catherine de Medici, and keeper of the Royal Cabinet of Curiosities at Fontainebleau. His most ambitious work, *La cosmographie universelle* (Paris: Huillier, 1575) in two volumes is over two thousand pages long and contains numerous illustrations and maps. The writing, however, is diffuse and tediously garrulous, and Thevet was again involved in scandal. Conservative Catholics felt this work was insufficiently reverential, and François de Belleforest, once employed by Thevet, maintained he had written much of what Thevet claimed as his own. Belleforest published *La Cosmographie universelle de tout le monde* (Paris: 1575), an augmented French translation of Sebastian Münster, *Cosmographia* (Basel: Heinrich Petri, 1544) before Thevet's cosmography reached print, preempting the market for Thevet's book. Thevet claimed Belleforest plagiarized his work while he employed him. Jean de Léry exposed and mocked inaccuracies and lies in Thevet's book, and Thevet's reputation suffered. His last significant publication, *Vrais pourtraits et vies des homes illustres* (Paris: I. Kervert et Guillaume Chaudiere, 1584) was not a success. Thevet died in 1592, leaving behind two unpublished manuscripts, "Grand Insulaire," a catalog of significant islands across the world, and "Histoire de deux voyages," a largely false account of his supposed travels, claiming he visited America twice.

Although the normal term of office for the Portuguese governor of Brazil was four years, Mem de Sá's abilities were so well respected that the king prolonged his term in office until Mem de Sá himself requested relief. He died in 1572, shortly after his successor arrived. His memory is still revered in Brazil.

The last substantial French effort to establish a colony in Brazil began in 1612, on a large island called today Ilha de São Luís in Baía de São Marcos, the estuary of several rivers. Daniel de la Touche, Seigneur de la Ravardière, explored the coast of Guyana in northern South America in 1604 and returned in 1609 with the grandiose title "Lieutenant General of All the Lands between the Amazon and the Orinoco" granted by the French king Henri IV. The king's assassination in 1610 ended any immediate plans to establish a colony. The regent for the young Louis XIII, Marie de Médicis, confirmed De la Touche's office, but she was not about to support financially his effort to establish a colony. De la Touche was a Huguenot, and thus out of favor. He turned to sympathetic nobles, François de Razilly and Nicolas de Harlay, seigneur de Sancy. In 1612, an initial expedition of five hundred colonists settled in northern Brazil. They named the colony Saint-Louis du Maragnan, but the Portuguese proved immediately hostile, and the French government, seeking good relations with

Spain, offered no aid. Despite the Portuguese hostility, three hundred more French immigrants joined the settlement, but the colony was not strong enough to resist the Portuguese forces and capitulated after just three years. The Portuguese resettled the site, which today is the major city of São Luís do Maranhão. The French eventually successfully settled and held territory to the north of the modern border of Brazil. That area today is French Guyana, an overseas department of France.

Sources

The original sources for Cabral's voyage to Brazil are gathered in J. R. Magalhães and S. M. Miranda, eds., *Os primeiros 14 documentos relativos à armada de Pedro Álvares Cabral* (Lisbon: Comissão Nacional para sa Comemorações dos Descobrimentos Portugueses, 1999). The complex questions surrounding Amerigo Vespucci's voyages are covered in Alberto Magnaghi, *Amerigo Vespucci: Studio critico, con speciale riguardo ad una nuova valutazione delle fonti e con documenti inediti tratti dal Codice Vaglienti,* 2 vols., 2nd. ed. (Rome: Treves, 1926); Lucianio Formisano, ed., *Letters from a New World: Amerigo Vespucci's Discovery of America* (New York: Marsilio, 1992); and E. Roukema, "The Mythical 'First Voyage' of the 'Solderini Letter,'" *Imago Mundi* 16 (1962): 70-75. *Mundus Novus,* a Latin translation of an Italian letter supposedly written by Vespucci to Lorenzo de' Medici, was published in 1502 or 1503, and *Lettera di Amerigo Vespucci delle isole nuovamente trovate in quattro suoi viaggi,* commonly referred to as the *Lettera al Soderini,* addressed to the Florentine politician Piero di Tommaso Soderini, was published in 1504 or 1505. The discovery during the eighteenth century of genuine letters by Vespucci has led scholars to conclude that the letters published in the early sixteenth century, though perhaps based on genuine letters of Vespucci, suffered from alteration and interpolation by anonymous editors.

Regina Johnson Tomlinson, *The Struggle for Brazil: Portugal and "The French Interlopers" (1500–1550)* (New York: Las Americas, 1970) covers the period before the establishment of the France Antarctique. A. R. Disney, *A History of Portugal and the Portuguese Empire,* 2 vols. (Cambridge: Cambridge University Press, 2009) provides a valuable overview, although the treatment of France Antarctique is summary.

Nicolas Durand de Villegagnon attacked the theologies of Calvin and other Reformation leaders and defended himself against attacks in the following works: *Ad articulos Calvinianae de Sacramento Eucharistiae tranditionis, ab ejus ministris in Francia Antarctica evulgatae, responsiones* (Paris, 1560); *Les propositions contentieuses entre le chevalier de villegaignon et Maistre Jehan Calvin concernant la vertié de l'Eucharististe* (Paris, 1561); (A French abridgment of the Latin work *Ad articulos Calvinianae*, made at the command of Catherine de Medici); *Paraphrase du chevalier Villegaignon sure la resolution des sacramens de Maistre Jehan Calvin* (Paris 1561); *Lettres du chevalier Villegaignon sure les remonstrances a la royne mere du roy, touchant la religion* (Paris, May 10, 1561); *De Coenae controversiae Philippi Melancthonis judicio* (Paris, 1561); La Réponse aux libelles d'injures publiés contre le chevalier de Villegainon (Paris, 1561); *De venerandissimo ecclesiae sacrificio* (Paris, 1562); *De consecration mystici Sacramenti et duplici Christi oblatione, advrsus Vannium Lutherologiae Professorem; de Judaici Paschatis implement, adversus Calvinologos; de Pocula sanguinis Christi et introit in sancta sanctorum, adversus Bezam* (Paris, 1569).

Villegagnon was ill served by a chief supporter, André Thevet. Thevet's *Singularités de la France Antarctique* (Anvers, 1558) contains relatively little about the colony and is concerned mainly about the Brazilian Natives and the new and wondrous plant and animal life of the region. Thevet drew somewhat on his own brief stay in Brazil and more on descriptions provided by others. His chief work focusing on the colony and events there is found in *Cosmographie universelle* (Paris, Chez Guillaume Chandiere: 1575), vol. 2, livre 21. At best, Thevet was a careless writer, frequently contradicting in one work what he had written earlier in another. At worst, he was a transparent liar, claiming to have been places and done things he had not and making obviously false accusations. For instance, he indicated he witnessed events in Brazil that took place after he returned to France, and he claimed the Geneva Calvinists instigated the failed revolt against Villegagnon that occurred before they came to Brazil. Thevet's inanities were easily refuted by Calvinist writers such as Jean de Léry and only served to damage Villegagnon.

The chief works by the Geneva Calvinists are Jean de Léry, *Histoire d'un voyage fait en la terre de Brésil* (La Rochelle: A. Chuppin, 1578); and Pierre Richer, *Petri Richerii Apologetici libri duo, contra Nico-*

laum Durandum qui se Villagagnonem vocat (Geneva, 1561) and *La Refutation des folles resveries, excecrables blasphemes, erreurs, et mensonges de Nicolas Durand, qui se nomme Villegagnon* (1562). De Léry's work is filled with material about the natural world and Indians of Brazil, some borrowed from Thevet's *Singularités,* but in style and language it is much more appealing to the reader, contributing to the uncritical acceptance of De Léry's account of Villegagnon's actions. Richer's attacks on Villegagnon were much more extreme, sometimes degenerating to mere insults.

Villegagnon was also attacked in Peter Boquin, *Justa degensio adversus injustam vim Heshusii et Villaganonis de judicio P. Melancthonis* (1562) and in anonymous pamphlets: *La Résponse aux lettres de Nicolad Durant; L'Estrille de Nicolas Durant; La Souffisance de maistre Colas Durand; L' Espousette des armoires de Villegaignon; L'Amende honorable de Nicolas Durand; Le Leur de Nicolas Durant,* all published in 1561 and listed in Johann Georg Theodor Grasse, *Tresor de livres rares et precieux ou, Nouveau dictionaire bibliographique: contenant plus de cent mille articles de livres rares, curieux et recherches, d'ouvrages de luxe, etc. avec les signes connus pour distinguer les editions originales des contrefacons qui en ont ete faites, des notes sur la rarete et le merite des livres cites et les prix que ces livres ont atteints dans les ventes les plus fameuses, et qu'ils conservent encore dans les magasins des bouquinistes les plus renommes de l'Europe* (Dresden: Rudolf Kuntze, 1859–1869).

Villegagnon attacked the theologies of Calvin and other Reformation leaders and defended himself against attacks in the following works: *Ad articulos Calvinianae de Sacramento Eucharistiae tranditionis, ab ejus ministris in Francia Antarctica evulgatae, responsiones* (Paris, 1560); *Les propositions contentieuses entre le chevalier de villegaignon et Maistre Jehan Calvin concernant la vertié de l'Eucharististe* (Paris, 1561). *Paraphrase du chevalier Villegaignon sure la resolution des sacramens de Maistre Jehan Calvin* (Paris 1561); *Lettres du chevalier Villegaignon sure les remonstrances a la royne mere du roy, touchant la religion* (Paris, May 10, 1561); *De Coenae controversiae Philippi Melancthonis judicio* (Paris, 1561); *La Réponse aux libelles d'injures publiés contre le chevalier de Villegainon* (Paris, 1561); *De venerandissimo ecclesiae sacrificio* (Paris, 1562); and *De consecration mystici Sacramenti et duplici Christi oblatione, advrsus Vannium Lutherologiae Professorem; de Judaici Paschatis implement, adversus Calvinologos; de Pocula sanguinis Christi et introit in sancta sanctorum, adversus Bezam* (Paris, 1569).

The first edition of Marc Lescarbot's *Histoire de la Novvelle-France* was published in Paris by I. Milot in 1609, followed by a second augmented edition by the same publisher in 1611 and 1612, and a third augmented edition also published in Paris by Adrian Perier in 1613. Lescarbot had no personal connection to France Antarctique. He was a moderate Catholic, but he did not hesitate to derive much of his account from Jean de Léry's work. Lescarbot also included two letters written by Nicolas Barré, who was one of the original colonists. His letters are particularly important as they were written at the time of events rather than after Villegagnon and the Calvinists had become bitter enemies and the colony had been destroyed. Nicolas Barré also published *Lettres sur la navigation du chevalier de Villegaignon* (Paris, 1558) and *Histoires des Choses Memorables advenues de la Terre de Brésil* (Geneva, 1561).

Jean Crespin, *Histoire des Martyrs* (Geneva: Pierre Aubert, 1619), contains a bitter condemnation of Villegagnon derived chiefly from Jean de Léry, Pierre Richer, and several of the anonymous pamphlets. There is nothing new or original in the account, but the work popularized the image of Villegagnon as a vicious persecutor. Crespin, *Histoire* is conveniently available in an excellent edition with an introduction by Daniel Benoit and notes by Matthieu Lelievre (Toulouse: Societe des Livres Religieux, 1887), 2:448-466.

Until recently, modern treatments of France Antarctique have chiefly relied on the works by De Léry and Richer picturing Villegagnon uncritically as a villainous tyrant. Thomas Edward Vermilye Smith, "Villegaignon: Founder and Destroyer of the First Huguenot Settlement in the New World," *Papers of the American Society of Church History* 3 (1891): 185-206, is typical of this approach. John McGrath, "Polemic and History in French Brazil, 1555–1560," *Sixteenth Century Journal* 27, no. 2 (Sumer 1996): 385-397, provides a valuable corrective, emphasizing documents contemporary with events rather than later memoirs, and his conclusions are now generally followed.

FIVE

Spanish Hidalgos *and* Covert Jews: Jamaica (1509–1655)

Background

In 1494, during his second voyage, Christopher Columbus touched briefly on the island that the Natives called Xaymaca, which Europeans gradually changed to Jamaica. Columbus observed that the Taíno people, also called Arawaks, who inhabited the island possessed a few gold ornaments and presumed that the island must be rich in the precious metal. The Taíno's gold, however, had been traded from other islands or gathered on Jamaica over many years. Little remained on the island, and that could only be extracted laboriously. Columbus came to Jamaica again at the end of his disastrous fourth voyage when his surviving ships were in poor condition, riddled by tropical shipworms. He beached them in St. Ann's Bay, and there he remained stranded for over a year until finally rescued late in 1504. Nevertheless, Columbus thought highly of the island and was glad to claim it for himself and his family. Columbus died in 1506.

In 1509, the Spanish King Ferdinand sought to allow Alonso de Ojeda and Diego de Nicuesa to draw supplies for their expeditions from Jamaica, but Diego Colón, Christopher Columbus's son, prevented the two from utilizing the island and sent Juan de Esquivel to take control of Jamaica in his name. This was the first of several of

Colón's ill-advised conflicts with royal power. During the same year, the Spanish founded their first settlement on the island, Sevilla la Nueva (New Seville) on the northern coast near St. Ann's Bay. The Spanish also settled in small numbers elsewhere on the island, establishing ranches wherever there was good water and grazing land. In 1511, the royal council recognized Colón's claims to Hispaniola, Puerto Rico, Cuba, and Jamaica and granted him titles that were honorific but bereft of authority. Colón and his supporters continued to clash with royal officials, and the king recalled him to Spain in 1514. He spent the next five years trying to establish his claims in the labyrinthine Spanish legal system. King Ferdinand died in 1516, and his successor, Charles, restored Colón to his offices in 1520. Colón, however, continued to offend royal officers, and he was once again recalled in 1523. He was still pressing his claims in Spanish courts when he died in 1526, leaving his young son, Luis Colón de Toledo, as his heir.

Luis Colón was concerned only with the income he could draw from the family holdings. Ten years after his father's death, he renounced all other claims in exchange for several honorific titles, an annual annuity, some territory in Panama, and the island of Jamaica as a royal fief. Luis Colón did little to administer Jamaica other than appoint the governor, who ruled with the assistance—or opposition— of a council, the *cabildo*, composed of leading citizens. Luis Colón died in 1572 and left children by four marriages who wrangled among themselves over the Columbus heritage. Felipa Colón de Toledo y Mosquera emerged as the Duchess of Veragua, Duchess of la Vega, and Marchioness of Jamaica. She died in 1577, and Nuño Álvares Pereira Colón succeeded her. He died in 1626, and Álvaro Colón became the fourth duke. After his death in 1636, Pedro Nuño Colón de Portugal became the fifth duke.

None of the descendants of Christopher Columbus involved themselves in the governance of Jamaica beyond appointing governors and a few other officials, always with the approval of the Spanish royal government, and sending occasional letters urging those officials to behave properly. The royal government could have easily filled the vacuum of leadership left by heirs of Columbus, but Jamaica was poor and obscure, and the royal government largely ignored it. In 1611, the abbot of Jamaica, don Bernardo Balbuena, wrote to King Philip IV a lengthy description of the island, including the information that the population was only 1,510, of whom 523 were Spanish men and women, 173 children, 558 Black slaves, 107 free Blacks and people of mixed heritage, only 74 surviving Taino (out of an original population numbering perhaps as many as 60,000), and 75 "foreigners," a vague category concealing "Portuguese," itself a deceptive description for "New Christians," Jews forced to convert to Catholicism, also called *conversos*.

New Christians and Crypto-Jews in Jamaica

After centuries of discrimination, the situation of Jews in Spain grew still worse after 1474, with the ascension of Isabella I of Castile, who married Ferdinand II "the Catholic" of Aragon. The royal couple introduced the Inquisition into Spain, Jews were soon isolated in ghettos, and expulsions began, first from Andalusia in 1483, then from all of Spain in 1492. Even before the edict of expulsion, some Jews converted to Christianity, either subject to forced baptism or seeking safety from Christian persecution. The Jews who converted were known as New Christians, conversos, or *marranos*, a particularly offensive term, applied to both pigs and New Christians. Spanish "Old Christians" often suspected that conversos were insincere and continued to practice Judaism in secret. Many Jews and those who had been forced into conversion migrated to Portugal, but they found little respite. In 1497, the Portuguese monarch ordered all Jews to convert to Christianity or depart from the country, leaving behind their children who would be raised as Christians, and in 1536, the Inquisition was introduced into Portugal. Many conversos migrated from Spain and Portugal to the New World, but the Inquisition followed them across the Atlantic.

Conversos and crypto-Jews had a long history in Jamaica. Some modern scholars argue that Columbus himself was descended from conversos, although not all agree. Juan de Esquivel, who led the conquest of the island in 1509, may also have been a descendant of New Christians. In 1511, more than a thousand Spanish colonists came to Jamaica, but disappointed at the insignificant amount of gold on the island, many moved on to Cuba by 1513, leaving behind some "Portuguese," who were personal servants. Although documentation is lacking, some of these Portuguese may have been conversos and even secret Jews, the first to settle in Jamaica. Others maintain that the first Jews only came to Jamaica after 1530. As Judaism was strictly prohibited and Jews could only worship in secret, decisive documentation is lacking.

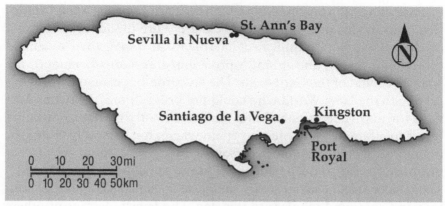

Early European settlements on Jamaica. Villa de la Vega was later known as St. Iago de la Vega and today is called Spanish Town.

The site of the initial settlement on Jamaica, Sevilla la Nueva on the northern coast, proved damp and unhealthy. In 1518, the settlers moved a short distance to higher ground, but the town was also vulnerable to raids by French, Dutch, and English pirates who haunted the waters around Jamaica and raided the island itself. Some Portuguese moved from the north coast to a plain near the south coast better suited for agriculture and less subject to pirate raids. In 1534, major changes came to Jamaica when most of the population left Sevilla la Nueva for a new capital, Santiago Villa de la Vega (Saint Iago Town on the Plain) later called Santiago de la Vega (Saint Iago on the Plain). Some people remained at Nueva Sevilla, but in 1555, French pirates massacred the remaining inhabitants, and the site was abandoned.

It was also during 1534 that Pedro de Mansuelo, the royal treasurer of Jamaica, suggested to King Charles that he send thirty more "Portuguese" families to Jamaica to join those already settled there. Mansuelo was using a euphemism for conversos to tell the king that Jewish businessmen were vital to Jamaica's success as a supply center for Spanish shipping. It sounds distressingly modern to stereotype Jews as merchants, however, Spanish and Portuguese Old Christians excluded Jews and New Christians from many professions but allowed them to be merchants. Despite the obvious importance of commerce, Iberian Old Christians notoriously despised merchants, assigning them a lower social status than peasant farmers.

In sending "Portuguese" New Christians to Jamaica, King Charles was breaking his own Limpieza de Sangre (Pure Blood) law. The first of these laws was established in Toledo in 1449, then extended throughout Spain, and in 1525 proclaimed at Santo Domingo, the Spanish capital of the Caribbean. The law prohibited anyone from migrating to the New World who could not prove "pure" Christian heritage for four generations. If one were sufficiently wealthy, one could resort to a famous monastery in Spain where, for a suitably large gift, the monks would examine a person's heritage and "discover" (a euphemism for forge) documents attesting to the donor's "pure blood." The monks did so with such skill that false documents continue to confuse and confound scholars to this day. The Jewish descent of others who possessed needed skills, such as translators, navigational instrument and map makers, and essential merchants, was quietly ignored, and so it was with the "Portuguese" of Jamaica.

Two classes emerged in Jamaica, Spanish hidalgos who raised cattle and horses on large ranches, and "Portuguese" farmers and merchants who chiefly supplied ships and sent food to the mainland in times of scarcity. The hidalgos were members of the minor aristocracy, the Spanish equivalent of English gentry. The word "hidalgo" means "son of somebody," in distinction to the commoners such as the conversos who were regarded as the sons of no one of note. During the first half of the seventeenth century, class conflict arose between the hidalgos and the Portuguese merchants. The hidalgos resented the commercial acumen of the merchants, whom they complained would join to purchase entire cargos from trading ships and reexport goods to other islands. It seems not to have occurred to the hidalgos that they could form similar combinations to buy what they wanted. With some justification, the hidalgos also accused the merchants of illicit trade and even supplying and doing business with pirates. Spanish law prohibited trade with other nationalities, but Spain was lax in providing its colonies with trade goods in sufficient quantity and quality. Traders of other nationalities offered goods in greater variety and were willing to barter for the island's produce, and pirates traded their loot for needed provisions. Ironically, the hidalgos themselves also seem to have engaged in illicit trade. Leather was always in demand in Europe, and cow hides are often mentioned as items of the illegal trade; hides came from the hidalgos' ranches.

The hidalgos wanted the Spanish royal government to assume control of Jamaica. The Columbus heirs owned the entire island, and the hidalgos had no real title to their ranches. If the Columbus family had ever arisen from its supposed sloth, it could have demanded rents from the ranchers as tenants or even expelled them. Under royal government, the land claims would be secure. The Portuguese, however, wanted nothing to disturb the current situation and favored the lax control by the Columbus family. The royal government showed no enthusiasm for assuming direct control of the poor colony so long as all remained calm and the farmers and merchants continued to provision Spanish shipping. It was thus in the interest of the hidalgos to agitate and cause conflict.

In 1596, two members of the Columbus family sued one another over their inheritance, including Jamaica, and no one in the family could legally appoint a governor until the lawsuit was concluded. The Spanish king sent his own man as governor, and the new governor paid attention to the hidalgos' complaints, such as accusations of heresy. Not all Portuguese farmers and merchants on Jamaica were New Christians, and not all New Christians were crypto-Jews, but some were, and accusations of heresy were likely to provoke the conservative Catholic authorities in Spain. In 1622, with the connivance of leading hidalgos, a synod transferred the jurisdiction over the Catholic Church on Jamaica to the archbishop of Santo Domingo, and the specter of the Inquisition reared itself before the conversos of Jamaica. The hidalgos also claimed that the Columbus family operated a secret gold mine and withheld the king's legal share of the gold. The secret mine became to Jamaica what the El Dorado story was to South America: one long and widely believed but ultimately elusive.

When the Portuguese royal house became extinct in 1580, the king of Spain also became the king of Portugal. In 1640, the Portuguese rose in revolt and reestablished independence, but the state of war between the two nations endured until 1668. The Spanish hidalgos of Jamaica could now denounce the Portuguese as enemy aliens, although some of their families had been resident on Jamaica for over a century. In response to hidalgo agitation, the Spanish royal government appointed Juan de Retuerta, judge of Santo Domingo, to report on the situation on Jamaica. His letter written to the Spanish king in April 1644 painted a dismal picture. Defense was weak: just six artillery pieces, no more than three hundred firearms (some obsolete), and little gunpowder. Pirates operated with impunity on sea and land. Retuerta testified that the current representative of the Columbus family, Pedro Nuño Colón de Portugal, the fifth Duke of Veragua, received only about 600 pesos income annually from Jamaica and consequently he could neither defend the island nor maintain justice nor enforce due obedience. Retuerta indicated the duke did what he could, and his letters, which Retuerta had seen, admonished and directed the observance of law and order, but the duke had neither money nor property in the island with which to uphold his instructions, and he was too far away to redress the harm done by his appointed officials. The duke paid officials a salary of only 500 ducats in quartos (small copper coins of little worth), which equaled just 250 in silver currency. The officials, to increase their incomes, committed many vexatious and troublesome acts against the poor citizens, Retuerta reported.

The judge continued: The principal church was in a state of disrepair. The administration of the aged abbot, the chief ecclesiastical authority on the island, was lax and disorganized, and records were so poorly maintained that no one could understand them. The judge concluded with a plea that the king should assume management of the island, but royal government continued to leave the Columbus family in control.

Conditions did not improve in the next years. Later in the decade, Governor Pedro Caballero feuded with Abbot Mateo de Medina Moreno about jurisdiction. Matters so deteriorated that the abbot excommunicated the governor, who publicly called the abbot a yokel, a rustic, and "a garlic-eating clown." A new governor, Jacinto Sedeno y Albornoz, soon replaced Caballero, but the feud continued until Caballero confronted the new governor and the abbot at the abbot's residence. When the infuriated Caballero rose from his chair, a Captain Blas de Figueroa, who was standing behind Caballero, drew the ex-governor's own sword from its scabbard and ran Caballero through from the back, killing him. A much different and less believable account of the affair maintained that as Caballero rose from a chair, he stumbled and somehow impaled himself on his own sword. As Caballero was "Titular Master of the Holy Office of the Supreme Council of the Holy General Inquisition," the Inquisition sent three agents to inquire into the affair. They arrested Sedeno and the abbot, but in the usual way of Spanish courts, after long and complex considerations, nothing came of it. The affair reveals tensions within the ranks of the Spanish elite on the island.

Jamaican Jews and the English Western Design

In view of the continuing hostility of the hidalgo class, fears of the Inquisition, and general mismanagement of Jamaica, the Portuguese merchants began to look to foreign powers in the seventeenth century. The Dutch were fully occupied with Brazil and elsewhere, but the rising economic and naval power of England offered a greater possibility.

The story of Columbus's secret mine in the mountains of Jamaica was generally known in Europe, and covert Jews may have used the tale to influence important English figures as early as 1623. In that year, George Villiers, the first Duke of Buckingham and the favorite of King James I, traveled to Spain with Prince Charles (later King Charles I) in a futile effort to arrange a dynastic marriage alliance with a Spanish princess. The two botched the attempt, but while they were in Spain, a secret agent informed them that if the English seized Jamaica, the Portuguese Jews would willingly reveal the location of Columbus's mine to the conquerors. Villiers was reputedly the handsomest and most graceful man in Europe, but he was certainly not known for his intellect. He seems to have been particularly entranced by the tale, and he began making elaborate overblown plans for capturing Jamaica as the first phase of the conquest of all Spanish America. Villiers's plans on this and other occasions, however, were unrealistic and generally came to nothing. In 1625, James I died, and Charles succeeded as king. He was occupied by more immediate concerns than Jamaica, and Villiers was killed in 1628 by a disgruntled army officer.

In 1643, the English privateer William Jackson easily captured Jamaica, seeking loot but not permanent conquest. On returning to England, he reported that the Portuguese welcomed him and expressed their hostility to Spanish rule. After Jackson departed, the Spanish accused the Portuguese of disloyalty and expelled a significant number from the island. This action, of course, further intensified the hostility of the Portuguese, both those remaining on Jamaica and those exiled.

Beginning in 1642, England was embroiled in civil war. In 1649, Charles I was executed, and in 1653, Oliver Cromwell became lord protector of the Commonwealth. In mid-1654, Cromwell sat with the Council of State in England to approve the Western Design, a plan to seize Spanish holdings in the Caribbean. Cromwell expected to strike a blow against Spanish Catholicism, establish bases that could interdict Spanish trade routes and treasure shipments, and establish profitable colonies that would serve England's growing mercantilist trade interests. William Penn was appointed commander of the naval forces, and Robert Venables was to command the army.

Realizing it was impossible to anticipate eventualities during the distant campaign, Cromwell and the Council of State did not direct Venables to invade any specific site in the Caribbean but simply instructed him to act in consultation with Penn to determine which Spanish territory to attack. Before the expedition departed, the English discussed possible objectives and sought information about the Spanish in the Caribbean. Among those consulted was Thomas Gage, an English Catholic who traveled to Spain where he joined the Dominican order. He served in South America until 1637, when he returned to England where he renounced the Dominican order and Catholicism, reconciling with the Church of England. He emphasized the vulnerability of Spanish forces in the Americas, but his information was almost twenty years out of date, leading Penn and Venables to believe the Spanish were weaker than they proved to be. Gage traveled with the expedition as chaplain and died on Jamaica in 1656.

Other important sources of English intelligence, often ignored or undervalued in modern accounts, were the New Christians and covert Jews. King John expelled Jews from England in 1290, but by the middle of the seventeenth century, several prominent, wealthy, and influential covert Jewish businessmen of Iberian origin had settled in London. A leader among them was António Fernandes Carvajal, resident in London since 1635. In addition to his widespread commercial interests, Carvajal ran a network of intelligence agents in several European countries and throughout the Caribbean. From the Netherlands, his spies reported on the Royalist exiles and conditions there, particularly significant to England during the First Anglo-Dutch War, 1652–1654. Other secret Jews in the Caribbean fed information into the network significant to the English invasion force. Simon de Caceres, an important merchant, passed on information about Jamaican defenses and told the English that Francisco de Carvajal (apparently no relation to António Fernandes Carvajal) was the sergeant major of the small Spanish force on Jamaica and a secret Jew. He could be relied on to make no resistance to an English landing. Campoe Sabada, a Jewish pilot who had previously served with the English privateer William Jackson in 1643, was ready to serve the English and guide them to safe anchorages.

The English expedition started with high hopes, but it was fatally flawed from the beginning. William Penn, an experienced naval officer, commanded the fleet of eighteen warships and twenty transports. Robert Venables was given command of the troops, but neither Penn nor Venables was given overall command, and disagreements between the two mounted to open hostility, exacerbated by Venables's hectoring wife. Rather than send experienced troops, the English formed five new regiments for the expedition, enrolling about 2,500 infantrymen. Only a minority, no more than about 1,000, had any military experience, and the majority were untrained, inexperienced, disorderly, and poorly armed. Though Venables complained about the quality of the troops even before the fleet set sail, his complaints were ignored, and the condition of troops further deteriorated during the voyage to the Caribbean, during which the soldiers subsisted in crowded conditions on poor rations for more than a month.

On arrival in the Caribbean, the English increased the number of men in their five regiments to about one thousand each and formed a sixth regiment of the same size by recruiting in the English-held islands in the region. Many of the new recruits were servants who were promised release from their indentures in exchange for enlisting. By the time recruiting was complete, provisions were in short supply, and the troops went to war with virtually no training. Many hoped for plunder, but much to their discontent, strict orders were issued that there would be no looting. The English intended to preserve captured Spanish colonies intact for English colonists.

Quarreling commanders leading poorly trained and disgruntled troops boded ill, and disaster soon followed. In mid-April 1655, the English fleet arrived off Santo Domingo, the capital of Hispaniola and all the Spanish Caribbean. The English landed some distance west of Santo Domingo—estimates vary from twenty-five to forty miles—in an area that lacked water, and the troops were not provided with canteens. The weather was hot, and the troops marched for three days to reach the city. Thirst drove soldiers to drink from any water source they encountered, most of which proved polluted. Dysentery spread among the troops, and even Venables fell ill. As an English detachment scouted the city's defenses, the Spanish attacked, and the detachment fled. The routed troops spread panic through the rest of the inexperienced British army, and Venables ordered a withdrawal. After regrouping, Venables ordered a second attack on Santo Domingo, preceded by a naval bombardment that proved ineffective. On land the Spanish ambushed the British troops as they moved toward the town. The British managed to break off the action, but the troops refused to move against Santo Domingo again, and Venables and Penn agreed to retreat from Hispaniola.

In May 1655, the English force moved to Jamaica, where, after a short bombardment, they landed more troops than the total population of the island. The Spanish garrison offered no significant resistance, and the Spanish officials began negotiating terms of surrender. They managed to delay for a week, during which time most of the Spanish were able to evacuate to Cuba with their goods. As they left, they turned their cattle loose, and their slaves took to the rough country in the center of the island where they formed Maroon groups that would long bedevil the English. A few of the Spanish also retreated to the mountainous areas on the islands, from which they launched raids against the English as late as 1661, but ultimately their resistance achieved nothing. One group of Jamaicans greeted the English with enthusiasm: the Portuguese conversos. During the next several years, regional Spanish forces made unsuccessful attempts to retake Jamaica, but the English maintained their hold on the island, much to the relief of the Jamaican Jewish community, no longer forced to conceal their religion.

Most modern commentators explain the English conquest of Jamaica simply: Penn and Venables knew it would not go well with them if they returned to England without accomplishing anything. Jamaica was unfortified and weakly garrisoned, and the English knew they could take it easily. Their decision, however, was not hastily extemporized, but rather they relied on Jewish information and assistance. Covert Jews provided intelligence about the island before the expedition left England and aid while it was in the Caribbean. After the English conquered the island, Simon de Caceres sent ships with supplies for the English army on Jamaica and wrote a cogent "Proposal for Revictualing and Fortifying Jamaica" for Cromwell that served well in the defense of Jamaica against Spanish attempts to retake the island. All would have important effects in England and Jamaica.

Penn and Venables hurried back to England, each anxious to avoid blame for the defeat on Hispaniola, leaving Colonel Edward D'Oyley in charge of Jamaica with the assistance of Vice Admiral William Goodson (or Goodsonn), who commanded a squadron of ships. In

England, Penn and Venables were charged with deserting their posts and promptly thrown into the Tower of London, but they ultimately suffered only the loss of their commissions.

Cromwell thought that English aggression in the Caribbean would not provoke war with Spain, but he was wrong. The Spanish royal government feared that Jamaica could serve as a base for further aggression against its western colonies and shipping and so declared war in 1656. France allied with England against Spain, and the Peace of the Pyrenees brought an end to hostilities in 1659. Spain ceded territory in Flanders and elsewhere to France, and England retained Jamaica. In 1658, Cromwell died, and the Commonwealth soon collapsed. Charles II returned to England as king in 1660, and peace with Spain was concluded in 1666, but England still retained Jamaica. The Spanish colony of Jamaica, first settled in 1509, was at an end, and a much different English Jamaica arose in its place.

Aftermath

In 1655, Cromwell recognized António Fernandes Carvajal's efforts by granting English citizenship to him and his two sons. During that same year, Menasseh ben Israel presented a petition to Cromwell "on behalf of the Hebrew nation" urging Jews be granted citizenship and freedom of trade, allowed to establish public synagogues and their own cemetery, and to follow Mosaic Law, and the repeal of all anti-Jewish laws. Prominent among the supporters of the petition was Carvajal. The petition was met with opposition from many, and Cromwell proceeded with caution, not approving the petition as such. Over the next few years, however, Jews in England were able to live openly, build synagogues in which to worship, establish a Jewish cemetery, and participate in trade. Many factors contributed to the improved status of Jews in England, and among them was surely the aid provided to the Western Design. When the monarchy was restored to England in 1660, there was no attempt to rescind the improved status of Jews. Full equality was, however, not attained, and the last of the anti-Jewish discriminatory laws were not abolished until the first half of the nineteenth century.

In Jamaica, English rule brought many changes, especially for the Jews who could now worship openly. Many conversos from Spain, Portugal, and elsewhere in Spanish America moved to Jamaica, where they returned to Judaism. A synagogue and Jewish cemetery were built at Santiago de la Vega, and subsequently other synagogues and cemeteries were constructed elsewhere on the island.

Santiago de la Vega gradually declined in importance, and its very name dropped out of use. Today it is known as Spanish Town. The English built a fort at the end of a peninsula in the harbor on the southern coast, and a community, Port Royal, grew up around it, crowding the peninsula and replacing Santiago de la Vega as the most important urban center of Jamaica. Many Jews moved to the town, establishing their businesses on what became known as Jews Street, which was also the site of a synagogue. Edward Long, secretary of the royal governor of Jamaica and judge of the Jamaican Admiralty Court, wrote that Jewish "knowledge of foreign languages and intercourse with their brethren over the Spanish and West Indian colonies have contributed greatly to extend trade and increase the wealth of the island." Nevertheless, English competitors complained about the Jews, accusing them essentially of being too successful. The authorities disregarded the complaints.

Port Royal not only served merchants and traders but also became a center for privateers and pirates. As Port Royal grew, it became known as the wickedest town in the world, crowded with taverns and bordellos, scenes of constant disorder and debauchery. In 1692, Jamaica suffered a tremendous earthquake. Port Royal was built on loose sand, the lower layers of which were permeated by seawater. The earthquake liquified the sand, foundations failed, buildings collapsed, and as much as two-thirds of the town subsided into the sea. More than twenty ships in the harbor were destroyed, and a tsunami swept through the town. About two thousand people perished immediately in the earthquake, and several thousand more soon died of injuries and diseases that spread among survivors. There was also widespread destruction elsewhere in Jamaica. Many buildings in Spanish Town collapsed. What remained of Port Royal was ravaged by a fire in 1703 and a hurricane in 1722.

After the earthquake, a new town, Kingston, was established across the bay. Merchants and traders moved there, and Kingston grew to become the capital and largest city of Jamaica. The Jewish community of Jamaica continues today, and some members can trace their heritage back to the seventeenth century.

The fabled Columbus family gold mine has never been found.

Sources

Until the publication of Frank Cundall and Joseph L. Pietersz, *Jamaica Under the Spaniards: Abstracted from the Archives of Seville* (Kingston: Institute of Jamaica, 1919) little was known of the history of the island between its initial occupation and the conquest by the English, reflecting the poor and underdeveloped situation of Jamaica under the Spanish regime. Cundall and Pietersz quote documents in translation from the Seville archive, and a valuable appendix lists the original documents by date. The materials utilized by Cundall and Pietersz do not mention the Portuguese New Christians and covert Jews and their conflict with the Old Christian Spanish that has emerged as an important element in the history of Spanish Jamaica. Padron Morales, *Spanish Jamaica*, trans. Patrick E. Bryan (Kingston, Jamaica: Ian Randle, 2002) provides a modern overview of Spanish Jamaica based on a much richer collection of original Spanish sources but still barely mentions the Portuguese conversos in Jamaica and their role in the English capture of Jamaica.

The situation and role of the New Christians and covert Jews can be appreciated in Mordechai Arbell, *Portuguese Jews of Jamaica* (Kingston, Jamaica: Canoe Press, 2000); Mordechai Arbell, Dennis Channing Landis, and Ann Phelps Barry, *Spanish and Portuguese Jews in the Caribbean and the Guianas: A Bibliography* (Providence, RI: John Carter Brown Library,1999); Harry A Ezratty, *500 Years in the Jewish Caribbean: The Spanish and Portuguese Jews in the West Indies* (Baltimore: Puerto Rico Omni Arts, 2002); Jonathan I. Israel, *Diasporas Within a Diaspora: Crypto Jews and the World's Maritime Empires (1540–1740)* (London: Hambledon Press, 1990); Daniel M. Swetschinski, "Conflict and Opportunity in 'Europe's Other Sea': The Adventure of Caribbean Jewish Settlement," *American Jewish History* 72, no. 2 (Dec. 1982): 212-240; and Lucien Wolf, *Cromwell's Jewish Intelligencers* (London: [W. Speaight], [1904]), reprinted in Lucien Wolf, *Essays in Jewish History*, ed. Cecil Roth (London: Jewish Historical Society of England, 1934). Zvi Loker, *Jews in the Caribbean: Evidence on the History of the Jews in the Caribbean Zone in Colonial Times* (Jerusalem: Misgav Yerushalayim, 1991) is an excellent source for period documents, and Edward Kritzler, *Jewish Pirates of the Caribbean* (New York: Anchor Books, 2008) provides a highly readable, engaging account of Jewish activity in Jamaica and elsewhere, deftly coordinating events in Europe, the Mediterranean, and the

Caribbean. More recently, Nuala Zahedieh, "Defying Mercantilism: Illicit Trade, Trust, and the Jamaican Sephardim, 1660–1730," *Historical Journal* 61, no. 1 (March 2018): 77-102, is of value, although largely concerned with events after the English conquest

The English invasion of Jamaica is well documented. Robert Venables, *The Narrative of General Venables: with an Appendix of Papers relating to the Expedition to the West Indies and the Conquest of Jamaica, 1654–1655*, ed. Charles H. Firth (London: Camden Society, 1900) is self-serving but of value, and Julian de Castilla, "The English Conquest of Jamaica: An Account of What Happened in the Island of Jamaica, From May 20 of the Year 1655, when the English laid siege to it, up to July 3 of the Year 1656, by Captain Julian de Castilla. Translated from the Original Ms. in the Archives of the Indies and Edited for the Royal Historical Society," trans. Irene A. Wright, *Camden Miscellany* 13 (1924): 1-29, provides a rare Spanish perspective on events. Anonymous, *Interesting Tracts, Relating to the Island of Jamaica, Consisting of Curious State-Papers, Councils of War, Letters, Petitions, Narratives, &c. &c. which Throw Great Light on the History of that Island, from its Conquest, Down to the Year 1702* (St. Jago de la Vega, Jamaica: Lewis, Lunan and Jones, 1800) is entirely concerned with the English invasion and subsequent events.

SIX

Courlanders *on* Tobago: Troubled Isle (1638–1654)

The Tobago Island

Tobago is a roughly oval island about twenty-five miles long and a little over six miles wide. It is about twenty-two miles north and slightly west of Trinidad, near the northern coast of South America at the end of the Lesser Antilles chain of islands. The northeastern portion of the island is hilly and rough, rising to about eighteen hundred feet. The southwest is relatively level and more conducive to settlement. Rain is frequent, and the island was originally covered with heavy tropical forest, much of which survives in the center and north. There are several good bays along the coast. Hurricanes only occasionally strike the island, but they can be devastating.

The Spanish called the Lesser Antilles including Tobago *islas inutiles*, useless islands. There were no precious metals, and the timbered land offered poor grazing for cattle, both chief concerns for any potential Spanish settlers. Moreover, the prevailing winds made it difficult to sail to Tobago from the prime areas of Spanish settlement in the Caribbean. Although the Spanish had little interest in settling in the Lesser Antilles, they did not want any other power great or small to take up residence in the area, which might serve as a base for further expansion or harassing Spanish shipping.

The island was not totally bereft of attractions. The forest contained rare and desirable hardwoods, and when cleared, the ground on the southern portion of the island offered good opportunities for the cultivation of tobacco, sugar, coconut, ginger, cinnamon, cacao, cotton, and indigo. At the time of first European contact, Kalinos Indians inhabited the island. They were relatively few, and their ethnic relationship to other groups is uncertain, although they were most likely one of the Carib tribes, and in time more Carib seem to have settled on the island. The Carib from other islands and the Arawak from Trinidad and South America, mutually hostile, frequently visited the island. Both groups were able warriors, and the Spanish maintained both were cannibals.

Earliest Attempts to Colonize Tobago

During his third voyage, Columbus sighted the islands of Trinidad and Tobago. The Spanish endeavored to settle in Trinidad several times during the sixteenth century, but they were repeatedly driven off by the local Indians. The first permanent Spanish settlement on Trinidad, San José de Oruña, was established in 1592. It survived, but it remained small, poor, and weak. Tobago was also visited by Europeans during the sixteenth century, although no attempt was made to establish a colony on the island until the early seventeenth century. Colonel John Scott, a villainous character of the seventeenth century but an able historian, records that in 1614, the Spanish Johannes Roderigo (Juan Rodriguez) tried to settle on the island. Attempts to trade with the local Caribs failed, illness spread among the soldiers, and the men mutinied. After just four months, Rodriguez abandoned Tobago and sailed with his men to Trinidad, where, according to Scott, they died.

In 1628, Jan de Moor, the burgomaster of Flushing in the Netherlands and member of the State Council of Holland, sponsored a colonizing expedition to Tobago, which they renamed Neue Walcheren after a Dutch island. The initial group of sixty-one was reinforced the next year by fifty-six more colonists. The Spanish governor of Trinidad and Guyana, don Luis de Monsalves, reported the development to Spain, but the royal government was notoriously slow to act so Monsalves encouraged the Caribs to harass the Dutch. The Indians drove the Dutch from their settlement and confined them to their fort. In 1630, the Dutch evacuated Tobago and fled to a settlement in Guyana.

In 1632, De Moor sent a second colonizing expedition to Tobago, commanded by William Gayner, an Irishman in Dutch service. The

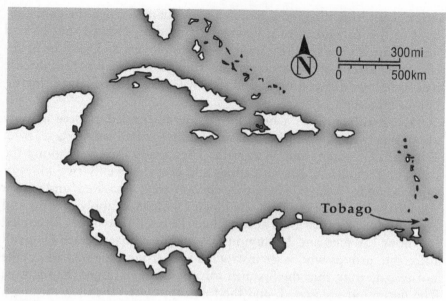

Tobago in the Lesser Antilles.

colonists were a mixed group, mostly Dutch but including significant numbers of English, Irish, and French. During the next few years, they also established two trading posts on the coast of Trinidad. In 1636, a new, vigorous governor, don Lopez de Escobar, arrived in Trinidad. An Indian informed Escobar about the existence of one of the Dutch posts and claimed the Dutch planned to expel the Spanish and transfer their colony to Trinidad as soon as they received reinforcements from Holland. Escobar had at his disposal only forty militiamen, poorly trained and not all fit. He gathered about sixty more Spanish, many of whom were badly armed and only a few of whom were experienced soldiers, and fifty Indians from Spanish settlements at Guayana and Margarita. Dividing his little force into two groups to reconnoiter the coast, they made their way in dugout canoes to the Dutch post, which they assaulted and captured, taking ten prisoners. The Spanish had scarcely burned the post when a Dutch ship came into view. Realizing the post had been taken, the ship sailed down the coast of Trinidad. The Spanish in their canoes shadowed the Dutch ship, which led them to the second Dutch trading post. Again, the Spanish took the post by

storm, capturing nine more Dutch and William Gayner, the commandant of the Tobago colony. Gayner, a Catholic, showed that he had
little sympathy for his Protestant Dutch employers and told the Spanish all the details of the settlement on Tobago: morale was low, disease
had decimated the colonists, and they were divided into disputing religious factions.

Don Escobar made a bold move. He assembled a force of only
about ninety men, Spanish, African, and those of mixed heritage, from
Trinidad, Guayana, and Margarita. They made their way along the
coast of Trinidad in dugout canoes and crossed twenty-two miles of
open ocean to Tobago. There they encountered, assaulted, and took a
subsidiary Dutch fort, which contained a welcome supply of arms and
ammunition. Escobar then approached the main Dutch fort, defended
by about 150 men and 28 cannons. At night Escobar divided his small
force into groups who were instructed to surround the fort and make
noise suggesting that the Spanish force was much larger than it was.
The deception succeeded, and the fort capitulated the next morning.
The colonists were appalled when they realized they had surrendered
to a force inferior in numbers and arms. Escobar destroyed the Dutch
colony and returned to Trinidad with his prisoners in the overloaded
dugouts.

Escobar guaranteed the safety of the captured colonists, who were
to be repatriated to Holland or the isle of St. Christopher, but before
that could happen international arrangements had to be made. When
the Spanish from Guayana and Margarita returned home, Escobar
lacked sufficient men and resources to guard, house, and feed all the
prisoners, so he sent fifty-three adult males and nineteen boys to Margarita. Don Juan de Eulate, the governor of Margarita Island, could
not cope with the influx of prisoners either, and after an unsuccessful
attempt to pass them on to the governor of the Spanish settlement of
Cumana, don Eulate resorted to a cruel expedient: he had the adults
slaughtered. Franciscans successfully pleaded with Eulate to spare the
boys, who were subsequently adopted into Spanish families and raised
Catholic. Don Escobar was outraged concerning the breach in the
terms of surrender and warned correctly that the act would provoke
revenge. In 1637, a Dutch reprisal force destroyed the Spanish settlements of Santo Tomé de Guayana and San José de Oruna on Trinidad.

Also, in 1637, a group of English Puritans appalled by the loose
morals of Barbados sought to colonize Tobago, but their venture col-

lapsed quickly. Disease and the local Carib discouraged the Puritans, who abandoned the attempt and withdrew.

The English tried again a few years later. Sources disagree whether this second attempt took place in 1639, the more likely date, or 1642. Robert Rich, Earl of Warwick, sent over two hundred colonists to Tobago under the command of a Captain Marsham or Marshall; again, sources disagree. The Carib decimated the colonists, and even Marshall was wounded. The surviving colonists abandoned the attempt. Some have seen these as two separate attempts, one in 1639 led by Marsham, the other in 1642 led by Marshall, but it is more likely this was a single expedition, the details of which were imperfectly recorded. Marsham is unlikely to have been the captain of that name active along the coast as early as 1597, but memory of him may explain the confusion of the name with Marshall.

The stage was now set for the most substantial and persistent attempts to colonize the isle of Tobago, sponsored by Jacob Kettler, Duke of Courland and Semigallia.

Courland

The Duchy of Courland and Semigallia was a vassal state of the United Kingdom of Poland and Lithuania in the eastern Baltic south of the Gulf of Riga. The native people of Courland and Semigallia were Balts who spoke Latvian, an Indo-European language related to but distinct from Slavic languages. During the thirteenth century, the German Fratres militiæ Christi Livoniae, the Brethren Militia of Christ of Livonia, generally known as the Brethren of the Sword, conquered and Christianized the area. The Brethren Militia merged with the Ordo domus Sanctæ Mariæ Theutonicorum Hierosolymitanorum, the Order of the Teutonic House of Saint Mary in Jerusalem, generally known as the Teutonic Knights. In 1562, the king of Poland and grand duke of Lithuania, Sigismund II Augustus, granted the duchy to the last grand master of the Teutonic Knights, Gothard Kettler. Although the duchy was technically a fief of the United Kingdom of Poland and Lithuania, the dukes were recognized as subordinate to the king only for the fief but not in person as vassals. To the modern mind, the concept of independent rulers of a dependent state seems an impossible contradiction, but it was in accord with late medieval and early modern usage, and in practice the dukes of Courland acted as independently as any minor power surrounded by greater powers could.

The population of Courland was diverse. In addition to the local Latvians, many Germans, Lithuanians, and German and Polish Jews migrated into the duchy over the years. The ruling class was largely German, and the government functioned primarily in German. Both German and Latvian were in common use in the port cities and larger towns, while Latvian continued to be the language of the countryside.

Jacob Kettler, born in 1610, was the grandson of Gothard Kettler and the son of Wilhelm Kettler, who, with his brother, Friedrich, jointly succeeded to the duchy on the death of Gothard. King James I of England was Jacob's godfather, and Jacob is regularly referred to as James in English documents. Jacob's mother died shortly after his birth, and his father Wilhelm was deposed in 1616 because of inept administration. When Wilhelm abandoned the duchy to live abroad, Jacob's uncle Friedrich adopted him. Jacob attended the University of Rostock and graduated from the University of Leipzig. Afterward he toured in western Europe, where he was greatly influenced by the ideas of royal absolutism and mercantilism. Returning to Courland, Jacob aided his foster father in the administration of the duchy, and as Friedrich aged, Jacob became coruler of Courland in 1638 and sole duke in 1642 after Friedrich's death.

As duke, Jacob had to contend with the nobility of Courland, who jealously protected their hereditary rights and privileges. Jacob strengthened his authority whenever possible, but he was cautious not to provoke the nobility to revolt. He also had to deal carefully with his powerful immediate neighbors, Poland and Sweden. He entered into treaties with most of the nations of Europe, and relations with France and England were particularly cordial. His interactions with the Dutch were complex. The Dutch were commercial rivals of Courland, exporting many of the same goods and hostile to England and suspicious of friends and allies of the English. The Dutch frequently interfered with Courland's commercial relations, but the duke had spent time in the Netherlands as a young man and was impressed by the progressive Dutch economy. He employed many Dutch experts in shipbuilding and other industries and projects.

By all accounts, Duke Jacob was an affable individual, courteous to all, moral, and honorable. In an age when royalty habitually and openly supported mistresses, the duke was an exception. He was an exemplary family man who was devoted to his wife, Louise Charlotte, and their children. The duke's contemporaries also describe him as en-

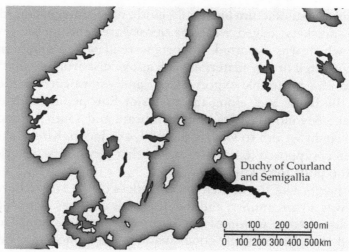

The Duchy of Courland and Semigallia.

ergetic, intellectual, and diligent. Later in life, however, he shared a fault common at the time: he failed to see the horrors of slavery.

Duke Jacob encouraged the economic development of the duchy. He spoke Latvian, toured the countryside, and encouraged advanced Dutch agriculture practices in the ducal domains such as the construction of drainage projects and the introduction of improved crop varieties. He enabled immigrants to bring previously uncultivated tracts into production by remitting rents and duties for years and even providing seed for initial planning. The duke also imported improved breeds of cattle and Spanish sheep and promoted pig breeding. Courland increased grain exports and also sold internationally meat, cheese, butter, hides, wool, and even beer and brandy.

Courland had a long tradition of shipbuilding, supported by the duchy's abundant timber resources, which the duke managed carefully. At its height, the duke's fleet consisted of over one hundred commercial vessels, forty-four armed warships carrying over fourteen hundred cannons, and fifteen unarmed warships. The armed warships were primarily frigates that conveyed and protected commercial ships and the ports of Courland, while the unarmed warships constituted a strategic reserve. In addition to building ships for his own navy and trading fleet, the duke built and sold ships mainly to France and England and chartered ships to Venice. The duke also established workshops under his control to manufacture linen sails, cloth, rope, tar, metal hardware, cannons, muskets, edged weapons, glassware, and amber jewelry, much of which was exported. Imports were kept to a minimum and usually consisted of raw materials such as Swedish iron ore that could be turned into profitable exports. Courland's ships carried goods to ports in the Baltic Sea, along the coasts of Europe, in the Mediterranean, and beyond to Africa, the Caribbean, and South America. All of this brought wealth to Courland and Duke Jacob. King Charles X of Sweden is supposed to have remarked that Jacob was "too rich for a duke, too poor for a king."

Duke Jacob, like the contemporary rulers of the larger European nations, was a mercantilist, and the desire for colonies was central to mercantilist theory. Colonies could provide raw materials for the homeland and also consume goods made in the homeland. The large powers, however, had settled the most attractive, profitable areas in the preceding century, and the opportunities for a small power such as Courland to establish colonies were few. Duke Jacob first turned his attention to Tobago, already the site of failed Spanish, Dutch, and English expeditions.

The Courland Colony on Tobago: First Attempts

The first colonial effort of the Courlanders at Tobago is poorly documented. England ceded its claim to the island to the duke, although the details of the arrangement are not clear. In 1639, the duke sent 212 men to colonize the island. Sources claim the colonists were conscripted criminals, although nothing specific is known of the circumstances of their supposed crimes. It was usual at the time to include men described as criminals in colonial efforts, and those conscripted usually ranged from individuals convicted of serious crimes such as counterfeiting or robbery to those described as beggars and vagabonds. John Scott, writing in the 1660s, described the fate of the first effort in picturesque language:

> The Duke of Corland Anno 1639 sent a ship thither accommodated with trade to buy it [the island] of the Indians and to take possession in his Right, being before this sufficiently informed of their inclination to trade with the Dutch or English, he purchased it and the natives gave him a cleare possession dispersing themselves to Guiana, to Trinidad and some of them to St. Vincents an Isle north North west fourty Leagues from Tobago. These people

[the Courlanders] being new hands as they phrase them in these parts and having noe experienced Planters in their Collonie, and people that came soe far fro the Norteward and not any amonst them that knew what was food or Physick in their proper seasons, did occasion their moldering to nothing.

The duke may have sent out this initial group as a declaration of his claim to the island. It is not apparent whether any remnants of the colony survived on the island until the second effort.

In 1642, Duke Jacob sent out a second expedition, of 310 colonists, under the command of a Dutchman, Cornelius Caroon, who had years of experience trading in Brazil. The population of Courland was small, no more than two hundred thousand, and those busily engaged in agriculture or working in the industries that Duke Jacob had established. Courland lacked surplus population, so the duke recruited three hundred colonists from Zeeland in the southern part of the Netherlands for a second attempt to colonize Tobago. John Scott claimed that the Indians had left the island at the time of the first Courland colony, but Carib were certainly present when the second colony arrived, and hostilities soon broke out between the two groups, perhaps because Caroon instituted friendly trade contacts with the Arawak on Trinidad. The second Courland colony endured until 1650, but by then the continuous harassment by the Carib and disease reduced the colony to seventy men. Caroon and the survivors abandoned Tobago and resettled with the Dutch in Guyana.

The Courland Colony in Gambia

Duke Jacob's next effort took place not on Tobago but in Africa. In the mind of the duke, both were part of the same plan. In 1651, Duke Jacob sent a colonizing expedition to the mouth of the Gambia River, an area not yet exploited by European powers. From the beginning, the duke ordered his colonizing effort to be conducted differently from the European norm. Rather than seizing territory, the duke's representatives bought an island in the river from the local king on which to erect a fort and rented still more land on the shore from the king. Through his representatives, the duke purchased or rented additional areas from other kings and established good relations with the local peoples. Shortly after the Courlanders arrived, two groups of English also sailed into the river, Royalist and Commonwealth. The Courlanders managed to remain neutral, and the English departed, although later Cromwell interfered with shipments from Gambia to Courland until a treaty with the duke was agreed on.

The Gambia colony was small. The garrison numbered about sixty, and almost all the soldiers were also craftsmen, fulfilling roles in the colony such as smiths, tailors, and carpenters. About three hundred colonists were sent to Gambia over the years, though the population at any one time was never that great, as deaths from tropical diseases were common. In addition to Courlanders, there were Scandinavians, Germans, and Portuguese among the colonists. The duke guaranteed religious tolerance. The Gambia colony exported several tropical products, but by far the most important were gold and, regrettably, slaves. Today slavery is rightly condemned as the horror it undoubtedly was, but in the sixteenth century it was almost universally approved. The duke decreed that no slaves were to be taken in the area surrounding the Gambia colony, but rather they were acquired, as customary at that time, from far inland up the Gambia River. The slaves were brought to the Caribbean either to work plantations on Tobago or be sold to other European colonies.

The Courland Colony on Tobago: The Successful Third Attempt

Duke Jacob attempted to establish a colony on Tobago a third time, in 1654. By that date, Courland was growing wealthy under the duke's enlightened leadership, and he was able to dedicate greater resources to the effort. The first contingent consisted of 124 Courland soldiers commanded by 25 Courland officers and 80 families, transported in the ship *Das Wappen der Herzogin von Kurland* (The Coat of Arms of the Duchess of Courland), constructed specifically to carry colonists and to transport products of the colony back to Europe. Again, the duke turned to foreigners, mainly Dutch Zeelanders and British, as the initial colonists, but there were also Swedes and Germans. Once the colony was well established, the duke also sent Latvians to settle there. The colonists swore loyalty to Duke Jacob and recognized the sovereignty of Courland, renaming the island Jaunkurzeme (New Courland in Latvian). The Courlanders established themselves on the northwestern coast of the island, where they erected a substantial fort, Jekabforts (Fort Jacob), and a settlement, Jekaba pilesta (Jacobstown). Initially there were a few clashes with Indians, but the Courlanders were soon able to establish peaceful trade relations.

The duke sent frequent ships bearing supplies, additional soldiers, and colonists. In 1655, a supply ship from Courland arrived in To-

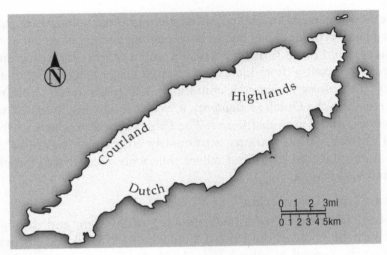

Tobago island.

bago, and the next year two ships from Courland carried 250 families and 120 more soldiers to the colony. Supply ships arrived in 1657 and 1658, also bringing an additional 150 families.

In 1654, two merchant brothers from Flushing in the Netherlands, Adriaen and Cornelis Lampsius, sent Dutch colonists to Tobago. They arrived sometime after the Courlanders and settled on the southern side of the island. The Courlanders accepted their presence, but in autumn 1655, the Dutch colonists attempted to conquer the island. The governor of the Courlander colony anticipated the Dutch move, and although outnumbered, the Courlanders so decisively repulsed the Dutch assault that the Dutch surrendered before the Courlanders could launch a counterattack. Duke Jacob allowed the Dutch to remain on Tobago, requiring them only to recognize him as the legitimate ruler of the island and to swear allegiance. In 1657, French refugees also arrived on the island from an unsuccessful attempt to establish a colony in South America. They were welcomed, and on taking an oath of alliance to the duke, they fully became members of the colony.

Duke Jacob also instituted liberal and enlightened opportunities for the colonists to improve their conditions of life and situation in society. The Latvians who came to the colony were from the poorest strata of Courland's society, serfs and farmers of small subsistent plots. The duke declared that Tobago colonists who had been serfs in Courland were now freemen, and all colonists were granted substantial parcels of land as freeholds. They received at least sixty acres, as much as most families could farm. Officers, officials, and any who had sufficient resources to develop more land were granted larger tracts. Within a few years, the colony prospered, containing 120 plantations, 3 churches (two more in the Dutch settlement), a works producing indigo, 7 sugar refineries, and 2 rum distilleries. The ships carried products of the island's farms and plantations, particularly large quantities of tobacco and sugar, back to Courland where they were reexported, largely to Poland and Russia.

Betrayal and Destruction

In 1654, Charles X Gustav became king of Sweden, and during the next year he invaded the United Kingdom of Poland and Lithuania, starting the Second Northern War (1655–1660). Sweden and the Polish-Lithuania coalition had a long history of hostilities dating back to the previous century, as both powers sought to dominate the eastern shore of the Baltic Sea. Duke Jacob quickly declared neutrality, which was recognized by both combatants. The war initially went well for Sweden. Charles X defeated the Polish armies and occupied all of Greater Poland, and the Polish king, John II Casimir, fled to Silesia. But Charles X had not counted on the reaction of the Polish people, who revolted against the Swedes. As the war surged back and forth across Poland, other powers—Denmark, Russia, Austria, and Prussia—saw opportunities to weaken Charles X and support Poland.

In 1658, the Swedes demanded the right of passage through the Duchy of Courland. The Swedish general again recognized Courland's neutrality and swore to observe it, but, ordered by his king, he treacherously seized the capital of the duchy, Mitau, and imprisoned the duke and duchess in Riga. Charles X's actions were condemned as dishonorable in all the courts of Europe. The Swedes quickly found it was easier to conquer the duchy than to administer it. Citizens of all classes refused to cooperate with the Swedes, and peasants proved the most effective in opposition. They formed military units, and guerrilla war broke out in Courland. In 1659, military units from Poland, Lithuania, and Prussia joined the peasants against the Swedes, and by the end of the year, the Swedes had lost control of almost all the duchy. In 1660, Charles X of Sweden died, and his successor quickly put an end to the war; the duke and duchess returned to Courland. The war, however, had devastated the duchy. The duke's industrial workshops had been looted and destroyed, and much of the navy and commercial fleet had been seized by Sweden or otherwise lost. Moreover, the war had been accompanied by a devastating epidemic, and it has been estimated that the war and disease had killed about a third of Courland's population. The colonies were also lost.

When the word arrived in Tobago that the duke was imprisoned and the Swedes had conquered the duchy, the Dutch promptly seized the colony. First, they corrupted the garrison, telling them that no more supplies would come from Courland and they would never receive their back pay. Then they offered a bribe of 500 rixthalers, large silver coins, which was promptly accepted, and the fort passed into Dutch hands. While the garrison and most officials lacked moral fiber to resist the Dutch, the common Courlanders in the colony were made of sterner stuff. They revolted against the Dutch, but because they lacked arms, organization, and training, the rebellion was suppressed with great violence and bloodletting by the Dutch.

The Dutch also tried to take the Gambia colony. The duke's commercial agent in Gambia, Henry Momber, was Dutch and readily agreed to his countrymen's plans, turning over the fortresses in the colony. The duke's governor, Otto Stiel, refused to go along with this betrayal, but again the Dutch resorted to propaganda and bribery, telling the garrison there was no hope of supplies from Courland and they would pay the garrison's back pay. Again the scarcely disguised bribe worked. The garrison revolted against Stiel, who was sent to Holland as a prisoner. A French privateer employed by the Swedes then captured the colony from the Dutch, looted everything of worth, including the artillery from the fort, and sought to sell the colony to a merchant from the province of Groningen in the Netherlands. The leaders of Groningen, however, wanted no part of such a dubious transaction. The provinces of the Netherlands exercised a great deal of autonomy, and it was not unusual for provinces to pursue differing courses of action, a source of weakness for the Netherlands as a whole. Groningen even supplied Stiel with a ship in which he sailed to Gambia with a small group of men and reclaimed the colony in the name of the Duke of Courland. The Amsterdam Dutch, however, sent three warships to Gambia to bombard the nearly defenseless fort, forcing Stiel to surrender.

The Amsterdam Dutch now controlled the island fort, but the remnant of the Courlander colonists and the native allies controlled the mainland and the only sources of water for the fort. They seized a Dutch watering party and then, with a strong force of native allies, attacked the Dutch in the fort. The Dutch surrendered, freed Stiel, and left, partially destroying the fort before their departure. Stiel held the colony in the name of the duke for eight months, but disease ravaged the surviving Courlanders until Stiel was left with only six Courlander men and women, about seventy Natives trained as soldiers, and six cannons salvaged from inland stations. Stiel managed to get a letter to Duke Jacob describing the situation in early 1661, but there was nothing the duke could do. The duchy was in state of ruin, and he could not send aid.

The restoration of Stuart rule in England happened in the same year, 1660, as Duke Jacob returned to Courland. Relations between the duke and the Stuarts had always been close. King James I was the duke's godfather, and the duke had visited Charles I, corresponded with him, and had even sent him substantial aid during the English Civil War, both money and warships, but new interests now overwhelmed old friendships. The Royal Adventurers of England Trading into Africa, a company formed by King Charles II's brothers Princes Rupert and James (the future King James II) and other influential and wealthy members of the court, sent a fleet of ships under Major Robert Holmes, a military man of ability but disreputable character, to the Guinea coast. Holmes sent two frigates to seize the fort, which he claimed to believe was held by the Dutch, although Otto Stiel explained to him that this was a colony of Duke Jacob of Courland, an ally of England and friend of the Stuarts. It made no difference; Holmes occupied the fort and colony, and subsequently England retained control despite the obvious injustice of the situation.

Twenty-Year Interval, 1658–1678

Duke Jacob spent the rest of his life working to rebuild Courland. Despite many obstacles, Courland's economy eventually recovered considerably, but never to the level the duchy had enjoyed before the Swedish invasion. The restoration had, however, required the exploitation of the duchy's resources, particularly the forests, beyond sustainable levels. Population loss also was not soon replenished. In 1661, the duke lodged protests with England about the loss of the colony in

Gambia, but matters dragged on until 1664, when the duke, understanding his weak bargaining position, accepted the best deal he could achieve. He surrendered his claim to Gambia, and in exchange King Charles II granted Tobago to Duke Jacob under the king's protection and further granted Courlanders the right to trade in all English domains subject to a 3 percent export fee. The king failed to live up to his promises. England provided Duke Jacob no help in recovering Tobago, and Courlanders were routinely shut out of trade in Gambia.

The Dutch merchants Adriaen and Cornelis Lampsius applied to Louis XIV of France for title to Tobago. The French king granted their request but stated that Tobago was a dependency of the Netherlands. In essence, the king of France granted a territory that he acknowledged was Dutch, not French, to Dutch citizens. This seems perplexing to the modern mind, but it satisfied the merchants, who felt they gained the support of the French king for their claim. Soon, however, France contended with the Netherlands for control of Tobago.

The involvement of England and France increased the chaos surrounding the troubled island. During the 1660s and 1670s, England, the Netherlands, and France fought wars and changed alliances with confusing frequency in Europe, and all three nations repeatedly invaded Tobago and displaced one another without any attention to Duke Jacob's claim. Caribs from other islands frequently came to Tobago also and often conducted bloody attacks on anyone who attempted to garrison and colonize the island, and buccaneers of various nationalities, and some of no nationality, raided and set up temporary camps on Tobago.

Duke Jacob always retained the hope of rebuilding his colony on Tobago, but early attempts proved futile. A group of colonists from Courland seem to have reached the island in 1667, and two more ships with colonists and supplies arrived in 1668. The colonists began the work of restoration, but they were soon attacked by the Arawak from Trinidad, who were now living on the island, and raided by pirates. The commander of the soldiers deserted with the duke's ships and sold the colony's goods in Barbados. The attempt to reestablish the colony collapsed. Another ship that the duke sent to Tobago was seized by the French in 1672. In 1675, the duke sent two more ships, but the commander proved corrupt, mortgaged the ships, and absconded with the money. In 1678, after a fierce and sanguinary conflict, the French took Tobago from the Dutch, depopulated the island except for a few renegades, and sailed away. The Treaty of Nymwegen was also signed that same year between the Netherlands and France, leaving each party with the territory they then possessed. France claimed the deserted island.

The duke sent another ship in 1681, but it was captured by Algerian corsairs. A second expedition in 1681 brought more colonists, many of whom were French Huguenots, and a contingent of well-armed soldiers. Over the next two years, the colonists were able to send back to Courland quantities of tobacco, exotic hardwood lumber, hides, dyes, and even coconuts, but the Indians continued to attack the colonists, causing casualties and limiting their activities. Courland's reduced population could not sustain the colonial effort, and the duke sought to sponsor an English soldier, Captain John Poyntz, to create a company in order to bring additional colonists from England. The scheme, however, came to nothing when the English government ordered Poyntz to cease and desist. Colonists became discouraged, and some evacuated to the English colony on Barbados or other destinations in the Caribbean. Courland maintained some interest in Tobago as late as 1691, but the colony slowly dissolved into nothing. As late as 1709, agents of the duchy tried to recruit colonists in England to settle on Tobago, but again the English government suppressed their attempt.

Aftermath

According to all accounts, Duke Jacob was a moral individual in regard to political and business transactions, and that served him badly in the world of power and politics. He sincerely and naively believed in the sanctity of personal relationships and written treaties, only to learn that the honor of kings was negated by current interests, and treaties were worthless without force to back them. The duke's attempt to revive the colony on Tobago encountered insoluble problems. The resources available to him were too few, and he could not overcome the dishonesty and incompetence of officers on whom he relied, the passive-aggressive antagonism of larger European powers, and the hostility of the Arawak and Carib, who had understandably become enemies of all Europeans without distinction.

In 1676, Duke Jacob's beloved wife, the Duchess Louise Charlotte, died. She had aided him in the administration of the duchy, and he felt her absence deeply. The duke's own health soon declined, and he died on January 1, 1682. He is still remembered with reverence in Livonia.

The duke's son and successor, Frederick Casimir, was highly intelligent, but like many individuals for whom much came easily, he never developed habits of diligence and sustained effort. His contemporaries characterized him as superficial and ultimately more concerned with maintaining a fashionable and pleasurable court than the welfare of the duchy. Courland continued to decline in significance during his administration and those that followed.

Tobago continued to be little inhabited and visited irregularly by Spanish, French, and English forces and pirates until 1763, when England finally annexed the island. A monument stands today on Tobago in honor of the colonists from Courland who came so far and for a brief time accomplished much before succumbing to powerful political and military forces.

Sources

For the Carib encountered by the colonists, see Louis Allaire, "The Island Caribs of the Lesser Antilles," 177–185, and Vincent O. Cooper, "Language and Gender among the Kalinago of Fifteenth-Century St. Croix," 186-196, in *The Indigenous People of the Caribbean*, ed. Samuel M. Wilson (Gainesville: University Press of Florida, 1997). For the Arawak, Betty J. Meggers and Clifford Evans, "Lowland South America and the Antilles," 543-591, in *Ancient Native Americans*, ed. Jesse D. Jennings (San Francisco: W. H. Freeman, 1978); William F. Keegan and Corinne L. Hofman, *The Caribbean before Columbus* (Oxford: Oxford University Press, 2017), particularly 11-15; J. D. Hill and F. Santos-Granero, *Comparative Arawakan Histories: Rethinking Language Family and Culture Area in Amazonia* (Urbana: University of Illinois Press, 2006).

The sources for Duke Jacob's colonization of Tobago are scattered and incomplete. Colonel (sometimes Major) John Scott, a reprehensible individual guilty of a host of serious crimes, began but did not complete an account of Caribbean colonization that survives in the original manuscript in his hand now in the British Museum. The work includes a report of the earliest efforts of the Dutch and Courlanders on Tobago: Major John Scott, "IV. Tobago and Trinidad. (i) The Description of Tobago," 114-119, in Vincent T. Harlow, *Colonising Expeditions to the West Indies and Guiana, 1623–1627*, works issued by the Hakluyt Society, 2nd ser., no. 56 (London: Printed for the Hakluyt Society, 1925; Nendelm, Liechtenstein: Kraus Reprint, 1967). This is a transcription of Sloan mss. 3662, folios 47b-49, British Museum, long dismissed as unreliable until George Edmundson demonstrated the accuracy of Scott's account in "The Dutch in Western Guiana," *English Historical Review* 16 (1901): 640-675. Wilbur C. Abbott has written a fascinating biography of this egregious character, *Colonel John Scott*, Society of Colonial Wars in the State of New York, pub. No. 30 (New Haven: Yale University Press, 1918).

Primary sources are effectively presented and utilized in Otto Heinz Mattiesen, *Die Kolonial-und Überseepolitik der kurlädischen Herzöge im 17. Und 18, Jahrhundert,* Schriftenreihe der Stadt der Auslandsdeutschen, Heft 6 (Stuttgart: Kohlhammer, 1940) and Edgar Anderson, *Senie kurzemnieki Amerika un Tobago koloniz cija* (Stockholm: Daugava, 1970), an excellent study based on original sources, but only available in Latvian. More accessible is Edgar Anderson, "The Couronians and the West Indies" (PhD diss., University of Chicago, 1965). Christoph George von Ziegenhorn, *Staats Recht de Herzogthümer Curland und Semgallen* (Königsberg: Joh. Jacob Kauter, 1772) is primarily important for documents concerning the general administration of Duke Jacob, including some material on colonization.

Alexander Valdonis Berkis, *The Reign of Duke James in Courland* (Lincoln, Nebraska: Vaidava, 1960) and more generally *The History of the Duchy of Courland* (Towsin, MD: Paul M. Harrod, 1969) provide excellent and sympathetic overviews of Duke Jacob's career and administration, but Berkis apparently did not know of John Scott's account of the earliest attempts of the Courlanders to colonize Tobago.

Rupert Douglas Archibald, *Tobago: Melancholy Isle*, vol. 1: 1498–1771 (St. Augustine: Trinidad and Tobago University of the West Indies, 1987) provides an excellent overview of the history of the island with good attention to the efforts of Duke Jacob and the Courlanders, but it should be read in accompaniment with Berkis, *The Reign of Duke James*. Ken Greger, "Too Rich for a Duke, Too Poor for a King: Duke Jacob and the Colonial Empire of Seventeenth Century Courland" (BA thesis, University of Wisconsin, 1995) accessed August 8, 2019, https://core.ac.uk/display/5062917, is based almost entirely on secondary sources but provides a lively and able overview.

Several recent studies examine different aspects of the significance of the Courland colony on Tobago: Harry C. Merritt, "The Colony of the Colonized: the Duchy of Courland's Tobago Colony and Contemporary Latvian National Identity," *Nationalities Papers* 38, no. 4

(2010): 491–508; Imbi Sooman, Jesma McFarlane, Valdis Teraud-kalns, and Stefan Donecker, "From the Port of Ventspils to Great Courland Bay: The Couronian Colony on Tobago in Past and Present," *Journal of Baltic Studies* 44, no. 4 (December 2013): 503–526; and Karin Jekabson-Lemanis, "Balts in the Caribbean: The Duchy of Courland's Attempts to Colonize Tobago Island, 1638 to 1654," *Caribbean Quarterly* 46, no. 2 (2000): 25–44.

For a good and detailed overview of Dutch colonization north of Brazil, see C. Ch. Goslinga, *The Dutch in the Caribbean and on the Wild Coast 1580–1680* (Assen, Netherlands: Van Gorcum, 1971).

SEVEN

The Graveyard *of* Colonists:
The Wild Coast (1576–1830)

THE MOUTH OF THE ORINOCO RIVER is separated from the mouth of the Amazon River by approximately nine hundred miles of jungle, swamp, and a multitude of rivers. The area was generally known to the indigenous population as Guyana, the Many Waters. The Dutch called it de Wilde Kust, the Wild Coast. For the French, the interior was l'Enfer Vert, the Green Hell. Early explorers describe the shore as brackish swamps densely grown with mangroves and scraggly courida trees and brush on the rare patches of slightly higher ground. Beyond the coast are swamps, jungles, and a highland of strange, isolated plateaus surrounded by high cliffs. The climate is challengingly hot and humid, a natural breeding ground for diseases, and torrential downpours flood large areas during the rainy season. The land is surprisingly fertile, but many of the flora and fauna are dangerous.

Before the first Europeans appeared, three ethnic groups dominated the Wild Coast. The Europeans referred to one group of related tribes as the Arawak, but they perhaps should more accurately be known as the Taino. They seem to have been less aggressive and more agrarian than the Arawak of the Caribbean but nevertheless capable of extreme violence when they felt aggrieved. They were frequently at war with the tribes that the Europeans called the Carib, but they could be more accurately called the Kalinago. They were generally held to be cannibals. The third, much smaller group were the Warao, who lived in villages built on stilts by the mouths of principal rivers. They were famed for building large dugout canoes of excellent quality, much desired by the Carib who traded with the Warao for these canoes and left them in peace. Carib and Arawak also lived in the interior, as did still other tribes.

The Spanish and Portuguese attempted few settlements, mainly on the periphery of the region, but they feared that if others settled there they would become rivals. Spanish encounters with foreign traders and colonists often resulted in violence. Nevertheless, foreign traders continued to ply the coast, and the empty middle territory attracted English, Dutch, and French colonists. Early European settlements were restricted to the coast and along major rivers, while the interior was dominated by indigenous Indian tribes and descendants of escaped African slaves who preserved much of their original cultures. Today the area is divided politically between southern Venezuela, Guyana, Suriname, French Guyana, and northern Brazil. Guyana and Suriname are independent countries, while French Guyana is an overseas department of France.

Early Explorers and Traders, Spanish and Dutch Hostility on the Wild Coast

Columbus touched on the northern portion of the Wild Coast during his third voyage in 1498. There he traded with the Natives for ornaments made of base gold that they indicated came from inland, the first manifestation of what would become a European obsession with the idea of undiscovered wealth in the interior of northern South America. He was followed in 1499 by Alonzo de Ojeda and in 1500 by Vicente Yáñez Pinzón, who earlier discovered the mouth of the Amazon. Both sailed along the Guyana coast without penetrating far into the interior.

In 1530, Pedro de Acosta attempted to establish a Spanish colony in the Guyanas on the Barima River that flows parallel to the coast before flowing into the Atlantic Ocean at the southern edge of the Orinoco delta. Acosta brought about three hundred men who established a village, but they proved no match for the Carib, who overran the settlement and killed many of the colonists. A minority escaped with their lives but little more, discouraging most subsequent Spanish attempts to establish colonies in the area, though exploration continued.

In 1594–1595, Sir Walter Raleigh explored in Guyana and eastern Venezuela. While there, he captured Antonio de Berrío, a Spanish explorer and official. Berrío related a garbled version of a Spanish tale to Raleigh that the latter repeated in his book *The Discoverie of the Large, Rich, and Bewtifvl Empyre of Gviana, with a Relation of the Great and Golden Citie of Manoa* (London: Robert Robinson, 1596). The story related the adventures of a man whose name Raleigh gave as "Johannes Martinez," probably to be identified as Juan Martin de Albujar, who was a member of an expedition in the region of the lower Orinoco led by Pedro de Silva in 1570. Raleigh's version is corrupt in many details, and the essential narrative in any form is incredible. Supposedly, Martinez was captured by Caribs who spared his life, and he lived among them for ten years, even taking a Native wife. The Indians, he claimed, led him blindfolded to the wonderful city of Manoa, so large that he and his Indian companions traveled a day and a half through the city before coming to the palace of the Inca emperor. Martinez lived for seven months in the palace before the emperor acceded to his request to return to his own people. On departing, the emperor loaded him and his companions with all the gold they could carry, but they were robbed of the treasure except for two gourds containing gold beads.

One can easily imagine the probable origin of the story. Juan Martin de Albujar, after long residence among the Indians, stumbled into a Spanish outpost, ill and without resources except for some gold beads. A tale of a golden kingdom, however, attracted interest and sympathy, and ensured he would not be ignored and left unattended. Raleigh exhibited no trace of critical thinking about the tale, but rather accepted the entire fable as true. He integrated the Martinez tale with an equally garbled version of the El Dorado legend, the account of a native ruler so rich that he cast gold and emeralds into a sacred lake and then dived into the lake to wash off his ritual coating of gold dust. For Raleigh, Manoa was the capital city of El Dorado. The Spanish had originally searched for El Dorado in the mountains of western Colombia and Ecuador, but they found nothing there that satisfied their imaginary vision, so now the search for the golden kingdom turned to Guyana.

Raleigh's book was immensely popular and influential, and it was quickly translated into Dutch, German, French, and Latin. In addition to the tale of Manoa and the treasure of El Dorado, Raleigh's publication exaggerated the extent of his discoveries and the wonderful

"Gviana sive Amazonum regio," published and republished beginning about 1638 by Hendrik Hondius, Gerhard Mercator, and Jan Janszoon, without substantial change. This printing is by Jan Janszoon (Iohannes Ianssonius). The map names many rivers but it is apparent that even more than a century after Columbus many were completely unexplored, their mouths only observed from the sea. Notable is the depiction of the large fictitious Lake Parime and the equally ficitious city labelled "Manoa, o' el Dorado" at the northwest corner of the lake. The existence of the lake may have been suggested by the seasonal flooding of the Rupununi savannah. (*Library of Congress*)

qualities of Guyana and its riches, giving rise to the notion that Guyana was a land of eternal spring, a kindly environment inhabited by happy, friendly Indians eager to trade exotic forest products and even gold for glass beads and cheap knives. Raleigh discounted or completely ignored the challenging climate, the warlike reputation of many Native peoples, and the dangers of hostilities with the Spanish, Portuguese, and pirates. The popularity of Raleigh's inflated account influenced many who colonized Guyana, both successfully and unsuccessfully.

In 1596, Lawrence Keymis, Raleigh's subordinate, sailed along the Guyana coast, making important observations and charting rivers.

Keymis also listed more than twenty Hispanic adventurers who attempted to explore the Guyanas before his voyage in 1596. None prospered in the endeavor, and Keymis reported their attempts succinctly and vividly: "Juan Corteso arrived at the river of Amazones or Orellana with three hundred men. He marched up into the country, but neither hee nor any of his companie did return againe." The contrast between the pragmatic, practical work of Keymis and Raleigh's romanticism could hardly be stronger. Raleigh was ultimately the victim of his own imaginative visions. In 1617, he embarked on a wildly unrealistic expedition to find the wealth he believed to exist on the Caroní River, a tributary of the Orinoco. All went wrong and ended with his beheading.

Throughout the seventeenth century and well into the eighteenth century, colonies continued to be founded along the Wild Coast and on the major rivers. Indians, reduced in number by European diseases, proved a declining menace, but Maroons—Africans and their descendants who escaped from slavery and formed their own communities—proved dangerous adversaries for plantation owners and even small towns. Of still greater threat were the frequent European wars of the period. The Spanish and Portuguese maintained their holds on the northern and southern fringes of the Wild Coast, while in the middle ground, English, Dutch, and French colonists found themselves dragged into the conflicts of their homelands. Colonies changed hands, some several times, and others were dispersed and destroyed during these international rivalries. Eventually, the English secured the territory just south of Spanish Venezuela that has become the nation of Guyana, while the Dutch dominated Suriname, and the French held what has become French Guyana.

It is impossible even to enumerate all the colonies that were founded and failed along the Wild Coast and on its numerous rivers. Sources for many are poor, some so little known that their very existence was more a matter of rumor than fact. Those described here are among the better recognized, more interesting, and illustrative of the varied activity in this dangerous area.

The Spanish Colony of Santo Tomé de Guayana, Destroyed Three Times (1576–1637)

In 1576, two Jesuit priests, Ignacio Llauri and Julián de Vergara, founded a mission, Santo Tomé de Guayana, by the confluence of the

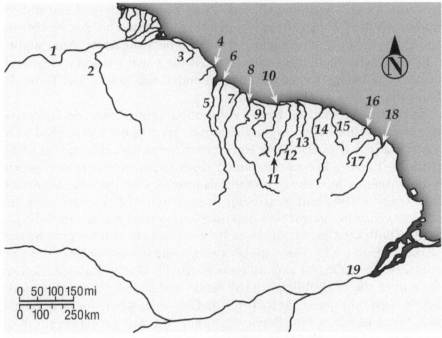

Chief rivers of the Wild Coast. 1. Orinoco, 2. Caroní, 3. Barima, 4. Pomeroon, 5. Essequibo, 6. Demerara, 7. Berbice, 8. Corentyne, 9. Nickerie, 10. Coppename, 11. Saramaca, 12. Suriname, 13. Commewine, 14. Maroni, 15. Mana, 16. Cayenne, 17. Approuague, 18. Oyapoc, 19. Amazon. In addition, there are hundreds of small rivers and thousands of creeks.

Orinoco and Caroní Rivers, a rare Spanish effort in the area. A mixed Spanish and Indian community quickly grew up around the mission, and a Dutch shipmaster, Captain Adrian Jansen, appeared at the new town to trade in 1578. The royal Spanish government prohibited trade with foreigners and regarded merchants like Jansen as illegal smugglers, but Spain was negligent in providing its colonies, especially the smaller communities, with adequate supplies. Wherever Spanish officialdom was weak, Spanish colonists proved eager to trade with all merchants no matter their national origin. The villagers, however, did not have much on hand to trade with Jansen, so he, like many other traders, extended credit. They could have their purchases now in exchange for tobacco, dyewood, or other goods that they pledged to have for Jansen when he returned in a year to conduct more business. When

Jensen returned, he found the town had been strictly ordered not to
trade with the Dutch. Jansen pleaded that he should at least be able to
collect his debts, and he anchored his ship near the town. After nightfall, he quietly landed his crew, looted the town's storehouses, and
burned the village to the ground. So ended the first Santo Tomé de
Guayana.

In 1595, Antonio de Berrío refounded Santo Tomé de Guayana
somewhat south of its original location. He has been described as a
man obsessed with the quest to discover the mythical kingdom of El
Dorado. Earlier, Berrío conducted three expeditions from western
South America into the mountainous interior and the headwaters of
the Orinoco River and its tributaries in search of El Dorado. On the
third expedition, he traveled downstream on the Orinoco to the confluence with the Caroní, where he believed he was near his goal before
he had to turn back. Berrío sought to continue the search from the east
coast, but in 1595, he was taken prisoner by Walter Raleigh. Before
the end of the year, Raleigh freed Berrío and sailed back to England.
Berrío then refounded Santo Tomé de Guayana, where he awaited his
son, Fernando de la Hoz Berrío y Oruña, who was gathering supplies
and men in Spain, and there Antonio de Berrío died in 1597, at least
seventy years old. His son carried on the fruitless hunt. The colony
survived and even grew moderately until Raleigh's quixotic, doomed
final expedition. At that time, 1618, Santo Tomé was a village of 140
homes, a church, and two convents.

After Raleigh was convicted of treason in a corrupt show trial early
in the reign of King James I, the king consigned Raleigh to the Tower
of London, where he spent sixteen years. The conditions of his imprisonment were liberal, even comfortable, but prison was galling for a
man of action. Always the romantic, Raleigh believed that there was
a rich mine of gold and silver to be found up the Orinoco near the
Caroní River, and in 1617, he and his supporters convinced James I
to release him to find it. The king, however, imposed impossible conditions on Raleigh's expedition. It was to penetrate deep into Spanish
territory, proceed up the Orinoco, locate the mine, load the ships with
high-grade ore, and sail back to Britain, all without conflict with the
Spanish.

With some difficulty, Raleigh and company sailed to the mouth of
the Orinoco, arriving in 1618. As fever spread through his fleet,
Raleigh fell seriously ill, and command of the land expedition fell to

Raleigh's loyal subordinate Lawrence Keymis, who was accompanied by Raleigh's son Walter, called Wat. The Spanish saw the sudden appearance of the English as a pirate raid, and a clash developed into a battle, which the English won. Wat Raleigh was killed during a brave but foolish charge against the Spanish position. Santo Tomé was partly burned during the battle, and the population fled into the jungle. Keymis and his troops remained in the half-ruined town for less than a month, unable to advance because of attacks by the Spanish and their allied Arawak. The English then burned the rest of Santo Tomé and retreated to the ships. Raleigh blamed Keymis for the death of his son and failure of the expedition, and Keymis was so distressed that he committed suicide. Raleigh returned to England, where the king ordered Raleigh's execution to satisfy Spanish protests.

In 1619, Fernando de Berrío intended to refound Santo Tomé de Guayana near its original location, but his agents were captured by British pirates and ransomed for tobacco. Thus delayed, the village was not reestablished until 1620. Santo Tomé seemed doomed to suffer troubles. In 1629, the Dutch Geoctroyeerde Westindische Compagnie, the Chartered West Indies Company, sent a fleet of nine ships and several smaller sloops commanded by Adrian Janszoon Pater to the Orinoco to attack Santo Tomé. They left the town burned to the ground again. Santo Tomé revived somewhat after this disaster only to be burned again by the Dutch in 1637. The situation at the confluence of the Caroní with the Orinoco, however, was too advantageous to remain undeveloped, and there was always some settlement in the vicinity.

The town was again officially refounded in 1764 as Santo Tomé de Guayana de Angostura del Orinoco. The name Angostura was derived from the Spanish for "narrowing," as Santo Tomé is located by the first narrowing of the Orinoco River, and it gave rise to the name of the most famous local product, Angostura Bitters. Today the town has been incorporated, along with several neighboring smaller settlements and a vast hydroelectric project, as Ciudad Guyana.

The English on the Oyapoc River: The Colony That Failed Three Times (1604–ca. 1635)

Charles Leigh was the younger brother of Sir John Oliph Leigh, a prominent London alderman. Beginning in the 1590s, Charles Leigh made several voyages to North and South America, although detailed documentation is lacking for all but a cruise in 1597 to Newfoundland waters, where he engaged in some piracy, capturing a ship from Brittany.

Leigh, like many others, seems to have been inspired by Raleigh's exaggerated claims about the excellence and wealth of the Wild Coast, and in 1604, he led the first English attempt to settle in Guyana. One small ship carried his expedition, numbering just forty-six men and boys, from England to the Wiapogo River, today called the Oyapoc River in English and the Rio Oiapoque in Portuguese. Now the river is the border between French Guyana and Brazil. Leigh and his company were greeted by friendly Indians, settled near their village, and agreed to aid them against their enemies. Leigh soon sent his small ship crewed by ten men back to England to fetch supplies and provisions. Meanwhile, the remaining settlers traded with the local Indians and with others upriver for a variety of goods, most notably dyewood, tobacco, cotton, parrots, monkeys, and a variety of plants thought to be of medicinal value. Leigh also explored for gold but found none.

A supply ship from England hampered by adverse winds and poor seamanship was blown to Barbados, from which it proceeded to St. Luca. Supposedly, the crew then got distracted from their mission by the prospect of finding gold among the Natives, only to fall into a Carib ambush. The survivors barely managed to sail the ship, which finally arrived at a Spanish port. Spain and England were then at peace, and the English sailors were treated well, but the ship never got to the colony in Guyana.

By the time Leigh's own ship returned to the colony, a tropical fever and dysentery were ravaging the settlers. Leigh was about to embark for England when he fell ill and died. The leaderless colony quickly dissolved. Some returned to England immediately; others persisted for a short while before taking passage with passing Dutch and French trading ships. By late 1605, the first English colony on the Oyapoc River was deserted.

In 1609, Robert Harcourt, eldest son of Sir Walter Harcourt, along with his younger brother Michael and colonists sailed from England to the Oyapoc River in three small ships, one of eighty tons, one of thirty-six tons, and a tiny shallop of nine tons crewed by only four men. At the mouth of the river, they were greeted by Indians who had a good opinion of the English dating back to the visit of Sir Walter Raleigh in 1595. Harcourt claimed all the land between the Amazon and Essequibo Rivers in the name of King James I of England, after explaining to the Indians that he had no desire to deprive them of their freedom but rather extended the king's protection against their enemies. After just a few days, Robert Harcourt departed for England, leaving behind his brother and the rest of the company to establish a colony on the Oyapoc, where they traded with the Indians and unsuccessfully sought the source of gold ornaments that the Indians reported came from deep in the interior.

In England, Harcourt encountered problems. As a Catholic, he was subject to penalties for failure to adhere to the Church of England, but he managed to obtain an exemption. He was also involved in a family dispute about control of resources. Harcourt did not return to the colony but rather tried to promote its development from England. He wrote an account of the establishment of the colony, *A Relation of a Voyage to Gviana. Describing the climat, bsession, fertilitie, prouisions, and commodities of that Country. [. . .] Together with the manners, customes, behauiors, and dispositions of the people.* (London: Edw. Allde, 1613). He also obtained letters patent from King James I establishing a legal basis for the colony, but evidently Harcourt was unable to provide sufficient support for the colony, and the colony was unable to create a viable financial basis. The end of this second effort is obscure, but the colony seems to have been abandoned within a few years except perhaps for a few who persisted in the area to trade with the Indians and passing ships.

Roger North, younger brother of Dudley North, third Baron North, sought to become leader of a third effort to establish an English colony on the Oyapoc. He had some experience of Guyana, taking part in Raleigh's last, disastrous expedition to the Orinoco River in 1617. In 1619, he obtained letters patent from the king permitting him to assert the king's right to the area previously claimed, to establish a colony, and to trade with the Natives. When the Spanish envoy objected strongly, the king commanded that the expedition be delayed until further notice, but North bribed the Duke of Buckingham, the lord high admiral, to give him a permit to leave, unbeknown to the king. After some time at sea, North learned from a Dutch vessel that he had been accused of disloyalty. He returned to England, where the king had his ship and its cargo of seven tons of tobacco seized, and he was imprisoned in the Tower of London for about six months until the Duke of Buckingham obtained his release. The Spanish envoy was unable to prove that North had obtained the tobacco illegally from Spanish territory, and the ship and cargo were returned to North. The tobacco had deteriorated during the interval, however, and North had a serious financial loss. The continuing disapproval of the king delayed the colonization project for years.

In 1625, Charles I succeeded James I, and in 1626, Roger North joined with Robert Harcourt in an attempt to obtain new letters patent from the king, but the effort failed. In 1627, important courtiers, George Villiers, Duke of Buckingham, and William Herbert, Earl of Pembroke, joined with fifty-five others to form a company, Governor and Company of Noblemen and Gentlemen of England for the Plantation of Guiana. This gained the king's approval, and Villiers was made governor and Roger North his deputy governor. Neither, however, went to the colony. The company managed to send colonists to the Oyapoc, where the Indians received them enthusiastically. The colony started well, but Villiers was assassinated in 1628 by a disgruntled army officer, and Herbert died in 1630. No equally influential leaders emerged to replace them, and when the colonists failed to find precious metals or produce substantial profits from trade, the lesser shareholders grew disillusioned and reluctant to make further investments. Poorly supplied, the settlers soon began to depart for other colonies or took passage on ships returning to the British Isles. The colony declined to a mere trading post and eventually was entirely abandoned.

Marshall's Creek (1630–1645): A Colony of Unanswered Questions

Accounts of colonies along the Wild Coast are frequently lacking in detail and related at several removes from original accounts. The history of the English Marshall's Creek colony on the Suriname River illustrates these difficulties. A source records that in 1630, a Captain Marshall established a settlement there to grow tobacco. Our best evidence for the colony comes from Dutch Captain David Pieterszoon de Vries, who in 1655 published a fascinating journal of his voyages to North and South America. De Vries records that in 1634, about sixteen miles up the Suriname River, he encountered Marshall and sixty colonists living in several buildings surrounded by a wood palisade. De Vries spend a day and night with Marshall, and later about six miles downstream he encountered fourteen or fifteen more Englishmen who were growing tobacco. It is not apparent whether these men were part of Marshall's colony, perhaps having arrived later, or an independent group. After De Vries's encounter, there is no further mention of the Marshall colony for some years.

Robert Rich, Earl of Warwick, who was also involved in the colonization of Providence Island in the Caribbean, sent a colony to Tobago Island, the date of which is variously given as 1639, 1640, or 1642. The correct date was almost certainly 1642; the others are probably due to confusion with an ephemeral English Puritan attempt to colonize Tobago a few years earlier. The effort on Tobago was led by a man whose name is written in various sources as Marshall or Marsham. Marshall is almost certainly the correct form, according to accounts of his subsequent activities in Suriname. There is no indication whether this was the same man active on the Suriname River in the previous decade or just a coincidence. The English colony on Tobago failed quickly owing to lack of supplies and the hostility of the Carib, so Captain Marshall moved the colonists to Suriname. No source indicates whether he found the colony established there in 1630 still in existence or whether he had to make a new start. The colonists seem to have begun well, but in 1645, they supported a neighboring French colony against indigenous Indians. The Indians retaliated, reportedly destroying both colonies in a single day. The name of the ill-fated colony survives in the Dutch form Marshallkreek as the name of a small district and a village in Suriname.

Cayenne (1604–ca. 1674): Commandant Brétigny, a Sadistic Monster or Perhaps Not

The sources for many of the Guyana colonies are unreliable, confusing, and even baffling. Nowhere is this more evident than regarding the accounts of the French efforts to colonize Cayenne. The town, now the capital of French Guyana, is on the estuary of the Cayenne River on what was once an island, now connected to the mainland by silting. In 1604, Daniel de La Touche, seigneur de la Ravardière, made an initial attempt to establish a colony in the area, but the Portuguese quickly ended the effort before anything substantial was accomplished. The Dutch made a small attempt to colonize the area in 1634, recorded by David Pieterszoon de Vries, landing only thirty men. They found some Dutch and English already in the area who joined the colony. This venture collapsed in less than a year when the English among the colonists attempted to seize control.

The main French attempt, subject of contentious accounts, began in 1643, when investors at the port of Rouen, capital of Normandy, formed the Compagnie du Cap au Nord, the North Cape Company, to establish a colony in Guyana. The corporation, sometimes referred to simply as the Compagnie de Rouen, chose Charles Poncet, seigneur de Brétigny, to lead the effort. Born about 1610, Brétigny rose quickly in the service of King Louis XIII of France, achieving the ranks of admiral and lieutenant general. He has, however, gone down in history as a sadistic madman, perhaps unfairly.

Brétigny arrived in Guyana early in 1644 with either three hundred or four hundred colonists. Uncertainty permeates every detail about the colony. Our knowledge of subsequent events is dependent on the accounts of survivors reported by authors who seldom resisted the temptation to dramatize stories. They depicted Brétigny as brutal, bloodthirsty, deranged, and megalomaniacal. They claimed that on the slightest provocation, he tortured and killed colonists and members of the neighboring Carib tribe, the Galibi, and that he even invented new means of inflicting pain and death. The colony was reportedly surrounded with gallows and other instruments of torment and execution, and as Brétigny grew increasingly paranoid, he insisted that colonists tell him their dreams, punishing brutally any he found threatening. Supposedly, when one colonist dreamed that the commandant had died, he had the man broken on the wheel, a gruesome death. Brétigny claimed the colonist would not have dreamed so if he did not intend to assassinate him.

How reliable are the survivors' reports? It is difficult to imagine that all the stories were simply invented, but one account characterizes the settlers as vagrants and adventurers. Brétigny would have had to exercise strict measures to maintain control of such an unpromising group, and discipline was generally harsh during the seventeenth century. Despite reports that Brétigny was equally cruel to the garrison, the soldiers remained loyal to him, and there was no revolt against the commandant. Groups of colonists, however, began to desert the settlement.

Events culminated with the death in 1645 of Brétigny, who, according to reports, is supposed to have died in three different ways. According to one account, a group of fleeing colonists found refuge with friendly Indians upstream from the community. Brétigny followed with a boatload of loyalists and demanded that the Indians surrender the fugitives. When they refused, Brétigny ordered his men to open fire on the Indians, who replied with such a shower of arrows and stones that Brétigny and all his companions were killed. Another account claims that the Galibi planned an uprising against Brétigny, but he was warned by an Indian woman—an element frequently found in colonial narratives—and so Brétigny was able to capture a group of the conspirators. The next day, however, more Indians attacked Brétigny with bows and arrows, killing him. A third story claims that an Indian named Pagaret, coming across Brétigny in a savannah near the colony, split open his skull with a hatchet.

Accounts of the Indians' actions after the death of Brétigny are equally contradictory and inspire equally little belief. Either the Indians then sent word to the colonists that they would live in peace with them, or the Indians attacked the colony, burning the crops and killing all who did not manage to flee. Confusion continues. Reportedly, a group of forty, unaware of events in the colony, arrived from France soon after. A Frenchman named Le Vendangeur later reported that Indians killed all the rest of the forty, and only he survived. The self-serving character of these reports is apparent, absolving the narrators from accusations of desertion. In 1652, colonists sponsored by the Compagnie de la France équinoxiale (French Equator Company) arrived in the area, where they found twenty-five colonists still living at Cayenne, hardly comprehensible if the Galibi were truly hostile.

Certainly, Compagnie du Cap au Nord colony at Cayenne failed, though its fate, like that of the character of Brétigny, remains in doubt. The colony may have been destroyed by Indians or simply deserted by the inhabitants who went to other settlements that offered brighter prospects. Brétigny may have been the monster as depicted, or he may have been vilified by deserters. Truth is often illusive in accounts of the Wild Coast.

A new Cayenne colony was founded in 1652 consisting of about 550 people who established themselves on the site formerly occupied by Brétigny's failed effort, but the new effort failed within a year, wracked by internal feuding, a virulent epidemic, food shortage, and Indian attacks. The survivors made their way to the English colony of Willoughbyland on the Suriname River, and from there to Barbados before the colonists returned to French islands in the Caribbean or France. Father Antoine Biet wrote an account of the colony and the survivors' misadventures.

About 1656, David Cohen Nassy led around 150 Jews, many of whom had left Brazil after the Portuguese reconquest, to settle at the abandoned Cayenne colony alongside some Dutch, but that settlement too proved short lived. In 1664, the French seized Cayenne, and the Jewish settlers left, moving to Jodensavanne on the Suriname River. During the next decade, the Dutch and English operating together captured the area, but it was restored to France by peace treaty. New colonists again came to Cayenne, which remained a French possession until the Napoleonic wars, when a combined English and Portuguese force captured the town. It was returned to France in 1814 and has remained part of French Guyana since then.

Jodensavanne: A Jewish Colony in Suriname

Jewish migration to Suriname was intimately connected with the Dutch presence in Brazil from 1630 to 1654. Many Jews who had been expelled from Spain and Portugal or forced to convert to Christianity migrated to the Netherlands, and from there some moved to Brazil anticipating new opportunities. Other conversos already in Brazil moved to the Dutch-controlled area and returned to their original religion. The Dutch guaranteed Jews freedom of conscience and of religious observance in the Netherlands and their holdings in Brazil, but in 1645, the Brazilian Portuguese revolted against the Dutch, leading to Portuguese reconquest in 1654. As Dutch fortunes waned in Brazil, Jews justifiably fearful of persecution and the Inquisition began to seek safer refuges. After the Portuguese reconquest, the surrender agreement included a provision allowing all who wished to depart three months in which to leave, and those Jews remaining in Brazil departed then. Many returned to the Netherlands; others migrated to the Caribbean islands, Suriname, and even to a recent English conquest in North America, New York.

It is not apparent when the first Jews settled in Suriname. The English encouraged migration to the area as early as 1639, but there is no evidence that Jews came to Suriname at that date. The earliest documentary evidence is a marriage contract written in Hebrew at Suriname and dated the equivalent of 1643. The Jewish immigrants settled initially south of a small settlement that became known as Thorarica, Torarica, and by other similar spellings. No shortage of ingenuity has been expended trying to explain the origin of the name. One theory claims the name was Jewish, a variation of Torah Rica, or Rich Torah.

"A New Draught of Surranam upon the coast of Guianna" (London: John Hydrgrapher, ca. 1675). The map shows the Suriname and Commewine Rivers and related waterways and the location of chief plantations. (*John Carter Brown Library, Brown University*)

Detail of the center section of "A New Draught of Surranam upon the coast of Guianna." The inscription "Iews" (Jews) shows the location of Jodensavanne.

Another version claims the name was a variant of *theriaca*, also spelled various ways, a compound of many ingredients highly popular during the early modern period, believed to be a panacea, a protection against all manner of diseases and poisons. The town was described as unusually healthy for the region, and Suriname was held to be the source of many plants believed to have medicinal virtues, hence the name.

By early 1653, the Jewish immigrants established a settlement along Cassapora Creek, a tributary of the Suriname River, and the next year they erected a synagogue of wood there. About the same time, Francis, Lord Willoughby, established an English colony, Willoughbyland, in the vicinity. There was no conflict between the two groups. There was an abundance of available land, and the presence of the substantial English colony increased the security of the area. About 1664, the Jewish population increased when Nassy led a group of migrants there. Many had left Brazil when the Portuguese reconquered that colony, then stayed for a few years at Cayenne, which they abandoned to settle in Suriname. Others had left Italy seeking better conditions in the New

Jodensavanne, called Jerusalem on the Riverside. Painting by Pierre Jacques Benoit, 1830. The synagogue is the large building visible in the background. (*Wikimedia Commons*)

World. In 1665, England recognized broad rights of the Suriname Jewish community to self-government, including the formation and maintenance of their own militia. Over the next two decades, the population moved a short distance to a fertile area that became known in Dutch as the Jodensavanne, the Jewish Savannah. The community there was also known as Jerusalem on the Riverside. Still more Jews came to settle at the Jodensavanne as wars among European nations disrupted Jewish settlers on the Pomeroon River and elsewhere in the region.

Tobacco was the chief crop in the Caribbean and the Wild Coast during the early seventeenth century, but it declined in importance by the 1650s. Abundant crops grown in the Caribbean depressed prices, and Virginia produced superior tobacco. Sugar, however, was in high demand and eventually replaced tobacco as the primary export of the Caribbean and the Wild Coast colonies. But sugar production was extremely labor intensive, and this labor, sadly, was provided by African slaves. Throughout the history of humanity, all nations and ethnic groups have held slaves, but thankfully, it was during this early modern period that slavery first began to become repugnant to modern consciousness. The Jews of Jodensavanne were reputably kinder to slaves than other groups and more likely to free them after a term of service. Many of these slaves and freedmen converted to Judaism, and interactions between Jewish men and female slaves often produced children who were also raised as Jews. Those of mixed ethnicity were permitted to attend services in the Jodensavanne Synagogue, Beracha Ve Shalom (Blessing and Peace), built in 1685, and in 1791 they formed their own synagogue, Darchei Yesharim (Way of the Righteous). In 1841, long after the demise of Jodensavanne, they were recognized as equal members of the Suriname religious community.

The Jodensavanne colony prospered during the seventeenth century. By 1700, the Jewish population was about six hundred. Many lived in the central community where the synagogue was located, and others were scattered among about forty Jewish-owned plantations along the interlocking waterways in the area. Estimates of the number of slaves vary greatly.

Jodensavanne survived the Dutch conquest of the neighboring Willoughbyland and continued to prosper during the first half of the eighteenth century, but the colony went into steep decline late in the century. Facing increased competition, sugar production became less profitable, and Maroons, descendants of escaped slaves who had formed their own communities in the hinterlands of Suriname, raided plantations to free slaves, loot, and kill plantation owners and overseers. By 1800, most of the population had moved to the growing town of Paramaribo, and only about twenty people remained at Jodensavanne. The beginning of sugar beet production in Europe at the beginning of the nineteenth century essentially destroyed what little market remained for sugar from Suriname, and Jodensavanne was deserted, although people returned periodically to maintain the synagogue and hold services there. In 1832, a fire spread through the remains of the old community, destroying the synagogue. After that the jungle reclaimed the site until the mid-1990s, when the World Monuments Fund drew attention to the remains of the colony. Since then archaeologists have cleared the overgrowth from the impressive ruins of the synagogue and the nearby cemetery, where about 450 graves have been uncovered, many covered with slabs of fine stone imported from Europe and engraved with inscriptions in Hebrew, Portuguese, or Dutch. Since independence, Suriname has suffered from racial factionalism and corruption. Many of the Jewish community of Paramaribo migrated to Israel, and today only about two hundred Jews reside in Suriname.

Willoughbyland: The Most Famous Failed Colony of Guyana

Francis, Lord Willoughby of Parham, was born about 1613. He first came into prominence during the opposition to King Charles I in the mid-1630s, when he sided with the Parliamentarians during the growing tensions that led to the English Civil War. Early in the war, Parliament appointed Willoughby lord lieutenant and commander in chief of Lincolnshire. Willoughby proved to be a mediocre military commander, winning little and losing more. On occasion, he had trouble accepting the appointment of a superior, and his troops were poorly disciplined.

As a politician, Willoughby also seems to have lacked insight. Always a moderate, he sought reconciliation between Parliament and king, a position that however morally admirable was also foolish. He seems not to have comprehended that civil wars are seldom reconciled but rather the contending parties become increasingly radical and bitter. Moderates soon find themselves distrusted, then hated, and so it was with Willoughby. The House of Lords elected him speaker in 1647, but the radicals among the Parliamentarians took control of London and impeached Willoughby and six other peers. When it became apparent that he would be tried for treason, Willoughby defected to the Royalist exiles in the Netherlands. He was then regarded as a traitor by the Parliamentarians and distrusted as a turncoat by the Royalists. He served briefly as vice admiral of the Royalist fleet in 1648, but he had no experience in naval matters and soon resigned. Meanwhile, Parliament confiscated Willoughby's estates in England.

In 1649, the Parliamentarians tried and executed King Charles I and proclaimed England a Commonwealth, but they had not secured control of the English holdings in the West Indies. Royalists flocked to Barbados as their fortunes waned in Britain, and there they seized control of the colony. In 1650, Charles II, in exile in the Netherlands, appointed Willoughby governor of Barbados, a post that included general supervision of British interests in the Caribbean and extended as far as the Wild Coast. Willoughby sought to reconcile the Royalist Cavalier and Parliamentary Roundhead factions in Barbados and even hoped to reach a cordial agreement with the Parliamentarians in England. Despite tensions, most Barbados planters, even more devoted to profit than partisan politics, found a way to maintain civility by informally banning political discussion, even agreeing that anyone who brought up politics owed a roast turkey dinner to all who were present.

Willoughby also faced problems in Barbados beyond politics. The islands were overpopulated, and the largest planters had been able to force many of the small proprietors into insolvency, taking over their lands. The islands' soil, never rich, was becoming exhausted, and the production of sugar, the economic basis of the colony, was sure to decline.

Willoughby knew that Parliamentary forces might be able to capture Barbados and turn him out of office, and he looked to the Wild Coast as both a potential refuge and a source of income. Earlier English efforts in the region had failed, but the fertility of the area; the European demand for tobacco, cotton, and exotic lumber; and the great market for sugar indicated a colony could be highly profitable. There was also the allure of the unexplored interior and the old rumors of gold there. Late in 1650, Willoughby sent an expedition under the command of Major William Rous (sometimes written as Rowse), long experienced in the Caribbean as a privateer, pioneer colonist, and planter, to investigate the possibilities of establishing a colony on the Suriname River. Rous returned with good reports and two Carib chiefs, who, suitably rewarded, agreed to allow the English to settle there.

In 1651, Willoughby sent Rous back to Suriname with one hundred men to prepare a site for the colony, to be called Willoughbyland. By the native village of Purmerbo they rebuilt an abandoned French fort, remnant of a previous effort, and built cabins. Purmerbo would eventually develop into modern Paramaribo, now the capital of Suriname. Willoughby had two small ships with which he regularly sent colonists to the site along with supplies and goods for trade to the Indians in exchange for cotton, tobacco, and hammocks, much in demand by ship owners. Rous even began to allot land to settlers and investors to establish plantations along the Suriname River and neighboring waterways. Jews, most of whom had left Brazil after the collapse of the Dutch attempt to colonize there, also established themselves in the vicinity as an independent colony. There was no conflict, as there was plenty of land for all.

In 1651, a Commonwealth naval force appeared at Barbados and blockaded the islands, forcing surrender after three months. The conditions were initially generous to Willoughby. In exchange for his acceptance of the Commonwealth, he was permitted to remain at Barbados and continue to develop his colony in Suriname, and his estates in England were to be restored. After only two months, however, the new Commonwealth governor and assembly broke the agreement and expelled Willoughby and Royalist sympathizers. Willoughby organized a disparate group of nearly three hundred people to migrate to his Suriname colony. There were people of all social classes, from aristocratic Cavaliers to servants and poor men and women hoping for an opportunity in the new land. The group included individuals and families, some long resident in the Caribbean and others only recently from England. Even some who sympathized with the Commonwealth left Barbados for the new opportunities in the Suriname colony. Willoughby remained in his colony only two months before departing for England to reclaim his estates according to the Barbados surrender agreement.

Anonymous portrait of Lord Willoughby of Parham, ca. 1647. (*National Portrait Gallery, London*)

In 1653, Antoine Biet, a French priest, accompanied by refugees from a failed colony at Cayenne, reached Willoughbyland, where they were received cordially and aided. Biet wrote an account of the failed colony, including his visit to Willoughbyland, which he described as a settlement of about fifty wooden buildings situated randomly near a fort with an outer wood palisade and a small interior stone keep. He also noted that plantations had been established as far as thirty miles upriver. Some were growing tobacco and others felling trees for lumber and to clear land. Sugar soon became the primary crop. A shipper agreed to transport the French to Barbados, but he charged them 150 pounds of sugar each. From there they moved to French holdings in the Caribbean or France.

When Willoughby returned to England, he could not resist involving himself in Royalist politics. He was twice imprisoned briefly on suspicion of conspiring to restore the monarchy, and he seems to have

been active in the Sealed Knot, a secret Royalist plot. Willoughby's dubious loyalty to the Commonwealth also led to problems getting his
rights to Willoughbyland confirmed. Nevertheless, he actively promoted migration to the colony, and by 1656, plantations extended
sixty miles upriver, twice as far as three years previously, and they were
established on neighboring waterways as well.

After Willoughby left the colony, Richard Holdip briefly served as
governor, but he was widely disliked. Anthony Rous was soon appointed governor in Holdip's place, but Rous left the colony to resume
his military career in 1654. With Willoughby occupied in England and
Rous departed, the colonists assumed the management of Willoughbyland by themselves. The male heads of the wealthier plantations annually elected a governor, a council of six men, and an assembly of
twenty-one men. The governor in conference with the council would
propose measures to which the assembly would agree or disapprove.
Such independence was highly unusual and looked upon with suspicion by authorities beyond the colony. The colonists were reportedly
overwhelmingly Royalists, but such autonomy seemed dangerously
like the ideas of the radical supporters of the Commonwealth.
Willoughby and the Commonwealth were occupied by much more immediate concerns to bother about the distant colony, where the ideas
of self-determination, even though limited to the wealthy White male
elite who were formally Royalists, proved intoxicatingly attractive.
Throughout the 1650s, Royalists and Parliamentarians in the colony
managed to cooperate, and the colony prospered.

In 1658, Oliver Cromwell died, and the Commonwealth soon failed.
Charles II returned to England as king in 1660 and promptly rewarded
Willoughby for his support by reappointing him governor of Barbados
and the other Caribbean islands then held by the British. Problems persisted, however, with the exact form of his grant to Willoughbyland.
Willoughby finally resolved matters by incorporating Lawrence Hyde,
the second son of the powerful Lord Clarendon, as coproprietor and
silent partner. The negotiations delayed Willoughby's departure for Barbados until 1663, where his administration was not universally popular.
Many residents of Barbados had supported the Commonwealth and
disliked new royal efforts to impose tighter controls on colonial administration and trade. Willoughbyland was exempted from the most onerous of these regulations, gaining a great advantage in trade. The
exemption was probably due to the influence of Lord Clarendon.

The letters patent granted to Willoughby specifically guaranteed religious liberty to the inhabitants of the colony, and Willoughbyland, once a refuge for Royalists, now became a haven for dissenters, Puritans, Quakers, and other Nonconformists. Many of these new arrivals were offended by the relaxed morality of the Royalists already resident in the colony. Two factions emerged, the Royalists and the Dissenters, and in 1657, William Byam, a wealthy planter, emerged as a political leader of the Royalists and the focus of Dissenter grievances. He was elected governor in 1657 and during the following two years. With the restoration of the monarchy in 1660 and the support of the thoroughly Royalist assembly, he announced he would continue in office until and unless contrary orders came from England. Byam's declaration and the migration of dissidents to the colony produced tensions and the formations of factions. Each group sent letters to England depicting the other in the worst light. It was impossible in London to know what was occurring in the distant colony, so the royal government sent an agent to investigate.

In July 1663, one of the most intriguing people of the seventeenth century came to Willoughbyland as a secret agent: Aphra Behn. Born Aphra Johnson in 1640, the daughter of a barber and a wet nurse, she grew up to be insubordinate, intelligent, tall, and attractive. Before the Restoration while she was still in her teens, a foster brother introduced her to exiled Royalists, and she became a copyist and secret courier. Her talent and discretion were soon recognized, and by age sixteen she became a Royalist spy, operating under the code names Astrea and Agent 160. Little is known about her marriage in or about 1664 to a Dutch man named Johan Behn. He seems to have died or disappeared in 1666, and she seems not to have regarded the marriage as an obstacle to her activities.

Aphra Behn was accompanied on her trip to Suriname by her mother, sister, younger brother, and maid. Her father may also have sailed with the family but died during the voyage, or that may have been a convenient story to explain why a young woman was traveling without a male guardian, customary at the time. She and her family took up residence at a plantation of Sir Robert Harley, a Royalist friend of Lord Willoughby's. Although serving as a Royalist agent, Behn soon formed a strongly negative opinion of William Byam, who continued to dominate the colonial government, and at the same time she praised William Scott, the most prominent supporter of the Commonwealth in the colony.

William Scott was the son of Thomas Scott, one of those responsible for the execution of King Charles I. In 1660, the Restoration government convicted Thomas Scott of regicide and had him hanged, drawn, and quartered. William Scott was also deeply involved in the Commonwealth, active in the bureaucracy and serving as a spy in France during the 1650s. After the Restoration, Scott escaped to the Netherlands, where he plotted with other Parliamentarians in exile, but he soon decided to seek more-distant refuge, migrating to Willoughbyland, where he earned a reputation as a voluble raconteur, reckless with money, and much dedicated to women and wine. There is some suggestion that he may have sought immunity from the royal government by acting as a spy, but specific evidence is lacking. England and the English colonies in this period were infested with spies, double, and even triple agents, playing deadly games with Royalists, supporters of the Commonwealth, and also foreign governments such as the Dutch and even the Spanish.

Although William Scott probably ranked at the top of the list of those Aphra Behn was to investigate, she rapidly formed a connection to him that led to scandalous rumors in the colony, especially since Scott was some years her senior and married with children. Behn also became very friendly with George Marten, whose brother was also a regicide. These friendships seem more than the attentions of a spy seeking to penetrate any designs these men might have, especially coupled with criticism of Byam and other Royalists. Behn was also interested in Indians, whom she saw sympathetically as living in the state of nature like Adam and Eve before the Fall. She was even more taken by the spectacle of African slavery. When she first arrived, there seems to have been relatively few Black slaves in the colony, but that was rapidly changing, as the recently chartered Company of Royal Adventurers Trading into Africa began importing slaves in large numbers from the west coast of Africa.

Aphra Behn's observations about the treatment of slaves in Suriname would years later form the basis for her most famous work, *Oroonoko: or the Royale Slave, A true History*. The novel, published in 1688, tells the story of an African prince, Oroonoko, who loves the virtuous Imoinda. Out of jealousy, Oroonoko's grandfather, the king, has the lovers sold into slavery in Suriname. The English slave owner recognizes Oroonoko's nobility of character, but his refusal to submit abjectly to slavery and struggle for freedom results in the destruction of both Oroonoko and Imoinda. Behn's work cannot be described as antislavery. Slavery was too well established and universal in her world for that, but she fiercely denounces the inhuman behavior of slave owners and the misanthropy and violence inherent in slavery. Behn and other contemporary observers such as Father Antoine Biet and George Warner saw that the masters not only brutalized and destroyed the African slaves but also that slavery corrupted the plantation owners, who frequently descended into indolence and alcoholism and whose fear of slave uprisings led to astounding cruelties.

William Byam was aware of Aphra Behn's antipathy, and after a brief trip to Barbados to consult with Willoughby, he expelled Behn from the colony in early 1664, shipping her back to England. William Scott also left the colony shortly thereafter. Scott could not go to England, as he was deeply in debt there and likely to be prosecuted for his actions under the Commonwealth. He went rather to the Netherlands, where he had relatives. Short of money, Scott apparently agreed to spy for the Dutch against England. Soon Behn traveled to the Spanish Netherlands to meet Scott to recruit him to spy for England against the Dutch, promising pay and a potential pardon.

Behn encountered problems in her role as a Royalist spy. The government of Charles II entertained itself luxuriously at home but was reluctant to pay its spies enough to sustain their efforts. Behn's appeals to the crown for money were ignored among the crises besetting England: the great plague of 1665–1666, and the fire that consumed much of London in 1666. Moreover, Scott, continually fearful of exposure or betrayal, began to drink heavily, and when intoxicated was not always discrete. The Dutch seem to have lost confidence in him and dispensed with his services. He was imprisoned for debt in the Netherlands in 1666, released in early 1667, and ordered out of the country. He went to Antwerp in Spanish Flanders, where he dropped out of sight. Behn returned to England.

In November 1664, Lord Willoughby returned to Willoughbyland after a decade-long absence. His reception was not as enthusiastic as he might have anticipated. Planters had come to regard their plantations as their own property rather than belonging to the proprietor who controlled tenure at his pleasure and to whom they were obligated to pay rents. One, John Allin, regarded Willoughby with particular hostility. A wealthy planter, Allin was known for biting sarcasm, swearing, drunkenness, violence, and paranoia. Convinced that Willoughby sought to take his plantation, he suddenly attacked Willoughby with a cutlass during a religious service early in 1665. Willoughby lost two fingers and suffered a glancing blow that laid open part of his scalp. Allin stabbed himself in a failed effort to commit suicide but later succeeded with the aid of drugs surreptitiously obtained. Willoughby convalesced slowly and left the colony in May 1665, leaving William Byam behind as lieutenant general and deputy governor.

Willoughby's visit exacerbated tensions in the colony. Some planters left Willoughbyland rather than accept the status as tenants, and others swore to oppose the new situation. Factions and cabals divided colonists against one another. A fever, perhaps brought with Willoughby's party, also swept through the colony, killing around two hundred men and many women and children. An even greater threat soon appeared: the Second Anglo-Dutch War (1665–1667).

England and the Netherlands, so much alike in many ways and formerly close allies, now contended with one another over global commerce, which the Dutch dominated and the English coveted. Conflict began on the African coast late in 1663 and spread to the Caribbean and North America during 1664. War was formally declared in January 1665. The Dutch, English, and French colonies along the Wild Coast had coexisted peacefully, but in late 1665, Charles II ordered attacks on the Dutch colonies. At the time, the Dutch had three colonies north of Willoughbyland by the mouths of the Pomeroon, Essequibo, and Berbice Rivers, and one south on the Approuague River. The last was scarcely more than a trading post.

Willoughby, now at Barbados, sent a force to attack the Dutch on Tobago Island, only to discover that the famous buccaneer Henry Morgan had already taken the colony. The expedition, led by Major John Scott, no relation to William Scott, was then diverted to the Dutch colonies on the Wild Coast, where the troops captured and burned the Dutch colonies at Pomeroon and Essequibo. John Scott was a thoroughgoing scoundrel with a long history of various crimes, but he was not without talent. A small force from Willoughbyland also destroyed the small Dutch colony on the Approuague River. English buccaneers attacked the Dutch at Berbice, but they were repulsed, and the colony survived. In 1666, the French allied with the Dutch against the English, and in April of that year, the French captured the English portion of St. Kitts. The Dutch and French along with Arawak allies recaptured Pomeroon and Essequibo and the small English garrisons there.

Willoughby ordered attacks on the three French colonies on the Wild Coast, and men from Willoughbyland destroyed the tiny French colony on the Sinnamary River, a minor waterway. With eight ships and about one thousand men, Willoughby set sail from Barbados to retake St. Kitts, but while they were near Guadeloupe, a hurricane devastated the fleet. Willoughby's flagship went down with all aboard, and when the storm abated there was no remaining English naval force in the Caribbean. A French fleet then ravaged English islands in the Caribbean, and in December 1666, the Dutch organized a fleet to attack Willoughbyland. It consisted of three substantial frigates, a yacht with thirteen guns, and four smaller ships that could function in shallow waters. The ships carried about 775 sailors and 225 soldiers. The force was modest, but William Scott may have informed the Dutch about the weakness of Willoughbyland, where fever still raged and the colonists were poorly armed. Byam had little with which to defend the colony: a badly situated and incomplete fort, a few cannons but not much powder or shot, and about three hundred poorly armed militiamen. Political divisions and personal resentments further weakened the colony. After a short bombardment from the ships and before the Dutch troops could even launch an assault, the fort surrendered. Byam later faced a court-martial but was acquitted, much to the disgust of William Willoughby, younger brother of the deceased Francis Willoughby and new governor of Barbados and the English Caribbean holdings.

Conflict between the French and English continued in the Caribbean, and in mid-1667, William Willoughby organized an expedition to capture the French colony at Cayenne and then to reconquer Willoughbyland. Cayenne fell easily to the English, Willoughbyland less so, but it was taken. The inhabitants of Jodensavanne, many of whom had lived in the Netherlands, wisely stayed out of the conflict. The new English occupation was short lived. Peace was made late in 1667, and as part of the arrangement, the Dutch reclaimed Willoughbyland and in exchange the English retained New Amsterdam, renamed New York. William Willoughby was outraged and ordered that the colony should be stripped bare of all that could be carried away and the rest burned and wrecked before it was handed over to the

Dutch. Willoughbyland was destroyed by its own inhabitants before they departed, almost all migrating to English islands in the Caribbean, only a few of the poorest remaining. In the chaos of the moment, hundreds of slaves escaped into the jungle, where they formed their own free Maroon communities.

The Dutch revived sugar production on the Suriname River, expanding the area farmed and importing vast numbers of slaves to cultivate and process the sugarcane. By 1735, there were as many as fifty thousand slaves on the Dutch plantations, and as the number of slaves increased, so also the fear of slave rebellion intensified. The Dutch sought to control the vast number of slaves by terror, punishing even the slightest infraction of rigid rules with brutal torture and grotesque forms of execution. Suriname became a byword for cruelty and horror. Despite all attempts to terrorize them, slaves escaped into the jungle to join existing Maroon communities. The Maroons made war on the plantation owners, freeing more slaves, burning crops and buildings, wrecking sugar mills, and killing plantation owners, their families, and overseers in ways that mimicked their own treatment as slaves. The Maroons forced the abandonment of plantations and even destroyed towns. With the collapse of the sugar market, even the most secure Dutch sugar plantations were abandoned, and large areas reverted to jungle. Today in many areas little remains of the great plantations beyond a few foundations and scattered gravestones. The Maroons, however, remain, still preserving much of their distinctive culture and independence.

Aphra Behn never received adequate compensation for her efforts as a spy. She turned to a new profession, unique for a woman of her day. She made her living as a writer, producing plays, novels, novellas, and poetry. During the 1670s, the number of her plays produced in London was second only to John Dryden, the poet laureate. In 1688, she published *Oroonoko*, which was not particularly successful when first published but today remains her most-remembered work. Behn used the names of real people who lived in Willoughbyland in the novel, such as William Byam, and she did not hesitate to describe them in harshly negative terms. She died in 1689 and was buried in Westminster Abbey, where her epitaph may still be read: "Here lies a Proof that Wit can never be Defence enough against Mortality." Her reputation suffered eclipse after the end of the Restoration period, but during the twentieth century she reemerged as a feminist hero.

Sources

Sir Walter Raleigh's *The Discoverie of the Large, Rich and Bewtiful Empire of Guiana* (London: Robert Robinson, 1596) is fundamental to understanding the subsequent history of the Wild Coast. His exaggerations and fantasies fueled the dreams and ambitions of generations of explorers and colonists. It has been reprinted many times and translated into most European languages. Lawrence Keymis published a much more sober work, *A Relation of the Second Voyage to Guinana, Perfourmed and written in the yeare 1596* (London: Thomas Dawson, 1596). Robert Harcourt, *A Relation of a Voyage to Gviana. Describing the climat, natives, fertilitie, prouisions, and commodities of that Country. [. . .] Together with the manners, customes, behauiors, and dispositions of the people* (London: Edw. Allde, 1613) is important both for an early description of the Wild Coast and for the English efforts to colonize the Oyapoc River. The work has been variously reprinted, such as in John Harris, *Avigantium atque itinerantium bibliotheca, or, A Compleat Collection of Voyages and Travels* (London: T. Osborne et al., 1705). Samuel Purchas, *Purchas his Pilgrimage. Or Relations of the Vvorld and the Religions Obseued in All Ages and places from the Creation vnto this Present*, fourth edition much enlarged with additions [. . .] by Sr. Ierome Horsey; [. . .] Master William Methold; [. . .] T. Erpenius (London: William Stansby, 1626) contains a wealth of information on early colonies. It has been frequently reprinted, best as Samuel Purchas, *Hakluytus Posthumus or Purchas His Pilgrimes Contaying a History of the World in Sea Voyages and Lande Travells by Englishmen and Others*, 20 vols., Hakluyt Society Extra Series nos. 14-33 (Glasgow: James MacLehose, 1905–1907). In the Hakluyt edition, volume 16 contains the accounts of the English on the Oyapoc River by Charles Leigh and John Wilson, one of the colonists.

John Scott was a rogue and criminal but nevertheless a good historian and an important source for early colonization along the Wild Coast. His work, never completed, is incorporated in Vincent T. Harlow, *Colonising Expeditions to the West Indies and Guiana, 1623–1627*, Works Issued by the Hakluyt Society, 2nd ser., no. 56 (London: Printed for the Hakluyt Society, 1925; Nendelm, Liechtenstein: Kraus Reprint, 1967). For a defense of Scott's reliability as a historian, see George Edmundson, "The Dutch in Western Guiana," *English Historical Review* 16 (1901): 640 – 675. José Rafael Lovera, *Antonio de*

Berrío. La bsession por El Dorado. Estudio preliminar y sellección documental (Caracas: Petróleos de Venezuela, 1991) is important for early Santo Tomé de Guyana.

For the unreliable history of Charles Poncet, seigneur de Brétigny, and his colony at Cayenne, see Paul Boyer, *Veritable relation de tovt ce qvi s'est fait et passéau voyage que monsieur de Bretigny fit à l'Amerique Occidentale* (Paris: P. Rocolet, 1654); James Rodway and Thomas Watt, *Chronological History of the Discovery and Settlement of Guiana 1493–1668* (Georgetown, Guyana: *Royal Gazette* Office, 1888); and James Rodway, *Guiana, British, Dutch and French* (London: T. Fisher Unwin, 1912).

Jean de Laon, Seigneur d'Aigremont, *Relation dur Voyage des François fait au Cap de Nord den Amerique* (Paris: E. Pepingué, 1654) details the unsuccessful attempt to colonize Cayenne in 1652. Antoine Biet, *Voyage de la France équinoxiale en l'Isle de Cayenne, entrepris par les François en l'année MCDLII* (Paris: F. Clovzier, 1664) provides a more candid and personal recollection of the same attempt and an important source for the early history of Willoughbyland.

There have been many contributions to the reconstruction of the history of the Jodensavanne colony. Among the most important are B. Felsenthal, "The Jewish Congregation in Surinam," *Publications of the American Jewish Historical Society* 2 (1894): 29-30; B. Felsenthal and Richard Gottheil, "Chronological Sketch of the History of the Jews in Surinam," *Publications of the American Jewish Historical Society* 4 (1896): 1-8; Richard Gottheil, "Contributions to the History of the Jews in Surinam," *Publications of the American Jewish Historical Society* 9 (1901): 129-142; J. S. Roos, "Additional Notes on the History of the Jews in Surinam," *Publications of the American Jewish Historical Society* 13 (1905): 127-136; P. A. Hilfman, "Some Further Notes on the History of the Jews in Surinam," *Publications of the American Jewish Historical Society* 16 (1907): 7-22; P. A. Hilfman, "Notes on the History of the Jews in Surinam," *Publications of the American Jewish Historical Society* 18 (1909): 179-207; Samuel Oppenheim, "An Early Jewish Colony in Western Guiana, 1658–1666: And Its Relation to the Jews in Surinam, Cayenne and Tobago," *Publications of the American Jewish Historical Society* 16 (1907): 95-186, and later reprinted as a book (New York: Publications of the American Jewish Historical Society, 1908). Oppenheim's work is of the most enduring value.

Notable among more modern works are Mordechai Arbell, Dennis Channing Landis, and Ann Phelps Barry, *Spanish and Portuguese Jews in the Caribbean and the Guianas: A Bibliography* (Providence, RI: John Carter Brown Library, 2000); Mordechai Arbell, *The Jewish Nation of the Caribbean: The Spanish-Portuguese Jewish Settlements in the Caribbean and the Guianas* (New York: World Jewish Congress, 2002); and Rich Gerber, *The Jews in the Caribbean* (London: Littman Library of Jewish Civilization in association with Liverpool University Press, 2018). Illustrations and an historical overview are to be found at Suriname Jewish Community, www.surinamejewishcommunity.com.

There are a variety of early sources for Willoughbyland. Most prominent are Antoine Biet, *Voyage de la France équinoxiale*, mentioned above; David Pieterzoon de Vries, *Korte historiael ende journaels aenteyckeninge van verscheyden voyagiens in de viere deelen des Wereldhts-Ronde, as Europa, Africa, Asia, ende Amerika gedaen* ('t Hoorn, Netherlands: Symon Corneliszoon Brekegeest, 1655), available in English as David Pieterzoon de Vries, *Voyages from Holland to America A.D. 1632 to 1644*, trans. Henry C. Murphy (New York: n.p., 1853); Henry Adis, *A Letter Sent from Syrranam, to His Excellency, the Lord Willoughby of Parham, General of the Western Islands, and of the continent of Guianah, &c. then residing at the Barbados: together, with Lord Willoughby's answer thereunto: with a commendable description of that county.* (London: n.p., 1664); George Warren, *An Impartial Description of Surinam upon the Continent of Guiana in America* (London: William Godbid for Nathaniel Brooke, 1667); Aphra Behn, *Oroonnoko: or the Royal Slave, a true History* (London: Will. Canning, 1688); and Charles Gildon, ed., *All the histories and novels: written by the late ingenious Mrs. Behn, entire in one volume: together with the history of the life and memoirs of Mrs. Behn never before printed*, 3rd ed. (London: Samuel Briscoe, 1698). V. T. Harlow, ed., *Colonising Expeditions to West Indies and Guiana 1623–1667*, Hakluyt Society, 2nd ser., no. 56 (London: Bedford, 1925) contains transcriptions of original documents bearing on Willoughbyland.

Matthew Parker, *Willoughbyland: England's Lost Colony* (London: Windmill Books, 2015) is by far the fullest and best treatment of Willoughbyland. Three important works on Aphra Behn are Maureen Duffy, *The Passionate Shepherdess: The Life of Aphra Behn* (London: Jonathan Cape, 1977); Angeline Goreau, *Reconstructing Aphra: A So-*

cial Biography of Aphra Behn (Oxford: Oxford University Press, 1980); and Janet Todd, *The Secret Life of Aphra Behn* (London: Pandora, 2000).

EIGHT

Puritans and Pirates
in the Caribbean:
Providence Island (1630–1641)

The Islands

Providencia, to use the current name, and St. Andres are two small, isolated islands in the western Caribbean separated by fifty-seven miles of water. Although both are remnants of an enormous, ancient-eroded volcano, they are different in character. St. Andres, about ten square miles in area, is low lying, the highest point only about 180 feet above sea level. Providencia to the north is only about eight and a half square miles in area. It is mountainous with rough ridges radiating from a central peak 1,190 feet high. The heights provide good opportunities to build defendable strong points and to detect approaching enemies. The best soil for farming is between the ridges near the shore where the land is nearly level. The island is surrounded by coral reefs, making approach dangerous for the unfamiliar or careless.

Alonso de Ojeda or Pedro de Nicuesa may have discovered the islands around 1510, and they were certainly included on the Spanish master map, the *Carta Universal*, of 1527. The Spanish initially named the islands Santo Andres and Santa Catalina, but otherwise paid little attention to them, as they contained no sources of wealth. Today there is a small island to the north of Providencia that was once connected to it by a low sand bank. In the late seventeenth century, pirates dug a moat through this sand bank to fortify the smaller prominence. Since then the sand bank has eroded away, leaving the smaller island separated by a little more than one hundred yards of shallow sea. Today it is called Santa Catalina (Saint Catherine) and in the local creole dialect Ketleena. Providencia and St. Andres are now part of the nation of Colombia, the mainland of which is over four hundred miles away. The coast of Nicaragua is closer, about 140 miles. English and an English-based creole are as often heard on Providencia as Spanish, an indication of the strange history of the island.

Discovery and Preparation

In February 1628, three ships, the *Earl of Warwick*, master Sussex Camock; the *Somers Islands*, master John Rose; and the *Robert*, master Daniel Elfrith, departed England with commissions as privateers to attack Spanish shipping. Cruising the western Caribbean, they kept alert hoping to sight Fonseca Island. They did not find it for the simple reason that Fonseca Island, despite appearing on maps for decades, never existed. Misidentified landfalls, cloud banks, and then inaccurate navigation created a fantasy. Instead, the English mariners first encountered St. Andres Island, where Captain Camock stayed behind with about thirty crewmen and the *Somers Islands* to secure the discovery. Daniel Elfrith, who was to play a major role in the colonization effort, assumed command of the *Earl of Warwick*, with John Tanner taking over the *Robert*. Elfrith was long familiar with the Caribbean. He first appears as a privateer in 1607, and despite occasionally descending to simply piracy, he was well respected as an able mariner and commander. He either was or was soon to become the father-in-law of Philip Bell, the governor of the Somers Islands, as the British then called Bermuda.

After leaving St. Andres, the three ships sailed on to Santa Catalina Island, which impressed Elfrith favorably. The climate was mild, the soil apparently fertile, and fresh water abundant. Lemons, oranges, papaya, and guava grew wild, and the forests contained a variety of exotic and valuable woods. There were no native inhabitants, large predatory animals, or noxious insects. The island, much of which was surrounded by cliffs, could also be easily fortified. On the northern promontory, Elfrith met a small group of Dutch mariners who had

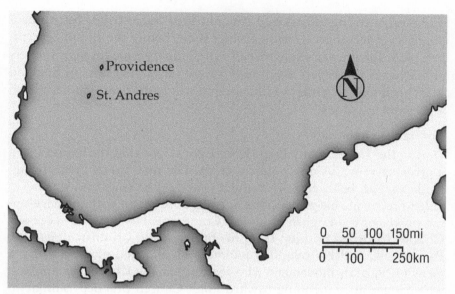

Providence and St. Andres Islands.

built a small stockade as a privateers' refuge. They were commanded by Abraham and Willem Blauveldt, father and son, members of an extended family of privateers. The Blauveldts would also be involved with the Providence colony. Abraham is also called Albertus in many sources, and he and his son are often confused. Their last name is variously spelled Blauveldt, Blauvelt, Blewvelt, Blauwveld, Blewfield, Bluefield, and other similar forms, some as deviant as Blaaeuwveldt. The English and Dutch fraternized peacefully, and Elfrith learned that the Dutch had no plans for planting a substantial permanent colony on the island.

Elfrith sailed to Bermuda to report the discovery to the governor, Philip Bell, who in turn wrote to Sir Nathaniel Rich, the business associate and agent of his cousin, Robert Rich, Earl of Warwick, who had underwritten Daniel Elfrith's privateering venture. In sponsoring privateers, Robert Rich combined English patriotism, the quest for profit, and the opportunity to harass Spain, the champion of conservative Catholicism and chief opponent of Protestantism. Rich was also deeply involved in financing American colonies and trading ventures. The three ships arrived back in England around the end of April 1629.

Their privateering efforts had brought little success, but Elfrith proposed a colonization effort to Robert Rich. Before the end of September 1629, Elfrith was ready to lead a preliminary expedition of soldiers and artisans to prepare the island for colonists. Investors in England were beginning to gather to finance and win authorization to establish a permanent colony.

Puritan Aristocracy

During the 1620s, many English were conscious that the nation faced a growing religious and political crisis. The first Stuart king of England, James I, believed fully in the divine right of kings and was never able to reconcile his pretensions of royal absolutism with the developing power of the English House of Commons. His son and successor Charles I learned nothing from his father's political difficulties with Parliament, and his religious inclinations alarmed members of the growing Puritan movement who feared that the Church of England was dangerously inclining toward High Church practices similar to hated and feared Catholicism. Robert Rich, Earl of Warwick, was a moderate Puritan who associated with other Puritans of similar high rank and opinion. Puritanism, which originated in the reign of Elizabeth I, was not a unified movement. The strictest Puritans regarded moderates such as Rich and his associates as too secular and questioned their commitment, but Rich and his associates were the most important, powerful, and influential Puritans in England.

The earl had invested in English colonizing schemes in Guyana, Virginia, and Massachusetts, and trading ventures as far away as the East Indies. While some of his privateering and trading ventures produced profits, the colonies were disappointing. He invested in a colony on the Oyapoc River in Guyana that failed. The Virginia colony, Jamestown, barely survived and required abundant support from England before it became financially viable. Bermuda had been colonized by accident when Sir George Somers grounded his sinking ship on a reef there to save the crew and passengers. The first colonists who intended to settle on the island arrived a few years later, primarily tenant farmers hoping for improved opportunities. They quickly discovered that English crops did not do well on the Caribbean island, and the colony also required significant support from England before it became self-sustaining. The Puritan colony in Massachusetts was a religious refuge, inward looking and self-serving, consisting largely of farmers of low social standing who eked out subsistence from rocky soil. It was far

The most prominent leaders of the Providence Island colonial venture depicted in contemporary and near-contemporary engravings. Top left, Robert Rich, Third Earl of Warwick, by William Faithhorne, published by Sir Robert Peake. Top right, Robert Greville, Second Baron Brook of Beauchamps Court, by R.S. Bottom left, William Fiennes, First Viscount Saye and Sele, by the Dutch artist Wenceslaus Hollar. (*National Portrait Gallery, London*) Bottom right, John Pym, by the Dutch artist Wenceslaus Hollar. (*National Galleries of Scotland*)

from the shining city upon a hill that could serve as an example and inspiration to all England that Robert Rich and his associates hoped to establish. Santa Catalina seemed to offer a variety of greater opportunities. The island could provide profitable tropical products and possibly serve as a base for privateers operating against the Spanish, and it offered the opportunity to become an ideal Puritan community, devout, righteous, and prosperous. The Puritans decided against establishing a colony on St. Andres, although they would support some agriculture there. They did, however, show interest in the mainland near Cape Gracias a Dios, where they might trade with the Indians and perhaps in the future sponsor a settlement.

During 1630, twenty Puritans, including titled aristocrats and members of both the House of Lords and Commons, met with the intention of founding a colony on Santa Catalina. The group sought to avoid the errors that frequently beset other colonial efforts. They invested substantially in the venture and focused on long-term development rather than the quest for short-term profits that blighted many other colonial ventures. Prominent among those attending were Robert Rich, Earl of Warwick; Robert Greville, Baron Brook of Beauchamps Court; William Fiennes, first Viscount Saye and Sele; and John Pym of the House of Commons, who was appointed treasurer. All were to be prominent in the outbreak of the English Civil War, but in 1630, that was yet far in the future.

Henry Rich, Earl of Holland, brother of Robert Rich, represented the investors at court. Largely because of his urging, King Charles I granted a patent to The Company of Adventurers of the City of Westminster for Plantation of the Islands of Providence or Catalina, Henrietta or Andres, and the Adjacent Islands Lying upon the Coast of America. The adventurers, those who "ventured" their capital, renamed the northern island Providence in acknowledgment of God's grace that led to Captain Elfrith's discovery and renamed St. Andres as Henrietta in tribute to Charles I's queen. International tensions remained high despite a recently established peace between England and Spain, and Charles I also granted letters of marque to the earl of Warwick entitling him or his agents to capture Spanish ships in the Caribbean. The king was to receive a fifth of all treasure so acquired. It was generally recognized that there was "no peace beyond the line," a phrase indicating that despite treaties that were observed in Europe, the Caribbean was still an area of conflict. English and Dutch privateers regarded all Spanish ships as fair game, and the Spanish regarded all privateers as pirates and dealt with any captured as such.

Plan for the Colony

The council of Puritan directors carefully prescribed the colony's form of government, economy, and even social organization, creating what might be described as religious socialism.

They established policies in London and sent instructions to a governor who administered the colony with the aid of a council of six military men and civilians. Members of the council could make proposals, but the governor had the right of veto. A company warehouse held goods and provisions brought from England for distribution to the colonists, who were divided into three classes: laborers, artificers, and apprentices. Laborers, more usually called planters, were allotted farmland. They would retain half their profits, the other half going to the company. The ownership of the land remained with the company, but the directors pledged that once cultivators were established on the land, their long-term tenure was assured. Artificers, men skilled in specialized trades such as blacksmiths, either worked for the company exclusively for provisions and wages of five pounds a year or worked independently for pay from other colonists. Those who worked independently also rendered half their profits to the company. Apprentices, usually called servants, were indentured to planters, artificers, and company officers, usually for two or three years to pay for their transportation to the colony and support there. The profits of their labor were shared equally between the planters who held their indentures and the company. During their indenture, the apprentices received meat, drink, and clothing, and afterward they could serve as artificers if they had special skills or receive a land allocation and enter the planter class, possibly having their own apprentices.

The initial group of colonists consisted entirely of men. Women and children came after the colony was established. Planters with apprentices lived on their farms, and men without apprentices were divided into "families" of six or seven who lived together. One member of each family designated as the leader was responsible to ensure that the family members prayed both in the morning and evening, avoided swearing and lewd behavior, and performed required public duties such as work on fortifications and public buildings. The directors were confident that the colonists would work gladly for the public good. The leader alone could draw stores for the family from the company warehouse, and such goods would be exchanged for the collective products of the family. The directors reminded colonists that settlers in Virginia and elsewhere, lured by the prospect of short-term profits, had imprudently neglected to plant enough food crops to cultivate tobacco, and that led to famine and deaths. Cultivation of tobacco was permitted, but each family was required to calculate how much food it would require and ordered to plant twice that amount.

Initial Colonization

Daniel Elfrith sailed from England to Bermuda, where he joined his son-in-law, Philip Bell. The directors had initially offered the position of governor to Elfrith, but he declined, recommending Bell for the position. The suggestion was accepted, and Bell resigned his position as governor of the Somers Isles to assume the post on Providence. Elfrith accepted the position of admiral, in charge of shipping, and Captain Samuel Axe commanded military matters on land. Elfrith went next to St. Andreas, where he discovered that most of the men had joined a Dutch ship and departed. A few remained, planting tobacco. Elfrith then sailed to Santa Catalina/Providence, where he arrived about Christmas 1629, bringing workmen who were to prepare the island for the permanent settlers. They set to work in the northern part of the island by a decent harbor where the largest stream on the island flowed across a plain to the sea. They named the nascent town New Westminster and built a church, governor's house, horse mill to grind grain, forge, cottages, and a variety of farm buildings, and planted fields of food crops and tobacco. They also constructed the island's primary fortification, Fort Warwick, which would later be improved and strengthened.

Meantime, two groups of colonists set sail for the island. One, from Bermuda, consisted of moderate Puritans and pragmatic men who hoped for enhanced opportunities on Providence. The other, a contingent of ninety strict Puritans, assembled in England and set sail in early 1631. They traveled aboard the *Seaflower*, owned by John Dyke, the only member of the twenty directors who was not a Puritan. The company provided funds for a generous supply of provisions to sustain the colonists while at sea and on land until crops could be harvested, but Dyke cheated by supplying provisions inferior in quality and quantity. After the *Seaflower* returned to England, the directors severed all connections to Dyke. On Providence, the colonists obeyed the injunctions to behave toward the Dutch with respect and friendship, and the Blauveldts and their Dutch buccaneers reciprocated by teaching the colonists to supplement their diet by butchering monk seals and large green turtles and to dine on turtle eggs.

A second group of colonists from Bermuda soon joined those on the island, along with another contingent of 150 Puritan colonists from England, including many artisans and the first women to come to the colony. They sailed on the *Charity*, commanded by Thomas Punt. The

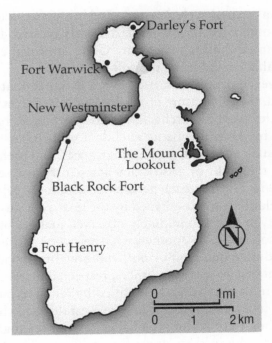

Providence Island.

directors tried to ensure that the captain treated the passengers honestly, but again the opportunity for profit prevailed, and the colonists suffered short rations of poor quality on the voyage. Punt too was dismissed by the company when reports of his behavior reached England. Subsequently, ships came to and went from Providence with some frequency. The directors tried to limit trade to their own ships, but on occasion necessity and profit eclipsed such regulations.

Problems in Paradise

The establishment of the colony on Providence Island was successful, despite Dyke's supply of inferior provisions and Punts' malfeasance, particularly when compared to the woes that typified the beginning of most other colonies. The great majority of other colonies suffered during their first months and years from chronic food shortages and great mortality. Jamestown, for instance, experienced a death rate of over 80 percent during the first three years of its existence despite three shipments from England of supplies, provisions, and reinforcements.

Providence was spared such disasters, and it is no wonder that Governor Bell and others felt they were particularly blessed. Bell called the island an Eden, and all felt that only God's approval could account for the favorable beginning of the colony.

Soon, however, problems arose from a dynamic that the sponsors least expected, the very nature of Puritanism. Seventeenth-century European societies were hierarchical. Status was largely based on birth and enforced by the entitlements attendant to membership in a privileged family, such as education, wealth, respect, and preferment. From king through the ranks of aristocracy and gentry and so on down to the lowliest tenant farmer, each person had a status in relation to every other. Each relationship was shaped by the relative statuses of the people involved even down to minutely observed matters of deportment: how one person spoke to another, what terms of address were used, whether one doffed one's hat or not, and how one stood in another's presence. Puritans, no less than others, respected hierarchical authority and felt it to be natural and sanctified by religion, but at the same time Puritans in their defiance of king and established church demonstrated that they were willing to challenge even the highest manifestations of hierarchy in their quest for godliness. The tension in the Puritan mind between their respect for the hierarchical elements of birth, status, and office, and their willingness to oppose it on moral grounds remained unresolved and probably unresolvable. This tension manifested itself in many conflicts. Puritans were notoriously argumentative and habitually disputatious, both within and beyond the Puritan community. This was true in England, in Massachusetts, and on Providence Island.

The structure of the island's government also contributed to the belligerency. The governor and council, often at odds themselves, were empowered to decide minor matters in the colony, but serious conflicts, never clearly defined, could be appealed to the directors in England. Predictably, everyone considered his cause to be serious, and the directors were besieged by masses of written complaints. None could be quickly resolved, as a letter from Providence had to cross the Atlantic, receive consideration, and get a reply from the directors. Since the initial complaint only contained one version of a matter, the reply often consisted of a request for more information from the other parties in the dispute. That too had to cross and recross the Atlantic before any decision was possible, and in the interval, disputes festered and intensified. Decisions were appealed, and even appeals were appealed. Nothing ever seemed to be definitively resolved.

It proved almost impossible to provide orderly clergy for the colonists on Providence. Puritan clerics were as a rule married, in distinction to the celibate Catholic clergy, but the directors had determined that women and children would not go to Providence until the colony was established. Married ministers could not be expected to abandon their wives and children, so the directors initially arranged for a young, unmarried Welsh minister, Lewis Morgan, who came to Providence with the first settlers. He proved a disaster, complaining about virtually everything, fomenting discontent between the planters and the governor, and even attacking the directors, charging they were interested in profit rather than godliness. After barely a year he was unceremoniously shipped back to England, where he was reprimanded and dismissed.

To replace him, three clergymen were sent to the island, Hope Sherrard to preside in New Westminster, Arthus Rous as teacher-lecturer, and a Reverend Ditloff, a Puritan from the Palatinate, to minister in the sparsely settled southwestern section of the island. Rous was soon criticized as a bully, more soldier than preacher, and accused of singing profane songs. He died of fever in 1634, before he became a major problem. Ditloff and Sherrard both contested the authority of Governor Bell and the councilors, seeking to substitute their own notions of congregational autonomy. Sherrard also accused Ditloff of singing secular songs, which he admitted, but claimed that Rous had taught them to him. He claimed that his English was limited so he had not understood the meaning of the songs and that he did not sing them on the Sabbath, despite Sherrard's claim that he did. Before the end of 1634, Ditloff was shipped back to England as unsuitable.

Sherrard remained on Providence until 1640, continually involved in controversies and endless complaints about company policies, officers, other colonists, and economic conditions. As leader of the strict Puritans, he aspired to establish a theocracy in the face of growing secular influences on the island. Sherrard's critics in turn accused him of divisiveness, disruptiveness, groundless excommunication of parishioners, negligence, and debility of memory. It is possible that in his case, the Puritan tension between respect for authority and the quest for spiritual perfection was complemented by some form of dementia. In 1640, Sherrard was forcibly seized and sent back to England. Other clerics were little improvement. For example, a Reverend Henry Root came to the colony in mid-1633 but left almost immediately in disgust when he discovered that most colonists were not sufficiently puritanical by his standards. He later offered to bring supporters to the colony to root out and deport heretical elements, but the directors failed to respond in the affirmative, and the suggestion remained in abeyance.

The Puritan tendency to quarrel was further exacerbated by the character of some of the upper-class colonists. No true aristocrats came to Province Island, but some of their lesser relatives did: younger brothers, cousins, and assorted others. Their claims to elevated social status were much more dependent on their family connections than individual achievements, and they were particularly defensive to even the least slight or smallest perceived breach of etiquette. Captain William Rudyerd was appointed commander of the first group of settlers during their transit from England to the island. He had some creditable military and colonial experience, but he was given the post chiefly because he was related to two of the twenty directors. Sir Benjamin Rudyerd, a member of Parliament, was his older brother, and the earl of Warwick was his cousin. On Providence, William Rudyerd was deeply offended when reproached by Reverend Lewis Morgan. Rudyerd's social status was far above that of Morgan, a mere minister, and he was indignant that Morgan presumed to criticize him. Rudyerd's arrogance subsequently caused even greater problems. He was accused before the directors of drunkenness, swearing, failure to respect Governor Bell, and physically punishing a servant so severely that he died, but no action was taken against him because of his influential relatives.

Despite his family connections, he eventually fell to the point where his main activity was kidnapping slaves from Portuguese and Spanish ships to sell on Providence. In another instance, during 1634, Lieutenant William Rous, John Pym's step-nephew, struck a blacksmith named Thomas Forman in front of Governor Bell. The council initially expelled him from his seat on the council and from his military position as second in command at Fort Henry. Rous refused to admit fault and apologize, but despite this he was readmitted to his offices at the direction of the proprietors before the end of the year. Rank continued to dominate over dissent.

The officers too were the subjects of complaints and complained about others, not least about one another. Governor Bell was naturally the target of most criticism. Councilors complained that Bell did not heed their concerns or suggestions and acted unilaterally, and Bell protested that the councilors were insufficiently respectful and shared confidential matters with others. Planters claimed that neither the governor nor the councilors paid attention to their grievances, while both Bell and the councilors protested that the planters were frequently lazy, shirked work on public projects, and complained without reason. Petty jealousies and personal feuds played roles too. Samuel Axe, in charge of the land defenses, resented that Daniel Elfrith received a larger salary than Axe did in the form of a portion of the tobacco harvest, although Elfrith had been designated as second in precedence to the governor and thus superior to Axe.

Two sources of dissatisfaction outweighed all others. The English Puritans criticized the Bermudians as insufficiently religious, and the Bermudians considered the English as impractical and ignorant of the realities of life in the tropics. The two groups divided into angry and mutually suspicious factions, and when Bell tried to mediate between them, both attacked him. Both, however, at least agreed about their grievances with the proprietors in England. The planters deeply resented their status as tenants who could not own the land they farmed, the requirement to render half their profits to the proprietors, and the obligation to labor on fortifications and other public works projects. The directors replied reasonably that they had expended large sums— as much as 1,250 each, a truly enormous sum at that time—and were entitled to recover their investment and that public works were, obviously, for the benefit of all. The directors also felt that only ownership of the island enabled them to control and guide the colony successfully, but the planters' tenant status discouraged investment to improve farms they did not own, encouraged the cultivation of tobacco for the most immediate gains, and created resentment toward public works projects.

Providence Island also proved to be less fruitful than expected. Although it encompasses about ten and a half square miles, much is covered with rocky high ground. There are only about three thousand acres of prime agricultural ground and an additional four thousand that are marginal. Colonists had been told they could grow three crops of corn a year, but generally only the first crop did well, while the other two often were damaged or destroyed by the usual summer drought that lasted five months; noxious weeds also proved a problem. The only crop that predictably succeeded was potatoes. Much of what was grown was then lost to rot, insects, and rodents, particularly conies, short-eared relatives of rabbits that inhabited the island. Tobacco, anticipated to be the island's cash crop, did not do well in quantity or quality. One colonist wrote that wood worms attacking the rafters in the drying buildings rained fine dust down on the tobacco, making it bitter. Apparently, tobacco farming and processing improved enough to serve as the island's chief item of trade, though it never did as well as hoped. By the 1630s, the market price for tobacco was also falling as large amounts of better-quality leaf from Virginia and the Caribbean exceeded demand. Cotton offered some profit, but hardly enough to justify the existence of the colony economically. Some colonists were quickly disillusioned by life on the island and left as soon as possible. At home, their accounts undoubtedly discouraged others who considered joining the colony, but even as some returned, others continued to go to Providence.

The First Spanish Attack

In late 1631, the *Seaflower* sailed from Providence for England. The ship had reached the Florida Straits between Florida and the Bahamas when it was attacked by a Spanish ship. During a desperate fight, the Spanish boarded the English vessel three times, only to be repeatedly driven off. The English lost a number of men to death and wounds, but the English ship managed to escape. Had their ship been captured, it is probable that the Spanish would have learned of the existence of the Providence colony long before they did.

Also in 1631, Daniel Elfrith, an inherently unruly character, hosted a visit to Providence by Diego "El Mulato" Martín. The Spanish particularly hated and feared El Mulato, as he was commonly known, whom they regarded as a renegade. He had escaped from slavery in Havana to join the Dutch, rising in their ranks to the command of a privateer. In early 1632, Elfrith took it upon himself to sail in a pinnace to Cape Gracias a Dios on the easternmost Mosquito Coast, today the borderland between Nicaragua and Honduras. There he attacked and captured a Spanish frigate, after which he abandoned the pinnace and sailed the frigate back to Providence Island. Bell and the colonists in general were alarmed that Elfrith's reckless conduct would bring the Spanish upon them, but the Spanish still did not know of the English colony. The company masked its operations so well that the Spanish remained ignorant of the establishment of Providence until the Spanish ambassador to England, Juan de Recolade, reported it to King Philip IV at the end of March 1634. This remarkable failure of the usually effective Spanish network of spies may be attributable to the private character of the Providence colony. Spanish intelligence tended to focus on the court and royal administration.

By early 1635, intelligence reached Spanish colonial authorities that privateers and pirates sailing from Providence Island, San Andres, and the Mosquito Coast were preying on Spanish shipping, but the royal government was deeply engaged with major efforts in Europe. France declared war on Spain that year, hostilities took place in Italy, and unrest was growing in Portugal, ruled by the Spanish kings since 1580. The Dutch had conquered much of Brazil, and the effort to prevent their further depredations and to expel them required substantial resources. The damages caused by the English from Providence Island were of little consequence in comparison, except to the Spanish residing in the area, and the royal government could not spare resources to deal with such a relatively minor menace. Local forces would have to suffice, so at Cartagena, Governor Francisco de Murga moved against the English. The first Spanish effort was against the isle of Tortuga off the northern coast of modern Haiti, over which the Province Company had nominal authority. The inhabitants, rough lawless men, hunted and dried meat to sell to privateers and pirates who stopped there and occasionally set forth in small ships to attack the Spanish. Murga's forces easily overran Tortuga and executed all except a few who managed to hide in the scrub that covered the island. The governor next sent Captain Gregorio de Castellar y Mantillar against Providence Island.

The colonists on Providence were aware of the potential strength of the Spanish and conscious of their own weakness, in part the result of their own failure to cooperate to create effective defensive measures. The colonists only reluctantly worked to strengthen the fortifications and failed to build sheds to shelter cannons and their carriages, implements, and gunpowder which were consequently ruined by rain and rot. Now more luck than readiness came to their rescue.

The First Spanish Attack on Providence

The Spanish force consisted of 225 troops and 20 sappers carried in two ships of the line and a frigate. Five small launches carried aboard the larger ships were to land the troops. Arriving at Providence, the Spanish formally demanded surrender, and Governor Bell formally refused. Impressed by the fortifications they had seen near New Westminster, the Spanish decided to land troops at an undefended locality on the eastern side of the northern promontory nearly opposite Fort Warwick. That required the ships to sail from near New Westminster around the promontory in the face of contrary wind and currents. As soon as the Spanish movement became apparent, the colonists moved artillery to a bluff overlooking the landing area from which they were able to bring heavy fire to bear on the Spanish ship carrying the landing force. The Spanish soon realized that the position on the bluff was virtually invincible and that a landing party would face cannon and musket fire without a chance to reply. The effort was canceled, and Castellar then sailed to St. Andres, where a few Englishmen had established themselves and planted crops. They promptly fled to the interior of the island, and the Spanish were only able to burn the little settlement and crops as well as capture three Englishmen and a Mosquito Indian boy.

The Spanish attack of 1635 ushered in profound changes on Providence. Administrative personnel changes, begun before the attack, gave the colony new but weaker leadership. The economy took new directions, with Puritan religious commitment and morality facing severe tests and temptations.

Changes

By 1634, the chorus of complaints convinced the directors that changes were required if Providence were ever to become the godly and profitable colony they envisioned. Some of the changes, however, were anything but godly.

Before the first Spanish attack in 1635, Governor Bell and the councilors on Providence had tried to limit privateering ventures for fear of bringing Spanish wrath upon the colony, though their efforts met with indifferent success. After the attack, however, there was no reason to restrain such ventures, and Providence victualed and supported privateers and even avowed pirates without hesitation. Most of the ships were small and did not attack major Spanish treasure fleets, but they caused significant damage to commerce along the coast of Central America and raided small coastal communities. In time their predations grew in number and boldness.

The increase in piratical activity quickly brought changes to the colony, both minor and profound. For example, the directors had initially prohibited cards, dice, gambling, and similar amusements, but the frequent commerce with privateers and pirates made it virtually impossible to prevent the importation of the banned items. By the mid-1630s, the directors no longer exhorted colonists on the subject, a seemingly minor matter but indicative of the erosion of Puritan morals.

More importantly, planters began to import Black slaves. Planters accustomed to the English climate quickly discovered that laboring in the tropics was enervating and debilitating. From the time of Columbus, a common opinion prevailed that Europeans and those of European descent were inherently unsuited to heavy labor in hot climates while Black Africans and their descendants well tolerated such work. Few observed that whips and guns enforced the work of slaves, who were no more suited to such labor than anyone else. In 1633, the company first allowed the importation of slaves to Providence Island. They warned the colonists that the introduction of too many slaves would be dangerous, but at the same time they suggested that twenty or forty slaves might be useful for public works, with the unspoken hope that that might end the colonists' objections to compulsory labor on such projects. After 1635, the importation of slaves increased greatly. Many Bermudians and other liberal colonists deserted agriculture on Providence for potentially more-rewarding privateering and piracy, and the resulting labor shortage created conditions close to famine on the island as well as an eager market for slaves. Privateers and pirates brought slaves to Providence taken from captured Portuguese and Spanish ships or bought from Indians on the Mosquito Coast who captured slaves fleeing from the Spanish. Slaves were also resold from Providence to other islands in the Caribbean, Virginia, and Massachusetts.

Among the Puritans there were a few abolitionists. Samuel Rishworth was a righteous Puritan who became a member of the governor's council soon after his arrival in 1632. Rishworth had definite ideas about morality, and he felt that slavery was contrary to Christian values. Robert Rich, Earl of Warwick, also had reservations about the morality of slavery, but the directors argued that it was lawful for Christians to keep pagans as slaves. Apparently, the directors felt it immoral to reduce Christians to slavery, although it is not entirely clear whom they regarded as Christians.

A unique Spanish source preserves the testimony of several African slaves who were captured by a pirate, sold on Providence, and escaped, returning to the Spanish. In 1634, a Spanish captain and eleven African slaves belonging to the widow doña Mariana de Armas Clavijo of Cartagena de Indias crewed the ship *Nuestra Señora del Rosario*, which was engaged in trade along the Rio Grande de la Magdalena. Several Spanish men were also aboard. A privateer or pirate captured the ship and, in an unusually magnanimous gesture, set the Spanish captain and his companions ashore; but the Africans were taken to Providence Island, where they were bartered for twenty pounds of tobacco and a pig each. The proprietors permitted the enslavement of pagans, but these newly acquired slaves were all Catholics. Either the colonists did not consider Catholics as sufficiently Christian, or they simply decided to disregard the instructions from the directors in London. They confiscated the Africans' rosaries and crosses and then forced them to attend church sermons even though they understood no English. The Africans testified that the governor, whose name the slaves gave as Félix Beles (Philip Bell), acquired four of the eleven while other officers took the remaining seven. They were among the first Black slaves on the island and testified that they saw no others during their sojourn of seven months.

The Africans disliked their life on Providence, claiming they were less free than among the Spanish, and had endured a monotonous diet of potatoes, which they and the colonists mainly ate raw. Five agreed to escape and return to the Spanish, though they were unable to include the others in their plans. They stole a boat and were ready to embark when they encountered a group of six English servants also discontent with life on Providence. They all agreed to leave together. After two days at sea they reached the mainland, where one of the Africans died. After traveling along the coast, they came to the mouth of the San Juan River. There one of the English revealed that four others conspired to kill the Africans, who precluded their plan by attacking first, killing one of the English while the other three fled. One of the two loyal English then went on alone while the others waited by the mouth of the river. He encountered a Spanish ship owner who brought the group to the proper authorities at Portobello.

During the interrogation that followed, the Africans revealed details about Providence Island, such as the location and description of fortifications, quality of armaments, ship traffic, the presence of about two hundred men on the island, and the existence of a militia organized in two units. One was commanded by the father-in-law of the governor, Captain Alfero (Daniel Elfrith), described as a small, older man, and the other by a younger man, Captain Rus (William Rous). Such details were important in the Spanish decision to attack Providence Island a few months later.

Eventually, hundreds of slaves labored on Providence, and the danger of a slave revolt became a substantial and continual source of anxiety. In reaction, the planters resorted to cruel measures to coerce and intimidate the slaves, which probably aggravated rather than relieved the danger. In 1638, there was a slave revolt, but rather than attacking the colonists, slaves simply escaped into the interior of the island, where the colonists hunted them down. Those captured were executed along with fifty more accused of conspiracy. Other slaves who escaped singly or in small groups stole boats to sail to the Mosquito Coast, where they were sometimes able to join Native American groups but on other occasions were captured and resold. One small group managed to hide in the rocky interior of Providence Island, where they planted small plots and raided the fields of outlying farms for food.

The growth of piracy and slavery transformed Providence from a community of farmers resembling a traditional English country village to something far different from Puritan ideals, a haven for piracy, a slave mart, and a plantation society based on slave labor controlled by violence.

The directors also decided to replace Philip Bell as governor, but it was not until 1636 that they sent a replacement, Robert Hunt. Hunt was a dependent of Lord Brooke and an extreme Puritan, rigid, and self-righteous. Despite specific instruction to reconcile differences on the island, Hunt did just the opposite. He made common cause with the most aristocratic and religious figures in the colony, Samuel Rishworth, William Rous, and the quarrelsome Reverend Hope Sherrard, while alienating the Bermudians and other moderates. The directors ordered Hunt to behave with courtesy toward Bell, but he gave credence to all complaints against him and confiscated his property and slaves. The directors nullified all actions against Bell, restoring his property. The chorus of complaints led the directors to replace Hunt after just two years.

The third governor, Nathaniel Butler, had both governmental and military experience. He arrived in autumn 1638 with orders to strengthen the defenses of the island and mediate the disputes that continued to divide the community. He was able to do the former, but the latter was probably beyond human capacity. Butler soon came to loath

Reverend Sherrard, whose theological rantings grew increasingly strident and served as the focus and cause of disorder. In a letter to Lord Saye, Butler summarized the cantankerous character of the Providence Island Puritans: "I never lived among men of more spleen, nor of less wit to conceal it." After seven months of trying to reconcile the irreconcilable, Butler left the island to go privateering on his own account, but he enjoyed little success. Finally, in early 1640, Butler departed to England, ostensibly to present the colonists' grievances to the directors, but he may have simply wanted to get away from the endless bickering and quarreling on the island. Butler appointed Captain Andrew Carter, muster master general of Fort Warwick, as acting governor, much to the horror of Reverend Sherrard and the other strict Puritans. Carter was a rough, irreligious military man who enjoyed drinking with pirates rather than attending Puritan services.

Second Attack of the Spanish, with the Portuguese

Despite growing tensions between the two Iberian nations in Europe, the Spanish and Portuguese were able to combine forces to move against the island. In mid-1640, a combined invasion fleet set sail, consisting of two galleons, three frigates, two supply ships, a caravel, and four launches. In addition to sailors, there were about six hundred or seven hundred troops and two hundred slaves to labor after the conquest. On the way to Providence, the fleet encountered heavy weather during which several light landing craft carried aboard the larger ships were swept away, and the frigates and several smaller ships were separated from the galleons and only able to reach Providence after the main action.

After initial reconnaissance, the commanders decided that the harbor by New Westminister was too strongly fortified for direct assault and determined to launch the invasion at the mouth of a small river a little north of Black Rock Fort. There the Spanish and Portuguese ships exchanged fire with Black Rock Fort and several neighboring artillery positions. The land fortifications suffered little, but a small ship was sunk, and other ships sustained some damage.

The earlier loss of landing craft in a storm prevented the invaders from disembarking more than about half of their infantry for the initial assault, and they quickly came under fire from Black Rock Fort and the mouth of the river. The Spanish, not knowing the colonists were desperately short of artillery ammunition and could not long sustain the bombardment, shifted their intended landing halfway between the river mouth and Black Rock Fort, an area less subject to direct cannon fire but also an area they had not sufficiently reconnoitered. The infantry struggled through the surf to find themselves on a beach covered with slimy rocks and facing a bluff manned by colonists armed with muskets. Slaves, promised their freedom if they would join in the fight, threw stones down on the attackers with dire effects. Several Spanish and Portuguese officers were killed or gravely wounded. A few officers and men managed to slip by the defenders onto the island, but most of the soldiers panicked and turned back to their boats. There was great slaughter of the Iberian soldiers in the surf. A Frenchman serving with the Spanish later reported that only two of three hundred escaped death or wounding. The colonists lost only two who died of wounds. Reverend Sherrard wrote disparagingly about the dead as sinners whom, he implied, got what they deserved.

The Spanish and Portuguese who had made it to shore soon surrendered when Carter promised to spare their lives, but after interrogation he had them all executed. The colonists condemned the betrayal with horror, yet they felt no moral compunction about reneging on their own promise to free the slaves who had fought beside them. Relations between masters and slaves on Providence predictably worsened.

Sherrard later wrote an account of the battle in which he accused Carter and other officers of cowardice and claimed he and his supporters had assumed control during the battle. It is difficult to accept his claims at face value since he was extremely hostile to Carter before the battle and hated him even more intensely because of events after it. Sherrard and several of his chief supporters, emboldened by the victory and the general indignation over the slaughter of the prisoners, attempted to remove Carter and substitute their own candidate as governor. Carter promptly jailed Sherrard along with his two chief followers and sent them back to England, where the directors freed them, condemned the slaughter of the prisoners, and ordered Carter to return to England.

While all of this was transpiring, relations between the Providence Island colonists, the Puritan Massachusetts colonists, and the directors in London were evolving in complex and often contradictory manners. The strict Puritans in both colonies sought to support one another in their hopes and intentions to establish intolerant theocracies, while the more liberal elements shipped captured loot to Massachusetts where it was often transshipped illegally, avoiding English customs' duties, to European ports. The directors in London found themselves alienated from the increasingly independent strict Puritan leadership of Massachusetts, particularly when it became apparent that the directors were attempting to recruit people from the Massachusetts colony to settle on Providence Island to relieve the labor shortage there. The directors went so far as to enlist John Humphry, one of the founders and leaders of the Massachusetts colony, to serve as the next governor of Providence, but before he could arrive, the Spanish had come again.

Third Spanish Attack: Conquest of Providence Island
Admiral Francisco Diaz Pimienta, an experienced and respected naval commander, arrived in Cartagena in 1640, assessed the situation, and returned to Spain to urge royal support to avenge the disgraceful defeat at Providence. Returning to Cartagena, he assembled a new force of seven large ships—three galleons, a ship of the line, and three troop transports—and smaller supply vessels, pinnaces, and shallops useful for communications and scouting. The fleet, manned by 600 sailors, carried 1,400 Spanish and Portuguese troops and landing craft lashed on the decks of the major ships. The admiral carefully prepared the campaign, gathering intelligence about the island. He set sail in May 1641, after the end of the less-predictable winter weather and the departure of pirates and privateers who passed the winter on the island.

Diaz Pimienta initially intended to land on the eastern side of the island, but an unseasonable storm forced cancellation on two successive nights and allowed the islanders to entrench the landing area. The admiral's subordinates urged him to give up the attempt, but instead he instituted a daring plan. He sailed up the eastern coast of the island, around the northern promontory, and unloaded his landing craft for an assault directly into the main harbor. He reasoned that if the landing craft were rowed quickly enough, the islanders would not be able to train their cannons on them. Coming ashore, the Spanish boats did take some damage and casualties, but losses were minimal. About 120 islanders opposed the landing of the Spanish, but they were soon overwhelmed. After about twenty were killed in the fight, the survivors retreated to Fort Warwick, and the Spanish took over New Westminster.

Diaz Pimienta now faced a problem. Over the years, the Puritans had greatly strengthened Fort Warwick. It was now a substantial defensive position, fully manned and well equipped with cannons and small arms, and Diaz Pimienta lacked the necessary supplies for a siege. The situation was quickly and surprisingly resolved when the interim governor, Andrew Carter, suddenly surrendered the fort, ending all opposition to the Spanish on Providence. Carter's pusillanimous performance gives some credence to Hope Sherrard's accusation that Carter had been a coward during the earlier Spanish confrontation.

Diaz Pimienta granted the islanders generous, humane conditions. He transported 398 English men, women, and children to Cartagena, and during the voyage they received the same rations as the Spanish mariners and troops. At Cartagena they were well treated, the men lodged in accommodations provided by the Jesuits and given a substantial allowance for food and drink. Families volunteered to take the women and children into their private homes, where they were treated with generosity. The contrast to the massacre of Spanish prisoners taken in the earlier confrontation could hardly be greater. The captured colonists were sent with the annual fleet to Cádiz, where they were released to return to England.

Before departing Providence, Diaz Pimienta loaded previously pirated goods from the warehouses of the island that when auctioned more than paid the cost of the expedition. Diaz Pimienta also took from Providence 380 slaves who were sold at Cartagena. The Providence Islanders, fearing a slave revolt, had shortly before sold about a thousand slaves to colonists on St. Kitts and Bermuda. Although Diaz Pimienta had been ordered to destroy the fortifications on Providence and then abandon the island, he quickly realized that if he did so it could quickly be reoccupied by the English or Dutch. On his own authority he left a garrison there, a decision later ratified by the royal government. In the aftermath of the destruction of the Providence Island colony, Spanish commerce and general prosperity in the region greatly improved.

Diaz Pimienta did not capture all the colonists or slaves on Providence. About 150 colonists fled to the hills, and a significant number of slaves also used the opportunity to escape. One group of slaves managed to take over a privateers' ship in the harbor, which they sailed to the Mosquito Coast. There it was wrecked, but they managed to get ashore. Other groups of slaves and colonists used small crafts to flee to the same area. Colonist refugees then dispersed in many directions, some to St. Kitts, others to Bluefields, Belize Town (today Belize City), and other places farther afield. Some escaped slaves remained on Providence Island, forming enduring villages inland that to this day speak an English-based creole, including words obsolete since the seventeenth century.

Ships bearing colonists from Massachusetts and from England arrived at Providence Island to find it occupied by the Spanish. They could only sail away. The directors were reluctant to abandon their hopes and dreams for the Providence colony, but the engagement of many directors in matters that led to the outbreak of the English Civil War precluded any action.

Aftermath

After the Spanish conquest, a small Spanish garrison remained on Providence Island, but there was no substantial settlement. In addition to the soldiers, who of necessity farmed plots of land to produce their own food, there were a few scattered individuals, such as Indian herdsmen and descendants of slaves who continued to live in the hills. Edward Mansveldt, whose name the English wrote as Mansfield, was a leading Dutch pirate and sometimes privateer. In 1666, nominally operating as an English privateer, he led the Brethren of the Coast (pirates) to Providence Island, and the aging Spanish garrison there quietly surrendered. Mansveldt left a small garrison on the island and then set out to find support for a major reoccupation of Providence. Soon after leaving the island, however, Mansveldt ran afoul of Spanish forces who captured and executed him. Juan Pérez de Guzmán, governor and captain general of Panama, dispatched a force under the command of José Sánchez Ximénez, the mayor of Portobello, who quickly forced the pirate garrison to surrender. The pirates held Providence just eighty-one days.

The Spanish then used Providence as a penal colony. In addition to a small garrison, slaves and criminals farmed plots of land merely to survive. Supplementary supplies arrived seldom and were never generous. One soldier who had been condemned to the island for some unspecified misdeed attacked Sánchez Ximénez as he slept, stabbing him to death.

In 1670, the famed pirate Henry Morgan, also acting nominally as an English privateer, came to Providence on his way to sack Panamá. He landed a thousand men, easily enough to overcome the small Spanish garrison. The ranking Spanish officer explained to Morgan that he would gladly surrender, but he needed to make at least a show of resisting if he expected to survive when reporting to his superiors. So a mock battle was arranged, the Spanish and the pirates merrily shooting at one another with blank loads until the garrison burned enough of their gunpowder to claim they had surrendered when they could no longer fight. Morgan let the Spanish officers and troops sail away and rounded up all the slaves that did not manage to escape into the hills. After deciding that he had no good reason to leave a garrison on the island, he destroyed the fortifications and all the other buildings except the church and after a couple of months sailed away, never to return. Promoters of modern tourism tell lurid tales of buried treasure on Providence, supposedly part of Morgan's loot from Panamá. None, of course, has ever been found. Pirates fought for gold to spend on rum and women, not to bury in holes in the ground. A Spanish reconnaissance of the island in 1688 found no signs of habitation, and other than occasional mariners landing to replenish water casks, the island seems to have remained deserted until resettlement began in 1787.

Conclusion

Although the Providence Island colony was better financed and planned than the great majority of colonies, it was fatally flawed from its inception. Daniel Elfrith and the others who first contemplated settlement on the island made the common mistake of assuming that abundant tropical growth indicated great fertility of the soil. European food crops did not do well, leading to the taunt that the islanders survived on potatoes and turtle meat. In the effort to develop the island's economy, the Puritan colonists turned increasingly to tobacco produced by slave labor. The oppression necessary to control hundreds of slaves altered and corrupted the ideals of the colonists but still failed to ensure the economic viability of the island. The possibility of Providence as a base for strikes against the Spanish had been contemplated in the initial planning stages, but the directors did not see the colony as primarily a base for privateers and pirates. As in the case of slavery, economic necessity drove change, and Providence became a favored resort for buccaneers. Catering to these rough characters and the consequence of trading in slaves and stolen goods further eroded Puritan morals, and colonists deserted the island in large numbers to take up with the sea rovers. The piratical attacks on Spanish shipping and settlements brought retribution on an already corrupted, disrupted, and dispirited community.

The inherent Puritan quarrelsomeness, evident throughout the eleven-year history of the colony, also contributed significantly to the failure. Despite the directors' vision of a united, orderly, devout religious community working in unity, the Providence Island colonists were bitterly divided from the beginning, and disagreements and mutual recriminations grew ever more intense. Some of the directors' stipulations for governing the colony, particularly the corporate ownership of land, contributed to dissatisfaction. Religious differences within the Puritan community also disrupted the colony.

The leading figures of the Puritan aristocracy who invested in the Providence Island colony played important roles in the outbreak of the English Civil War in 1642. Robert Rich, Earl of Warwick, became commander of the Parliament fleet. After Charles I was executed and the victorious Parliamentarians abolished the House of Lords, Rich retired from public life, although his family was intricately connected to Cromwell. Rich's grandson and heir married Cromwell's daughter Francis. Rich died in 1658. His brother, Henry Rich, Earl of Holland—who got his title for his role in arranging Charles I's marriage to Henrietta—sided with the Royalists during the civil war. He was captured by the Parliamentarians and executed in 1649. Robert Greville, Baron Brook, became a general of Parliament forces and was killed in early 1643 by a Royalist marksman. William Fiennes, First Viscount Saye and Sele, supported Parliament during the civil war, but he was a moderate who tried unsuccessfully to arrange a compromise between the king and Parliament. He retired from public life after the execution of Charles I, although he came out of retirement to serve Charles II as a privy counselor. He died in 1662.

In the years leading to the outbreak of the civil war, John Pym became the leader of the opposition to Charles I. He died of natural causes in 1643 but was so reviled by the Royalists that after the Restoration in 1660, they desecrated his grave.

Philip Bell left Providence soon after being relieved as governor. In 1641, he became the governor of Barbados, where he enjoyed success as an administrator.

After some years of experimenting unsuccessfully with various crops, the Barbadians turned to sugarcane. Sugar, produced by slaves, brought high prices in Europe and made the Barbados plantation owners wealthy. During the English Civil War, Bell long managed to maintain neutrality on Barbados, but that finally began to break down after the execution of Charles I in 1649. Royalists took control of the island in 1650, and Bell was replaced as governor. He returned to England, where it is reported that he died in 1678.

Daniel Elfrith was formally removed from his official position on Providence in 1637, but he continued his career as a privateer and occasionally as a pirate. He was last mentioned in 1641, and his fate remains unknown.

The Blauveldts remained prominent privateers and occasional pirates. Abraham Brauvelt commanded his own privateering vessel operating out of New Amsterdam (later New York) in 1644, and after Spain and the Netherlands made peace in 1648, he used Rhode Island as his chief port for piratical endeavors and became a friend of Roger Williams's. In 1650, he commanded a French privateer and after that served with the Swedes in the Caribbean. He was last reported in 1663 to be living at Bluefields, the settlement on the Mosquito Coast named after his family, in modern Nicaragua.

After his return to England in 1640, Reverend Hope Sherrard continued to be argumentative, cantankerous, and unable to tolerate anyone who did not agree with his strict Puritan views. Predictably, he was not popular as a minister and had to move from town to town. In one case, parishioners petitioned the House of Lords for his removal. He was still active as late as 1658, but the date of his death is unknown. It is unlikely that he was widely mourned.

Francisco Diaz Pimienta returned to Madrid, where King Philip IV awarded him the Order of Santiago for the capture of Providence Island and his other services to the crown. He went on to have a distinguished career until he was killed in 1652 during the Catalan Rebellion.

Sources

The history of the Providence Island colony was long confused by the misattribution of relevant documents to New Providence in the Bahamas and even to Providence, Rhode Island. The British Public Record Office only sorted out the error in 1876 and now has organized the documents in two large volumes, *The Records of the Providence Island Company*. The first lengthy treatment of the colony is A. P. Newton, *The Colonising Activities of English Puritans* (New Haven: Yale University Press, 1914). The work remains useful, particularly regarding activities of the directors. The primary sources for the colony are now gathered in Karen Ordahl Kupperman, ed., *Papers Relating to the Providence Company and Colony, 1630–1641*, in the series British Records Relating to America in Microform, W. E. Winchinton, gen. ed. (London: Microform Academic Publishers, 1989). Karen Ordahl Kupperman is also the author of the comprehensively researched and fully documented *Providence Island 1630–1641: The Other Puritan Colony* (Cambridge: Cambridge University Press, 1993). The work also contains an extensive and useful bibliographic essay. Tom Feiling, *The Island that Disappeared: The Lost History of the Mayflower's Sister Ship and Its Rival Puritan Colony* (Brooklyn: Melville House, 2017) is a lively account of the island and the fate of the colony that owes a great deal to Kupperman's research.

William Sorsby, "Old Providence Island: Puritans, Pirates and Spaniards 1630–1670" is a peculiar and somewhat mysterious work. It is an unpublished and undated typescript; each chapter is individually numbered. Judging from the type and paper, it appears to have been written in the 1970s. A copy, missing the title page and first page, is available at www.scribd.com from a photocopy of the typescript in the Biblioteca Luis Angel Arango, Bogota, Colombia. The work is well researched, contains valuable insights, and is particularly strong regarding the Spanish activities and sources. The author is apparently William Shuman Sorsby, whose PhD thesis, "The British Superintendency of the Mosquito Shore," was accepted in University College, London, in 1969. We have found no information about another book he mentions having written, *The Zambo Mosquito Empire*, dealing with the Mosquito Coast of Honduras and Nicaragua from 1502 to 1908.

David Wheat, "A Spanish Caribbean Captivity Narrative: African Sailors and Puritan Slavers, 1635," in *Afro-Latino Voices: Narratives from the Early Modern Ibero-Atlantic World, 1550–1812*, ed. Kathryn Joy McKnight and Leo J. Garofalo (Indianapolis: Hackett, 2009) translates and provides a commentary on the unique account of the African slave-sailors kidnaped to Providence Island and their subsequent escape to return to the Spanish.

NINE

Burghers *in the* Tropics: Dutch West India Company *in* Brazil (1624–1654)

Portuguese Background

Portuguese colonization began in 1415 with the conquest of Ceuta, a trade center in North Africa. In addition to expanding holdings in North Africa, the Portuguese explored down the Atlantic coast of Africa, colonizing the Madeira and Azores Islands, establishing trading stations on the African mainland, and bringing gold and slaves back to Portugal. In 1498, the Portuguese navigator Vasco da Gama reached India. The journey around Africa was long and difficult, but the spices and other exotic imports from India made Portugal wealthy. Large numbers of Portuguese fishermen also participated in the northern cod fisheries. The Portuguese first came to Brazil in 1500. Initially, they harvested dyewood and captured or traded for Indians whom they reduced to slavery, but they viewed Brazil as not particularly productive in comparison to the trade in Africa and India and even the cod fisheries. The Dutch and French, however, were initially attracted to Brazil as a source of dyewood, important to their cloth industries. As early as the 1520s, the Portuguese began experimenting with growing sugarcane in Brazil, and by the middle of the century, Brazil was becoming a significant source of sugar. The demand for the sugar was great and growing in Europe, where it was regarded not merely as a confection but also as a potent medicine. Sugar production elevated the importance of Brazil to the Portuguese and to potential rivals. During the second half of the sixteenth century, Portuguese began to penetrate inland from their costal settlements to establish sugarcane plantations.

Despite the growing economic importance of Brazilian sugar, the Portuguese population remained modest. Estimates of the Portuguese population of Brazil around 1600 varied from about thirty thousand to sixty thousand, the great majority of whom were concentrated in the provinces of Pernambuco and Bahia. There were also about fifteen thousand to twenty thousand African slaves held by the Portuguese and some Indian slaves, but the Portuguese found the Indians much less profitable to enslave than Africans. By the early seventeenth century, the number of Indians in the coastal region had declined precipitously. In the Native cultures of the area, all agricultural work was done by women, and male Indians saw the Portuguese attempt to use them as plantation workers as emasculating, provoking intense resistance and frequent attempts to escape. Indians, unlike recently imported Africans, knew the local languages and were familiar with the countryside and possible refuges.

In 1578, the disastrous battle of Alcácer Quibir in North Africa resulted in the death of the Portuguese King Sebastian and many of the Portuguese nobility. Sebastian left no direct heir, and the throne passed to his granduncle, Henry, who was sixty-six years old, a cardinal of the Catholic church, and of course childless. He died two years later. Three grandchildren of Manuel I, king of Portugal from 1495 to 1521, claimed the throne, but one of the three, Philip II, the king of Spain, had vastly more power than the other two. Philip's forces invaded Portugal, and he had himself proclaimed king there, beginning a period from 1580 to 1640 during which the Spanish monarchy dominated Portugal and its overseas colonies. To lessen Portuguese aversion, it was agreed that Portugal would remain nominally independent. The joining of the two nations under one monarch, however, remained problematic. Many Portuguese felt with reason that the Spanish taxed Portugal excessively, exploited Portuguese military and naval resources, ignored matters vital to Portugal, and pursued policies that benefited Spain at the expense of Portugal. Portuguese who actively cooperated with the Spanish government were resented by their compatriots.

A French attempt to plant a colony in Brazil from 1555 to 1560 miscarried because of a religiously quarrelsome French commandant and a strong Portuguese response led by an able governor. A subsequent French effort in 1612 was quashed in 1615. A much more powerful force, however, soon challenged Portuguese domination of Brazil.

Dutch Background

The Netherlands revolted against Spanish rule in the second half of the sixteenth century. The major causes of the revolt were Spanish attempts to impose more-centralized bureaucratic control on the Netherlands while abolishing centuries-old provincial and municipal rights and privileges; high taxation, which injured growing Dutch trade and capitalism, and the growth of Protestantism in the northern provinces of the Netherlands at the time Spain was emerging as the chief center of conservative Catholicism and social hierarchy. The first stirrings began in the early 1560s, and by the early 1580s, the Netherlands declared independence.

During the first years of the revolt, the Dutch fared poorly. The revolt had begun in the southern provinces of the Netherlands, but the Spanish were able to restore their permanent control in that area. The southern provinces, Flanders, Brabant, and Luxembourg, the so-called Spanish Netherlands, have become modern Belgium and Luxembourg. As the Spanish reasserted control, many of the merchant and economic elite, among whom Protestantism spread widely, fled from the south to the northern provinces, especially Holland, fueling a vast expansion of the economy. Initially, Spanish forces also conquered much of the southern and eastern portions of the northern provinces, but they were ultimately not able to retain them. In 1590, the Dutch began to institute military and economic reforms that radically altered the situation, and the Dutch reforms coincided with increasing Spanish conflicts with France that drew financial and military resources away from the Dutch revolt.

The Dutch war for independence, the so-called Eighty Years' War, lasted from 1568 to 1648, though there was the Twelve Years' Truce from 1609 to 1621. Most of the other European nations recognized the sovereign independence of the Dutch Republic at the beginning of the truce, but Spain did not acknowledge the Netherlands' independence until 1648 as part of the settlement of the Thirty Years' War that involved much of Europe.

Over two decades, 1590–1609, the Netherlands rose to become a major power. Dutch naval and economic mastery spread across the globe. Dutch trade grew as merchants from the Netherlands penetrated the Mediterranean and soon played such a large role in Turkey that English and French merchants purchased Dutch coins struck specifically for foreign trade to do business there. The Dutch opened important trade connections in Persia, India, Ceylon (modern Sri Lanka), Indonesia, China, and Japan. In 1606, the Dutch made the earliest documented discovery of Australia, and soon they circumnavigated that continent and discovered New Zealand and the Fiji Islands. In North America, they founded the colony of New Netherlands, the capital of which they named New Amsterdam, today New York City. In South America, the Dutch cast covetous eyes on Brazil.

In 1590, despite continuing attempts to repress the Dutch revolt, Spain's King Philip II repealed the embargo of Portuguese trade with the Dutch to aid the Portuguese economy. Able and aggressive Dutch merchants soon came to dominate the export of pepper, spices, and sugar from Portugal to northern Europe, further enabling the Dutch to assume a major role in trade with Russia. At the same time, Jews fleeing from persecution in Spain and Portugal settled in the Netherlands, where they were able to practice their religion. They were tolerated but not universally welcomed, as the most fanatic Dutch Calvinists preached against them. Sephardic Jews retained connections to Christiah merchants in their homelands and were able to promote and facilitate trade.

In 1602, the Dutch formed the Verenigde Oostindische Compagnie, the United East India Company, normally known just as the VOC. The company was neither entirely independent nor a government monopoly, but rather a blend of the two. The directors of the company, known as the *Heeren XVII*, the Seventeen Gentlemen, had great freedom of action, but they also had to report regularly to the Dutch Estates General, the ruling organ of the Dutch government that had the right to approve or veto all treaties, alliances, and instructions to the governors of VOC holdings. The VOC exercised a monopoly of trade from the Cape of Good Hope in Africa eastward and enhanced Dutch economic and military power, largely at the expense of Portugal.

In 1598, Philip II, alarmed at the growing strength of the Netherlands, reimposed the embargo of trade with the Dutch, following which the Dutch became more active along the west coast of Africa, exporting gold and ivory. Dutch ships also began to move in greater numbers into the Caribbean and along the coasts of northern South

America and Brazil. Portuguese and Spanish trade with the Dutch was strictly prohibited, but the Iberian governments inadequately supplied their colonial settlements in South America, so settlements remote from governmental control were eager to trade with the English, French, or Dutch. Indians also traded with anyone who could supply their wants and needs, and as early as 1600, the Dutch established fortified trading ports near the mouth of the Amazon River. The Dutch exported from South America a range of goods: silver, sugar, dye-woods, exotic lumber, tobacco, hides, and salt. The latter, formerly obtained from Portugal, was needed in quantities for the important Dutch herring fishery and to set the dyes used in the Dutch textile industries.

The Twelve Years' Truce delayed the formation of a company to deal with trade in the Americas, but when the truce expired, the Dutch promptly chartered the Geoctroyeerde Westindische Compagnie, the Chartered West Indies Company, generally known as the GWC (or in English WIC). Structured much like the VOC, the GWC was governed by the Heeren XIX, the Nineteen Gentlemen, and given control of Dutch trade on the west coast of Africa and the Americas. By the time the GWC was established, the Dutch were already carrying half of Brazil's exports to Europe and had achieved a dominant position in the Brazilian sugar trade, exporting Portuguese sugar to the Netherlands, where it was further refined and exported to much of the rest of Europe. Under GWC direction, the Dutch role in trade to the Americas grew even greater, and the Dutch soon attempted to wrest control of Brazil from the Portuguese and establish their own colony there.

In addition to Dutch traders, Dutch privateers and pirates flourished in the Atlantic, and a favorite target was Portuguese ships carrying products, particularly sugar, from Brazil. One Brazilian source maintained that the Dutch had captured eighty Portuguese ships trading with Brazil during 1625–1626, sixty of which had been captured when fully laden with sugar and other Brazilian products on the return voyage to Portugal.

First Years of the Dutch in Brazil, 1624–1625, 1630–1636

The first Dutch attempt to establish a colony in Brazil came in May 1624, when a GWC expedition of 26 armed ships carrying 3,300 men attacked and easily overwhelmed the Portuguese Brazilian port of Salvador da Bahia de Todos os Santos, generally just called Salvador, in central Brazil. The Dutch, however, underestimated Portuguese resolve and left an inadequately supplied and poorly led garrison. In April 1625, a Portuguese fleet of 52 ships with over 12,500 men appeared at Salvador, and the Dutch quickly surrendered. The Dutch, however, would soon return to Brazil.

In 1628, Piet Pieterzoon Heyn, vice admiral of the GWC, captured almost all the annual Mexican treasure fleet. The fleet carried a little gold, an enormous amount of silver, and a variety of expensive trade goods such as indigo and cochineal, both valued as textile dyes. The share that went to the Dutch government supported the army for eight months, and stockholders in the GWC received two dividends equaling 50 and 25 percent of their investment. The company retained sufficient funds to finance a larger, bolder attempt at turning the Portuguese colonies in Brazil into a Dutch colony.

The Dutch took substantial time to organize the new invasion of Brazil, and they were further delayed by fighting against a Spanish advance in the Netherlands. By the time the fleet sailed, the Portuguese in Brazil were aware it was coming, although the exact target of the anticipated invasion was unknown. Finally, in early 1630, a GWC fleet of sixty-seven ships carrying over seven thousand men attacked the Portuguese at Pernambuco, the richest sugar-producing colony in Brazil. The Spanish royal government had wasted the opportunity to strengthen defenses in Brazil, doing little but issuing orders to the Brazilian Portuguese. The court in Madrid, however, did appoint an able man to the governorship of Pernambuco, Matthias de Albuquerque. He found the situation at Pernambuco desperate even before the Dutch arrived. Many of the fortifications had been dismantled, their materials spirited away for other constructions, and there were only about 200 regular soldiers and 650 unenthusiastic militiamen. He tried to recruit more men and eventually ended up with about two thousand, but most were untrained and many armed with only an ill assortment of hunting guns.

When the Dutch landed they quickly swept Albuquerque's forces away, and in less than three weeks, the Dutch had ended Portuguese resistance in the area and taken control of the capital, Olinda; the important port Recife; and the nearby, strategically located island of António Vaz. After the initial shock, however, Albuquerque was able to rally the previously somnambulant Portuguese. He established fortified camps that halted the Dutch advance and served as bases for retaliatory raids. The strongest base, Arraial do Bom Jesus (Encampment of the Good Jesus), was only three miles from Recife in an easily defensible position deep in a swampy, tropical forest. A violent stalemate ensued that occupied much of 1630 and 1631, each side raiding the other. Both suffered from lack of provisions so extreme that soldiers were close to starvation while awaiting substantial reinforcements from Europe. The Portuguese and Spanish quarreled about their respective contributions in aid of Brazil, and in the Netherlands, the Nineteen Gentlemen and the Estates General were indignant at the continuing military stalemate, undervaluing the fighting spirit of the Portuguese and mistakenly regarding them as weak and irresolute.

In 1631, the Iberian kingdoms sent an armada to Brazil. They first unloaded eight hundred soldiers at Bahia, and then their fleet of fifty-six ships—twenty warships, twelve transports, and twenty-four sugar ships in convoy—steered north toward Pernambuco. The Dutch had sent a much smaller force and met the combined Spanish and Portuguese fleet with only sixteen ships, engaging before they realized the full strength of the opposing fleet. Many of the Iberian ships, however, remained out of the battle, protecting the transports and sugar ships. The main battle involved only about five ships on each side. Two major Dutch ships caught fire and were destroyed, and three of the Iberian fleet were sunk and one captured. Both sides withdrew, but the Dutch ships remained in Brazil while the Iberian fleet sailed back to Spain. In November 1631, the Dutch decided that Olinda, located on rocky hills, could not be readily fortified or defended. They abandoned the town, burning it as they left, and concentrated their defenses around Recife.

In 1632, substantial reinforcements arrived from the Netherlands, and the Dutch took the offensive. The Dutch forces incorporated mercenaries of many origins, including the exiled Polish nobleman Crestofle d'Artischau Arciszewski, who proved himself an intelligent and courageous leader. The Dutch had trouble with his name, spelling it as Arquixofle and similar forms, and the Portuguese found it totally impossible, referring to him commonly as Artichoke. The Dutch found another able commander in the German mercenary Sigismund von Schoppe. Arciszewski and von Schoppe worked together well and listened with respect to a third important commander, Domingo Fernandes Calabar, of Portuguese and Black parentage, who had initially fought for Portugal and had even been wounded in its service. The reason for his defection to the Dutch is unknown, but he was acquainted with the territory intimately and proved an able leader, commanding Dutch, Indians, and former slaves in battle.

Like the Dutch, the Portuguese also recruited foreign mercenaries, and at one point both sides printed leaflets in English and French encouraging the other's mercenaries to defect. The Portuguese were also aided by three hundred Italian troops under the command of Giovanni Vincenzo de San Felice, count of Bagnuoli. Despite evidence that Bagnuoli and his troops conducted themselves credibly on most occasions, they were generally regarded unfavorably by the Portuguese. In particular, the priest Manoel Calado do Salvador, an important source for events, was excessively scornful of Bagnuoli and the Italians. Both sides also employed Indians, African, and Afro-Brazilians, either those who had escaped from slavery or were promised freedom for their service.

The Portuguese continued to resist resolutely, but by the end of 1634, the Dutch gained control of the captaincies of Rio Grande, Itamaraca, and Paraiba, second in productivity only to Pernambuco. As the Dutch won control of the coast, the Portuguese lost the ability to be resupplied by sea. Supply ships had to be unloaded far to the south, and porters carried provisions north on mere footpaths through forests, jungles, and swamps. Much of the provisions were consumed in their transport, and the situation of the Portuguese opposing the Dutch grew ever more desperate. The Spanish and Portuguese monarchy, faced with crises in Europe and the East, as well as three years of drought and famine in Portugal, could do little to relieve the situation in Brazil. As the Dutch advanced their control inland some Portuguese submitted, and others, including many of their troops, retreated to the south. During the retreat, they overwhelmed a small Dutch position and captured and executed Domingo Calabar, who had been so important to the Dutch successes.

Despite Dutch advances, the Portuguese continued to fight, employing guerrilla tactics. Warfare grew increasingly bitter, with both sides burning sugar plantations and farms that might offer aid to their enemies. Colonel Arciszewski, with clearer strategic vision than most of his fellows, argued that the only way to deal with the agile Portuguese guerrillas was a strong campaign to drive them far to the south, but the councilors in charge of the government at Recife were too hesitant to make the effort.

Meantime, another crisis threatened the Dutch effort to colonize Brazil: the GWC was failing financially. Their privateers captured hundreds of Iberian ships, damaging Spain and Portugal significantly, and bringing rich loot back to the Netherlands. The expense of maintaining the naval forces, however, exceeded the worth of the booty, and the value of sugar, dyewood, and other Brazilian products exported to the Netherlands was not enough to finance the war. The Dutch provinces agreed to subsidize the GWC effort in Brazil, but they failed to fulfill their agreements, and the Estates General of the Netherlands lacked the authority to enforce them.

If Dutch Brazil was to survive, an able administrator was needed to execute a bold plan to end the war and stop the financial hemorrhage. The Heeren XIX chose Johan Maurits, count of Nassau-Siegen.

Johan Maurits, Governor of Dutch Brazil, 1637–1641

Johan Maurits van Nassau-Siegen came from one of the most famous noble families in the Netherlands. He was well educated, although the Thirty Years' War interrupted his university attendance. A convinced Protestant but by no means a fanatic, he was very much a man of the Northern Renaissance, interested in the humanities and science. From the age of sixteen, Maurits took part in important campaigns and battles, winning a reputation for intelligence and courage. But he had no experience in colonial matters.

Initially, the GWC and the Estates General hoped to send him to Brazil at the head of a large force, but financial exigency dictated otherwise. The GWC scraped together 12 ships and about 2,700 men to accompany Maurits, and even then, not all could be dispatched at once. Maurits, always impatient, proceeded to Recife with just two ships. There he acted quickly, moving against Porto Calvo to the south, which was garrisoned by the Italians, who soon retreated. Maurits was able to clear all Pernambuco of opposition, extending Dutch control down to the Rio São Francisco, which formed a convenient border between the Portuguese and the Dutch—for the time being.

During 1637, at the invitation of Indian allies, the Dutch invaded the captaincy of Ceará to the north, a relatively poor area exporting primarily cow hides. The Portuguese force in the area was totally inadequate to repel the Dutch advance. That same year, Maurits dispatched Colonel von Schoppen to invade Sergipe to the south, where the overmatched Italian troops offered little resistance before again retreating precipitously. Von Schoppen ravaged Sergipe but did not occupy it permanently. Largely depopulated, it became a no-man's land

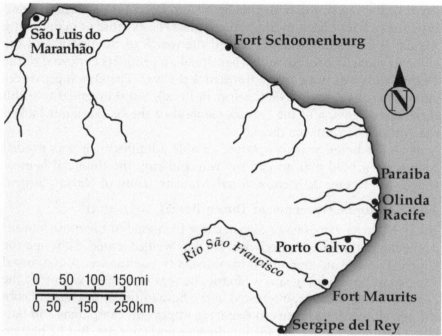

Major towns and forts of Dutch Brazil.

between the opposing forces. These two campaigns provided a safe margin around the rich sugar-producing area controlled by the Dutch, but the center of Portuguese power, Bahia, remained yet unchallenged.

In April 1638, Maurits launched an invasion of Bahia, attacking the one large town and capital, Salvador de Bahia de Todos os Santos. The garrison outnumbered the attackers, and after a bloody battle that left many dead, the Dutch withdrew. The Heeren XIX of the WIC assured Maurits that the Spanish were so heavily engaged against the French and Dutch in Europe that he need not fear any substantial attack, but Maurits was not convinced, and the defeat at Bahia and the reassignment of six hundred troops from Brazil to the West Indies left his force dangerously weak. The Heeren XIX had badly underestimated their enemies. Despite constant quarreling between the Spanish and the Portuguese, the Iberian kingdoms sent an armada of forty-six ships, twenty-six of which were large galleons bearing five thousand troops, against the Dutch in Brazil. This favored the Dutch in two regards. The leader of the Iberian fleet, dom Fernão de Mascarenhas, conde da Torre, was poorly qualified for the post, and when the fleet paused at the Cape Verde islands, disease swept through the troops. About three thousand died or were so ill they had to be left behind. The Conde da Torre rejected the advice of many of his officers to attack Recife immediately and preferred sailing to Bahia in the hope of recruiting more men there. It was Maurits, however, who received reinforcements—1,200 men brought by Arciszewski from the Netherlands. For reasons unknown, Maurits conceived a dislike of Arciszewski and sent him back to the Netherlands, depriving himself of an able commander.

Portrait of Johan Maurits, graaf van Nassau-Siegen, engraved in 1647 by the Dutch artist Pieter Claeszoon Soutman. At that time, Maurits was forty-three years old. The Latin motto surrounding the portrait, *Qua Patet Orbis* may be translated "As Far as the World Extends." This has subsequently become the motto of the Dutch marines. (*New York Public Library*)

Maurits's ships managed to capture a small Portuguese vessel carrying dispatches that revealed the Iberian force was suffering a variety of serious problems. The Conde da Torre was not popular, even accused of cowardice for his failure to attack Recife; provisions were in short supply; disease had again broken out among the troops, many of whom deserted; and discipline rapidly disappeared. Through summer 1639, the Conde da Torre worked to restore order and recruit men as he received supplies from the Azores and from Spanish areas of South America. He also sent guerrillas to positions inland of the Dutch with orders not to attack until he landed troops on the coast, but then to burn all and kill without quarter. Through captured documents and deserters, the Dutch learned of these plans.

In November 1639, the Iberian fleet set out to attack the Dutch. It was an impressive array, consisting of twenty strong galleons, thirty-four armed merchantmen transporting about six thousand troops, and twenty-three smaller ships. The Dutch put to sea with forty-one ships, all smaller than the Spanish and Portuguese grand galleons, and about twelve hundred men drawn from the Recife garrison. The two fleets came together in a desultory five-day battle that cost each side several ships but yielded no decisive victory for either side. During the battle, however, currents and winds drove the fleets north. The Dutch ships were able to return to their port, but the heavy Iberian galleons could not proceed south through adverse winds and weather. They landed about 1,250 troops with orders to find their way back to Bahia through Dutch territory, a march of nearly 1,200 miles. With the aid of Portuguese living in Dutch territory, most troops survived the long march and reached Bahia. Several hundred, however, fell behind because of illness, wounds, or exhaustion. They were slaughtered, just as the Iberian guerrillas and their allies had been ordered to treat the Dutch.

The Conde da Torre abandoned this fleet to their own resources, returning to Bahia in a small vessel. The Iberian fleet scattered, some to the Azores, others to the Portuguese territory of Maranhão, north of the Dutch, and others to Spanish holdings in the Caribbean. Disease decimated the ships's crews, which were already short of food and water when the fleet broke up. Many ships never returned to Spain or Portugal, and those that did suffered many dead. Da Torre returned to Portugal in disgrace.

In Brazil, both the Dutch and the Portuguese received reinforcements and provisions from Europe. A new Portuguese commander arrived in Brazil, dom Jorge da Mascarenhas, marquês da Montalvão, bearing the title of viceroy of Brazil. He and Maurits entered negotiations to end the no-quarter orders issued by both sides, when startling information came from Portugal that Mascarenhas forwarded to Maurits: In December 1640, Portugal revolted against the rule of the Spanish King Philip IV, proclaiming João, duque da Bragança, as King João IV of Portugal. Portugal did not reestablish its independence quickly or easily; war with Spain went on with varying intensity until 1668, but the Portuguese revolt altered the situation in Brazil immediately and profoundly. Portugal could no longer depend on Spanish resources to aid in a war against the Dutch, and, whatever their differences in Brazil and elsewhere, the mutual hostility of the Netherlands and Portugal toward Spain suggested they should resolve their differences and perhaps even form an alliance. The Portuguese quickly proposed a ten-year truce with the Netherlands preliminary to establishing a permanent peace and alliance. The Portuguese also suggested that they

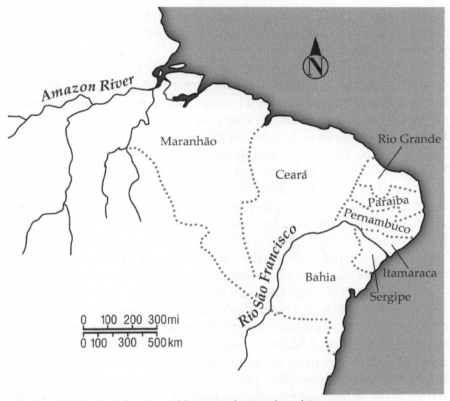

Chief captaincies Brazil contested between the Dutch and Portuguese.

reclaim Brazil by compensating the Dutch to withdraw. After negotiation, a truce to last ten years was agreed on, though the status of Brazil was not addressed in the agreement, and the parties failed to establish a permanent peace.

Among many other provisions, one seemingly innocent stipulation shaped the future relations of the Portuguese and Dutch and the future of Brazil. The truce began immediately in Europe, but in Brazil, Africa, and the East Indies, the truce would become operative when proof of its ratification by both nations reached those regions. Dutch leaders in the Netherlands sent orders to Maurits to move aggressively against the Portuguese before formal ratification reached Brazil, but the orders were not necessary as Maurits had already begun to do so on his own authority. The Dutch sent munitions to Portugal, and Dutch and Portuguese soldiers fought side by side in Europe, but in Brazil, Maurits coolly invaded and occupied Sergipe, left largely unoccupied since Von Schoppen devastated the captaincy.

Maurits did not feel his forces were sufficient to assault Bahia successfully but moved against a distant target that would both damage the Portuguese and benefit Dutch Brazil. Sugar production depended on African slaves, and Maurits sent a naval expedition to conquer São Paulo da Assumpção de Loanda on the coast of Angola, the chief slave market for the Portuguese and Spanish in Africa. The Dutch already had a port, Elmina, on the African coast, but the slaves available there were fewer in number and less tractable than the people taken from the Bantus to the south. The Dutch force of twenty-one ships and about three thousand men, including a contingent of Brazilian Indians, took Loanda with ease and went on to capture the islands of Anobam and São Thomé and Axim on the Guinea coast of Africa from the Portuguese before climate and disease put an end to the expedition.

Official notification of the truce had still not been received in Brazil late in 1641, although knowledge of it was common, when Maurits dispatched forces to conquer Maranhão to the north. The area fell easily to the Dutch, and Maurits now controlled half of all the settled areas of Brazil. The truce between the Netherlands and Portugal was finally formally announced in July 1642. Dutch advances in Brazil and Africa made before the formal announcement may have been technically legal, but they certainly were less than honorable, violated the spirit of the truce, and doomed any possibility of an alliance between the Netherlands and Portugal and any possibility of a peaceful settlement in Brazil. The old and brutal proverb "No peace beyond the line" again proved true.

The Internal Administration of Johan Maurits, Governor of Dutch Brazil, 1637–1644

Johan Maurits quickly developed a great love for Brazil, proclaiming it the most beautiful place in the world, and he intended to proclaim its wealth and attractions to the entire world. He imported a corps of artists, craftsmen, and scientists to study and publicize this new world so little known in Europe. Maurits's scholars made collections and classified the flora and fauna of Brazil, studied its geography, recorded meteorological data, and investigated diseases endemic in the region and their treatments, while artists sketched and painted local inhabitants of every sort and recorded local life. Some of this material was published during Maurits's lifetime, and other material remains in the great museums of Europe. The studies of Brazil sponsored by Maurits remained the standard works on that country into the nineteenth century and still offer the investigator valuable material today.

Maurits also built a new city adjoining Recife on the island of António Vaz, which he connected by means of a long bridge that remained in use into the nineteenth century. He carefully laid out the new city, called Mauritsstad. Streets were paved, and the town was serviced by two intersecting canals, enabling convenient movement of provisions and goods. Frequent bridges over the canals enabled convenient movement on land. Maurits erected his own home there, an impressive building suitable to his rank and status, important for impressing Portuguese and Dutch alike. He surrounded his palace with extensive gardens containing Brazilian and foreign fruit trees and flowering plants and an equally impressive collection of animals of all sorts native to Brazil.

From the beginning of his administration, Maurits attempted to reconcile those Portuguese who remained in the Dutch territory, promising them peace, freedom of worship with their own clergy (excluding Jesuits), security of property, the right to bear arms, and reduced taxes in exchange for swearing loyalty to the Dutch. Many submitted, but tensions predictably remained high. Maurits also increased law and order in Recife, turning what had been a rough garrison town into a well-regulated port and business center, although corruption among minor officials and judges continued to bedevil Maurits. That was perhaps unavoidable. Recife had become an expensive boom town, and the wages of minor GWC officials were grossly inadequate. Corrupt minor officials proved to be one of the major grievances of Portuguese residents in Dutch Brazil.

Trade prospered under Maurits, but a controversy arose between advocates of free trade and the GWC that wanted to enforce a monopoly. The GWC argued that it was bearing all the expenses of the continuing war against the Portuguese, and indeed faced the prospect of financial ruin, and thus required and deserved the profits from trade with Brazil. Free traders argued that a GWC monopoly would make it impossible to reconcile the Portuguese to Dutch rule and discourage migration, which would be necessary for the long-term survival and prosperity of Dutch Brazil. A compromise of sorts allowed free trading but required that exports be carried on GWC ships, which earned freight charges, convoy tax, and other fees. The GWC also retained a trade monopoly in certain commodities: dyewoods, munitions, and, ominously, slaves. Like most compromises, it satisfied no one.

Despite dissatisfaction about trade rules, sugar production began to revive in Dutch Brazil after 1635, and with it came the demand for African slaves to harvest the sugarcane and work the labor-intensive sugar mills. Dutch clergy exhibited some initial opposition to the slave trade and insisted on humane treatment. But such sentiments were soon forgotten, and Dutch slave traders in Africa and plantation owners in Brazil proved just as ruthless as other nationalities.

Religion in Dutch Brazil

While the Netherlands and Dutch Brazil have long been celebrated for their religious tolerance during the seventeenth century, recent scholarship has shown that all was far from ideal. Dutch Brazil was a cacophony of religions. Portuguese Catholics despised Dutch Calvinists as hell-bound heretics, while the Dutch Protestants similarly regarded the Catholics as doomed minions of Satan. Both loathed Jews, who had no reason to hold Christians of any sort in high regard. Sadly, Dutch Brazil was at the same time the most tolerant area inhabited by Europeans anywhere in the world.

Johan Maurits, though by personal conviction a sincere Dutch Calvinist, recognized that the Portuguese would never be reconciled to Dutch rule unless granted freedom of religion. Maurits also had a personal commitment, rare in the seventeenth century, to tolerance. He certainly went to extraordinary lengths to reconcile Catholic clergy to his administration and even invited one priest, Father Manuel Calado, to live in his palace. The priest declined but lived close to Maurits and often consulted with him. Maurits's tolerant attitude toward Catholicism outraged the Calvinist clergy in the Netherlands, whose followers were prominent among the leadership of the GWC. Maurits's reply to the chorus of complaints from the intolerant clergy revealed him as a master of administrative bureaucracy. He repeatedly promised to curb all unauthorized Catholic activities but did nothing. Maurits's commitment to the peaceful coexistence of Protestants and Catholics was not shared by all in Brazil, and tensions between the two groups remained significant, as indeed did disagreements between fanatics and moderates within each group.

On one matter, most Protestants and Catholics agreed: their dislike and contempt for Jews. The Jewish community in Dutch Brazil was overwhelmingly Sephardic. Some had migrated from the Iberian kingdoms to the Netherlands and from there to Brazil, while many had been forcibly converted to Catholicism in Portugal and had subsequently migrated to Brazil. The latter were known in Spain, Portugal, and throughout Latin America as New Christians or *conversos*. New Christians were subject to constant scrutiny by Old Christians and the Inquisition. The slightest suspicion could result in charges of crypto-Jewish worship considered heresy by the Catholic Church. Even baseless accusations by personal enemies or business rivals could result in imprisonment, torture, and death by fire. Many Portuguese New Christians returned to the Jewish faith in Dutch Brazil, and Jews proved resolute supporters of the Dutch regime, serving in the military and offering their goods and money in support.

In the Netherlands, the Dutch extended freedom of conscience and freedom of religious worship to Jews, although Jews remained largely segregated, subject to prejudice, and condemned by fanatic Calvinists. Jews in Brazil, who were more integrated in society, enjoyed similar protections, although regulations remained against Jews openly criticizing Christianity, or opening their stores or schools or having their slaves work on Sundays.

Despite prejudice, Jews in Dutch Brazil took part in most areas of society. Some purchased or developed sugar plantations, owned stores, and served in the army or navy. Many Jews in Brazil who came from the Netherlands knew both Portuguese and Dutch, while few Dutch knew Portuguese and virtually no Brazilian Portuguese spoke Dutch. Jews fluent in both languages could deal with both communities, and some bought sugar from the Portuguese and resold it to Dutch exporters. They also served as translators and important intermediaries between the two communities, but toleration of Jews was often based only on pragmatic need of their trade connections and linguistic abilities. As Dutch Christians in Brazil learned the Portuguese language, the intermediary role of Jews became less vital. Christians then complained that Jews were too prominent in the sugar trade and sought regulation to suppress them.

For three years, 1642–1645, the Jewish community in Recife was led by Isaac Aboab da Fonseca. He was born in Portugal in 1605 into a Jewish family that had been forcibly converted to Christianity. The family moved to Amsterdam when he was seven and there returned to Judaism. He studied Judaism with prominent scholars and so excelled that he was appointed rabbi for Beth Israel, one of three congregations in Amsterdam. In 1642, Aboab, as he was generally known, migrated to Recife, where he became the spiritual leader, *hakham*, of Recife's synagogue Kahal Zur Israel (Rock of Israel), the first synagogue in the Americas, established in 1636. Aboab was a powerful speaker, scholar, poet, and much-beloved leader. The Recife Jewish community also had two religious schools, the Talmud Torah and Etz Hayim, and a Jewish cemetery.

The Loss of Dutch Brazil, 1642–1654

Despite the dishonorable conquests in Brazil and Africa before the Dutch-Portuguese cease-fire was announced, the truce went into effect formally in 1642. The GWC, bled white financially by the expenses of war in Brazil and by Johan Maurits's lavish administration, sought to trim costs. In 1643, the Heeren XIX ordered him recalled and reduced the number of troops in Brazil significantly. Maurits was genuinely popular with all groups in Brazil, even the Portuguese, who saw him as their defender against radical Dutch Calvinists, and his departure was mourned by all.

The Dutch hold on Brazil seemed relatively secure, relying on their unquestioned naval superiority and, even more importantly, the evident weakness of Portugal, but both sides suffered from vulnerabilities. The Netherlands revolted against Spain at least in part because of Spanish attempts to abolish medieval provincial and municipal rights and privileges. The government of the Dutch Republic had to respect those same rights, but those very rights weakened the government. The Dutch Republic was oligarchic with a diffused structure that inhibited quick and decisive action. Each of the seven provinces was dominated by the local elite, composed of the traditional aristocratic families and the wealthy merchants, often closely aligned and intermarried. Although called the United Provinces, the provinces exercised a large degree of independence. Interprovince rivalries and jealousies were frequent and enduring. Holland was by far the largest and richest province and sometimes allied with Zeeland, the other primarily maritime province. The five inland provinces had different economic and defense concerns and were often united in opposition to Holland and Zeeland, which were not above intimidation of the poorer provinces.

Resolutions had to be referred to each provincial assembly, and no general resolution could be passed unless there was unanimous approval. Even if a province agreed to a resolution, there was no means to enforce its adherence, and provinces frequently defaulted on their promises. Repeatedly, provinces pledged money to support the GWC in its efforts to hold Brazil, only to fail to fulfill their pledges on time, or entirely.

The organization of the GWC paralleled and imitated that of the Dutch Republic. Each province had a chamber of the GWC that provided its own capital for trading, managed its own shipping, and controlled its own finances. Rivalry and jealously among the chambers were common, and the Herren XIX, who were supposed to coordinate policies and responses to events, could not overrule provincial chambers that refused to agree with them. Delay and inefficiency characterized the GWC response to crises.

King Joo IV of Portugal was often accused of passivity and even timidity, but in fact he carefully and intelligently dealt with daunting difficulties. Portugal, with a much smaller population than Spain and fewer military resources, would have had little hope of retaining its independence if Spain were not preoccupied with hostilities against the Netherlands and France. Joo IV needed an alliance with the Dutch in Europe to preserve Portuguese independence and so had to endure aggressive Dutch behavior elsewhere. Even in colonial matters, Joo IV was more concerned with protecting valuable enclaves in India, Ceylon, and even farther east than with Brazil.

Events in Brazil were not driven by decisions taken in the Netherlands or in Lisbon, but rather by the Portuguese in Brazil. In 1642, the Portuguese in Maranhão, captured by the Dutch the previous year, revolted. Desultory warfare went on well into 1643 before the Dutch withdrew from the area. The success encouraged Portuguese elsewhere. While leading Portuguese planters in Dutch Brazil were the first to plot revolt, Antonio Telles da Silva, who became governor of Bahia in August 1642, was the principal figure behind the Portuguese uprising. All indications are that he acted without the knowledge of the royal government in Lisbon.

In early 1645, Telles da Silva dispatched a force of loyal Afro-Brazilians to the hinterlands of Dutch Brazil, spreading the report that they had deserted the Portuguese. He then sent allied Brazilian Indians ostensibly to track down the deserters. Instead, they joined forces and awaited the arrival of Portuguese Brazilian troops. The Dutch were initially suspicious of these actions, and soon reports led to alarm among administrators, who appealed to the homeland to send men and munitions. After a few minor skirmishes between the Portuguese guerrillas and Dutch forces, the Dutch withdrew from much of the countryside to the area around Recife and Mauritsstadt, where they constructed strong points surrounding the two contiguous towns. The Dutch also continued to hold fortified posts along the coast.

Most of the Portuguese who lived on plantations in the countryside initially hesitated to join in the revolt, waiting to see which side was likely to prevail, but two events alienated the Portuguese from the Dutch and strengthened the rebellion. The Dutch had long allied with the fierce Tapuya Indians from the interior, who attacked and massacred Portuguese residents in the Rio Grande region without regard for age or gender. The Dutch administration proclaimed this was done without their knowledge or connivance, but the claim was met with Portuguese skepticism. Henceforth atrocities became common on both sides. The second event was the Battle of Monte das Tabocas. There some four hundred Dutch troops, largely mercenaries, and three hundred Brazilian Indian allies attacked a Portuguese force of about one thousand led by João Fernandes Vieira. Vieira had initially risen from humble origins to a position of power in Dutch Brazil, even becoming a member of the town council of Mauritsstad. He accumulated power and property but even more debt before changing sides and becoming a leader of the rebellion. At Monte das Tabocas, the Portuguese enjoyed a numerical superiority and the advantage of a good defensive position on the high ground, but they were poorly equipped and had few firearms. The battle went on for a full day before the Dutch retreated during the night, leaving behind about two hundred dead. The Portuguese victory led to the spread of the revolt among those who were previously reluctant to join, and henceforth the Dutch were on the defensive.

As the war progressed, the Portuguese dominated on land, forcing the surrender of about 270 Dutch troops and some Indian allies at Casa Forte. The Portuguese gave the Dutch quarter but massacred the Indians. The Portuguese also forced the surrender of many of the Dutch coastal posts. At sea, the Dutch had one success, destroying a convoy of Portuguese transports, but by the end of 1645, the Portuguese had recovered almost all of Brazil, except the area immediately around Recife and a couple of Dutch coastal positions that managed to hold out.

When news of the revolt in Brazil reached Europe, the reactions of the Portuguese monarchy and the Dutch Republic were quite different. Portugal was still nominally at war with Spain, and King Joo IV was conscious of the continuing weakness of his position. The population and wealth of Portugal was much less than that of Spain, and Spanish hostilities with the Netherlands were in large part responsible for preventing Spain from turning the full weight of its forces against Portugal. It was important that Joo IV take no action that would end the Portuguese truce with the Dutch and perhaps drive the Dutch to some reconciliation with Spain. Opinion was divided among the Portuguese elite between those who wanted open support of the Brazilian revolt and those who, more concerned with the precarious position of Portugal in Europe, argued for caution. Joo IV, striving to maintain the truce with the Netherlands, informed the Dutch that he had not authorized the revolt and was taken unaware by it. The Dutch were unconvinced.

In the Netherlands, news of the revolt was greeted by a resolution to send a strong force of ships and men to Brazil, but the decentralized structure of the Dutch Republic soon manifested itself. As the initial enthusiasm waned and the individual provinces counted costs, pledged funds came in late, in lesser amounts, or not at all. It proved difficult to recruit mercenaries to serve in Brazil, and winter 1645-46 was so bitter and stormy that forces could not be dispatched to Brazil until May 1646, and even then, the number of ships and men that arrived in Brazil were inadequate to deal effectively with the rebellion.

In Brazil, the Dutch and their mercenaries demolished Maurits's palace and gardens and many other buildings in Mauritsstadt to provide clear fields of fire against the Portuguese besieging Recife and Mauritsstadt. The Dutch defenders, cut off from the resources of the hinterland and inadequately supplied from the Netherlands, began to starve. Just as provisions were on the verge of utter exhaustion in July 1646, ships arrived from the Netherlands with supplies. One can get an appreciation of the relief felt by the besieged from an emotional poem written in Hebrew by Rabbi Aboad da Fonseca, but the aid failed to alter the basic situation. Other ships from the Netherlands arrived in August and through autumn, but the Dutch in Brazil were still closely besieged and dependent on uncertain support from the Netherlands.

Despite João Fernandes Vieira's leadership in the early phases of the revolt, many of his fellow insurrectionists criticized him sharply. They had not forgotten his early enthusiastic support of the Dutch and did not trust him, claiming he had supported the revolt solely to avoid his debts. His critics also claimed that he extorted money from the inhabitants in the territory he controlled and took loot from the Dutch for his own benefit. The Portuguese in Brazil were also running short of money, munitions, and men. In Portugal during 1647, King João IV suppressed the accusations against Vieira but appointed a new commander of the revolt in Brazil, Francisco Barreto de Menezes, and dispatched him with some aid for the revolutionaries—far too little, however, to be decisive. Barreto was a young officer whose experience was limited to command of a cavalry regiment, but he would prove a good choice. His early experience, however, was painful and discouraging. While still at sea, Zeeland privateers attacked the Portuguese ships, and Barreto was severely wounded and taken captive to Recife. There he slowly recovered, and in 1648, he managed a daring escape along with two comrades and made his way to the revolutionaries. He duly became commander with the title *mestre de campo general*, master of the camp general, and relied on João Fernandes Vieira and André Vidal de Negreiros as his chief subordinates.

As the war continued, the Dutch sought to make landings along the coastline now held mainly by the Portuguese and at one point even threatened the Portuguese hold on Bahia. The income from Brazilian sugar, exported through Bahia, was vital for the war effort in Brazil and for financing the army and navy in Portugal. Had the Dutch been able to take Bahia, they would have won the war.

In April 1648, the Dutch commander in Brazil, Sigismund von Schoppe, was determined to break the siege of Recife by forcing a decisive battle against the Portuguese. The First Battle of Guararapes is named after a group of rugged hills where the confrontation took place. The Dutch troops, whose pay was long overdue, were demoralized and inexperienced in fighting in a tropical climate, while the Portuguese were badly outnumbered and poorly equipped. The battle, much of which was fought at close quarters, raged from early morning until about noon, when combat broke off. After nightfall, the Dutch retreated, leaving behind about 500 dead, including 48 officers, and they suffered over 550 wounded. The Portuguese admitted to about 400 wounded but only 80 dead, which seems suspiciously low. The siege of Recife went on.

The Dutch threat to Bahia led the Dutch and Portuguese to prepare major expeditions in the hope of winning a decisive victory. In Portugal, Joo IV made the maximum effort by sending the Armada Real, the royal fleet, to Brazil, virtually denuding Portugal of naval forces. The weakness of Portugal, however, is revealed in the small size of the Armada Real: just eight galleons, two frigates, three armed merchant ships, and two caravels, manned by about one thousand sailors and carrying fewer than three thousand troops. Subsequently, seven more ships, several under charter from English owners, carried another six hundred troops.

The Dutch prepared a fleet incorporating both GWC and Estates General ships, but they encountered the usual problems: disagreements among the provinces, failure to provide pledged funds, difficulties in recruiting troops, and harsh winter weather that delayed the dispatch of forces. In the Netherlands, the provinces of Holland and Zeeland, formerly close allies, disagreed bitterly over peace proposals made to Spain, and the VOC, forced to contribute to the defense of Brazil, quarreled with the GWC about respective rights and obligations. The GWC, deeply in debt, did all it could to reduce the expenses, but as a result the troops arrived in Brazil weakened and diseased, poorly armed, and dispirited.

The Portuguese fleet commander had been ordered to land the troops and then conserve the Armada Real by acting only on the defensive, so he anchored his fleet where it was protected by land batteries. The Dutch fleet raged helplessly at sea, accomplishing nothing of significance. At one point, the fleet landed troops who ravaged territory normally controlled by the Portuguese, burning sugar mills and looting, but the damage was ultimately of little importance to the outcome of the war. Privateers chiefly from the Dutch province of Zeeland did much greater damage to the Portuguese than the combined fleet of the GWC and the Estates General. In 1647 and 1648, the Portuguese lost 220 ships engaged in the Brazil trade to pirates and privateers, mainly to the Zeelanders. Most of the ships were caravels, small ships, but every capture entailed the loss of ship and cargo, a blow to Portuguese ship owners and Brazilian sugar growers. The Portuguese were able to send ships and men to Africa where they recaptured São Paulo da Assumpção de Loanda on the coast of Angola, but that was of little immediate significance to Dutch Brazil. The port was an important slave mart, but there was no demand for slaves in tightly besieged Recife.

Again, the Dutch sought to break the Portuguese siege, leading to the Second Battle of Guararapes. The Dutch force, consisting of a little over 3,000 European troops, 200 Brazilian Indians, and about 250 sailors manning about half a dozen light artillery pieces, occupied the Guararapes hills without opposition and took up position on the top of a prominent rise. The Portuguese advanced with about 2,600 men, occupying swamps and uncultivated wooded and brushy land around the foot of the hill. The Dutch hoped they could provoke the Portuguese to attack them on the high ground, but the Portuguese remained in their position while the Dutch sweltered in the sun on the bare hilltop. In the midafternoon, punished by heat and thirst, the Dutch began to retreat, falling into a Portuguese ambush. Dutch resistance soon broke and became a general rout. The Dutch lost 957 dead and 89 captives. Among the slain were about 100 officers, including the Dutch commander and the second in command of the fleet, who led the naval contingent. The Portuguese claimed they suffered only about 250 casualties, mostly wounded.

Even before the news of the disaster reached the Netherlands, the Dutch Republic was deeply divided about the policy to be followed in Brazil and, more profoundly, about the governance of the republic itself. Prowar and propeace parties argued, and within each group there were divisions about how best to achieve goals. Monarchist and Republican elements contended within the Netherlands, and Holland, the richest and most populous of the provinces, sought to assume a dominant position. Moreover, relations between the Dutch Republic and England were rapidly deteriorating, and war between the two nations seemed a real possibility. The flow of provisions to Brazil was infrequent and insufficient.

At Recife, soldiers, sailors, and civilians again faced starvation. Men deserted, and sailors seized one of the fleet's warships and sailed back to Holland. Civilians left Brazil in large numbers. Jews could only anticipate the worst if the Portuguese prevailed, and by 1648, half of their number left Dutch Brazil. The condition of the Dutch fleet, long at sea or in harbor in tropical waters, rapidly deteriorated. In 1649, the admiral took it upon himself to sail for the Netherlands with his two best ships. On other ships, sailors of the fleet mutinied and forced their officers to sail for home. By the end of 1649, the Portuguese Armada Real, although also deteriorating, was the only significant naval force in Brazilian waters.

During that same year, the Portuguese founded the Companhia Geral para o Estado do Brasil, the General Company for the State of Brazil, generally called the Brazil Company, a trading company established on the model of the VOC and GWC. The company commenced to raise funds for the Portuguese cause in Brazil and instituted a convoy system to protect shipping. In November 1649, the Brazil Company dispatched an enormous fleet of eighteen warships and sixty-six merchant ships to Brazil. Some of the ships were newly launched, others purchased, and a number chartered from English owners. Once the fleet arrived, it followed the pattern established by earlier Portuguese fleets, assuming a defensive position rather than cooperating with the land forces besieging Recife.

In 1651, the ten-year truce between the Netherlands and Portugal expired. Some Dutch, particularly the more fanatical Calvinists, piratical Zeelanders, and shareholders in the GWC, urged the immediate declaration of war against Portugal, but others who were engaged in active trade with Portugal and Brazil were adamantly opposed. It may seem surprising now that while the Portuguese and Dutch were at war in Brazil, Dutch merchants were routinely engaged in trade with Portugal and even with the Portuguese in Brazil, but it surprised no one in the seventeenth century. Then it was a common saying that the Dutch would trade with the devil in hell if they could find a way to avoid burning their ships' sails. Any question of a declaration of war against Portugal was, however, quickly forgotten in 1652, when war broke out between England and the Netherlands, provoked by the increasing trade competition between the two nations, particularly in the East Indies, and the rise of mercantilism.

The war against England occupied the Dutch warships, as they provided protection for convoys, defended the Netherlands, and fought epic sea battles, but the Dutch lacked naval resources to fight the English and simultaneously send a strong fleet to Brazil. They did continue to send supply ships to Recife, which arrived irregularly but in sufficient numbers to feed the colony. This provided an opportunity for the Portuguese; the Brazil Company raised money for another convoy for Brazil. Most of the sixty ships in the new convoy were transports, but several strong galleons accompanied and protected them. Shortly after the arrival of the Brazilian Company's fleet at Bahia early in 1652, Dutch warships at Recife departed for the Netherlands without waiting for the arrival of any replacements. Most had been in Brazilian waters since 1650, and wooden ships deteriorate quickly in tropical waters. If they had not left, they soon would have become useless.

The Dutch had little concern about leaving Recife without strong naval protection. The Portuguese fleets had consistently remained on the defensive in Brazil and seemed no threat. This time, however, the Portuguese had determined that the fleet would take an aggressive role. The Brazil Company fleet with the addition of some serviceable ships already at Bahia appeared off Recife on December 20, 1653. On land, the besiegers faced difficulties: some had served since 1645, war weariness had long since set in, and they were chronically short of provisions and armaments. Two factors, however, bolstered their confidence: the appearance of the Portuguese fleet and the presence of a French military engineer who had come with the fleet. He instructed the besiegers in constructing approaches to the Dutch strong points, which began to surrender one after the other.

Within Recife, the Dutch forces were dispirited and demoralized. Many had been stranded in Brazil long beyond their contracted period of service, and their pay was chronically in arrears. They were further intimidated by the Portuguese fleet and by the sudden sophistication of the besiegers. No effective resistance could be mounted against the steady advance of the Portuguese forces on land, and there was no hope of succor by sea. On January 22, 1654, the Dutch asked for a parley and signed surrender documents four days later. Two days later, Francisco Barreto entered Recife with his troops.

One Dutch officer escaped from Recife by night just before the surrender and spread word to the Dutch garrisons to the north, causing fears that the Portuguese would massacre the Dutch. Thoroughly alarmed, the northern garrisons and Dutch population in the area seized ships and fled to the Caribbean. Their fears were unfounded. Despite the long and bloody war, the Portuguese behaved with utmost chivalry and courtesy. Barreto and his subordinates so controlled their troops that there was no looting or even insults toward the conquered, and the terms of surrender were generous. Any Dutch who chose could remain in Brazil as Portuguese subjects. Protestants were guaranteed freedom of conscience, though open Protestant worship was prohibited. The same offer was extended to Jews, but none decided to remain, reasonably apprehensive about the eventual appearance of the Inquisition. Those who wished to leave could take their possessions or avail themselves of three months in which to sell possessions before leaving.

The Dutch were permitted to retain sufficient cannons to defend their ships on the return to the Netherlands. The Dutch effort to colonize Brazil was at an end, but diplomatic wrangling would long endure.

Aftermath

The fall of Dutch Brazil in 1654 coincided closely with the end of the First Anglo-Dutch War, freeing Dutch naval resources. In the Netherlands, strong forces urged the declaration of war against Portugal and the invasion of Bahia or the blockade of Lisbon, the capital, chief port, and trade center of Portugal. Dutch action was, however, temporarily preempted by a crisis in the Baltic between Denmark and Sweden. Baltic trade was vital to the Netherlands, far more so than Brazil. King João IV died in 1656, leaving a three-year-old heir and his queen as regent. Often accused of timidity and indecisiveness, João IV was rather realistically conscious of Portugal's weakness in confrontation with Spain and the Netherlands, despite which he was able to maneuver successfully to preserve the independence of his nation.

Easing of the Baltic crisis led to renewed Dutch pressure on Portugal, demanding restoration of Portuguese reconquests in Brazil and Africa. The queen regent rejected the Dutch demands, and the Netherlands declared war in October 1657. France and England feared that Dutch naval power would lead to the fatal weakening of Portugal with profound consequences, contrary to their interests. Spain would be able to reconquer Portugal, and the Netherlands would be enriched by the acquisitions in Brazil and Africa. France and England pressured both parties to make peace. There was virtually no fighting, and negotiations to end the war began in 1658, although it took until 1662 to reach an accord, formally enacted in 1663. Portugal agreed to pay the Netherlands four million cruzados, a substantial sum, over sixteen years as an indemnity for the loss of Brazil and granted the Dutch trade privileges in Portugal and the Portuguese overseas possessions. The indemnity was onerous, and Portugal was not able to make the final payment until the first years of the eighteenth century.

The GWC continued to flounder after the loss of Brazil. In 1664, the English seized the GWC's colony of New Amsterdam and renamed it New York. In view of the continuing decline of the company and its difficulty in paying its debts, the Dutch Estates General restructured it in 1674 under a new charter, after which the "new" GWC engaged mainly in the slave trade from West Africa. The company was never truly prosperous, but it survived until 1792, when the Dutch government took it over. The Portuguese Brazil Company, Companhia Geral para o Estado do Brasil, was taken over by the Portuguese government in 1657 and transformed into the Junta do Comércio, in 1662.

Most Dutch returned from Brazil to the Netherlands, but some settled on the Wild Coast (modern Surinam, Guyana, and French Guyana), others on the islands of the Caribbean. They brought with them knowledge they had acquired in Brazil of how to refine sugar. The demand for fine white sugar was great, and it brought a much higher price than brown sugar. These new sources of refined sugar competed with the Brazilian product and reduced the role of Brazil in the international sugar market

Most of the Jewish population of Dutch Brazil returned to the Netherlands, but some went to locations in the Americas and the Caribbean, including Surinam, where they developed a colony, Jodensavanne (Dutch for Jewish Savanna) that long thrived until changing economic conditions led to its end. Others went to various islands in the Caribbean, where they, like the Dutch, spread knowledge they had acquired in Brazil about the production of sugar of high quality. One group migrated to New Amsterdam in North America, the first Jews to settle in what would become New York.

When the Jewish community left Brazil after the fall of Recife, the first synagogue in the Americas, Kahal Zur Israel, closed. Some of its records still exist, carried to Amsterdam by refugees. The building that housed the synagogue was put to other uses, gradually becoming dilapidated until it was torn down early in the twentieth century and a new building erected on the site. In recent years, that building was removed and archaeologists discovered the foundations and even the mikveh, the ritual bath, of the original structure. The synagogue has now been rebuilt. The details of the original upper portions have, of course, not been preserved, but they have been reconstructed based on other surviving contemporary Sephardic synagogues. The handsome building is again a place of worship and pilgrimage.

One can cite many reasons that Portugal eventually managed to defeat the attempt to turn Brazil into a Dutch colony. Both the Dutch Republic and Portugal suffered from profound vulnerabilities, and the conflict went on so long because these weaknesses tended to offset one another.

Two factors, however, are frequently underrated: The Dutch conquests in the interval between the truce of 1640 and the proclamation of the truce in the colonies profoundly offended the Portuguese sense of honor and made any accommodation with the Dutch virtually impossible, and the Dutch, judging based on conflicts with Portuguese in the East Indies, radically underestimated the military prowess of the Brazilian Portuguese, who were fighting for their homes. It was not until about 1648 that the Dutch began to realize they were fighting men who were their equal and better motivated.

Every nation forms the narrative of its own history, and the account of resisting and overcoming the Dutch invasion makes up an important part of the Brazilian narrative.

Sources

The sources relevant to the Dutch attempt to establish their colonial hold on Brazil are exceptionally rich. The Algemeen Rijksarchief at The Hague holds manuscripts of the WGC, although many of the records were destroyed in 1674 when the company was rechartered. Arquivo Historico Ultramarino (formerly Arquivo Colonial) at Lisbon is the primary repository for the Portuguese archival material on the Dutch period, and the Revista Gabinete de Estudos Ultamarinos, Biblioteca Nacional, Rio de Janeiro, holds the Brazilian manuscript material, some of which is found in Archivo Nacional do Brasil (Rio de Janeiro) and Bibliotheca Nacional de Brasil (Rio de Janeiro), *Documentos Historicos*, published beginning in 1928.

Four printed works have long been recognized as basic to the history of Dutch efforts in Brazil. Johannes de Laet, *Historie ofte Iaelyck Verhael van der Geoctroveerde West-Indische Compagnie* (Leiden: Bonaventuer ende Abraham Elsevier, 1644) covers the GWC from first organizational efforts in 1621 until 1636. De Laet was an important scholar of great ability and wide-ranging interests. At one time he was a member of the Heeren XIX and had access to documents many of which do not now exist. Caspar van Barle, *Rerum per octennium in Brasilia et albi nuper gestarum, sub praefectura Illustrissimi Comitis I, Mavritii Nassoviae &c. Comitis, nunc Vasaliae Gubernatoris e Equitatus Federatorum Belgii Ordd, sub Auriaco Ductoris, historia* (Amsterdam: Ioannis Blaeu, 1647) continues De Laet's work, covering the governorship of Johann Maurits. The Latin text of Van Barle's work was later reprinted, and the work was also translated into German, but these later editions omitted portions of the original text and should not be trusted. Like De Laet, Van Barle had access to documents not now extant, but he was a less objective writer. Van Barle deeply admired Maurits, although he went to great lengths to be fair to others, such as Colonel Crestofle d'Artischau Arciszewski, whom he quotes at length. Arciszewski's own writings supplement Van Barle's account: "Missive van den kolonnel Artichofsky aan Graaf Maurits en den Hoogen Raad in Brazilië, 24 Juli 1637," *Kroniek Historisch Genootschap Utrecht* (1869), 25:222-248; "Memorie door den kilonnel Artichofsky, bij zijn vertrek uit Brazilië in 1637 overgeleverd aan Gref Maurits en zijnen Geheimen Raad," *Kroniek Historisch Genootschap Utrecht* (1869), 25:253-349; "Apologie van Artichofsky tegen de beschuldiging vanden Raad van Brazilië, ingeleverd aan de Staten Generaal in Augustus 1639," *Kroniek Historisch Genootschap Utrecht* (1869), 25:351-392.

Johannes Hendrik Nieuhof, *Gedenkweedige Brasiliaense zee- en lantreize. Behelzende al het geen op dezelve is voorgevalle, beneffens een bondige beschrijving van gantsch Neerlants Brasil* (Amsterdam: Jacob van Meurs, 1682) provides an excellent account of Dutch Brazil from the time of Maurits's departure in 1644 until 1647, much of which he witnessed himself. Nieuhof remained in Brazil until 1649, but he was killed in Madagascar in 1672, apparently before he could complete the text. The work does contain a much inferior and often confused account of the years 1648 and 1649, apparently hastily composed from Nieuhof's notes by an inferior hand.

Hendrik Haecxs was a Dutch merchant and trader who lived in Recife before returning to the Netherlands. The Heeren XIX appointed him one of four councilors who along with a president were to govern Dutch Brazil after the departure of Maurits. Haecxs kept a journal covering the years 1645 to 1654, which was published in S. P. L'Honoré Naber, ed., "Het Dagboek van Hendrik Haecxs, lid van den Hoogen Raad van Brazilië, 1645-1654," *Bijdragen en Mededeelingen van het Historisch Genootschap gevestigd te Utrecht* 46 (1925):126-311. Despite some lacunae when Haecxs failed to make notations in his daybook, the work is important for understanding the last years of Dutch Brazil and the many rivalries and divisions in Dutch society in the homeland and Brazil. Leeuw van Aitzema, *Historie of Verhael saken van staet en oorlogh in ende omtrent de Vereenigde Nederlanden*, 7 vols. (The Hague: I. Veely, 1657–1671) is one of the basic sources for Dutch history in the seventeenth century. Its coverage of the Dutch in Brazil is uneven but at points important.

Among important Portuguese eyewitness accounts, the following are particularly interesting:

Duarte de Albuquerque Coelho, marques de Basto, *Memorias Diarias de la Guerra del Brasil, par discurso de nueve años, empeçandos desde el de M.D.C.XXX* (Madrid: Diego Diaz de la Carrera, Impressor del Reyno, 1654) provides a fascinating account of the first years of the confrontation between the Dutch and Portuguese. The author was the *donatário* (developer) of Pernambuco and the brother of Matthias de Albuquerque, governor of the province at the time of the Dutch invasion.

Frei Manoel Calado do Salvador actively cooperated with the Dutch in the early years of the conflict, only to return to the Portuguese side when events turned in its favor. Among his other distasteful characteristics was vehement anti-Semitism and frequently unfair criticism of the Italians serving the Portuguese. Nevertheless, his account provides a unique and shifting perspective, *O Valeroso Lucideno e triumpho do Liberdade. Primeira Parte. Composta par o P. Mestre Frei Monoel Calado da Ordem de S. Paulo primeiro Ermitão, da Congregação dos Eremitas da Serra d'Ossa, natural de Villauiçosa.* (Lisbon: Paulo Craesbeeck, 1648). Only the first part was ever printed.

Francisco de Sousa Coutinho, an important diplomat, served as Portuguese envoy to The Hague. His diplomatic correspondence, *Correspondencia diplomática de Francisco de Sousa Coutinho durante a sua embaixada em Holanda, 1643–1648,* 2 vols., ed. E. Prestage and Pedro de Azevedo (Coimbra, Portugal: Imprensa da Universidade, 1920–1926), provides important insights to the maneuvering of the Portuguese and Dutch governments.

José Honorio Rodrigues, *Historiografia e Bibliografia do domínio Holandés no Brasil* (Rio de Janeiro: Departamento de Imprensa Nacional, 1949) lists still other first-person accounts. The Dutch involvement in Brazil gave rise to extensive pamphlet literature, most of which is of little importance except to document the extent of divisions within the Netherlands. A few pamphlets contain alleged eyewitness accounts of events or extracts purportedly from intercepted letters. The pamphlet literature is also treated in Rodrigues, *Historiografia e Bibliografia,* which additionally provides a critical bibliography of materials, primary and secondary, up to 1949. Also important for bibliography is Hermann Wätjen, *Das holländische Kolonialreich in Brasilien. Ein Kapital aus der Kolonialgeschichte des 17. Jahrhunderts*

(The Hague: M. Nijhoff, 1921), an earlier work that provides somewhat different evaluations of sources. These are ably supplemented by
the narrative, bibliographical note, and bibliography in C. R. Boxer,
The Dutch in Brazil 1624–1654 (Oxford: Clarendon Press, 1957) and
A. R. Disney, *A History of Portugal and the Portuguese Empire*, vol.
2 (Cambridge: Cambridge University Press, 2009), which provides a
good secondary bibliography. Boxer remains the best single-volume
account in English.

Several recent histories of the Netherlands during the seventeenth
century touch on Brazil only lightly: Helmer J. Helmers and Geert H.
Janssen, *The Cambridge Companion to the Dutch Golden Age* (Cambridge: Cambridge University Press, 2018); James C. Kennedy, *A Con-
cise History of the Netherlands* (Cambridge: Cambridge University
Press, 2017); Simon Schama's entertaining and thoughtful *The Em-
barrassment of Riches: An Interpretation of Dutch Culture in the
Golden Age* (New York: Alfred A. Knopf, 1987); and Jonathan Irvine
Israel's truly massive *The Dutch Republic: Its Rise, Greatness, and Fall
1477–1806* (Oxford: Clarendon Press, 1995).

Much has been written about the Jewish community in Dutch
Brazil. Two authors, Arnold Wiznitzer and the prolific Jonathan Irvine
Israel, are particularly prominent. Wiznitzer's publications include *The
Records of the Earliest Jewish Community in the New World* (New
York: American Jewish Historical Society, 1954); "The Number of
Jews in Dutch Brazil (1630–1654)," *Jewish Social Studies* 16 (1954):
107-114; *O livro de atas das congregacoes judaicas Zur Israel em Re-
cife e Magen Abraham em Mauricia, Brasil: 1648–1653* (Rio de
Janeiro: Biblioteca Nacional, Divisao de Obras Raras e Publicacoes,
Ministerio da Educacao e Cultura, 1955); "The Jews in the Sugar In-
dustry of Colonial Brazil," *Jewish Social Studies* 18, no. 3 (1956): 189-
198; and "Jewish Soldiers in Dutch Brazil," *Publications of the
American Jewish Historical Society* 46, no. 1 (September 1956): 40-
50. Among Jonathan Irvine Israel's many publications are *Empires and
Entrepots: the Dutch, the Spanish Monarchy and the Jews: 1585–1713*
(London: Hambledon Press, 1990); *The Dutch Republic: Its Rise,
Greatness, and Fall 1477–1806* (Oxford: Clarendon Press, 1995);
Dutch Primacy in World Trade, 1585–1740 (Oxford: Clarendon
Press, 2002); *Diasporas within a Diaspora: Jews, Crypto-Jews and the
World Maritime Empires (1540–1740)* (Leiden, Netherlands: Brill,
2002); and *European Jewry in the Age of Mercantilism, 1550–1750*

(London: Littman Library of Jewish Civilization, 2014). The bibliographies contained in these works provide a good guide to further reading.

TEN

Phillippe de Longvilliers de Poincy: A Rogue Knight *of* Malta *in the* Caribbean (1651–1665)

Introduction

In 1651, the Supremus Militaris Ordo Hospitalarius Sancti Ioannis Hierosolymitani Rhodiensis et Melitensis (Sovereign Military Hospitaller Order of Saint John of Jerusalem, of Rhodes and of Malta), generally referred to as the Knights of Malta or simply the Order, bought four Caribbean islands, St. Kitts, St. Croix, St. Martin, and St. Barts, from the financially distressed Compagnie des Îles de l'Amérique (American Islands Company). While the French king remained the nominal sovereign of the islands, the Knights of Malta became the official proprietors. In 1665, the Order sold their proprietary right to the Compagnie française des Indes occidentales (French Western Islands Company), ending one of the most peculiar failed colonial ventures. Central to these events was Phillippe de Longvilliers de Poincy, who was both a Knight of Malta and the royal French governor of the islands. An extraordinary character, he controlled the islands long before the purchase by the Knights of Malta and acted independently of both France and the Order. De Poincy was at once an able colonial administrator, skilled politician, self-serving pragmatist, indulgent bon vivant, defiant rebel, and charlatan.

Phillippe de Longvilliers de Poincy, Early Life to 1638

Phillippe de Longvilliers de Poincy was born in 1584 in France to an aristocratic family. Many members of his mother's family joined the Knights of Malta, and in 1606, after submitting proofs of aristocratic heritage, De Poincy was admitted to the Order. Over the next few years, he completed four obligatory "caravans," military campaigns that served to train new knights. During these expeditions, the Order's leaders observed the newcomers' obedience, courage, and potential as commanders. In 1610, with financial aid from family, he acquired his own ship and license from the Order to attack the Muslims in the Mediterranean. De Poincy spent about a decade raiding Islamic ships and towns. The Order was impressed with his activities and awarded him the first of three commanderies, estates with lifetime tenure, that he eventually received. The Knights of Malta awarded commanderies to support knights and enable them to engage in the work of the Order. By 1622, De Poincy had also served in the French navy, acting as captain of several ships and steadily advancing his position in both the Order and the navy. In 1632, he became an investor in the Compagnie de la Nouvelle France (New France Company) and traveled to Isaac de Razilly's newly established colony of La Hève in Acadia (today La Have, Nova Scotia), where he served as commander of Fort Ste. Marie de Grace. Back in France, De Poincy became vice admiral and commander of the fleet in Brittany stationed at Brest, but he soon quarreled with the influential Henri d'Escoubleau de Sourdis, who was both the archbishop of Bordeaux and commander of the French Atlantic fleet. De Poincy was relieved of his position as vice admiral, and the demotion seems to have led him in 1637 to accept the offer of the Compagnie des les de l'Amérique to become governor and lieutenant general of St. Kitts in the French Antilles. The circumstances may also have embittered De Poincy, who on St. Kitts exhibited negative aspects of his personality not previously apparent.

The early life of De Poincy parallels to a remarkable degree that of another French Knight of Malta, Nicolas Durand de Villegagnon, who sought to establish a colony in the New World a century earlier. Both were born into aristocratic French families, and both had family connections to the Knights of Malta. Both joined the Knights of Malta and held high ranks in the French navy, and both left France for the New World after quarrels with superiors that damaged their opportunities at home. Both were also interested in the new intellectual developments that characterized the Renaissance. Villegagnon, however, was intensely engaged by theology while De Poincy became worldly in the extreme.

St. Kitts before the Arrival of De Poincy

In 1493, Christopher Columbus became the first European to discover the island today generally called St. Kitts. The island is formally known as Saint Christopher in English, Saint-Christophe in French, and San Cristoforo or San Christopharo in the Italian documents of the Order, and there are a number of variant spellings. The island is among the most fertile and well watered of the Lesser Antilles. It is roughly oval in form, about eighteen miles long and five miles across, with a long tail stretching toward the neighboring island of Nevis, separated by a shallow channel about two miles wide. The name Nevis comes from the Spanish Nuestra Señora de las Nieves, Our Lady of the Snows, supposedly suggested by the white clouds that usually surround Nevis's highest point. Kalinago Caribs inhabited the islands when Europeans arrived as colonists.

In 1619, Englishman Roger North, brother of Dudley North, third Baron North, endeavored to establish a colony on the Oyapock River that today separates Brazil's northernmost Atlantic coastal state from French Guyana, but that attempt failed before anything was accomplished. Thomas Painton and Sir Thomas Warner served as captains under North, and Painton suggested to Warner that an island in the Lesser Antilles would be a more favorable location. In 1623, Warner led a group of colonists to St. Kitts, where they established the first enduring English colony in the Antilles. At first the Kalinago Caribs welcomed the English colonists, but soon tensions began to develop. In 1625, two members of the lesser French aristocracy who had turned privateer, Pierre Bélain d'Esnambuc and Urbain de Roissey de Chardonville, arrived on St. Kitts after a naval clash with the Spanish. Warner, apprehensive of both the Kalinago Caribs and the Spanish, welcomed the French, who established their own settlement. D'Esnambuc and De Roissey returned to France, where they formed the Compagnie de Saint-Christophe (Saint Christopher Company) to colonize the island. Among the investors was the powerful Cardinal Armand Jean de Plessis de Richelieu, the king's chief minister. In 1627, D'Esnambuc and De Roissey brought 250 settlers to St. Kitts. Subsequently, De Roissey dropped from notice—he may have died at St. Kitts—and D'Esnambuc became the French leader.

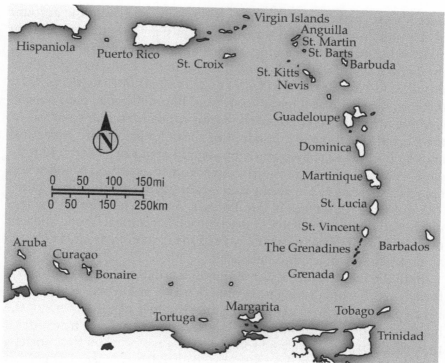

St. Kitts and surrounding islands.

The French and English agreed to divide the island between them. The English occupied the central portion—their two areas of settlement near the north and south coasts were separated by the mountainous central core of the island—while the French settled in west and east areas. Both groups agreed not to attack one another even if war broke out in Europe unless they were specifically ordered by their home government, and in that event, they pledged to provide warning before commencing any hostilities. The two communities sometimes cooperated effectively, though often they remained wary and mutually suspicious.

In a notable but discreditable example of cooperation, the English and French collaborated to eliminate the Kalinago Caribs from St. Kitts. According to the European accounts, the Kalinago, in alliance with other Caribs from neighboring islands, conspired to massacre the English and French, but an Arawak woman slave who had fallen in love with Sir Thomas Warner betrayed their plot, and the Europeans were able to strike first. The story is dubious, especially the account of the Indian woman who saves the colonists, a tale that appears in many other colonial accounts. According to the European accounts, the French and English threw a party for the Kalinago, got them drunk, and later at night killed over a hundred in their sleep. Over three thousand Caribs, many from neighboring islands, then congregated to attack the colonists, who again struck first. In a great battle, the Caribs killed about a hundred of the colonists before retreating, and the Europeans subsequently massacred about two thousand Kalinago, sparing only the most attractive women as slaves. Modern ethnologists suggest the European accounts of Carib intentions are fiction. The massacre took place in late January, a time when the Caribs regularly gathered on St. Kitts in preparation for annual Taino raids on other islands. The colonists likely used the gathering as an excuse for an unprovoked attack and massacre.

Both the French and English communities initially relied on tobacco for export. Eventually sugar, in high demand in Europe, replaced tobacco as the dominant crop. After the slaughter of the Kalinago, the inhabitants of St. Kitts imported large numbers of slaves from Africa to work the fields. The island soon became a typical plantation society, wealthy, dependent on slave labor controlled by violence, and perpetually fearful of slave revolts. During the 1620s, English immigrants came to St. Kitts in large numbers, and by 1629 there were about five thousand English on the island but only about four hundred French. In September that year, the Spanish invaded and burned the English settlements, but most of the population successfully retreated to the mountainous center of the island. The Spanish soon abandoned St. Kitts, and the English rebuilt. Although they never returned, the Spanish did not surrender their formal claim to the island until 1670. In 1634, the French Compagnie de Saint-Christophe reorganized as the Compagnie des Îles de l'Amérique. The reorganized company promoted immigration to St. Kitts, and by 1636, there were about three thousand French on the island.

St. Kitts is known as the "mother colony of the Antilles." From there the English colonized Nevis, Antigua, Anguila, Monserrat, Tortuga, and St. Luca. The Monserrat colonists were mainly Irish Roman Catholics who left St. Kitts because of religious disputes. Only the St. Luca colony failed, destroyed by Indians after just two years. From St. Kitts, the French colonized Guadeloupe, St. Barts, and St. Martin.

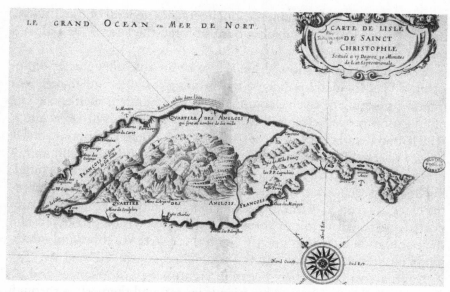

Earliest printed map of St. Kitts, 1650, entitled "Carte de Lisle de Sainct Christophle," Nicolas Sanson cartographer, Abraham Peyrounin engraver, and Pierre Mariette publisher. The English occupied the center of the island, while the French held two widely separated territories on the opposite coasts. (*Library of Congress*)

Phillippe de Longvilliers de Poincy on St. Kitts

D'Esnambuc died in 1637, and the next year the Compagnie des les de l'Amérique appointed Phillippe de Longvilliers de Poincy captain general of St. Kitts, and King Louis XIII named De Poincy Gouverneur et Lieutenant Général de Sa Majesté pour toutes les sles de l'Amerique (Governor and Lieutenant General of his Majesty for all the Isles of America). When De Poincy arrived on St. Kitts in January 1639, he was already fifty-four years old, a considerable age in the seventeenth century, but the usual tenure in office for a colonial governor was only three years. There were, however, some indications that De Poincy planned for a much longer residency. He was accompanied by his immediate family, other relatives, friends, a company of soldiers, and a contingent of artisans, including carpenters, masons, and smiths. Most notable of De Poincy's companions were his two nephews, Robert de Lonvilliers de Poincy and Charles de Tréval de Poincy, and a banker named Desmartin who invested heavily with De Poincy. De Poincy soon acquired three parcels of land on St. Kitts from Jacques Dyel du

Parquet, nephew of D'Esnambuc and lieutenant general of Martinique, the most significant of which would become the site of De Poincy's residence.

De Poincy quickly showed himself to be an able, farsighted administrator. He provided for defense by enrolling the able-bodied men in a militia consisting of twelve companies of two hundred men each. The militia soon proved essential. There was a slave revolt in 1639 about which few details survive other than it was quickly suppressed. De Poincy selected Basseterre as his administrative center and built an impressive town hall there. He also improved the port at Basseterre, building docks, warehouses, streets, and a hospital. Basseterre soon became the chief town on St. Kitts, and it remains so today. De Poincy also supported the construction of three new churches. Trade prospered and the population increased greatly. Soon there were six thousand inhabitants on French St. Kitts, and the population continued to grow.

Upon arrival, De Poincy began to create a web of alliances and influence. He, his family, and his friends ingratiated themselves through favors, appointments, financial manipulations, and even marriage alliances. De Poincy obligated subordinates by loaning substantial amounts of money to finance their migration to St. Kitts and establishment there. At the same time, he borrowed large amounts from the wealthy, such as the banker Desmartin, until they were so invested that they had to continue to support De Poincy or face catastrophic losses. Other "loans" to De Poincy may have been bribes. Certainly, many were not repaid, and there is no evidence of more than rare attempts to collect loans during De Poincy's lifetime. In those sporadic instances where a lender attempted to collect an outstanding loan, De Poincy usually showed himself to be a master of evasion and delay.

De Poincy was a pragmatist concerning the island's economy and his own interests. He allowed privateers and even pirates to shelter, refurbish their ships, and sell their loot at St. Kitts and later at other islands he came to control. Some modern commentators have suggested that De Poincy himself was engaged in piracy, but there are no documentary sources that support such a claim. It is, however, likely that De Poincy received substantial gratuities from the buccaneers, like many other colonial governors who similarly allowed port privileges to pirates.

Even in matters of religion De Poincy was pragmatic. Although a member of a leading Catholic military order, he allowed French Protes-

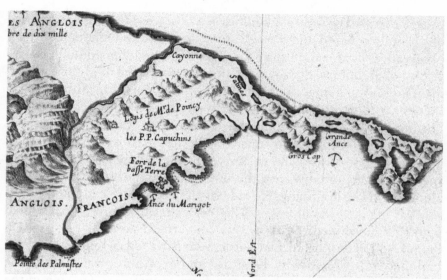

Enlargement of the southeastern section of the French map of 1650 showing the location of De Poincy's palace near the border with the English zone, an establishment of the Capuchin friars, and the fort at Basseterre that became the chief French settlement on the island.

tant Huguenots and Jansenists, a dissident movement within Catholicism, to settle on St. Kitts and the other islands in the French Antilles, where they contributed to economic prosperity. He also supported the successful efforts of the Huguenot François Le Vasseur to expel the English from Tortuga, after which De Poincy appointed Le Vasseur governor, and the two signed an agreement proclaiming religious tolerance on Tortuga and free trade between Tortuga and St. Kitts. The Capuchins complained bitterly about this toleration, highly unusual for the time, and thereafter De Poincy regarded them with hostility. A few years later, the Capuchins supported a failed attempt to replace De Poincy, but the governor in alliance with the Jesuits was able to expel the Capuchins, and the Jesuits replaced them.

An ideal Knight of Malta was ascetic and abstemious; De Poincy was frankly hedonistic. As a residence he constructed a fabulous baroque palace on St. Kitts called La Château de la Montagne, the Mountain Mansion. De Poincy chose a high position for his home with a view of Basseterre, the chief town and his administrative center. Guests approached the chateau along an avenue lined on both sides by cedar trees. The central building on a raised terrace was constructed of carefully squared and dressed stone, four stories high, and with an observation platform on the roof. This main building contained a reception hall, library, displays of paintings, maritime maps and instruments, private living chambers, and storerooms. On Sundays, De Poincy customarily entertained forty guests in a large separate banqueting hall where they would dine on the finest foods and wines and enjoy entertainment by a troupe of slave acrobats that De Poincy had imported from Africa. The palace was protected by two surrounding walls, cannons mounted on the inner one, and a water-filled moat along the most approachable side of the compound. A company of soldiers manned the defenses. The former residence of D'Esnambuc, who first developed the area, was converted into a chapel, and De Poincy had elaborate formal gardens constructed behind the central building and planted with beautiful and exotic tropical plants. The central feature of the gardens was a large fountain, so striking in the colonial Caribbean that De Poincy's establishment was often called Château de la Fontaine (Fountain Chateau). The estate was also equipped with a sizable kitchen building, water cisterns, a house for a resident surgeon, a pharmacy, workshops for artisans, barracks for the soldiers, magazines for arms and equipment, and storehouses. A large staff of servants waited on De Poincy and his guests, and three hundred slaves lived in the "ville d'Angole" (Angolan village) outside the walls of the château. Also outside the walls were stables for horses, barns for storing fodder, pens for cattle and pigs, a tannery, and a butcher shop.

De Poincy became the major producer of tobacco on the island and pioneered the refining of sugar, a complex process. It was particularly difficult to produce the highest quality of pure white sugar, called regal sugar, which brought the highest price in Europe. When De Poincy arrived on St. Kitts, the technique was unknown to the French. Jean-Baptiste Du Tertre, a Dominican missionary and botanist active in the Antilles during De Poincy's administration, wrote that De Poincy learned the secret of producing the finest sugar from a Portuguese who had committed a crime and was condemned to hang. De Poincy bargained to spare his life if he would reveal the method of refining sugar. For a licensing fee, De Poincy then passed on the technique to a few close associates and supporters. Sugar made St. Kitts wealthy, and regal sugar contributed to De Poincy's expensive way of life.

De Poincy's palace on St. Kitts. Charles de Rochefort, *Histoire naturelle et morale des iles Antilles de l'Amérique*, Second Edition (Rotterdam: Chez Arnould Leers, 1665), between pages 52 and 53.

Du Tertre also wrote a short but revealing evaluation of De Poincy's character, describing him as "a man of spirit, a great politician, generous on certain occasions, affecting to appear magnificent in his entertainment and in his buildings, beneficent towards his friends and domestics, to whom he gave fortunes, the object of fear, and severe to excess towards those who were not in his interests." Those who opposed De Poincy's autocratic rule soon discovered that while he could be a generous ally, he was a much worse enemy. Several men who opposed him died unexpectedly amid rumors of poison—perhaps baseless, as sudden death from natural causes was far from unknown in the Caribbean during the seventeenth century. It is undeniable, however, that a judge critical of the governor was mysteriously assassinated. Men of discretion who could not get along with De Poincy found it expedient to leave St. Kitts, and those who did not leave of their own volition were likely to find themselves in court and condemned to exile or worse.

One wit named Querolan wrote satiric verses to mock De Poincy's affair with a local beauty of convenient virtue. He barely escaped the island, fleeing on an English ship to the Dutch colony on St. Eustatia. When the Dutch governor refused to return the writer to St. Kitts, De Poincy's supportive judges condemned the author to death in absentia and confiscated his belongings. De Poincy then had an effigy made of the man and ceremoniously beheaded it.

François Le Vasseur, the Huguenot whom De Poincy aided to secure Tortuga and appointed governor there, foolishly denied a request from De Poincy, who never forgot a slight. Pirates looted a magnificent silver statue of the Virgin Mary from a Spanish ship, and it passed into the possession of Le Vasseur. News of the statue reached De Poincy, who wrote to Le Vasseur asking for the image, suggesting it would be more appropriate in the keeping of a Catholic and Knight of Malta than a Protestant. Le Vasseur replied flippantly by sending a wood copy of the statue to De Poincy, with a note that Catholics were too spiritual to regard the material from which their images were made, while he could not part with such a beautiful object. Le Vasseur may have intended to convey a more important message, that he was so well established on Tortuga that he was now independent of De Poincy. Whatever Le Vasseur's intent, he insulted and challenged De Poincy.

Relations between the two worsened until a chance event in 1652 offered De Poincy the opportunity to rid himself of his onetime ally. Captain Timoléon Hotman de Fontenay, coincidentally a Knight of Malta, arrived at St. Kitts in a well-armed frigate. De Poincy made a pact with Fontenay to oust and replace Le Vasseur. Word of the intended invasion soon reached Tortuga, but as the force got ready to set sail, news arrived that Le Vasseur's subordinates had assassinated him, supposedly because of behavior that embarrassed his family. When Fontenay took over Tortuga, he and De Poincy agreed not to investigate the circumstances of Le Vasseur's death and to allow his family to retain his property. The murder was surprisingly convenient for all concerned, and it was equally apparent to all that one did not lightly disregard Phillippe de Longvilliers de Poincy.

Despite some negative reports reaching France, the growing prosperity of St. Kitts led the Compagnie des Îles de l'Amérique and Louis XIII in 1642 to renew De Poincy's appointment as governor for three more years. By 1644, however, the chorus of complaints against De Poincy had grown loud, but the company and even the royal govern-

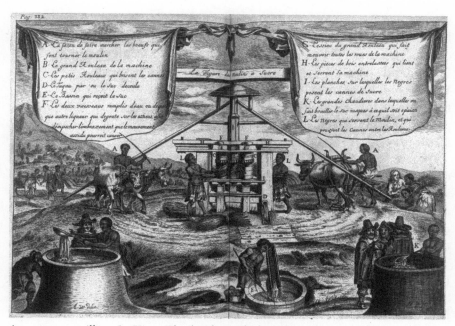

A sugarcane mill on St. Kitts. Charles de Rochefort, *Histoire naturelle et morale des iles Antilles de l'Amérique*, Second Edition (Rotterdam: Chez Arnould Leers, 1665), between pages 332 and 333. (*John Carter Brown Library, Brown University*)

ment had to act circumspectly in regard to a governor so distant and so entrenched. At the time, France was deeply involved in a war with Spain and riven by internal divisions. King Louis XIII's chief minister, the great Cardinal Richelieu, died in December 1642, and Louis died in May 1643. Louis XIV was only five years old when he became king, and the regent, his mother, depended entirely on the Italian Cardinal Giulio Mazarin, an effective advocate of the growth of royal power but also resented by the nobles as foreign. In 1648, civil war broke out in France, flaring intermittently thereafter even while the war with Spain continued. French naval forces were weak and fully occupied in Europe. The royal government, immediately concerned with pressing problems at home, had little time and less resources to deal with a distant colonial governor. De Poincy well appreciated the situation.

In early 1645, Louis XIV, or rather Mazarin acting in the name of the king, with the agreement of the Compagnie des les de l'Amérique, sent a letter signed by the king and countersigned by the secretary of state to De Poincy ordering him to return to France, where he would be employed in other important (but unspecified) services for the crown. This was followed shortly by an announcement that Noël de Patrocles de Thoisy would succeed De Poincy as governor of St. Kitts. When De Poincy made no reply, directors of the company sent an officer to order him to return to France. De Poincy simply had him expelled from St. Kitts. A second official letter that same year ordered De Poincy to leave St. Kitts, and again he ignored it.

In late November 1645, De Thoisy arrived at St. Kitts bearing royal orders that he was to assume the position of governor. De Poincy's loyal officers and militia repeatedly prevented De Thoisy's emissary, the captain of his small guard, from landing on the island, and even the English on St. Kitts turned away De Thoisy's officer when he attempted to land there. Lacking the means to enforce his orders, De Thoisy retreated to Guadeloupe. The situation grew increasingly bizarre.

De Thoisy persuaded the French governors of Guadeloupe and Martinique to join him in a scheme to invade St. Kitts to seize De Poincy's nephews, who were major supporters of his administration. De Thoisy with two companions and the governor of Martinique landed on St. Kitts, where they were joined with nearly four hundred local inhabitants who either disliked De Poincy's rule or saw no future in opposing the royal government. They captured De Poincy's nephews and sent them to Nevis, but De Poincy counterattacked with two thousand men, French and English, and quickly scattered De Thoisy's small force and took prisoners. De Thoisy escaped, but the governor of Martinique was less fortunate. After barely evading De Poincy's men, he fled to the English portion of the island, where the English governor promptly surrendered him to De Poincy, who recovered his nephews by arranging an exchange of prisoners.

In the aftermath of the defeat, the governor of Guadeloupe reconsidered the potential cost of opposing De Poincy, and De Thoisy's presumption to act as an independent power on Guadeloupe further alienated the governor. The governor expelled De Thoisy from the island, and he fled to Martinique. In January 1647, De Poincy sent eight hundred men in five ships to capture De Thoisy. De Poincy then sent him back to France on a ship captained by a man whom De Thoisy had once punished for disobedience. It was not a pleasant voyage. All that Mazarin and the royal government could do was make a face-saving gesture, first allowing De Poincy an additional year as governor to prepare to return to France or Malta, and then, after a short interval, recognizing him as governor for his lifetime. Undoubtedly, the royal government reasoned that De Poincy was already an old man and would not live much longer. De Thoisy never returned to St. Kitts, and De Poincy had no intention of ever leaving the island.

Expansion: St. Barts, St. Martin, and St. Croix

De Poincy increased his efforts to strengthen his support on St. Kitts, rewarding friends and forcing enemies to leave. In 1647, he sent sixty-six men, partisans of De Thoisy, to what is now the American Virgin Islands, ostensibly to establish a colony. De Poincy provided little support for the colony, and it is apparent that his main concern was to rid himself of dissidents. In January 1648, the Spanish sent a force from Puerto Rico that burned the small colony and killed or captured all but eighteen who managed to escape to the woods. Most of those eventually settled on St. Martin. In addition to strengthening his hold on St. Kitts, De Poincy involved himself in other places around the Caribbean, particularly intervening in the affairs of Tortuga and Martinique, and at the same time he embarked on a campaign of expansion.

In 1648, the year after he had ejected De Thoisy, De Poincy annexed St. Barthélemy and St. Martin. St. Barthélemy is generally known today as St. Barts. Pierre Bélain d'Esnambuc left some colonists on the island briefly in 1629, but their settlement came to nothing, and D'Esnambuc soon removed them to St. Kitts. De Poincy now sent fifty men to St. Barts commanded by Jacques Gente, and the initial settlement was soon reinforced by more settlers. In the seventeenth century, the island seems to have been more heavily forested and may have enjoyed more rainfall than it does now, but St. Barts has always been regarded as a dry island. Streams run only after rains, and the settlers had to build cisterns to store rainwater. The island population was never large, measured in the hundreds rather than the thousands, but they successfully grew tobacco as their chief export crop and exploited other natural resources of the island.

St. Martin lies a short distance to the southeast of St. Barts. Columbus sighted the island during his second voyage, but the first recorded landing did not take place until 1624, when the Dutch saw St. Martin (Sint Maarten in Dutch) as a port of convenience for their ships traveling between New Amsterdam (later New York) and their holdings in Brazil. St. Martin, like St. Barts, is a dry island, and the soil is poor. None of the typical Caribbean export crops such as sugar, tobacco, indigo, coffee, cacao, or cotton could be grown there profitably, but St. Martin had a great abundance of one resource in high demand: salt. The island has naturally occurring salt ponds that can be easily exploited. Within a few years of the initial landing, there was a modest Dutch colony and small French and British settlements, but the Spanish still claimed the island, disliked any foreign intrusion, and did not want to lose control of the salt trade they had long dominated. In 1627, they destroyed the small French and British settlements, and in 1633, they drove the Dutch, with whom they had long been at war, off the island. The Spanish, however, found St. Martin barely worth the trouble it took to occupy it, and when general peace was made in Europe in 1648, they abandoned the island.

The Dutch hastened to reestablish their settlement on St. Martin, and De Poincy sent his nephew Robert de Longvilliers de Poincy with two ships and three hundred armed men, arriving a little later. Initially there were some hostilities between the Dutch and French, but they soon realized it made more sense to share the island, and the Treaty of Concordia was signed in 1648 granting the French the greater portion in the north of the island and the Dutch a slightly smaller share in the south. Over the years an amusing legend grew up about how the island was apportioned. Supposedly a Frenchman and a Dutchman agreed to meet at a starting point and each walk along the coast in opposite directions. A line would be drawn from the starting point to the meeting point, dividing the island. The Frenchman refreshed himself with wine while the Dutchman drank gin, fell asleep, and covered less territory. In reality, the division simply reflected the prevailing balance of power at the time of the agreement. Both sides generally abided by the concord, although relatively minor disagreements arose about the exact dividing line between the two areas, which was resurveyed and revised sixteen times by 1816. Today the island remains divided into two areas, the Collectivité de Saint-Martin (Collectivity of Saint-Martin), preserving its relation with France, and Sint Maarten, a constituent county of the Kingdom of the Netherlands. Relations between the two areas are cordial, and each displays its distinctive culture, architecture, and cuisine.

During Columbus's second voyage to the Americas, he landed men on the island that he named Santa Cruz, where they clashed with the local Indians and quickly withdrew. The French version of the name of the island, Sainte-Croix, has become the modern norm as Saint Croix. In the early years of the seventeenth century, Spanish slave raids led the local Caribs to abandon the island. The English and the Dutch along with some French Huguenots settled on the island during the early 1620s, and the two groups coexisted uneasily until 1645. Then, according to the English, the Dutch governor murdered the English governor during a peaceful visit. No detailed account of this mysterious event survives, but it provoked a battle between the Dutch and English during which the homicidal Dutch governor was severely wounded, dying a few days later. His successor went to the English under a flag of truce to seek a resolution of the crisis. The enraged English seized the new Dutch governor and executed him. English forces prevailed in further fighting, and the Dutch and French withdrew from the island.

The English did not control St. Croix for long; the Spanish expelled them in 1650. Shortly afterward, the Dutch, mistakenly believing that the Spanish had not garrisoned the island, landed a small troop without caution and were bloodily repulsed. De Poincy was more successful. He sent one of his officers, a man named De Vaugalan, with 160 men in two ships. The ships became separated and landed their men in different parts of the island. The Spanish defeated and killed almost all the smaller group, but De Vaugalan, with great boldness, advanced on the Spanish fort and demanded surrender. The Spanish, assuming that the French were there in great strength, surrendered and were repatriated to Puerto Rico. De Poincy subsequently sent three hundred colonists in 1651, but the new French colony was almost immediately struck by an epidemic that killed most of the settlers, and several governors in succession. At that time, much of St. Croix was covered by a heavy growth of forest, which the French blamed for oppressive humidity and hosting disease. De Poincy ordered the burning of much of the woodland to fight the infection and open the land for agriculture. Subsequently, more French colonists migrated to the island.

The Knights of Malta Purchase the Islands

By 1650, the Compagnie des les de l'Amérique was on the verge of collapse. The French Caribbean islands were legally required to send and receive goods only on French shipping approved by the company, but smuggling was widely practiced, and the Dutch dominated trade in the Caribbean to the detriment of the company. The long war between France and Spain further disrupted the company's trade, and the shift from tobacco to sugar production required increased investment in African slaves just at the time the company could least afford to finance it. The Compagnie des Îles de l'Amérique fell into debt, and interest on loans compounded the problem. Moreover, De Poincy effectively usurped control of the company's holdings in the Caribbean, and nothing could be done to remedy the situation. The only possible solution was to sell the holdings in the Caribbean and dissolve the company, and there was only one potential buyer.

The Knights of Malta had two major inducements to invest in colonies within the Caribbean. First, the Order's continuing campaigns against Islam were expensive, and the loot from raided towns and captured ships was insufficient to fund them. European contributions to the Catholic Order declined as the north became mostly Protestant, and the south, while remaining Catholic, engaged in long internecine wars. The Caribbean islands seemed to offer good prospects for substantial profit to make up the shortfall. The hard work of settling them was complete; communities were well established; the island crops, particularly sugar, tobacco, cotton, and indigo, were in demand in Europe; and newer products—coffee, cacao, ginger, and rum—were growing in popularity. All could redound to the Order's benefit.

The second inducement was more complex: the desire to secure De Poincy's estate. In 1650, he was sixty-seven, a substantial age at the time. Knights of Malta were supposed to leave four-fifths of their property to the Order, reserving only a fifth for their families. Unless the Order was forcefully present at the time of the governor's death, De Poincy's family, who surrounded him on St. Kitts, would be able to take immediate control of his estate. Creative accounting was already well developed in the seventeenth century. It seemed evident to the Knights of Malta and to everyone else that De Poincy's estate would be truly substantial. His great wealth was proclaimed by the princely chateau, the household staff of three hundred, luxurious daily life, lavish entertainments, substantial gifts to his supporters, ownership of seven hundred slaves, employment of one hundred free workers, fields of tobacco, indigo, and sugarcane, six sugar mills, and several facilities for processing indigo. De Poincy also bought and sold land at a profit, drew money from the three commanderies in France that the Order had awarded to him, and benefitted substantially from his office as governor, even instituting a remarkably modern source of income: a sales tax.

De Poincy exercised care to ensure that his personal reputation, including his standing as a man of wealth, remained unimpaired. Jean-Baptiste du Tertre, a Dominican missionary, arrived in the Antilles in 1640 and served primarily in Guadeloupe until 1647. He observed De Poincy's activities in detail and sympathized with De Thoisy, and he, along with the other Dominicans, was expelled in the aftermath of the De Thoisy affair. After returning to France, Du Tertre wrote a book about the Antilles and his experiences, but the realities of rank and power in the seventeenth century ensured that Du Tertre could not denounce De Poincy boldly. He could, however, subtly criticize the governor's actions. Du Tertre first circulated his work in manuscript form, and word of the work may have reached De Poincy or his friends and supporters. The manuscript mysteriously disappeared. Du Tertre rewrote the book, which appeared in print as *Histoire générale des isles de Christophe, de la Guadeloupe, et le Martinique et autres* (Paris: Chez I. Langlois, 1654). De Poincy countered by cooperating with the French Huguenot Charles de Rochefort, who published anonymously a much more favorable account in *Histoire naturelle et morale des Iles Antilles de l'Amérique* (Rotterdam: Arnould Leers, 1658). Du Tertre subsequently returned to the Caribbean in 1656–1657, and later expanded his work to *Histoirie Générale des Antilles habitées par les Français*, 4 parts in 3 vols. (Paris: T. Iolly, 1667–1671). Although Du Tertre and De Rochefort presented opposing views of De Poincy, both attested to his wealth and magnificent lifestyle. For example, Du Tertre exaggeratedly estimated that De Poincy's income over twenty years was 1,800,000 livres—a free laborer could be hired for 200-300 livre a year—and De Rochefort published magnificent engravings of De Poincy's estate and holdings.

During 1649, rumors circulated of De Poincy's ill health and approaching death. De Poincy wrote to an old acquaintance and fellow Knight of Malta, Jacques de Souvré, the Order's *chargé d'affaires* in France, and to the grand master of the Order, Jean-Paul Lascaris de Castelar. De Poincy indicated he could not expect to live much longer and requested the Order send two knights to assist him in his administration, to receive his estate upon his death, and to assume the governorship when he died. The request was clearly impossible, as the Order was not the sovereign of the Caribbean isles and only the Compagnie des les de l'Amérique and the French royal government had the legal right to appoint a new governor. Yet if the Order did not have a commanding figure in place at the time of De Poincy's death, it might well lose most or all of his estate to his relatives and to the company. The Order in consultation with the royal French government nominated an ideal figure to preserve the financial interests of the Order and respect French sovereignty: Charles-Jacques Hualt de Montmagny. A member of an aristocratic French family, De Montmagny, like De Poincy, served in the French navy, achieving high rank and great respect. He also joined the Knights of Malta, although he did not take the vows of knighthood until 1651. In 1636, De Montmagny became the first governor of Nouvelle France (New France, the name then given to French Canada), succeeding Samuel de Champlain, who held the position of lieutenant general. De Montmagny was several times renewed in this position, remaining as governor until 1648. His administration was well regarded by the French and Indians, and the Iroquois translated his name into their language as Onontio (Great Mountain), which became the Indians' title for all the subsequent French governors of Canada. Gabriel de La Haye Coulonces, another respected Knight of Malta, was nominated along with De Montmagny to travel to St. Kitts, where they would morbidly wait for De Poincy to die. La Haye, however, withdrew before the mission began.

In spring 1650, as representatives of the Order, the Compagnie des les de l'Amérique, and the French royal government discussed the situation with De Poincy, the idea emerged for the Knights of Malta to purchase the proprietary rights to the islands from the company while France retained titular sovereignty. De Montmagny sailed from France in August 1650 with the additional role as the Order's chief negotiator with the company and the French government for the purchase of the islands. De Montmagny's first report to the Order has not survived, but it appears he was cordially received, and negotiations moved forward quickly.

In May 1651, the Knights of Malta purchased the "right of domain and *seigneurie*" of the French portions of St. Kitts, St. Martin, St. Barts, and St. Croix for 120,000 livres, accepting all assets and liabilities, and French sovereignty was recognized by a provision that the Order agreed to present a golden crown worth 1,000 écus to each

French king upon his accession to the throne. The Order awarded De Poincy the high and honorific rank of *bali* and confirmed him as governor for life with De Montmagny as his deputy. De Montmagny traveled back to France in July 1651 to be inducted as a Knight of the Order, and in early 1653, he returned to St. Kitts, where De Poincy continued his autocratic rule, ignoring De Montmagny and his official role. Shut out of the administration, he retired to a planation near Cayonne on the far side of St. Kitts, where he had little to do. De Montmagny requested replacement and return to France, but permission was slow in coming, and he died on St. Kitts in 1657. De Poincy had him buried with great pomp and ceremony, though it may not have been clear to observers whether he was celebrating De Montmagny's life or that De Poincy had outlived his presumed successor. `

In 1656, Caribs, provoked by European predations, attacked St. Barts. They overran the settlement by night and massacred almost all the three hundred colonists, a pitiful few escaping to St. Kitts. After peace was made with the Caribs, De Poincy was able in 1659 to send thirty settlers to St. Barts, and subsequently the French population increased but remained small. In 1664, there were little more than one hundred colonists on the island. All was not well on St. Croix either. In 1657, some two hundred discouraged colonists seized a ship and sailed away, though their destination and fate remain uncertain. Concessions and an energetic new governor improved conditions on the island, and the population grew, but slowly.

At the end of 1657, the Order dispatched two knights, Charles de Sales and Jean de Limoges Saint-Just, to succeed De Montmagny. De Limoges Saint-Just played little role in subsequent events; his health may have suffered in the Caribbean, and he left St. Kitts in 1660. De Sales was genially received by De Poincy, who accorded him a more active role in his administration than De Montmagny.

In 1660, Phillippe de Longvilliers de Poincy, age seventy-seven, full of years and guile, finally died, having long outlived the expectations of friends and enemies. He ultimately willed everything to the Order, and by accepting the heritage, the Order acquired De Poincy's assets and debts, including even a provision granting an annual payment of 10,000 livres to a niece. De Poincy seems to have taken good care of his other relatives before his death. The inventory of his estate filled 113 pages, but there proved to be many outstanding loans and unpaid obligations. When De Sales made a final accounting, it became apparent debts exceeded assets, and there was no fabulous legacy coming to the knights. We can only imagine the sense of frustration as the Order's administrators realized they were victims of an elaborate fraud.

While the officers of the Knights of Malta evaluated what to do with their dubious purchase, they appointed De Sales governor, but his accession was not unanimously popular. He was approached by petitioners who wanted recent changes in regulations abolished, which he promised to consider when time permitted. A group headed by a certain Du Bisson were so openly disrespectful that De Sales ordered him arrested, but Du Bisson shot at De Sales with a pistol. At the crucial moment, De Sales's horse reared, and the bullet passed through his thigh rather than his body. De Sales recovered, and Du Bisson was hanged and quartered.

Despite the early opposition, De Sales proved an excellent administrator. Sugar production increased, and the economy of St. Kitts and the other islands prospered. De Sales argued that the islands could produce enough income to pay De Poincy's outstanding debts, support the administration of the colony, and still leave a significant income for the Order. His projections, however, were premised on the production of sugar and other commodities during normal years, but many years were not normal. Even as he wrote, St. Kitts and the other islands were suffering from drought and fires, and the growing discord in Europe between England and the Netherlands, the latter of which was allied with France, threated war. Additionally, De Poincy's creditors kept emerging with new debts that had to be paid, and by spring 1663, the Order had reimbursed over 58,000 livre and still owed considerably more. Despite all, the grand master of the Knights of Malta, Nicolas Cotoner, wished to retain the colonies, which he felt contributed to the Order's status and prestige, as well as offering the possibility of substantial profit in the future. Other forces, however, would determine the fate of the Order's colonial ambitions.

The End of the Maltese Colonial Venture

Prestige and profits also motivated others. As early as 1662, the French monarchy expressed tentative interest in the reacquisition of St. Kitts and the other islands. As Jean-Baptiste Colbert emerged as the chief minister of Louis XIV during the 1660s, he devoted himself to the economic reform of the government and the nation. Colbert came to dominate all areas of the administration other than war, and in 1665, he became the comptroller general of finance. Among his other projects, Colbert expanded the French navy and promoted overseas commerce and the development of colonies.

As the old Compagnie des Îles de l'Amérique moved toward its final dissolution, a new corporation emerged in 1664, the Compagnie française des Indes occidentales. A project of Colbert, the new company was an instrument of the French monarchy. Louis XIV provided over half of the initial funding, and royal officials financed the rest. Colbert hoped to use the company to break the near monopoly of trade that the Dutch enjoyed in the Caribbean and, along with other French companies, to make France a major commercial country. The crown granted the company a trade monopoly on all French possessions on the Atlantic coasts of the Americas and Africa and in the Caribbean, and the sugar production of St. Kitts and the other islands was a central element in Colbert's plans to finance the company. Colbert wanted the islands for France, and the Knights of Malta could not ignore the firmly expressed wish of the French monarchy. Most of the knights were French, much of the Order's property was in France, and French hostility could easily cripple the Order or even threaten its continued existence. The Knights of Malta could only hope to strike the best possible deal. The initial French offer of 400,000 livres was regarded as too little, although the Order had paid just 120,000 livres in 1651. The islands had provided some income, but the knights had also encountered great expenses, particularly paying De Poincy's debts. After much negotiation, the French offer was raised to 500,000 livres, and the deal was concluded. The Order learned the lesson made apparent to Duke Jacob of Courland just a few years earlier: minor powers might aspire to have colonies, but major powers could take them away whenever they wished. The Knights of Malta's colonial venture was at an end.

Aftermath

After reclaiming the islands, the French crown retained Charles de Sales as governor, but in 1666, he suffered a sad fate. In 1665, the Second Anglo-Dutch War had broken out, and in January 1666, France entered the war against England. News of the war first reached the English of St. Kitts, and the English governor informed De Sales. When a large English force arrived at St. Kitts from St. Eustatia, obviously prepatory to an attack on the French, the French seized the initiative, attacking the English on the northeastern side of the island with eight hundred troops and several hundred slaves. Initially they made fast progress, driving the English from their positions and burning houses and cane fields. The French, however, advanced incautiously and fell into an ambush that virtually wiped out their advance guard. When De Sales saw the commander fall, he rushed forward to the rescue, but he was shot twice and died on the spot.

The French counterattacked victoriously and became masters of the island. English property owners who wished to remain on St. Kitts had to swear an oath of allegiance to the king of France. Many others fled to Nevis, St. Barts, Anguilla, Jamaica, or the English colonies in North America. An English fleet carrying troops under the command of Francis, Lord Willoughby, set sail to reconquer the island, but a hurricane destroyed the fleet, and later the French easily repulsed a second English attempt to retake it. French attempts to capture Nevis from the English were also unsuccessful.

The Treaty of Breda, 1667, restored to the English their former share of St. Kitts, although the situation was massively complicated by conflicting claims about the ownership of plantations, lost slaves, and destroyed and purloined property. The economy was thoroughly ruined, capital was in short supply, and few plantation owners could afford to replace the slaves who were carried off, escaped, died, or simply disappeared during the war. The English and French remained mutually suspicious and sullen. The population, both English and French, was much reduced, and the economy recovered only slowly. Nevis, which suffered less destruction during the war, was more productive than St. Kitts until the early eighteenth century.

Despite the central role Phillippe de Longvilliers de Poincy played in the history of St. Kitts and the other islands, little trace of him remains today. No portrait survives of the man, and his grave is unmarked and unknown. His great palace was shattered by an earthquake in 1690 and ravaged by hurricanes. Only a few lower courses of the main building now survive, serving as the foundation of the plantation house on Fountain Estate. Ironically, his most visible heritage is two groups of entertainers, The Actors and The Clown Troupe, successors of the acrobats with whom De Poincy entertained his guests. Regarded as national treasures, they perform at traditional festivals and the great carnival every December.

Sources

Several archives contain documents bearing on De Poincy and the Order's activities in the Caribbean: in France, the Archives des affaires étrangères and Archives Nationales de France; on Malta, the Magistral Archives and Library of the Order of Malta, the Notarial Archive, and the National Archives of Malta, Rabat, and Medina; and in the Vatican, the Archivio Segreto Vaticano, renamed in 2019 the Archivio Apostolico Vaticano. The Dominican Jean-Baptiste du Tertre's two works, *Histoire générale des isles de Christophe, de la Guadeloupe, et le Martinique et autres dans l'Amerique.* (Paris: Chez Iacques Langlois, 1654), and *Histoire générale des antilles habitées par les Francois*, 4 vols. in 3 parts (Paris: Chez Thomas Jolly, 1667[–1671]), and the Huguenot Minister Charles de Rochefort's anonymously published *Histoire naturelle et morale des iles Antilles de l'Amérique*, 2nd ed. (Rotterdam: Chez Arnould Leers, 1665) provide a connective narrative account of events. Charles de Rochefort identified himself in later editions of the work. He has sometimes been confused with Count Charles-César de Rochefort. The second edition of Rochefort's work contains excellent illustrations of De Poincy's chateau, a sugar mill, and other aspects of St. Kitts.

Thomas Freller and William Zammit, *Knights, Buccaneers, and Sugar Cane: The Caribbean Colonies of the Order of Malta*, Maltese Social Studies Series 23 (Malta: Midsea Books, 2015) is the sole book-length treatment of De Poincy and the involvement of the Knights of Malta in the Caribbean. The authors are sympathetic to the Order, and even their criticisms of De Poincy seem mild. Their work is based on excellent research, and the authors have helpfully included in an appendix several important documents that are otherwise difficult to locate. A more comprehensive index would have been useful.

Several significant articles deal with the Maltese colonies: David F. Allen, "The Social and Religious World of a Knight of Malta in the Caribbean, c. 1632–1660," in *Malta: A Case Study in International Cross-Currents*, ed. Stanley Fiorini and Helen J. Nicholson (Malta: University of Malta, 1989), 147-157; Michel-Christian Camus, "Le general de Poincy, premier capitaliste sucrier des Antilles," *Revue française d'histoire d'outre-mer* 84 (1997): 119-125; Jean-Claude Dubé, "L'Ordre de Malte dans les Antilles, 1638–1666," *Proceedings of the Annual Meeting of the French Colonial Historical Society* 18 (1993): 26-35.

Philip P. Boucher, *France and the American Tropics to 1700: Tropics of Discontent?* (Baltimore: Johns Hopkins University Press, 2008) contains a broad overview of French activities in the Caribbean. The very breadth of the work inevitably required broad interpretive generalizations, which are both the strength and the weakness of the work. Thomas Southey, *Chronological History of the West Indies*, 3 vols. (London: Longman, Rees, Orme, Brown, and Green, 1827), although oblivious to resources that have subsequently come to light and to modern interpretations, contains a wealth of information that is often ignored, and the annalistic organization juxtaposes materials usually considered in isolation.

Georges Bourdin, *Histoire de St. Barthélemy* (Pelham, NY: Porter Henry, 1978), now available in English as *History of Saint Barthélemy* (n.p.: William von Mueffling, 2012) provides a useful though unfootnoted overview of the history of St. Barts and St. Martin. It must be used with caution as there are occasional errors and oversimplifications.

Florence Lewisohn, *St. Croix under Seven Flags* (Hollywood, FL: Dukane Press, 1970) presents a well-written, full account of the history of the island. Brian Dyde, *Out of Crowded Vagueness: A History of the Islands of St. Kitts, Nevis and Anguila* (Oxford: Macmillan Caribbean, 2005) provides some good insights, although his skepticism about the accuracy of Charles de Rochefort's depiction of De Poincy's estate is unwarranted. The contemporary manuscript plan of the complex drawn on St. Kitts and preserved in the Vatican, published in Freller and Zammit, *Knights*, 79-86; and an anonymous account of De Poincy's estate from the later 1640s, also published in Freller and Zammit, *Knights*, 109-113; and the 113-page inventory of De Poincy's estate all support the accuracy of Rochefort's engraving.

ELEVEN

The Fate *of a* Nation:
Scots *in* Panama (1698–1700)

Background

With the death of Queen Elizabeth I in 1603, King James VI of Scotland also became King James I of England. Although he reigned in both kingdoms, each remained a separate nation, Scotland the lesser in every sense: size, wealth, and royal attention. During the Commonwealth (1649–1660), the situation grew worse for Scotland. An English army occupied the country, and extractions to support the army significantly impoverished the land. Under the restored Stuarts, the Navigation Acts of 1660 and 1663 excluded Scotland from free trade with England, further depressing the economy. As the seventeenth century drew toward a close, Scots dreamed of finding some way to strike out on their own economically, and prominent among the dreamers was William Paterson. In 1693, the Scottish parliament passed An Act for Encouraging Foreign Trade, granting valuable concessions to companies that might be constituted for that purpose. In 1695, the Scottish Parliament passed an act establishing the Company of Scotland Trading to Africa and the Indies, based on a draft written by Paterson.

William Paterson

By all accounts, William Paterson was pedantic, garrulous, boring, utterly humorless, abstentious in a hard-drinking age, and someone with few social skills, but at the same time intelligent, enterprising, an original thinker, and possessing good organizational skills. His origins and early history were a matter of dispute. He was born to a farm family in 1658, wealthy and respectable according to his supporters, poor and lowly according to his detractors. He did indisputably receive a good education, indicating his family enjoyed some status. He spent time in the Bahamas as a merchant according to supporters, while enemies claimed he had been a pirate. After Paterson left the Bahamas he traveled in Europe before moving to London, where he enjoyed considerable success. He was a prime mover in a plan that provided a water supply for London, made money developing property, and became a founder and one of the first directors of the Bank of England, although he soon resigned after alienating the other directors. In London, he associated primarily with successful merchants, and there he promoted the idea that foreign trade could be greatly enhanced by the establishment of overseas "plantations"—that is, colonies.

During the seventeenth and eighteenth centuries, the dominant economic theory was mercantilism. Colonies were intended to trade only with the home country, exporting cheap raw materials and importing expensive finished goods. This would produce a positive balance of trade for the homeland, increasing its monetary reserves, prosperity, and power. Paterson, however, was a man out of touch with his own age. He envisioned the establishment of a great international emporium of free trade open to all and benefitting all. He hoped that the Company of Scotland Trading to Africa and the Indies, generally known as the Company of Scotland, would be a joint venture primarily of English and Scottish investors but even include others, such as the English entrepreneur Joseph Cohen D'Azevedo and the wealthy French Huguenot Paul Domonique.

Planning the Colony

In November 1695, the Company of Scotland opened a subscription book in London for investors to reserve stock in the venture. The entire issue of 300,000 was quickly pledged, but the effort alarmed the two great English trading companies, the East India Company and the Royal African Company, that enjoyed British trade monopolies in their respective areas. These companies exercised their considerable influence in the English Parliament, and before the end of the year, the Lords and Commons presented a protest to King William III against

Portrait of William Paterson, left, from J.H. Innes, *New Amsterdam and Its People: Studies, Social and topographical, of the town under Dutch and early English Rule* (New York: Charles Scribner's Sons, 1902), page 272, described as a wash-drawing in the British Museum. Paterson's Latin moto, *Sic vos non vobis* appears below the portrait, literally, "Thus you but not for you," with the meaning "Thus you (labor), but not for yourself." The coat of arms illustrates the myth that pelicans pierced their own breasts to feed their young with their own blood, regarded as an archetype of self-sacrifice and of Christ's sacrifice for mankind. Right, Arms of the Company of Scotland Trading to Africa and the Indies. The Rising Sun was the chief emblem of the Company. The coat of arms bears a ship and pack animals: horse, elephant, and camel. The flanking figures are fanciful representations of a Central American Indian and an African, each holding a cornucopia. The Latin motto may be translated as "Throughout the extant of the world, the power of unity is stronger." (*National Library of Scotland*)

the Company of Scotland. In January 1696, the English Commons denounced the company as a treasonous conspiracy threatening the trade and prosperity of England and passed a resolution condemning as high crimes the company, its directors, and efforts to raise money in England to launch the company. English participation collapsed, and the 300,000 of pledges were withdrawn.

The Scots, notoriously proud and easily offended, saw the English resolution as an insult and challenge. A new subscription opened in Edinburgh for 400,000, and in a great nationalistic rush, the entire stock offering was fully subscribed in just a few months. The sum was immense for a country as small and relatively poor as Scotland, and it represented between a quarter and half of the country's capital. In the

Lowlands, the purchase of stock was equated with patriotism and defiance of the English, and it involved all levels of society. Those who could not afford the price of the minimum investment combined their resources with those of their neighbors, while the rich invested their wealth and in some cases much of their substance, mortgaging or selling property. Highland gentry, however, were inherently suspicious of Lowland schemes and invested little, and the common Highlanders, many speaking only Scots Gaelic, were too isolated and often too poor to invest even in combination.

In July 1696, Paterson laid before the directors of the Company of Scotland his great accumulation of reports, maps, and testimonies and a plan he had long cherished, the establishment of a colony where the narrow Darien isthmus offered the opportunity to join the trade of the Atlantic and Pacific worlds. Paterson had never visited Darien, today southern Panama, but he had learned about the area from the sources he had gathered and most particularly from the writings of Lionel Wafer.

Wafer, born about 1640, became a ship's surgeon and after voyages in the Pacific settled down briefly in Jamaica before returning to the sea as a surgeon on privateers and pirate ships. Wafer participated in an attack on the Spanish on the Pacific coast, but the expedition did not go well, and Wafer along with other buccaneers decided to return across the isthmus to the Caribbean. During the crossing, Wafer was injured in a gunpowder explosion. Unable to keep up with the rest, he and several others were left behind. Kuna Indians, also referred to as the Tule, took him in and healed him, and he lived with them for some time. He was a keen observer of nature, and when he eventually wrote about his adventures, he included vivid descriptions of the people, land, flora, and fauna. Wafer's account circulated in manuscripts before it was finally printed following the launch of the Scottish colonizing effort as *A New Voyage and Description of the Isthmus of America* (London: Printed for James Knapton, 1699).

Paterson was much impressed with Wafer's positive description of Darien, its fertility and wealth of resources, and its geographic position on the narrow isthmus between the Atlantic and the Pacific. To Paterson, the area seemed ripe for an ambitious power to colonize, and the directors of the Company of Scotland were impressed with Paterson's vision.

Paterson and the directors, however, ignored Wafer's negative comments about the area—the long rainy season, widespread flooding, hazardous rivers, oppressive heat, stifling humidity, hordes of mosquitoes, dangerous animals, and poisonous plants—and even more importantly, they ignored the realities of Spanish interests in the area. La Ciudad de Panamá, Spain's chief port on the Pacific, was connected by a road across the isthmus to Portobello on the Caribbean coast, not far northwest of the Scots' proposed colony. These two Spanish towns and the road connecting them were the essential link between the Pacific coast of South America and Spain, and the silver that flowed along that route was Spain's lifeblood. Spain, although no longer the power it had been a century earlier, was still formidable and could not tolerate a foreign presence in the area.

Although the directors were impressed with Paterson, events led them to act without his substantial participation. Late in 1696, Paterson journeyed to Hamburg for the company intending to engage German and Dutch merchants in the colonization scheme. His efforts were unsuccessful, largely because of the actions of the English governmental representative in Hamburg. While there, Paterson left a trusted associate, James Smith, behind in Britain with a substantial amount of the company's money. Smith promptly embezzled £8,000. After a long examination, the company exonerated Paterson of any personal involvement but ended his official connection to the company based on his poor judgement in trusting Smith.

Nevertheless, the plan moved forward, and the company purchased great stores of salt beef and dried cod, tons of hard biscuit, and barrels of beer, wine, and hard liquor. Provisions were, however, difficult and expensive to obtain. Scotland was in the second year of a seven-year period of bad weather and failed crops that led to famine and starvation in the countryside. The company also bought a wide variety of materials for the colonists: axes, knives, mattocks, tools for artisans, an ample supply of weapons of all sorts, medicines, and a great assortment of clothing, including wigs, hats, hose, shoes, and an abundance of cloth of many sorts and sewing materials. Trade goods for the Indians included axes, knives, combs, cloth, and an assortment of ornaments. Later men would satirize the Scottish company for sending material such as wigs, as if the company expected to trade them to the Natives. In fact, they were intended for the colonists, who expected to have a town well established shortly after arrival in which they would live as they had in Europe, and proper wigs were essential components of correct dress. All this was loaded onto five ships the company purchased or had built to order to carry the mass of material and the men and a few women to their new homes.

It was not difficult to recruit colonists. King William III's long war against France had finally ended, the Scots regiments had been disbanded, the navy was reduced in size, and thousands of unemployed men crowded the streets of Scottish towns and cities. Twelve hundred men were chosen, along with several boys who served primarily as servants, and a few women, chiefly wives of the most important officials. A quarter of the men were gentlemen volunteers, members of the gentry, often younger sons or members of cadet branches of the family who had to find their own way in the world. Officially, they were to have the same rank and duties of the planters (i.e., farmers) and entitled only to social precedence. Virtually every colonial endeavor in the sixteenth and seventeenth centuries included a significant contingent of such gentlemen volunteers, but they seldom proved an asset. Their social status was due only to their lineages, and they often lacked relevant skills, experience, and talent. Perhaps because their claims to social distinction were often tenuous, they tended to be defensive of their status, quick to feel affronted, quarrelsome, disdainful of those they regarded as social inferiors, and contemptuous of manual labor.

Most colonists were planters. Each was to be allotted at least fifty acres of farmable land and a house lot in the town. More than a third of the planters were discharged soldiers, who often enlisted along with the officers under whom they had previously served. Many were Highlanders who spoke only Gaelic, while the Lowlanders spoke Scots English and often did not know Gaelic. Officially, the company could only engage soldiers if permitted by the King's Privy Council, but in view of the evident animosity of the English, the company did not even request permission. The discharged officers selected for the colony retained their rank and authority, and in case of necessity would serve along with the soldiers who had followed them to the colony. Officers received stock in the company and larger allocations of farmland and house lots according to their ranks. The colonists also included seamen, both ships' officers and common sailors. Many came and went with the ships transporting the colonists and supplies, but others were recruited as permanent colonists, necessary to man and maintain ships in the service of the colony.

The government of the colony consisted of a council of seven men. The directors of the company chose the councilors on grounds that had surprisingly little to do with the intelligent management of the colony. Several had little to recommend them other than high standing in the Scottish Presbyterian Church. Others owed their appointment to important relatives or friends. Most were distinguished more by pride than by achievements. Three were seamen, one of whom, Captain Robert Pennecuik, would prove a corrosively disruptive element.

The Drummond brothers, Robert and Thomas, members of an impoverished branch of a once-prominent family, were also troublesome members of the expedition. Robert Drummond had been a lieutenant in the Royal Navy and like many others was discharged at the end of the war against France. The company directors gave him command of one of the ships carrying the colonists to Darien. Thomas Drummond had been a captain of grenadiers during the war and later served in the Highlands under Robert Campbell of Glenlyon. He played an extremely brutal role in the infamous massacre of the MacDonalds of Glencoe in 1692. Despite many Scots' abhorrence of Thomas Drummond, he was accepted to go to Darien, as were several other officers and some private soldiers complicit in the massacre. Drummond, acknowledged as a rough and implacable man even by his friends, soon became the leader of a faction known in the colony as the "Glencoe Gang." Initially, Thomas Drummond was not a member of the council, though a close friend of a council member, and he was able to intrude himself into the governance of the colony through his friend and his leadership of the Glencoe Gang. His proposals for the colony were sometimes sound, but he and his clique were a constantly divisive force, and too often his activities promoted stalemate and inaction.

There were many potential lines of tension among the colonists: gentry and commons, officers and soldiers, Highlanders and Lowlanders, landsmen and seamen, councilors and the governed, and still other divisions arose because of personalities and competition for power such as quickly developed between Robert Pennecuik and the Drummond brothers. All these divisions would come to the fore during the troubled life of the colony. A notable contrast was a beneficial member of the expedition, Benjamin Spense, a Jewish interpreter fluent in six languages and most particularly in Spanish and Portuguese. He would prove important to the colony when it faced severe trials. William Paterson also came to the colony along with his wife and clerk, not as an official of the company but as a simple colonist.

The Voyage

The ships, supplies, and colonists gathered at Leith, the port of Edinburgh. Captain Pennecuik was the commander of the *Saint Andrew* and acted as the commodore of the fleet. Robert Drummond commanded the *Caledonia*, another of the major ships, and Captain Robert Pincarton captained the third large ship, the *Unicorn*. The two small ships, the *Dolphin* and *Endeavour*, were commanded by Thomas Fullarton and John Malloch respectively. Pennecuik arranged for their appointment, and they remained his unquestioned supporters. The first colonists boarded the ships early in June, but there were inevitable delays caused by late-arriving supplies, various deficiencies, and rounding up laggards who spent their days ashore in taverns rather than belowdecks on ships. The fleet finally set sail on July 14. The ships moved north along the eastern coast of Scotland to the Orkneys and then into the Atlantic west of Ireland before heading toward the Madeira Islands off the coast of Africa to conceal their destination from the English. The effort was pointless; the English government well knew where the Scots were going. When the fleet was at sea, the councilors discovered that the supply of available provisions was much less than anticipated. The directors had put enough on board to last nine months, but the crews and colonists had consumed substantially during the weeks before the ships departed from Scotland, and damp and poor storage had spoiled still more. It was now estimated that the provisions would last no more than five and a half months.

The councilors gathered in their first meeting to discuss the situation and quickly revealed a lack of unity, a pattern of petty bickering, and the beginning of factionalism. Pennecuik, who as captain of the flagship acted as commodore while at sea, was arrogant and blustering, and there was little the rest of the councilors could do until the colony was established on land. The Drummond brothers refused to defer to Pennecuik, and they quickly came to loathe one another.

As the fleet passed around the northern coast of Scotland, it encountered a strong storm that left the passengers seasick and miserable. Later the ships encountered frequent calms and intermittent storms before arriving in late August at the island of Madeira, where they took on fresh water and what few provisions were available and affordable. While there, Pennecuik accused the Drummond brothers of plotting against him and tried to have them stripped of their commands and left ashore. The councilors declined to take any decisive action, a pattern that would soon become the norm, and they merely assured Pennicuik that the Drummonds would recognize his authority while at sea. One of the councilors had been too ill to leave Scotland, and now at Madeira the councilors elected Paterson to fill the empty position. Paterson held himself aloof from the growing feuds but was unable to do much to promote conciliation.

The fleet took advantage of the trade winds and sighted first land in the West Indies on September 28. By that time, however, "flux"—diarrhea or dysentery—had begun to spread among the colonists, and forty had died. By seventeenth-century standards that was not surprising or excessive for a crossing with so many passengers. The fleet stopped briefly in the eastern Caribbean at the Dutch colony on St. Thomas, today part of the US Virgin Islands. There Pennecuik again attempted to have the council set the Drummonds ashore, and again the councilors temporized between the feuding factions, effectively doing nothing. After leaving St. Thomas, the fleet set course southwest for Darien, experiencing sweltering calms and violent gales while more died of flux and fever. The fleet finally reached the location chosen for the colony on November 2, 1698.

The Colony—First Effort

The Roman name for Scotland was Caledonia, and the colony was called New Caledonia, the adjacent haven Caledonia Bay, and the actual settlement grandly titled New Edinburgh. The Kuna tribe regarded the Spanish as enemies but had good relations with British buccaneers and so greeted the strangers as friends. Several Indians knew a little Spanish, and Benjamin Spense was able to translate, assuring both parties of their goodwill. Three days later, the first contingent of colonists came ashore to cut timber for buildings, and along with them came the sick, who hoped to recover on shore. The event should have been a triumph for William Paterson, but it brought only sadness. His clerk had died shortly before, and his wife lived just long enough to be buried on land.

By the time the ships reached Darien, the colonists had long been on short rations, and most were weak from hunger. Barrels of pork and beef spoiled in the hot and humid holds of the ships, and mold covered hard biscuit and dried fish. Edible provisions were dangerously depleted, and rations were only marginally supplemented ashore by hunting, fishing, and trading with the Indians for plantains and fruit. Beer, wine, and hard liquor were issued in quantity, but drunkenness was not an adequate substitute for a nutritious diet that could rebuild strength and health. It was soon apparent that the sailors who remained on their ships were better fed, and the colonists on land suspected with good reason that the seamen were retaining a disproportionate share of the remaining provisions. The rift between seamen and landsmen grew and deepened. The councilors enjoyed cabins aboard the ships rather than the hardships ashore, and they provided themselves and the officers with more and better food and liquor than the common colonists received. Such class distinctions were common at the time but still led to resentment and bitterness.

Scots wilted in the unfamiliar heat, and flux and fever continued to claim victims. The general term "flux" now included not only diarrhea and dysentery but also typhoid and cholera, while "fever" in the colony seem to have encompassed smallpox, measles, malaria, and yellow fever. In December, the rainy season began early, slowing work and aggravating the illnesses, which spread from the men ashore to the ships. The Scots built huts and cabins roofed with palmetto fronds and began to build a fort deep in the bay, but they soon realized it was a poor site and began another nearer the mouth of the bay that would become the colony's chief defense against naval attack. Thomas Drummond, appointed commander of the land forces, pushed forward work on the fort mercilessly, as hard on himself as he was on his men. He also set men to work creating a fosse, a great moat across the base of the peninsula, 8 feet deep and 12 feet wide, laboriously cut through about 180 yards of hard coral limestone and further defended by an earthen fortification.

The colonists initially believed Caledonia Bay was an excellent anchorage and a great asset to a trading colony, but they soon learned differently. The prevaling winds in the area came from the north, blowing directly into the mouth of the bay. It was easy for a sailing ship to enter Caledonia Bay, but it might have to wait for weeks before it could depart. Ships that should have been up and down the coast peddling the Scots' trade goods sat idle, trapped in the harbor. A helmsman mishandled the *Unicorn*, which drifted onto a sunken rock, damaging the ship severely. Afterward the ship leaked badly, could not be repaired adequately, and was never completely sound again.

An English ship visited the colony, perhaps to spy on the Scots, soon followed by a French ship and a Dutch ship, not to trade but rather

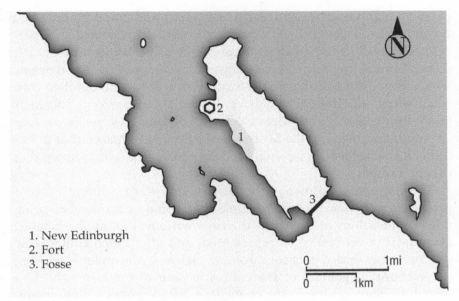

1. New Edinburgh
2. Fort
3. Fosse

New Caledonia Bay on the Darien coast.

bringing news that the Spanish were aware of the new settlement, although they had a much-exaggerated assessment of the Scots' strength. In addition to the fort, the colonists established a battery on the opposite side of the bay and anchored their ships in a battle line between the two strong points. One day while the crew and officers of the French ship were drunk, the ship was badly mismanaged and was impaled on the same sunken rock that had earlier damaged the Scottish ship. The ship sank and rumors spread that it had contained sixty thousand pieces of eight. Colonists wasted time fishing for treasure when they could have more profitably spent the time fishing for something edible.

Meanwhile, the council dithered, in part because of an impractical structure that made each member the president for a week in rotation. Quarreling and quibbling had degenerated to a point where each president spent much of his week in office undoing the work of the previous holder of the office. A second English ship entered the harbor bringing a small but welcome cargo of flour and preserved beef to barter against the Scottish goods. Later the partners who owned the ship would argue with the Scots about their trade goods, which the partners maintained were greatly overpriced and could be obtained for much less in Jamaica. The partners eventually obtained a 30 percent rebate. Other small ships occasionally came and went from the colony, and as the rainy season began to wane and the unfavorable winds from the north abated, the Scots were able to send out their own small ships, but trade was elusive. Potential customers found their goods uninteresting and prices too high. Scotland was hardly a center of manufacturing, and the Scots were beginning to realize that it was difficult to establish an international center of trade with nothing that others wanted.

The partners who owned the English ship were willing to take a passenger to Jamaica where he could find a ship to Scotland to bring news of the colony more vividly than any written account. Predictably, every faction wanted to be represented, and after much controversy the councilors settled on a compromise: they sent Alexander Hamilton, the accountant general of the colony, a man of integrity who had joined no faction. One of the councilors, Major James Cunningham, whose carping criticisms had rendered him obnoxious to everyone, also left the colony at the same time. His departure was regarded as desertion both in Darien and in Scotland. Cunningham's departure left the council with just six members, making it even harder to gain a majority and promoting the already prevalent tendency to do nothing.

Hamilton brought many letters to Scotland that, despite all the death and deprivations, were generally optimistic. Letters told of the "fruitfulness" of the land and passed on Indians' accounts of gold deposits only a few days' march away. Complaints of food shortages, noxious insects, torrential rains, and other problems were largely discounted in Scotland, where preparations for the dispatch of a second group of colonists went forward enthusiastically.

First Spanish Response

Although the Americas were the chief source of Spanish wealth, Spain was often reluctant to spend treasure in defense of its colonial holdings, and as Spain grew weaker in the course of the seventeenth century, the royal government was less able to maintain even the most essential elements of defense. The Armada de las Islas de Barlovento y Seno Mexicano (Fleet of the Windward Islands and Gulf of Mexico) was the chief Spanish naval force in the Caribbean and the Gulf of Mexico, established in 1635 and revitalized in 1664. At its greatest it had been a grand fleet of fifty ships, but when news of the Scots colony reached the Spanish, the commander, don Andrés de Pez y Malzarraga, could only muster four warships and some transports to carry troops. He sailed with this little force from Cartagena in Colombia to Portobelo, but by the time the ships arrived, don Pez's aged flagship and a second warship were leaking so badly they had to be careened and subject to repairs that would take months. The Spanish had no accurate knowledge of the Scots' strength, and rumor credited them with forces far greater than in reality.

There was little don Pez could do with his deteriorated fleet, so he approached don Pedro Luis Henríques de Monroy y Guzmán, conde de Canillas de los Torneros de Enríques, generally known simply as the Conde (count) de Canillas. He served as presidente de la Real Audiencia de Panamá (president of the Royal Appellate Court of Panama) and readily agreed to the plan don Pez proposed. Don Pez sent five hundred soldiers from Portobelo by road to Ciudad Panamá, where they joined two companies of gentlemen volunteers raised in Panamá. The Conde de Canillas had already stationed four companies of militia at Toubacanti, an improvised fort deep in the jungle between the Pacific coast and the Scottish colony. Now the additional troops were carried by ship from Panama to San Miguel Bay where they disembarked, following a plan to attack the Scottish colony overland from the south. The shores of San Miguel Bay were only about fifty miles from New Caledonia, but it was impossible to move directly toward the colony. The Spanish troops had to trek about 150 miles following the least difficult terrain, first up a river where Indians in dugouts carried their supplies while the troops had to hack their way through heavy growth along the banks, then into the trackless jungle. Many of the troops were fresh from Spain and totally unacquainted with Central American climate and wilderness and found the heat and humidity just as oppressive as the Scots did.

At the crude fort, the Spanish soldiers joined with the militia, bringing their total number to about 1,500. They then crossed the central spine of the isthmus. The mountains are not high, but they are rugged, and the ever-present heat and humidity contributed to the exhaustion of the troops. Each had to carry ten days' rations in a basket strapped to his back in addition to his weapons and ammunition. After the mountains they slashed their way through more jungle until they camped about six miles from their objective on marshy ground for lack of a better place. There they built crude huts in which to rest and recoup before the planned attack. Then the rains came, three days of unremitting downpour that flooded the marsh and washed away their shelters. A column of Black slaves arrived bringing supplies of hard biscuits and cheese, but the long trek and the rains left the biscuits soaked and the cheese moldy. The men were miserable, fatigued, and dispirited, and even the officers had no confidence of success in the coming confrontation. The conde ordered the main force to pull back to better ground, leaving only a rearguard of about twenty soldiers along with some allied Indians and Black porters.

Meantime, in New Caledonia, Indians reported the presence of the Spanish, although they seemed to have no accurate notion of their numbers. The Scots immediately sent an officer and councilor, James Montgomerie, with a hundred men to join the Indians and raised sixty more from the healthiest men on the ships to follow. As the Scots and Indians approached the area where the Spanish had camped, the Indians, according to their tradition, shouted defiance, alerting the tiny Spanish rearguard and giving it the opportunity to retreat. The Scots charged an empty camp. The Indians followed the retreating Spanish, and the Scots followed the Indians, only to receive a volley of musket fire from the forest, after which the Spanish rearguard successfully continued its retreat. The Scots lost two dead and ten wounded, although Montgomerie reported only nine, gallantly omitting his name from the list despite a thigh wound.

The condition of the main body of Spanish soldiers continued to deteriorate, but the officers were deeply concerned to preserve their honor and save their careers. Reason spoke in the person of don Juan Martinez Retes de la Vega, a commander of a company in the Panama garrison and veteran of more than thirty years' service who had worked his way up from private to commissioned officer and had fought in major battles in Europe. He advised discretion: retreat now, fight later in better circumstances. The other officers agreed, and the conde ordered withdrawal. The Scots, particularly Montgomerie, believed they had won a victory but still feared a Spanish attack and so launched a diplomatic effort, sending formal letters to the Conde de Canillas and others claiming legitimacy of their settlement and inviting negotiations. The Spanish reply was polite but negative, and the Scots soon received word that the Spanish had captured the *Dolphin*, one of the expedition's small ships that had been sent out to seek trade.

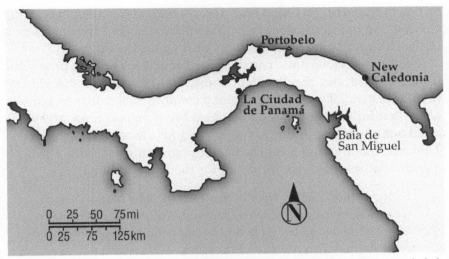

New Caledonia in relation to the Spanish ports of Portobelo and La Ciudad de Panamá and the Baia de San Miguel.

The Scots sent a Highland officer bearing a demand that the ship be returned and empty threats against the Spanish if they did not comply. The Scot's presumption insulted and infuriated the Spanish. There would be no peaceful understanding.

End of the First Colony

Matters continued to deteriorate in the colony. The council remained quarrelsome and ineffective. The disputes among the councilors became so acrimonious that two quit, and the remaining members decided to choose four new members, increasing the size of the council. Thomas Drummond and three of his allies were elected. Drummond was now a major power on the council, but the rancor that had long characterized the council continued unabated.

In the five months between the landing of the colonists in November 1698 and March 1699, two hundred colonists died of disease. In April, both the fort and the moat across the base of the peninsula were completed, but many men were left debilitated by the combination of heavy labor and scanty rations, most of which were contaminated by insects and rot. Also in April, despite the deaths, illnesses, and hunger, the colonists took the time to debate and pass "Rules and Ordinances et the Parliament of Caledonia, for the Good Government of the Colony," an optimistic document that envisioned the enduring success of the colony, despite fever that was causing deaths every day.

The colonists long anticipated the arrival of ships bearing provisions from Scotland, but they had not come, and hunger and disease had become general. The councilors sent a small coastal trader to Jamaica with what little money they could muster to purchase food, and when it did not return promptly, they sent a dugout canoe to seek the trader. The men encountered a Jamaican sloop and returned with a proclamation that sounded the death nell for the Scots' colony:

> By the Honorable Sir William Beeston, Kt., His Majesty's Lieutenant-Governor and Commandant-in-Chief in and over this his Island of Jamaica, and over the territories depending thereon in America, and Vice-Admiral of the same.
>
> A Proclamation.
>
> Whereas I have received commands from His Majesty, by the Right Honourable *James Vernon* Esquire, one of His Majesty's principal Secretaries of State, signifying to me that His Majesty is unacquainted with the intentions and designs of the *Scots* settling in *Darien*; and that it is contrary to the peace entered into with His Majesty's Allies, and therefore has commanded me that no assistance be given them. There are, therefore, in His Majesty's name and by command, strictly to command His Majesty's subjects, whatsoever, that they do not presume, on any pretense whatsoever, to hold any correspondence with said *Scots*, not to give them any assistance of arms, ammunition, provisions, or any necessaries whatsoever, either by themselves of any other for them or by any of their vessels, or of the English nation, as they will answer the contempt of His Majesty's command, at their utmost peril. Given under my hand and seal of arms this 8th day of April, 1699, in the eleventh year of our Sovereign Lord William the Third of England, Scotland, France, and Ireland King, and of Jamaica, Lord Defender of the Faith, etc.
>
> William Beeston

Other governors issued similar proclamations. The Scottish colony was effectively prevented from trading with or even purchasing provisions from England, any English colony, and even from individual Englishmen. Ostensibly, the Scots had established a colony on territory long claimed by Spain, in violation of the treaties of friendship and alliance between England and Spain, but William III and his advisers had other important considerations as well: English trading companies wished to crush the Scottish company before it could develop into a competitor, and those same companies even contemplated planting their own trading colony on the isthmus.

The English proclamation destroyed any hope of relief. The colonists were starving, beset by illness, and by June they had buried nearly four hundred of their fellows. The survivors no longer had the strength to defend the colony or even adequately man the fort. Reluctantly facing reality, the Scots decided the colony should be abandoned. Among the leaders only Paterson and Thomas Drummond argued the contrary, wishing to leave at least a token presence at Darien, but Peterson was gravely ill and often delirious, and Drummond was sick with malaria. Their own conditions nullified their arguments. In early June, the colonists began to load the ships. In mid-June, the *Saint Andrew* left first, and the *Caledonia*, *Unicorn*, and *Endeavour* soon followed. A few weeks later, a Spanish officer in a small ship entered Caledonia Bay, investigated the abandoned colony, and burned it to the ground.

On the *Saint Andrew*, fever raged through crew and passengers. The ship's officers died, and a land soldier with no naval experience suddenly found himself in command of the ship. By the time it reached Jamaica, 140 of those aboard had perished, including the argumentative and now unmourned Robert Pennecuik. At Jamaica, the survivors found no solace as the proclamation was rigidly enforced. Those who were still somewhat able deserted the *Saint Andrew* to seek births on other ships, enlist in the English navy, or indenture themselves for food and clothing. Those too ill crawled ashore to die or died on the rotting ship that could sail no farther.

The *Endeavour* proved unseaworthy soon after leaving the colony, and the captain had to order the crew and passengers to abandon the sinking ship. The *Caledonia* was nearby at the time and was able to rescue the colonists and crew. The overcrowded *Caledonia* reached New York in seven weeks. By the time the ship docked, 116 of the passengers and sailors were dead and the survivors near death from starvation and illness.

The *Unicorn*, never fully repaired after an early accident, was overloaded with 250 passengers. The ship suffered additional damage in storms and was partly dismasted. It was barely kept afloat by constant pumping of the water that leaked into the damaged ship. Flux and fever ran rampant, despite which the captain had to press colonists into service to sail the ship. It was driven by weather to Cuba, and translator Benjamin Spense went ashore to plead with the Spanish. They seized him and held him prisoner for fifteen months, though he eventually returned safely to Scotland. The captain, later praised for his skill and humanity, nursed the damaged ship from Cuba to the coast of North America and finally reached New York ten days after the *Caledonia*. Nearly 150 passengers and crew died on the voyage.

The governor of New York, Massachusetts, and New Hampshire, Richard Coote, Earl of Bellamont, generally did not allow the Scots to leave their ships, although exceptions were made for some gentlemen. He allowed the purchase of provisions for immediate needs on credit, but the commoners had no access to credit. Some slipped off the ships and made their away ashore to start new lives in New York or New England, where many Scots already resided. Others, confined to the pestiferous ships at the height of summer and fed only on the miserable remaining stores, continued to die. The *Unicorn* was ultimately abandoned on the Jersey Shore, and Robert Drummond worked to make the *Caledonia* seaworthy enough to return to Scotland.

The Drummond brothers, always roguish, also attempted to highjack a small ship so that Thomas and some followers could sail back to Darien. The plot failed, and they were barely able to talk their way out of trouble by claiming it was a drunken misunderstanding. With the aid of two New York merchants, Thomas Drummond acquired a sloop and set sail surreptitiously with a crew of thirteen and a few volunteers to return to Darien. They stopped at St. Thomas, where Drummond hired a second sloop to carry provisions. A few days after they left the island, a Spanish ship of twenty guns attacked Drummond's lightly armed sloop. After receiving a battering, Drummond was able to escape at night. The two sloops reached Darien in November, where they met members of a second Scottish expedition that had set sail in May 1699.

Robert Drummond worked with typical energy, pressing his men to ready the *Caledonia* for the return to Scotland. The governor of New York allowed him to purchase enough provisions for the voyage, which sailed from New York in October. About three hundred survivors were aboard, many still ill and weak, including William Paterson. The voyage was beset with storms, and there were more deaths during the voyage, but the ship reached Scotland in about five weeks.

Of the twelve hundred men and women who left Scotland, about fifty died on the voyage to Darien. Nearly four hundred died at the colony and more than four hundred on the ships after abandoning the colony. Still more perished in the ports or ashore at Jamaica and New York. Fewer than three hundred returned to Scotland, where they received a rude welcome, accused of having abandoned the colony and betraying the homeland.

The Second Expedition to Darien

While members of the first expedition were dying aboard the ships, Scotland, still unaware of the disaster, prepared a second expedition. Even before the major new effort was launched, several ships were sent bearing provisions and some colonists. The first small ship, the *Dispatch*, was driven back to Scotland by adverse winds and wrecked on Texa island. Two sloops, the *Olive Branch* and the *Hopeful Binning*, set sail in May 1699 with provisions for the colony and three hundred eager colonists packed into the small ships. The close quarters fostered disease, and there were deaths during the crossing.

Four larger ships were to carry the main group of men and women to Darien. The greatest was the *Rising Sun*, named after the central emblem on the arms of the Company of Scotland Trading to Africa and the Indies. The *Rising Sun* was a large ship of 450 tons burden and was magnificently decorated and armed with thirty-eight cannons. The company built it to specifications to carry colonists and trade goods. James Gibson was captain and overall commander of the fleet. James Byres, who was to play a central role in Darien, also sailed on the *Rising Sun*. The *Hope of Bo'ness* and the *Duke of Hamilton*, both chartered for the trip, were each over three hundred tons. The *Hope*, a smaller but still substantial vessel owned by the company, completed the group. They were loaded with provisions, trade goods, equipment for the colony, and about 1,300 settlers.

Collectively, the second group of colonists resembled those who had traveled to Darien a year earlier. Again, many of the colonists were men who had served in King William's War against the French and had been discharged at the end of that conflict. A sizable contingent were Highlanders, perhaps as many as a third, and again many spoke only Scots Gaelic. Officers, ensigns and lieutenants, were again chosen primarily from the younger sons of prominent families, and there was the usual contingent of gentlemen volunteers who held no office or rank but hoped for promotion. Among the colonists was also another Jewish interpreter, David Dovale, fluent in Spanish, Portuguese, Dutch, French, English, and several Indian languages of Central America. One major difference involved women, only a few of whom went in the first contingent to Darien. About a hundred now took part in the second voyage, some accompanied by husbands and children. Others expected to join their husbands waiting for them in Darien; many would soon discover they were widows. A council was again formed to govern the new colonists, and again the directors chose councilors for reasons irrelevant to guiding a colony or even working cooperatively.

The ships set sail in mid-August 1699, just about the same time that the wretched survivors of the first expedition reached New York. Rumors reached Scotland that the Darien colony had been abandoned, but they were dismissed as errant nonsense spread by English enemies. Definitive word of the colony's fate would not reach Scotland for weeks. Almost immediately after setting out, the fleet was held up by adverse winds. For over a month the ships sat immobile while the colonists consumed provisions and fever began to spread in the crowded conditions.

The *Olive Branch* and the *Hopeful Binning* arrived at Darien, where the colonists expected to be received at a well-established community. One can only imagine the shock and horror as they confronted a ruined fort, a burned colony, and hundreds of graves, all reverting to jungle. An accident set the *Olive Branch* ablaze, destroying the ship and all the provisions it contained. The two captains decided to leave an officer, a Lieutenant Oliphant, and twelve men at Darien and take the rest of the colonists aboard the *Hopeful Binning* to Jamaica. The voyage was long and unhealthy. Many died before arriving at the island and many more afterward.

Thomas Drummond arrived with two sloops shortly after the *Hopeful Binning* departed, and the main fleet not long after that. Their voyage had been rapid, but not without troubles. They had touched briefly at Montserrat, where the English governor prevented them from obtaining provisions. More significantly, about 160 of the colonists had died during the crossing. Scotland was suffering through years of crop failure and famine, and many of the colonists may have been in weakened condition even before embarking.

In Scotland, the directors had appointed four councilors to govern the main body of colonists while on the voyage and to yield power on arrival to the established council at New Caledonia. Of the four, James Byres was by far the most dominant. On arrival, the colonists found no colony and no council except Thomas Drummond, who had returned with two small ships, *Ann of Caledonia* and *Society*. Neither Byres nor Drummond were the sort to surrender power willingly, and they differed in opinion about what to do. Drummond wanted to rebuild the colony, starting with the fort, and then move aggressively against the Spanish before they could act. Byres first proposed that all should withdraw to Jamaica, leaving behind two hundred or three hundred troops to garrison the colony. The other councilors agreed on two points: first, Drummod would not be seated as a fellow councilor, holding that his appointment ended when the first colonists abandoned Darien and sailed to New York, and second, the fort should be repaired and then all but five hundred men withdrawn to Jamaica.

The colony soon found itself divided into factions supporting either Drummond's aggressive approach or Byres's plans for withdrawal. Drummond proposed taking 150 men into the jungles who, in alliance with Indians, would attack the Spanish, moving even against Portobelo or Cartagena. Byres and the other councilors rejected the plan. Alarmed at loose talk by supporters of Drummond, Byres had a simple carpenter arrested on grounds of sedition, brought before a court-martial, convicted, and hanged. The object was clearly to intimidate Drummond's supporters. Byres then had Drummond arrested and imprisoned on the *Duke of Hamilton* with three other officers.

Fever spread throughout the men ashore and on the ships. Hundreds fell ill, and many died. For weeks the colonists, ill and discouraged, did nothing significant to strengthen the defenses at Darien. Indians, whom Byres foolishly dismissed as weak and worthless allies, reported that the Spanish were making major preparations to attack the colony, and a trading ship from Jamaica brought more news of great Spanish preparations in Portobelo for a campaign against the Scots. Fear finally motivated the colonists to action, and they repaired the fort and mounted cannons brought from the ships. Amid this activity, Byres boarded the *Society* and set sail, saying he was going to get provisions from Jamaica. He did not return to the colony and apparently never intended to do so. His departure, however welcomed by some, left the colony bereft of leadership. The three remaining councilors were irresolute, weak personalities. They did not release Drummond or his colleagues and took no decisive actions themselves.

The Reaction in Spain

Carlos II El Hechizado (The Bewitched), the last of the Spanish Habsburgs, was king from 1665 to 1700. Cursed by familial inbreeding and disease, he had no direct heir. He lived longer—or rather, died more slowly—than anyone anticipated, precipitating a long-developing crisis that resulted in the War of the Spanish Succession. During his last years, the Spanish government had to react to the Scots' attempt to colonize Darien amid the greater concerns of a dying king and a coming war. Spain was certainly weaker than it had been a century earlier, but its power was not inconsiderable, and by seventeenth-century standards, Spain was relatively well organized and staffed by able bureaucrats, seamen, and soldiers. The government in Spain considered the Scottish incursion a serious challenge, threatening the Spanish route through the isthmus to South America and potentially portending a general assault by European powers on Spanish political control and trade in the Americas. Spain also considered itself the bastion of Catholicism and looked on the Scottish Presbyterians as heretics who would lead the ignorant away from the true faith.

In 1698, the Spanish royal government ordered don José Sarmiento Valladares Arines-Troncoso de Romay, duque de Atrisco, conde de Moctezuma (jure uxoris) y de Tula, Viceroy of New Spain, to colonize Pensacola Bay on the Gulf Coast to prevent the French from seizing the site. Don Martín de Aranguren Zavala, General of the Carrera de Indias, was ordered to the Caribbean with a modest reinforcement for the Armada de Barlovento to take part in the Pensacola Bay expedition, but he arrived too late to participate. The Conde de Moctezuma redirected his effort against the Scots, but don Zavala pleaded that after the voyage from Spain and an epidemic among his sailors he was unable to participate in the first Spanish attempt by don Andrés de Pez and the Conde de Canillas to expel the Scots. The Conde de Moctezuma ordered sailors recruited in Mexico for don Zavala's ships, and they were reinforced by two warships, a transport, and five companies of infantry brought from Spain by don Juan Díaz Pimienta y Zaldivar, newly appointed governor of Cartagena. In June 1699, his contingent reached Panamá, where he would play a central role in subsequent events. In the same month, the royal government in Spain began to prepare a larger expedition to oust the Scots.

News of the Scottish withdrawal took time to reach Spain, and by the time information was confirmed there, rumors were circulating of the second Scottish expedition to Darien, so preparations continued. In August 1699, don Melchor Portocarrero y Lasso de la Vega, conde de Monclova, the Viceroy of Peru, sent nearly six hundred troops to Panamá and traveled there to take command of the campaign. More troops came from Guatemala, and still more were raised locally. Don Zavala returned to Spain, but ships and troops he brought remained and played a role in the coming Spanish confrontation with the Scots.

The Spanish government intended that a fleet carrying troops would embark from Spain in December 1699, but inevitably there were delays. New ships had to be completed and equipped, and existing vessels needed to be refitted for the voyage. Military units had to be brought up to strength by recruiting and even impressing men, who then had to be clothed, equipped, trained, and moved to ports, where they had to be fed and housed until embarkation. Ships' crews also had to be recruited or impressed. All required money, but the recent end of the Nine Years' War left the royal government with depleted resources, and it had to finance the expedition in large part through various expedients such as donations, grants, and loans. Theoretically, loyal citizens offered these monies freely, but governmental pressure was necessary to extract them from merchants, trade organizations, and religious institutions. Spain also had other expensive concerns. There was an ongoing war in North Africa against the king of Morocco, and Navarra had to be heavily garrisoned against the ambitions of Louis XIV of France. The departure of the fleet from Spain was delayed from December 1699 to March 1700, and then again until June 1700. Every country commonly experienced such delays in preparing a major expedition, and the delays do not indicate that Spain was substantially less efficient than others.

The expedition finally set sail with don Pedro Fernández de Navarrete y Ayala in command. The fleet consisted of ten ships crewed by nearly eighteen hundred men and carrying a little more than three thousand troops. Navarrette was directed to proceed to Cartagena and there to join forces with the ships and men that had previously come from Spain and with other troops from South and Central America. He was then to move under the direction of the viceroy of Peru against the Scots. Navarrette arrived in September 1700 to discover that the Conde de Canillas and don Juan de Pimienta had already organized the naval and land forces available to them and dealt with the Scots. Although the fleet from Spain ultimately proved unnecessary, the efforts demonstrate the willingness and ability of the government to deal with what it perceived as a significant threat.

The Spanish Colonial Reaction and Alexander Campbell of Fonab

Faced by illness and rations little better than starvation, individuals and small groups deserted the Scottish colony. In mid-January 1700, two such deserters fell into the hands of the Spanish. Interrogated by the Conde de Canillas, they readily gave the Spanish a fully detailed account of the situation and strength of Scots at New Caledonia. The conde was pleased to hear that the Scots were fewer in number and far weaker than anticipated. He could now unleash Juan de Pimienta, who had long wished to move against the Scots. Fever, then widespread throughout Central America, much reduced Pimienta's forces, but he remained confident that he had enough healthy sailors and soldiers to overcome the Scots. The Spanish plan envisioned a coordinated attack by land and sea. Troops from Cartagena, Portobelo, and Ciudad de Panamá rendezvoused with troops at Toubacanti, the jungle fort used during the first Spanish assault on New Caledonia. From there they moved to attack the colony on land as the Barlovento fleet attacked by sea.

When the directors of the company in Scotland learned that the first contingent had abandoned the colony, they felt it necessary to send a letter encouraging the second group to rebuild the colony. In October 1699, they dispatched that letter in the care of Alexander Campbell of Fonab and Monzie, generally called Fonab. Formerly a lieutenant colonel in a Scots brigade, he was liked and respected. It took him four months to reach New Caledonia, sailing first to Barbados; from there he took a sloop to the colony. He found the Spanish fleet of twelve ships assembled outside Caledonia Bay, but he managed to evade it and slip into the bay.

The three feckless councilors were overjoyed to relinquish power to Fonab, who immediately ordered the release of Drummond and the other imprisoned officers. Drummond, however, had fallen ill during his incarceration. He declined Fonab's offer to share command and wanted to get to Scotland to defend himself against Byres's negative reports. Fonab determined to attack the Spanish at Toubacanti before they could act, and he appointed Lieutenant Robert Turnbull his second in command. Turnbull had become good friends with the Indians and was able to persuade them to take part in the attack. Two days after landing in the colony, Fonab and Turnbull led two hundred Scots and Indians into the jungle. The climate and conditions were utterly new to Alexander Campbell, and none of the Scots other than Turnbull had been far from the colony. Indians suggested that they and the Scots set an ambush for the Spanish when they ventured out of the fort to march on the colony. Fornab rejected that as unworthy and ignominious, exhibiting the quixotic sense of honor typical of a Highlander, but increasingly less practical in an age of numerous and improved firearms.

The Spanish had developed Toubacanti into a formidable star-shaped fort with redoubts and bastions, walled with a palisade of vertical logs set into the earth. The Scots and Indians had no idea of the size of the Spanish garrison within, but Fonab ordered an immediate attack. The Scots fired one volley and then attacked the wall with axes and claymores as the Indians threw spears over the walls from the flanks. The Spanish put up a creditable resistance until the Scots and Indians cut their way into the fort, at which point the Spanish retreated out the rear gate and into the forest. The action took place late in the afternoon, and there was little pursuit. Seven Scots were killed in the assault and fourteen wounded. No one thought to record whether there were Indian casualties. Both Turnbull and Fonab were among the wounded, both shot in the shoulder, Fonab's wound the more serious. The Scots and Indians looted the fort and freed all but three of about thirty Spanish prisoners. The colonists greeted the returning forces triumphantly, but the victory had little significance. The Spanish were chagrined and embarrassed by the setback, but their land forces were still stronger than the Scots, and their naval forces immensely powerful.

Fonab, gravely wounded and now feverish, organized the defense and strengthened the Scots' fort, but an accidental fire burned much of New Edinburgh, depriving colonists of shelter and supplies. A Jamaican sloop that had taken refuge in the bay now left, slipping by the Spanish at night. With it went Thomas Drummond, who promised to send supplies from Jamaica. Unlike Byres, his word was good.

On March 1, 1700, the Spanish landed some artillery and about two hundred men four miles from the peninsula under the command of an engineer to establish a base of operations. They advanced cautiously on reconnaissance and encountered the Scots near the moat across the base of the peninsula. Three times the Scots charged the Spanish, and three times the Spanish drove them back. The Spanish commander counted seventeen dead Scots. His force lost only thirteen wounded. He pulled back and began constructing a fort.

Two days later, Pimienta came ashore with three hundred additional troops and sent a formal request for the Scots to surrender, which they refused. Pimienta continued to increase his forces and pushed skirmish lines forward, followed by artillery. Fever increased in the colony, carrying away more men than the increasingly frequent clashes with the Spanish. On March 18, the Spanish crossed the moat without resistance and moved within sight of the huts of New Edinburgh before stopping to dig entrenchments. The Scots sent a message to Pimienta asking for terms, and proposals were exchanged back and forth for several days, but no agreement was reached. Pimienta demanded that the Scots yield their weaponry and ships, and to this they would not agree. The Spanish continued to strengthen their position, even landing artillery directly on the peninsula, and the Scots did what they could to strengthen their fort.

The Spanish advanced to within pistol range of the fort, cutting the Scots off from their source of fresh water. Within the fort, shallow wells held only brackish, polluted water, and the scanty remaining provisions were moldy and noxious. The Spanish were also suffering. Many of Pimienta's troops were ill with fever and exhaustion. Again the Spanish commander formally suggested surrender. Again the Scots refused, writing that to give up their artillery and ships would be dishonorable, and they would rather die honorably. Pimienta shared the same chivalric values as the Scottish officers and so now felt obliged to make an equally chivalric gesture. The Spanish commander agreed to the Scottish surrender with all military honors, retaining their belongings and ships. The Scots surrendered the fort and then were allowed two weeks to load their ships, after which they were to depart on the first favorable wind. The Scots accepted, and the tattered colonists left the fort.

When Thomas Drummond reached Jamaica, he found two of the company's sloops there, one recently arrived from Scotland and the other controlled by Drummond's enemy, James Byres, who had dawdled there irresolutely. Drummond managed to obtain provisions and forced the reluctant Byres to follow him back to the colony. The sloop

THE FATE OF A NATION

commanded by Drummond managed to slip into Caledonia Bay at night, but rather than follow, Byres threatened the captain of the second sloop with a club and sailed back to Jamaica. Drummond gave the provisions he had brought to the colonists but expressed his disgust at their surrender by refusing even to speak to them.

Over the next weeks, the Scots loaded their ships. Fonab, stricken with fever and still suffering from his wound, had to be carried aboard on a stretcher, still protesting the surrender. The Scots were so weak that the Spanish had to aid in warping the ships out of the bay in the face of an adverse wind. Many of the colonists were ill when they came aboard the ships, and when crowded belowdecks, flux and fevers quickly spread among them. The *Hope of Bo'ness* began to leak badly and had to transfer passengers to the *Rising Sun*, increasing the crowding and misery on that ship. Pumping out water and barely afloat, the *Hope of Bo'ness* managed to make port at Cartagena, where the captain surrendered the ship to the Spanish in exchange for them releasing him and his crew. The *Ann of Caledonia* sailed directly to New York, avoiding the Caribbean ports where fever ranged. Fonab was on that ship and was among those who survived the journey. The sloop *Speedy Return* that Drummond had brought to the colony sailed quickly to Jamaica, followed more slowly by the *Rising Sun*, *Duke of Hamilton*, and *Hope*. Nearly 250 colonists died aboard the ships and about 100 more after arriving in Jamaica. Facing starvation, many colonists and some crew members indentured themselves to planters on the island.

The governor of Jamaica did nothing to hinder the departure of the Scottish ships, but he also did nothing to aid. Drummond in the *Speedy Return* left first, eager to discredit Byres to the company in Scotland, followed by the second sloop, the *Content*, that Drummond had chartered. The *Rising Sun*, *Duke of Hamilton*, and *Hope* also set sail, but the *Hope*, in poor condition and battered by squalls, was driven ashore on a Cuban island. The Spanish rescued the survivors. The *Rising Sun* was dismasted in a storm. Leaking badly and dependent on a jury-rigged mast, the ship reached Charleston in Carolina, where the *Duke of Hamilton* and the *Content* had previously arrived. A few, including Byres, went ashore and remained safe, when several days later a hurricane hit Charleston. The *Duke of Hamilton* sank at its anchorage, and the *Rising Sun* was driven out to sea, where it went down with all aboard. Of the thirteen hundred who left Scotland on the second effort to colonize Darien, well over one thousand perished on land or at sea, and few of the survivors ever returned to their homeland.

News of the failure of the colony reached Scotland, where Fonab and Drummond were regarded as heroes, though Fonab remained outspoken in his criticism of the company. William Paterson was restored to favor, and James Byres was roundly condemned. But the Scots reserved their greatest hostility for England and the English.

Aftermath

The Darien project was fatally flawed. None of the colonists, not even William Paterson, had ever been to Darien before the Scots sent the first contingent of twelve hundred people there. Relying on little more than Lionel Wafer's account, and even that read selectively, the Scots had no realistic appreciation of the challenges they faced. Paterson envisioned an international trade center, but the Scots had little to offer that interested potential customers, and even that little was too expensive. Provisions were inadequate in quantity and deteriorated in the heat and humidity, and illness ravaged the colonists. The governance of the colony was poorly conceived, and the councilors poorly chosen. Finally, the Scots failed to understand the strength of foreign opposition to the project, both English and Spanish. Paterson's vision of a great project uniting the commerce of the Atlantic and Pacific was not realized until more than two centuries later when the Panama Canal was completed.

The fate of the Darien colony gave rise to a great pamphlet war. Authors, some anonymous or publishing under pseudonyms, condemned or defended the actions of the Scots or the English, supported the legitimacy of the Darien scheme or sarcastically mocked the effort. The pamphlets added much heat but contributed little light to the hostility between Scots and the English.

The Company of Scotland Trading to Africa and the Indies was left practically destitute by the Darien disaster, and the investors had to count their funds as lost. In 1703, the company granted a license to Captain John Ap-Rice of the *Annandale* to trade in the East Indies in the company's name. The English East India company seized the vessel and its cargo, charging breach of its monopoly of trade. When the English ship *Worcester*, trading under an English East India Company license, put into Scotland, the Scots seized the ship, claiming it had sold East Indian goods in Scotland in violation of the Company of Scotland's monopoly. The Scottish population grew increasingly vociferous against the English, and the officers and crew of the *Worcester* were charged with piracy. There was no proof of the outrageous accusation, but the crowd demanded English blood, and Scottish officials cowardly shirked duty and justice. The captain, first mate, and gunner were condemned in a trial—which may have been technically legal but was grossly unfair—and then hanged.

Amid the deteriorating relations, the royal English government, assessing its self-interest, proposed the unification of England and Scotland. England was engaged in the long War of Spanish Succession, and the increasing alienation of the Scots raised the prospect of revolt and renewal of the "old alliance" between Scotland and France. In such an event, England would face a war in the north. Moreover, in 1702, King William III died, and the succession was far from clear. Anne, the second daughter of James II, succeeded as queen in England, but there was some question whether the Scots would accept her and the eventual accession of the Hanoverian George I. All could be resolved by the union of Scotland and England.

Scottish and English commissions negotiated the merger of the two nations. As part of the proposed union, the English government agreed to provide money, called the Equivalent, to be paid on ratification of the agreement. The Equivalent was a vastly complex matter involving national debt, taxes, subsidies, and repayment of investments in the company along with a 42 percent interest premium. All the capital counted as lost by investors would be recouped along with a generous bonus—provided the union was ratified. The greatest payments, of course, would go to the greatest investors, who were also the members of Scottish Parliament that would vote on the union. The English government took additional steps to ensure passage, creating peerages, awarding government appointments and pensions, and even resorting to simple bribery to ensure favorable votes. The English government also made threats to prohibit Scottish exports to England if the union were not passed.

Most Scots opposed the union. Some honorable men in the Scottish Parliament denounced the Equivalent as no more than a bribe, but they were outnumbered and outvoted by those who benefited financially, and the Act of Union passed in 1707. The scurrilous measures taken to ensure its passage have never been forgotten in Scotland, and in recent years the movement for Scottish independence has grown considerably. In 1997, a referendum led to the reestablishment of a Scottish Parliament, and in 2007, the Scottish National Party, which supports independence, gained control of that parliament. A referendum on Scottish independence narrowly failed in 2014, but after the British referendum to withdraw from the European Union passed in 2016, the Scottish Parliament authorized the Scottish government to seek a second independence referendum. Arguments continue in Britain about the legitimacy of that authorization. History is relevant, and Robert Burns's lament "Bought and sold for English gold" is once again heard in the streets of Scotland.

William Paterson retained an almost childish faith in the Company of Scotland Trading to Africa and the Indies and in the possibility of founding colonies that would make Scotland and all Britain rich, but the Darien scheme had consumed much of Scotland's capital, and no one was in the mood for a new venture. Paterson eventually moved to London, where he spent his last years earning small fees for teaching mathematics. He died in 1719.

Alexander Campbell of Fonab and Monzie recovered his health. The company presented him with a gold medal, but he remained irreconcilable in his criticism of the company and the events that led to the abandonment of the colony. He also continued his military career, fighting with the Loyalists against the Jacobite rising of 1715. Later he played an important role in the formation of the Independent Highland Companies that were subsequently joined to form the 42nd (Royal Highland) Regiment of Foot, better known as the Black Watch. He died in 1724.

James Byres was able to continue as a merchant despite harsh criticism by the company. He died at sea in 1706.

The directors of the Company of Scotland cleared the Drummonds of any blame, and Thomas Drummond was respected for his reluctance to abandon the colony and his return to Darien with a sloop filled with provisions. The company subsequently employed the Drummond brothers on a trading voyage to Africa. Robert Drummond was appointed commander of the *Content*, and Thomas Drummond sailed on the *Speedy Return* as the company's representative in charge of the cargo and trading. The company expected the Drummonds to trade for gold, ivory, and spices, but instead they loaded the ships with slaves. After selling their human cargo, they sailed to a notorious pirates' island off the coast of Madagascar. There they agreed to lend their ships to John Bowen, a pirate, who intended to raid East India-men, ships engaged in trade with India and the Orient. On more sober consideration, the Drummonds decided to renege on the agreement, but Bowen sailed away with their ships while the Drummonds were ashore. Fire destroyed the *Content* on the Malabar Coast, and when Bowen captured an Indiaman, he kept the larger vessel and scuttled the *Speedy Return*. The Drummonds made no effort to inform the company about the fate of their ships and cargoes and simply disappeared. It has been suggested that they may have changed their identities and become pirates, and there was even a rumor that some MacDonalds tracked them down and avenged the Massacre of Glencoe.

The Kuna remember the Scots as allies. They still refer to New Cale-donia Bay as Puerto Escocés, the Scottish Port. In 2011, the Panaman-ian government officially renamed the bay Puerto Inabaginya in honor of a prominent Kuna leader of the early twentieth century, but for the Kuna it remains Puerto Escocés.

Sources

Many of the original sources detailing the business dealings of the Company of Scotland Trading to Africa and the Indies survive in the National Library of Scotland, the archives of the Royal Bank of Scot-land, Glasgow University Library, and London University Library. Sev-eral other institutions hold less material. The Royal Bank of Scotland is particularly to be lauded for its historical consciousness and appre-ciation of the importance of banking and finance. Many modern ac-counts have been written about the Darien scheme, each with its emphasis. John Prebble's classic *The Darien Disaster: A Scots Colony in the New World, 1698–1700* (New York: Holt, Rinehart and Win-ston, 1969) provides a detailed account of the events at Darien, while Douglas Watt, *The Price of Scotland: Darien, Union, and the Wealth of Nations* (Edinburgh: Luath Press, 2014) is primarily concerned with the economic effects of the Darien scheme and the attendant political results. Both provide extensive lists of the original sources and their locations, including a full list of the pamphlets published after the fail-ure of the colony. George Pratt Insh played a vital role in the recovery and organization of the Darien papers. In addition to *The Company of Scotland Trading to Africa and the Indies* (London: C. Scribner's Sons, 1932), which emphasizes the history of the company, and *The Darien Scheme* (London: Historical Association by Staples Press,

1947), Insh published an account of his discoveries as *Historian's Odyssey: The Romance of the Quest for the Records of the Darien Company* (Edinburgh: Moray Press, 1938), a pure expression of a historian's joy of research and discovery.

Lionel Wafer's account of Darien, printed as *A New Voyage and Description of the Isthmus of America* (London: Printed for James Knapton, 1699), was instrumental in forming William Paterson's vision and encouraging the entire colonization effort. Paterson's extensive and somewhat repetitious writings are gathered in Saxe Bannister, ed., *The Writings of William Peterson, Founder of the Bank of England*, 3 vols. (New York: Kelley, 1968).

Hugh Rose, secretary and clerk during the first colonial effort, kept an official journal that covered the voyage and early days of the colony. Alexander Hamilton carried the journal back to the directors of the company in Scotland, departing on December 29, 1698, about two months after the initial landing. Robert Pennecuik also kept a journal that well reflects his pompous, bullying character. These journals are printed in John Hill Burton, ed., *The Darien Papers: being a selection of original letters and official documents relating to the establishment of a colony at Darien by the Company of Scotland Trading to Africa and the Indies, 1695–1700* (Edinburgh: n.p., 1849), and in George Pratt Insh, ed., *Papers Relating to the Ships and Voyages of the Company of Scotland Trading to Africa and the Indies, 1696–1707*, Publications of the Scottish History Society, ser. 3, vol. 6 (Edinburgh: T. and A. Constable for the Scottish History Society, 1924).

The Reverend Francis Borland's *The History of Darien* (Glasgow: John Bryce, 1779), written mostly in 1700, is vital for understanding events during the second occupancy of Darien. Borland, fanatical and self-righteous, provides a vital account of events amid an abundance of singularly distasteful, sanctimonious, smug assurances of his own moral excellence and merciless condemnation of the suffering colonists as sinners punished by a wrathful God.

Francis Russell Hart, *The Disaster of Darien* (London: Constable, 1930) is of importance for the appendix printing the most important Spanish documents relevant to the campaign against and destruction of the Darien colony. C. D. Storrs, "Disaster at Darien (1698–1700)?: The Persistence of Spanish Imperial Power on the Eve of the Demise of the Spanish Habsburgs," *European History Quarterly* 29 (1999): 5-38, provides a sympathetic and detailed account of the preparation in Spain of the campaign against Darien based on extensive research in the Spanish archives.

Nate Edwards, *Caledonia's Last Stand: In Search of the Lost Scots of Darien* (Edinburgh: Luath Press, 2007) should not be missed. This excellent travel book gives a vivid account of the land the Scots attempted to colonize and testifies to the importance of the memory of Darien to modern Scots.

TWELVE

Sir Gregor MacGregor: Cacique *of the* Never-Never Land *of* Poyais (1820–1838)

Gregor MacGregor's Early Years

The colony of Poyais on the Mosquito Coast of modern Honduras was the creation of Gregor MacGregor, and any account of the colony must begin with him. MacGregor was born in 1786 in Scotland to a family locally prominent and prosperous but not truly wealthy. He seems to have had good, basic education, and in 1803, at sixteen, the youngest possible age, he joined the British army. His family purchased the rank of ensign in the 57th Foot for him, which likely cost the substantial sum of £450. Within a year he had been promoted to lieutenant, as the regiment recruited more men in anticipation of renewed war against Napoleon. In 1805, he married Maria Bowater, a member of a distinguished and affluent family, who brought a large dowry. Two months later, MacGregor purchased the rank of captain for £900. He always maintained he had paid from his own funds, but subsequent events showed his word was not to be trusted. He was not universally popular with other officers, who saw him as arrogant, pretentious, and a heavy drinker whose behavior deteriorated with alcohol.

In 1809, MacGregor went with the 57th Foot to Lisbon, but he soon left the regiment. According to a later published report, he quarreled with a superior officer, the matter becoming so serious that Mac-Gregor was transferred to a Portuguese regiment, part of the combined British and Portuguese army serving under William Carr Beresford, first Viscount Beresford. MacGregor was granted the rank of major in the Portuguese regiment but did not serve there long either. He seems to have quarreled again with other officers, and reportedly Beresford indicated that MacGregor's services were no longer required. He resigned from the army, sold his rank for £1,350, and returned to England.

Shortly afterward, the 57th Foot won fame for its role in the Battle of Albuera in Spain, earning the men the nickname "Die-Hards." Mac-Gregor was no longer a member of the regiment and had returned to England by that time, but later he frequently bragged of his service with the regiment and did nothing to deny the report that he had served nobly during the famous battle.

MacGregor returned to Scotland and took up residence at Edinburgh, where he assumed the title of colonel and styled himself Sir Gregor MacGregor, claiming he had been awarded knighthood in the Portuguese Ordem Militar de Cristo (Military Order of Christ). It is not apparent whether that was a legitimate claim, and MacGregor subsequently let the impression stand that his knighthood was British rather than Portuguese. MacGregor's attempt to break into the upper strata of Edinburgh society failed, as the dour Scots saw him as a poser. MacGregor and his wife soon relocated to the Isle of Wight, where they experienced more social success. By the second half of 1811, Mac-Gregor and wife moved again, this time to London, where he claimed to be the heir of a Highland baronet that included an estate and castle—all false. In December 1811, MacGregor's wife died. The expenses required to maintain his social pretenses in London rapidly drove him toward bankruptcy. ·

MacGregor in South America

Shortly after the death of his wife, MacGregor came into an inheritance that would not support his extravagances for long, but it was enough to finance a trip to Venezuela. There he might win fame and fortune in the revolution against Spanish rule. In 1810, a junta deposed Spanish colonial officers in Venezuela and in 1811 declared Venezuela

278 Neither Hee Nor Any of His Companie Did Return Againe

an independent republic. General Sebastián Francisco de Miranda y Rodríguez de Espinoza, usually known simply as Miranda, rose to become the chief military figure in the Venezuela independence movement. MacGregor attached himself to Miranda, who granted him the rank of colonel and appointed him commander of a cavalry battalion.

The republican movement, however, quickly faltered. Large portions of the country remained under Royalist control, trade with Spain ceased, the economy deteriorated, and two strong earthquakes struck Venezuela, doing the greatest damage in the republican areas. The first quake struck late in 1811 and the second on Maundy Thursday of 1812. The junta had been initially established on Maundy Thursday two years earlier, and the superstitious, encouraged by the clergy, saw this as divine punishment for rejecting royal rule.

As Royalist forces moved toward Caracas, MacGregor and his cavalry acquitted themselves well, victorious in one engagement and defeated in another, but having fought well, and Miranda promoted MacGregor to brigadier general. During a lull in activity, MacGregor met and was married to doña Josefa Antonia Andrea Aristeguieta y Lovera. Less than a month later, amid discord, betrayal, and incompetence, the first Republic of Venezuela floundered and failed, and MacGregor and wife escaped from to Curaçao aboard a British ship. Miranda fell into the hands of the Spanish forces and died in a Spanish prison in 1816.

Simon Bolivar, now the de facto leader of the Venezuelan independence movement, also fled to Curaçao. He was a cousin of MacGregor's new wife, but not yet famous, and for the moment unable to take action. MacGregor offered his services to Antonio Amador José de Nariño y Álvarez del Casal, generally known as Nariño, who was fighting for the independence of Gran Granada, the core of which would eventually become the modern nation of Colombia. Nariño made MacGregor the commander of the military district of Socorro near the border of Venezuela, far from active fighting. MacGregor improved discipline among the troops but made himself unpopular with other officers by his pretentiousness.

After about a year, Nariño's effort collapsed, and MacGregor withdrew to Cartagena in Colombia. As the Spanish Royalists closed in on the city, the local government declared martial law and appointed MacGregor commander of a regiment. The Spanish besieged the city from August through early December, by which time famine left the

Portrait of MacGregor. Mezzotint, ca. 1820, by Samuel William Reynolds, after a painting by Simon Jacques Rochard. This portrait is used as the frontispiece of Thomas Strangeways, *Sketch of the Mosquito Shore, Including the Territory of Poyais, Descriptive of the Country; with Some Information as to its Productions, the Best Mode of Culture, &c. Chiefly Intended for the Use of Settlers* (Edinburgh: William Blackwood, 1822).

garrison too weak to sustain defense. MacGregor and two other officers commanded an escape. Aboard gunboats they slipped by the Spanish ships guarding the mouth of the bay and, once clear, sailed to Jamaica. There the British inhabitants celebrated MacGregor as a hero, his reputation enhanced by his own embellished accounts of his activities during the siege and escape.

While MacGregor was engaged in Gran Granada, Bolivar made another unsuccessful attempt to liberate Venezuela and then raised new forces at Santo Domingo for yet another attempt. MacGregor approached Bolivar, who restored him to his old rank of brigadier general, and he sailed with Bolivar's invasion force. Bolivar had thirteen ships but relatively few soldiers and hoped to raise more troops in Venezuela. After a minor victory at Carúpano, Bolivar sailed to Ocumare west of Caracas, where MacGregor was assigned to recruit Indians at the nearby town of Choroni. There he commanded about

1,500 men, consisting of some troops brought from Santo Domingo, Spanish creoles recruited in the area, and many local Indians armed only with bows and arrows.

Once again, the Royalist troops proved more than a match for Bolivar's hastily raised and poorly trained forces. Defeated in the battle of La Cabrera, Bolivar retreated to his ships and sailed to Choroni, where he hoped he could make a stand or at least evacuate MacGregor's forces. When Bolivar arrived, about July 20, he discovered that MacGregor had left the town on July 16, 1816, and was withdrawing toward Barcelona about two hundred miles to the east. MacGregor's retreat was the one genuine military achievement of his life.

MacGregor had no wagons or pack mules and only a few horses, so his men had to carry their provisions on their backs along with their arms and ammunition as they traversed a coastal mountain range, a large expanse of swampy jungle, and plains covered with tall grass and thick brush. The men found little to eat during the trek, and Royalist soldiers harassed the retreating revolutionaries from the beginning of their march. MacGregor's men were able to repel attacks, but they took casualties and had to abandon the wounded, as they had no way to transport them.

On July 27, the revolutionaries encountered a strong Royalist force outside the little town of Chaguaramas, south of Caracas. Driven by hunger and desperation, MacGregor's men fired a volley at the enemy and then charged furiously. Surprised by the assault, the Royalists panicked and fled into the town. The next morning MacGregor demanded surrender. When the Spanish commander refused, MacGregor prepared to besiege the town, but at night he withdrew his forces and continued the march toward Barcelona. The Royalist forces did not begin to follow until July 30, when they were reinforced.

The climax came on August 10 near Quebrada Honda, where the Royalists, with five hundred mounted dragoons and about seven hundred infantry, forced MacGregor to make a stand. He had about the same number of men, but most were Indians armed only with bows and arrows. MacGregor chose the field of battle with care. A small stream flowed across his front, and he anchored one flank on an inconspicuous morass. The Spanish dragoons blundered into the swamp and had to abandon their horses and fight on foot. As the Royalist infantry attempted to cross the brook, the Indians showered them with arrows. The battle continued for over two hours until MacGregor reverted to the tactic that had succeeded a few days earlier, a furious assault. He led the charge on one of the few horses, and his wife, Josefa, rode beside him on another, brandishing a lance and exhorting the troops. Again, the Royalists broke and retreated precipitously.

The battle by Quebrada Honda was the last Royalist attack on MacGregor's forces, who soon afterward reached the main body of the revolutionary army, entering Barcelona on August 20. MacGregor had undoubtedly conducted the long retreat with skill and courage, though it should be noted that in addition to fighting for his men and his wife, he was saving his own life. The Spanish government issued a decree that "all foreign adventurers taken with arms in their hands in our territories . . . shall be condemned to death."

MacGregor took control of Barcelona and issued a grandiloquent proclamation recounting the heroic retreat and exhorting the citizenry to support the revolution, but his moment of glory was short lived. Before long, two generals senior in rank arrived and displaced Mac-Gregor from command. One, Manuel Carlos María Francisco Piar Gómez, soon won a glorious victory over Royalist forces near Barcelona, eclipsing MacGregor's achievement. Ambitions thwarted, MacGregor resigned from the army, left his men, and withdrew to the island of Margarita and from there sailed to the United States.

MacGregor in Florida: The Amelia Island Affair

By March 1817, MacGregor was in Washington, DC, where he graduated from braggadocio to fraud. MacGregor promoted a scheme to seize Amelia Island as a preliminary to the annexation of all Florida to the United States, and, more importantly, he realized he could raise money to finance the venture. Amelia Island is a barrier island at the mouth of the St. Marys River, at the extreme northeast of Florida, bordering on Georgia to the north. It is about thirteen miles long and a little over four miles wide at its broadest point. There is a decent harbor and one small town, Fernandina, where the Spanish maintained a garrison of fifty-four mainly superannuated men, a fort near the harbor, and two blockhouses inland defending the landward side of the town. The small population included a few respectable merchants and farmers and a motley assortment of buccaneers, slavers, hunters, felons, and general miscreants.

The United States had an interest in Amelia Island and Florida that predated MacGregor's involvement. In 1812, President James Madison and George Mathews, a former governor of Georgia, planned to annex the Spanish province of Florida Oriental (East Florida) to the United States, starting at Amelia Island. Mathews led a force of civilian volunteers who seized the island, and the president sent gunboats and troops who took possession of the island from Mathews in the name of the United States. Congress, however, feared that Spain might go to war with the United States over the seizure, a daunting prospect as the United States was then at war with Britain. In 1813, Madison returned the island to Spain, an unpopular act, particularly in the southern states.

MacGregor obtained a document signed by representatives of the Latin American independence movements in Venezuela, New Granada, Rio de la Plata (Argentina), and Mexico encouraging him to take possession of Florida from the Spanish. He claimed the US government also commissioned him to take possession of Florida in the name of New Granada and provided him with funds to do so. According to MacGregor, Spain was willing to cede Amelia Island to the United States but would not do so openly for fear of encouraging independence movements elsewhere and offending the British, who had previously held Florida. Spain would not oppose MacGregor's taking Amelia Island in the name of New Granada and Venezuela and holding it for a short time, after which the United States could occupy the island. MacGregor asserted that during March 1817, he met daily with the US secretary of state and Spanish ambassador in Washington working out the details of this arrangement. MacGregor's claims were almost entirely fiction. Neither the American secretary of state nor the Spanish ambassador were in Washington when MacGregor claimed to have met with them daily, and subsequently both the United States and Spain denied any role in his Amelia Island scheme.

MacGregor's initial attempt to raise money and men did not do well in Philadelphia, where people were little concerned with Florida, and MacGregor's plans seemed vague and unconvincing. He succeeded at Charleston, South Carolina, and Savannah, Georgia, however, playing upon his knighthood and rank of general, his carefully enhanced military reputation from the British and South American campaigns, and his ability to portray a charming British aristocrat. He sold documents for $1,000 each entitling the holder to two thousand acres of Florida land or money back with interest once the conquest was accomplished, and he approached a commercial firm identified by a contemporary only as C. and Co. of Savanah, convincing them to pay $30,000 for a grant of thirty thousand acres of particularly choice farmland in Florida. His efforts raised about $160,000, ostensibly to finance his expedition. The war with Britain had recently concluded, and many soldiers had been discharged from the army. It was difficult for the recently released military men to find employment, so MacGregor easily recruited about 150 men, ranging from officers to dock workers. Many, however, soon lost their enthusiasm and deserted. One of MacGregor's associates preceded him to Amelia claiming MacGregor would soon arrive at the head of a thousand well-equipped troops. MacGregor actually sailed with just fifty-five men equipped with only small arms.

They landed on the island without opposition and advanced on the fort. The Spanish captain had ordered his men not to fire and quietly surrendered. MacGregor had the Spanish soldiers transported to the mainland and released and then followed his victory by issuing a pompous declaration styling himself "Brigadier General and Commander-in-Chief of all the forces both naval and military, destined to effect the independence of the Floridas, duly authorized by the constituted authorities of the Republics of Mexico, Buenos Ayres, New Grenada and Venezuela." He established a government on Amelia Island, the chief purpose of which seems to have been to raise money. He sold letters of marque allowing pirates to pose as revolutionary privateers and established an admiralty court to declare prizes taken by such revolutionary privateers as legitimately captured so they could be put on the market openly. For this service, MacGregor charged 16.5 percent of the value of the prize vessel and the goods it contained. He also passed time designing a flag, a green cross on a white field; dress insignia for his troops; and military decorations for himself, but he made no effort to take the rest of Florida from the Spanish.

More men joined MacGregor on the island, although he never had more than two hundred under arms. He had the local printer issue Amelia Island banknotes with which he paid his men, much to their discontent. Discipline deteriorated, soldiers extorted residents of the island, and desertions became common. When it became apparent that the Spanish at St. Augustine were mounting an effort to retake the island, MacGregor departed to Nassau, leaving behind about 120 men, many debts, and no money except his worthless paper currency.

MacGregor left Amelia in the hands of Ruggles Hubbard, on leave from his office as New York City sheriff, and Jared Irwin, formerly a

284 Neither Hee Nor Any of His Companie Did Return Againe

member of the Pennsylvania House of Representatives who had served with the rank of colonel during the War of 1812. The Spanish attacked in September 1817 with two gunboats and about three hundred men who erected a battery of four cannons on a hill outside of town. Hubbard and Irwin mustered ninety-four men who manned the fort at Fernandina supported by an armed schooner. The artillery duel resulted in the death of two Spanish troops and wounding of several more. The Spanish commander abandoned the attack and returned with his men to St. Augustine.

Shortly after the battle, Louis-Michel Aury came to Amelia Island. A French-born pirate, he ostensibly claimed to be operating as a privateer for the revolutionary Republic of Mexico. Hubbard and Irwin initially welcomed Aury as an ally against the Spanish, but tensions soon arose. Hubbard died of yellow fever in October, and Irwin could not stand alone against Aury, who took command of the island in the name of the Mexican Republic. The United States and Spain were at the time in negotiations concerning the future of Florida, and Aury's activities threatened to disrupt a potential agreement. Consequently, in December 1817, US forces intervened to take possession of Amelia Island. Aury soon departed to continue his revolutionary and piratical activities elsewhere, and in 1819, Spain agreed to cede Florida to the United States.

MacGregor to Portobelo

MacGregor soon departed from Nassau for London, stopping only briefly at Dublin and Liverpool, where he promoted his image as a hero of the Latin American wars of liberation. In Britain, the end of the long wars against Napoleon left many officers and common soldiers and sailors unemployed. In more peaceful times, they could have learned skills in their youth that would have enabled them to earn a living in civilian society, but early and often involuntary enrollment in the military left them unqualified for any other employment. As Bolivar and other leaders of the South American independence movements were at last making substantial advances against Spanish forces, unemployed men from many nations were eager to join the South American revolutionaries. Some, primarily educated officers, were idealists, but others were willing to serve simply for mercenaries' wages and the hope of loot. The situation suited MacGregor well.

In London, MacGregor met with Luis López Méndez, Bolivar's close friend and diplomatic agent, and persuaded him to advance him

£1,000 so he could raise troops and charter ships to carry them to Venezuela. MacGregor, however, squandered the money on luxurious living. He next associated himself with several dubious characters who sold officers' commissions and raised troops in Britain and Ireland. In late 1818, MacGregor, along with his wife and a headquarters staff, set sail, followed shortly by other ships bearing about five hundred officers and men, designated by MacGregor as the "Army of New Granada." All rendezvoused at Aux Cayes, Haiti.

MacGregor had men, but he lacked the arms required to turn them into a fighting force and the eighty Spanish silver eight-reales pieces ("dollars" in the common parlance) he had promised each man on his arrival. The sum seems small, but, of course, had much greater purchasing power then. Grumbling and near mutiny were somewhat dispelled when patriotic South American merchants provided arms and ammunition to his troops and credit so he could pay and feed them. The president of Haiti gave MacGregor a sloop on the condition that whenever he took territory from the Spanish, he would free all slaves. Relieved of all immediate concerns, MacGregor failed to move for a month until he had exhausted all his credit in Haiti.

MacGregor sent his force to remote St. Andres Island while he proceeded to Jamaica in an unsuccessful attempt to raise more money. After nearly another month passed, he arrived at St. Andres, where he announced the army would forthwith attack Portobelo on the isthmus of Panama. Portobelo had once been a major port, but it had long since declined and was now of little importance. The town did, however, offer MacGregor two inducements: it was lightly defended, and its name was still famous. A victory there, although of little significance, would redound to MacGregor's fame and prestige.

Adverse winds delayed the ships' final approach to Portobelo. His ships were sighted, and the Spanish had the opportunity to prepare for the attack. MacGregor's second in command, William Rafter, landed with two hundred men and soon encountered about the same number of Spanish troops in a strong defensive position. Rather than making a suicidal frontal attack, Rafter flanked the Spanish position through terrain so difficult that the Spanish thought it impassable. The Spanish abandoned their position, and Rafter and his men marched into Portobelo unopposed. MacGregor remained aboard ship, reportedly drinking wine, until after the town was secured. He announced that the army would soon move on Panama City and conquer the isthmus, but he made no plans for any such advance. Rather, MacGregor passed time sending grandiloquent accounts of his victory to newspapers in Jamaica and Britain and creating his own chivalric knighthood, the Order of the Green Cross, with, of course, himself as its head. Henceforth, MacGregor would grant his own knighthoods to supporters and potential contributors. Reportedly, his evenings were spent gourmandizing and drinking.

As news of the victory spread, more men flocked to Portobelo. Although a substantial amount of money was recovered in the town, MacGregor initially distributed none as pay or bonuses. Eventually, as the troops grew agitated, he paid them just twenty dollars each. MacGregor remained otherwise indolent, and discipline disappeared among the troops, who often ignored orders. Men spent their time drinking, gambling, and brawling. Refugees from Portobelo informed the Spanish at Panama City of the situation, and they sent a force that retook the town with ridiculous ease. They marched to the central square unnoticed until they opened fire on MacGregor's troops. MacGregor precipitously escaped by jumping out of a second story window and, using a log for flotation, tried to swim to the ships. He almost drowned before he was noticed and rescued. William Rafter rallied over three hundred men who defended themselves in the fort, though they had few weapons and little ammunition.

MacGregor later maintained that he took command of the situation and ordered the ships to engage the Spanish with their cannons, but Rafter betrayed him by surrendering before he could do anything. The accounts of the survivors differ in virtually every particular. They maintained that Rafter sent a message to MacGregor requesting that he have the ships bombard the Spanish, but MacGregor precipitously sailed away, and the other ships followed. Rafter had to surrender. Many of the prisoners died during a forced march to Panama City. William Rafter and other officers were executed by firing squads and the common soldiers forced to labor in chain gangs until the Spanish withdrew from the area in 1821, when they were released. Of the 340 prisoners captured at Portobelo, only 121 survived.

MacGregor at Rio de la Hacha

MacGregor sailed to Port-au-Prince, Haiti, where his reception was unenthusiastic. He was in debt to merchants there and had no prospect of paying. Nevertheless, for the moment matters seemed hopeful as about nine hundred new recruits arrived from Ireland and Britain, and a supporter in England sent a ship loaded with arms and munitions to equip the men. Then matters quickly deteriorated. After quarreling with the captain and legal owner of the sloop that carried him from Portobelo, MacGregor seized the vessel. Accusations and counteraccusations flew back and forth between the two men until the president of Haiti, disgusted with the entire affair, ordered MacGregor and the ship out of the port. He sailed to Aux Cayes, where the crew deserted, the ship grounded on the beach, and the locals stripped everything to the bare hull, which MacGregor could sell for only $500. To compound McGregor's troubles, the Haitian government declared the cargo of munitions and the ship carrying them as contraband and impounded them.

MacGregor now lacked ships and arms and had little money. Once again, a lassitude overtook him, and he did little but assume the title "Captain-General and Commander-in-Chief of the Land and Naval Forces of New Granada" while his men languished on short rations, protested the lack of pay, grew increasingly disorderly, and deserted until only about 250 remained. As matters were beginning to look hopeless, another contingent arrived from England carrying about sixty troops and forty able officers, including Lieutenant Colonel Michael Rafter. At that time, Rafter did not know the details of Mac-Gregor's actions at Portobelo, but he knew his brother William had been taken prisoner by the Spanish and hoped to rescue him. The president of Haiti agreed to release the impounded ship and its cargo of arms, probably just to get MacGregor and his men to leave the country, and MacGregor decided to attack Rio de la Hacha, on the northern Caribbean coast of Colombia.

The attack proved to be a sad and bloody reprise of the failure at Portobelo. On September 29, 1819, MacGregor and his revolutionary troops sailed in a small, single-masted vessel and two medium-sized ships, one of which had carried recent recruits from England and the other that transported arms. MacGregor hoped and expected the town would welcome him as a liberator, but shore batteries fired on the ships as they approached. He retreated to a safe distance and cruised offshore until after nightfall. MacGregor then ordered a landing to be made on a convenient beach about three miles from the town, indicating he would come ashore and assume command once the landing was completed.

William Norcott commanded the effort, ably assisted by Michael Rafter and other officers. By about 3:00 AM, 210 officers and men had landed without opposition, although skirmishing soon broke out between MacGregor's troops and Royalist Spanish soldiers and local militia. MacGregor left his ship about 4:00 AM, but a few Spanish stranggers fired at MacGregor and his headquarters staff as they attempted to land. Although the body of his troops were only a few hundred yards farther down the beach, MacGregor and his companions scurried back to the ships, and once aboard, MacGregor ordered the ships to move farther offshore. While the troops remained waiting for their commander on the beach, the Spanish infiltrated close enough deliver a sudden volley that killed and wounded fifteen officers and men. Norcott ordered the men into the jungle to counterattack the Spanish, who withdrew. As his men approached the town, an artillery battery fired on them causing many casualties, and the battle raged for five hours before the revolutionaries captured the battery and the Royalist forces broke and scattered. Seventy-eight of the attackers were killed or wounded.

As dawn broke, MacGregor and the ships remained far offshore, even after the flag of New Granada flew over the town. To the troops on shore, it appeared that MacGregor was on the point of abandoning them. Norcott had to row out to MacGregor's ship before he consented to enter the harbor, and even then he would not come ashore immediately. When MacGregor finally alighted, he received a rude welcome from the troops, some of whom threatened to shoot him while others spat and swore at him. His response was to draw up another bombastic and self-congratulatory proclamation, which he signed with a new and singularly bizarre title: "His Majesty the Inca of New Granada."

MacGregor justified this new title of "Inca" by claiming that an ancestor had participated in the unsuccessful Scottish attempt to colonize the isthmus of Panama, the Darien colony, over a century earlier, and there he married "an Indian Princess." MacGregor may have had an ancestor who participated in the Darien colony and who had a child by an Indian woman, but there is no record of a marriage, and the local Kuna Indian tribe was not related to the Incas in any way. General Miranda mentioned "Inca" among other possibilities as a possible title for a Latin American head of state as it might appeal to Native peoples, and MacGregor may have fastened on Miranda's suggestion.

Whatever the origin of MacGregor's new title, the ridiculousness of the narcissistic claim was evident to everyone other than the "Inca" himself.

MacGregor then fell into days of indolence and inaction. Soldiers broke into stores of liquor and drunkenly refused to obey orders, and neither Norcott nor Rafter could maintain order without MacGregor's support. Most of the inhabitants fled from Rio de la Hacha, fearing both the occupiers and the inevitable Spanish attempt to recapture the town. When a Spanish schooner sailed into the harbor, not realizing the town had fallen into enemy hands, it was quickly seized, and Norcott, Rafter, five naval officers, and twenty-seven soldiers and sailors, all thoroughly disgusted with MacGregor, resigned and sailed away in the schooner.

News that the Spanish were approaching with a force of soldiers, militia, and Indian allies finally roused MacGregor, who delivered a speech in which he promised to lead the men personally in the coming battle. Afterward he said he would escort an officer's wife and children to one of the ships for safety and return with more men to defend the town. He took the family to the ship, but then he boarded another one and deserted Rio de la Hacha and all who remained there. The Spanish and their Indian allies quickly overwhelmed the leaderless defenders, and a general slaughter ensued. Few survived to be taken prisoner, and they were summarily executed shortly thereafter. MacGregor held Rio de la Hacha for just about one week, and the adventure cost hundreds of lives.

MacGregor sought to blame Norcott and Rafter for the disaster at Rio de la Hacha, claiming they looted the town before deserting in the face of the enemy. Those who left the town before the disaster testified that MacGregor's account was false, and he was now despised throughout the Caribbean. The Haitians seized one of his ships, and he barely escaped the island. Bolivar ordered that if he came to South America, he should be arrested for treason and hanged, and the British government of Jamaica issued a warrant for his arrest as a pirate. In England, where witnesses were not available, it was difficult to judge between conflicting accounts, but even there MacGregor had no immediate prospect other than debtors' prison.

His Highness, Gregor, Cacique of Poyais

MacGregor next appeared in the early months of 1820 at Capo Gracias á Dios at the mouth of the Rio Coco, today the border between

Honduras to the north and Nicaragua to the south. Spain claimed the area but had never settled it, and during the seventeenth and eighteenth centuries, English buccaneers established cordial relations with Mosquito Indians there who saw them as trading partners and allies against the Spanish. The leading Mosquito family adopted English names and the title "king," often sent sons to England for education, and sought to have England recognize the area as an English colony. The English government provided some slight supervision for British citizens who settled along the coast but saw no real advantage in formally annexing the area, which would certainly alienate the Spanish government and could even lead to war.

MacGregor met with the Mosquito king, George Frederick, also known as George Frederick II and George Frederick Augustus I, who ruled from 1816 to 1824. During an alcoholic evening, he granted MacGregor permission to form a colony in the area known as Poyais, consisting roughly of the drainage basin of the Black River (today the Rio Sico). The name Poyais is derived from the name of the local Indians, known variously as Poyas, Payas, Popyya, Poyai, Poyers, and Pawyers. This coastal area is swampy and covered with heavy jungle, while territory farther inland is less sodden but heavily forested. In 1732, William Pitt, probably a distant relative of the like-named English politician, made a settlement at the Black Lagoon (today the Laguna de Bacalar) on the shore of Poyais. It was generally known as the Black Lagoon Settlement, but late in its history, when the Spanish held the town, it was called San Juan or St. Joseph, and under that name it would feature in MacGregor's plan.

The Black Lagoon Settlement grew to be moderately prosperous with a population at its height of about 1,300, mostly Black slaves. In 1786, Spain and Britain agreed that the British would evacuate the Mosquito Coast in exchange for added security for Belize and expanded logging and fishing rights. The British at the Black Lagoon were replaced by forty Spanish families and a garrison of forty-eight men manning a small earthen fort. The Spanish effort was a failure, mainly because of unwillingness or inability to supply the Mosquito Indians with the trade goods on which they relied. In 1800, the Indians attacked and burned the community, killing some of the inhabitants while the rest fled. The area was not resettled, and wild growth quickly obscured the slight remains of the community. By 1820, when MacGregor persuaded the Mosquito king to grant him the right to establish a colony in the area, the Black Lagoon settlement and the rest of Poyais had reverted to a state of nature.

In 1821, MacGregor and his wife returned to England. There were still disgruntled creditors there, and the previous year, Michael Rafter published an exposé, *Memoirs of Gregor M'Gregor* (London: J. J. Stockdale, 1820), but MacGregor's carefully nurtured reputation as a hero of the South American liberation movement, undeniable personal charm, glib tongue, brilliant display of military medals (many he invented himself), and intriguing plan for a colony at Poyais abolished most doubts. The creditors were quieted with promises of payment soon, and MacGregor countered Rafter's work with his own accusations and highly fictional account of events at Rio de la Hacha published in the *Edinburgh Courant* magazine in September and October 1821.

MacGregor's accounts of his adventures and those of his wife, Josefa, an exotic, dark-haired beauty and cousin of the now-famous Bolivar, charmed London society. During winter 1821, the two were widely celebrated and invited to the most fashionable gatherings. Mac-Gregor informed his new friends that the king of the Mosquito Coast had appointed him *cacique* of Poyais, which was an independent principality established by the royal authority. "Kasike," more usually spelled "cacique" in the Spanish fashion, was a Native American word meaning chief. As such, MacGregor signed correspondence as "Gregor the First, Sovereign Prince of the State of Poyais."

MacGregor explained that after a brief Spanish interlude, the British had returned to build a modern city on the European model, St. Joseph, on the western side of the lagoon just a few miles from the original Black Lagoon settlement. Major buildings in the city included a large cathedral, opera house, theater, the Bank of Poyais, government offices and parliament, a regal palace, and mansions built by entrepreneurs who had begun moving to Poyais, attracted by its abundant resources. The city, MacGregor assured his audiences, was graced by the latest European architectural styles and broad avenues. Protected by natural barriers and in agreement concerning borders with the neighboring Spanish provinces, Poyais remained in peace and security while the rest of Latin America was convulsed by revolutions and warfare. All that Poyais needed was an infusion of able, honest, and industrious British citizens to bring the blessings of Western civilization to the rest of the country beyond St. Joseph, and a good start had already been made at the town of Poyais, to the south on the banks of the Black River. In Poyais, fertile farmland was available at low prices, one hundred acres for £11 5s., and one acre for 2s. 3d. The average worker earned about £1 a week in industrial cities, more in London, and even agricultural workers earned at least 10s., the equivalent of half a pound, a week. A ten-acre plot was available for £1 2s. 5d., little over two weeks wages for an average working man. Three acres of cotton, potential emigrants were assured, would produce enough profit to support a family. Good British working men and women would of course need leaders, and MacGregor was also eager to recruit bureaucrats, military men, and cultural figures.

At first, MacGregor did not seek to raise money but indicated he just wished to inform his prominent new friends about Poyais and all its advantages and potentials. They, of course, were not likely to migrate, but MacGregor hoped they would encourage others, and he showered honors on those who aided him. For example, Major William John Richardson, a wealthy and honest gentleman, was so impressed with the MacGregors that he invited them to use his country estate near London as their official residence while in England. Mac-Gregor conferred on Richardson the rank of commander of the Most Illustrious Order of the Green Cross, the title Baron Tinto (Rio Tinto was a Spanish name for the Black River), and an estate of 12,800 acres in Poyais. He also appointed Richardson major of the Poyais Royal Regiment of Horse Guards and chargé d'affaires of the Legation for the Territory of Poyais in Great Britain. Richardson must also have received one of the medallions MacGregor had struck to commemorate his glorious triumph on Amelia Island and distributed to supporters. Such awards now appear ridiculous, but in the aristocratic world of nineteenth century Britain, they were important and highly sought, especially among men such as Richardson, wealthy and of some prominence but not truly a member of the elite. Any improvement in such a person's status enhanced the prospects of the entire family, especially allowing sons and daughters to aspire to marriages into families of still higher status and greater wealth.

MacGregor publicized the attractions of Poyais through interviews granted to newspapermen. He also placed advertisements in newspapers, printed pamphlets and handbills that were distributed on street corners, and even paid street entertainers to sing ballads about the marvelous land. The most impressive work was Thomas Strangeways,

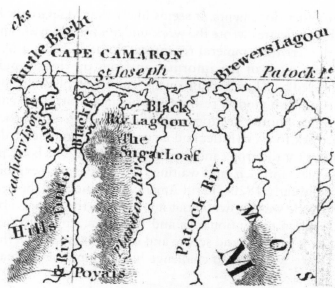

Detail from "A Map of Mosquitia and the Territory of Poyais with the Adjacent Countries," Leith: Wm. Reid, 1822. The map was sold independently in Edinburgh and London and included in Strangeways, *Sketch of the Mosquito Shore*. The map depicts the fictitious towns of St. Joseph and Poyais, south on the "Black River." Even the river systems bear little resemblance to a modern map of the region. The "Planlian Riv." on MacGregor's map appears on other maps as the Black River and today is known as the Rio Sico, while the river called the "Black River" on MacGregor's map is a much shorter, minor waterway. The Sugar Loaf Mountain, today the Pilón de Azúcar, is also misplaced and grossly exaggerated. It is a heavily forested, conical hill on the Rio Sico. MacGregor's map shows the outlet of the Black Lagoon in the middle of the lagoon. That outlet has since closed, although its location is apparent on a high-resolution satellite photograph, and a new outlet has appeared at the eastern end of the lagoon.

Sketch of the Mosquito Shore, Including the Territory of Poyais, Descriptive of the Country; with Some Information as to its Productions, the Best Mode of Culture, &c. Chiefly Intended for the Use of Settlers. (Edinburgh: William Blackwood, 1822). In addition to the publisher in Scotland, a bookshop in London was provided an ample supply for sales in England. The author is described on the title page as K. G. C. (Knight of the Green Cross), Captain of the 1st Native Poyer Regiment, and aide-de-camp to His Highness Gregor, Cazique of Poyais. Other than the name on the title page, however, there is no trace of Thomas Strangeways. No one seems ever to have met him, and he appears in no other documents. It seems likely that MacGregor himself or one of his associates wrote the work under a pseudonym. The book describes the territory, mineral resources, flora, and fauna of the region, deriving most of the information from previously published books, followed by a long section on agriculture emphasizing how migrants starting with modest resources could in a short time make substantial profits. Shorter sections described the Natives as docile and willing to work for very little, and an account of commerce depicted markets eager for the crops and products of Poyais. The book presents Poyais as a pleasant, rich land waiting for Europeans to exploit its resources. In the early 1820s, Latin America was much in the news, but remarkably little was known about it except for the reports about the conflicts between revolutionaries and Royalists. Poyais, MacGregor explained, was peaceful and secure and so did not appear in the headlines, and there was little to challenge his accounts of the marvelous land.

MacGregor particularly sought to recruit emigrants from Scotland. He claimed that an ancestor had participated in the failed Scottish attempt to colonize the isthmus of Panama, the Darien colony 120 years previously, a disaster that resonates to this day in the Scottish consciousness. The current effort at Poyais, MacGregor said, would restore Scotland's honor. This emotional appeal from a fellow Scot, hero of the Latin American wars for freedom, seems to have overridden all sense of suspicion, and many Scots enthusiastically purchased deeds to land in Poyais and exchanged good British pounds for Bank of Poyais banknotes. Beautifully printed by the company that manufactured banknotes for the Bank of Scotland, the impressive Poyais dollars, redeemable in "hard dollars" (silver Spanish eight-reales pieces, the famous "pieces of eight"), inspired confidence and seemed evidence of a well-organized and functioning economy.

MacGregor required funds, of course, for printing, distribution, the establishment of offices in England and Scotland to encourage emigration, the arrangement of transportation of emigrants to Poyais, and there were also personal expenses, including a staff of liveried servants and the fine wines and banquets with which he entertained friends and supporters. The obvious solution was to have the government of Poyais issue interest-bearing loan bonds secured by income from future taxes and excise fees. Newly independent Latin American countries, such as Colombia, Chile, and Peru, as well as long-established European nations, including Russia, Austria, Spain, and Denmark, all issued such national loan bonds. After the end of the Napoleonic Wars, London emerged as the world's leading financial center, and in the early 1820s, the London financial economic markets were flush with cash looking for lucrative investments. The Latin American loan bonds, including the Poyais bonds, offered the highest interest.

Poyais loan bonds with the face value of £200,000 were issued on October 23, 1822, in the amounts of £100, £200, and £500, and sold initially at 80 percent of the face value. The bonds were to mature in thirty years and pay annual interest of 6 percent, secured by the revenues of the government of Poyais and the sale of land in Poyais. Buyers only had to make a down payment of 15 percent, with the remaining sum due in two installments in 1823. Beautifully printed, endorsed by the famous and celebrated Gregor MacGregor, the bonds proved popular, and the few voices of skepticism and caution were ignored or ridiculed. Not all the bonds were sold initially, but enough were to finance MacGregor and provide for the dispatch of settlers to the Poyais colony.

Colonists at Poyais

Even before the first bond sales, in late August 1822, seventy colonists set sail from London for Poyais on the *Honduras Packet*, a ship owned by an old acquaintance of MacGregor's. MacGregor appointed Hector Hall as leader of the colonists, commissioning him as lieutenant colonel of the 2nd Native Regiment of Foot, lieutenant governor of the Town and District of St. Joseph acting in the name of His Highness Gregor in his absence, and president of the Ordinary Council. Hall was a former officer in the British army, like so many others mustered out at the end of the Napoleonic Wars. He was accompanied by a group of young men whose families purchased officers' commissions for them in the Poyais army. There were also clerks who anticipated posts in the government bureaucracy, several doctors, and others eager to begin new lives in the land that offered such great promise.

The *Honduras Packet* crossed without incident to the shore of Honduras, where the captain quickly located the Black Lagoon, although he noted that MacGregor's printed map of the area agreed only poorly with the official charts. The ship's company then waited for a boat from shore to greet them, but no one came. The captain ordered a cannon fired to attract attention, but again no one appeared. Assuming

View of Poyais depicting the entrance to the Black Lagoon with a view of the imaginary town of St. Joseph and Sugar Loaf Mountain, grossly exaggerated and misplaced. Strangeways, *Sketch of the Mosquito Shore*, page 2.

that the town must be some distance away, the emigrants disembarked and began landing their supplies. A storm arose before the unloading was complete, and the captain could not take the ship through the shallow entrance of the lagoon into the protected waters, and so had to run before the storm. Afterward, he did not return.

Marooned by the mouth of the Black Lagoon, the emigrants sent out parties to locate the town of St. Joseph without success. They met two Americans who had established a modest farm a few miles up the river that emptied into the lagoon, but they knew nothing of the towns of St. Joseph or Poyais. The searchers also met Natives, some of whom wanted to have nothing to do with the new arrivals. Others were friendly, and in response to questioning indicated they had heard of St. Joseph and guided them to the location. There, all the colonists found were the eroded remnants of an earthen fort, a couple of rusted cannons, and foundations of buildings burned long ago. Convinced that there was some misunderstanding, Hector Hall set out to travel overland through about 150 miles of jungle to Cape Gracias á Dios, where the Mosquito king resided and where, according to the reports from the local Indians, the captain of the *Honduras Packet* was busily

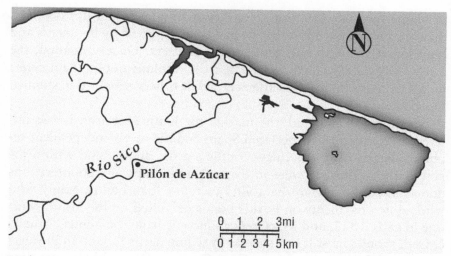

Modern map of the area of "Poyais" drawn from a satellite photograph. Pilón de Azú-car is the modern name of the Sugar Loaf Mountain, badly misrepresented on the engraving of the view of Poyais and mislocated on MacGregor's map of Mosquitia and the Territory of Poyais. It is a conical hill of moderate size heavily covered with tropical forest.

selling the emigrant's supplies and provisions. At the Black Lagoon, the emigrants set up tents and built bamboo huts thatched with reeds, and waited. They were still waiting when the second shipload of emigrants arrived.

Another old acquaintance of MacGregor's, Captain Henry Crouch, set sail from Leith, Scotland, on January 22, 1823, on the *Kennersley Castle* with nearly two hundred eager emigrants on board. Farmers purchased deeds to land that they could never have afforded in Britain, and artisans were attracted by reports of high wages and the potential of becoming owners of their own businesses. Most were relatively poor and had sold their meager possessions to pay for their passage and exchanged their remaining British pounds for the official paper money of the Bank of Poyais. Like the first group, there were also a minority of more-affluent and educated individuals who expected to become the leaders of the colonial movement. They arrived at the Black Lagoon on March 20 and found the puzzled members of the first group, still trying to understand what had happened. Like many other people in similar circumstances, they were reluctant to admit that they had been fooled and victimized, seeking any excuse to acquit MacGregor of blame for their situation. He, they maintained, had not deceived them about Poyais, but rather he had been ill-served by his agents and representatives who had exaggerated matters. Once unloaded, the *Kennersley Castle* sailed away. The most resolute among them determined to create their own settlement, while others remained in stunned inaction.

Meantime in England, the market for Latin American bonds faltered. Even as conflicts between Spain and the newly independent republics began to resolve, new conflicts arose among and within the new nations. Borders were in dispute, and coups and countercoups damaged confidence in the ability to repay loan bonds. Many who made down payments on Poyais bonds defaulted on the installments due in early 1823, and MacGregor's income from the bonds virtually ceased, though he still had success in selling deeds to land in Poyais.

In April, Hall returned from Cape Gracias á Dios with discouraging news. He had no explanation for the situation at the Black Lagoon, had missed the *Honduras Packet*, and the Mosquito king provided no aid. The rainy season began in late April, for which the colonists' poor huts and tents were ill suited. Shallow wells in the sand provided only brackish water and were easily contaminated. Malaria, yellow fever, and dysentery spread among the colonists, and dissension grew.

Hall decided to return to the cape, but he failed to acquaint the colonists with his purpose of going there. He realized long before most others that the resources and supplies were inadequate to establish a viable settlement under the current circumstances or even to remain long at the Black Lagoon. The colonists needed rescue but were not ready to admit that. If Hall had announced he was trying to arrange evacuation, he would have faced revolt, but by keeping his purpose secret he inevitably encountered resentment and distrust. He did inform the settlers that the *Skeen*, a ship from Britain, was supposed to arrive soon with supplies for those who chose to remain and the ability to carry away any who wished to leave. But the *Skeen* did not appear, and by late April many colonists were sick, eight had died, and any sense of community disappeared among them. Some looted the general stores and stole from one another, and few attempted to do anything to improve their situation.

About two weeks after Hall departed, the schooner *Mexican Eagle* approached the entrance to the lagoon by chance. Among its passengers was Marshal Bennet, the chief magistrate, colonel of the militia, and senior judge of the Supreme Court of Belize. He and others on board knew nothing of any plans for a settlement on the Mosquito Coast, had never heard of any such title as the Cacique of Poyais or anything called the Territory of Poyais, and while they thought it possible that the Mosquito king might provide land for settlement, they were certain he would not grant sovereignty of territory to anyone. Bennet indicated he had no authority to order the colonists to do anything, but he would offer advice: they could seek to evacuate to Belize, where at least the skilled artisans would find ready employment at high wages, or they could remain where they were and die. A few days later Hall returned, and the Mosquito king and his tribal elders came with him.

The king brought bitter news. He had granted MacGregor the right to settle in the area, but all the rest was false. He had not conceded sovereignty to MacGregor nor granted him the title cacique. MacGregor had no right to sell land in the area or bonds, and the towns of St. Joseph and Poyais did not exist. There was no government of Poyais, no cleared land to farm, and no infrastructure to move crops to market. The king, moreover, now revoked the grant to MacGregor because of his misrepresentations and informed the settlers they must either leave the king's territory or swear allegiance to him.

All dreams of Poyais were now dead. A few grumbled and considered resisting, but even these sentiments disappeared quickly. The *Mexican Eagle* could not carry all the colonists, but sixty were crowded aboard, priority given to families. The trip to Belize Town took only three days, but the temperature was sweltering while the sun was up, and it poured rain every night. It required second and third voyages in increasingly bad weather to evacuate the rest of the refugees, and many who arrived in Belize were exhausted and ill. Over the next few weeks, as many as 180 of the approximately 270 colonists died, some at the Black Lagoon but most in Belize, despite efforts of doctors and the primitive hospitals there. The highest official in Belize announced an official inquiry into the Poyais affair and sent an urgent account to the government in England, but this inquiry arrived just after five more ships carrying emigrants departed Britain for Poyais. Ships from the Royal Navy were able to intercept them and order their return, preventing an even larger tragedy.

Several skilled artisans remained in Belize, and a few scattered to other locations. Fewer than fifty returned to Britain, where, astoundingly, some continued to defend MacGregor, claiming that his agents and employees were responsible for the disaster but surely not the much-decorated, heroic, charismatic General Sir Gregor MacGregor. Major Richardson, who still considered MacGregor a friend, denounced the exposés in English and Scottish newspapers as gross libels. While the details of the disaster were not yet available in England, MacGregor tried to blame the debacle on a supposedly larcenous stockbroker and on merchants in Belize who feared competition. He even attempted to launch a second Poyais loan bond offering, but there were few takers, and as more became known, he reverted to previous behavior: fleeing—this time to France.

MacGregor in France

MacGregor announced that his wife was ill, and doctors advised he take her to Italy to recuperate before winter began in England. He absconded with the remaining Poyais funds, traveling not to Italy but rather just as far as Paris. There he allied with a dubious investment group, Compagnie de Nouvelle Neustrie (Company of New Western France), to promote French migration to Latin America. According to an admirer, MacGregor claimed to confer with the French prime minister, Jean-Baptiste Guillaume Joseph Marie Anne Séraphin, le Compte de Villèle, and with the Spanish ambassador to Paris, José Miguel de Carvajal-Vargas y Manrique de Lara Polanco, Duque de San Carlos, in an attempt to have the Spanish renounce any claim to Poyais, but the Spanish government was unable to reach a decision in the matter. There is little likelihood MacGregor ever met these officials and no evidence beyond his word.

McGregor continued to claim that complex negotiations were underway between the French and Spanish governments to guarantee the sovereignty of Poyais. He hoped to retain credibility among his aristocratic supporters in England and to prepare the way for a new Poyais fraud in France. He next stated that he ceded a large tract of Poyais to the Compagnie de Nouvelle Neustrie for colonization by French emigrants, who would pay a modest tax after they established farms there. This scheme would be financed by a £300,000 loan managed by a small London bank attracted by the high fees for its services. The Compagnie de Nouvelle Neustrie commenced to sell plots of land in Poyais to farmers eager to migrate, but French authorities put an end to the scheme before it was far advanced. Alerted by applications for passports to travel to Poyais, not acknowledged by France to be a real country, the French arrested two of MacGregor's associates, and the managing director of the Compagnie de Nouvelle Neustrie, M. Lehuby, fled to Belgium. After MacGregor spent several months in hiding outside of Paris, the authorities found and arrested him in early December 1823.

MacGregor, his two associates, and the director of the Compagnie de Nouvelle Neustrie were finally brought to trial in early April 1824, charged with defrauding the public by the Poyais emigration ploy. The director remained in hiding in Belgium and was tried *in absentia*, which enabled MacGregor's lawyers to blame him for all malfeasance. The French judges concluded there was no definite proof that Mac-Gregor and colleagues were guilty of fraud, but just on the verge of acquittal, the prosecution managed to deport Lehuby from Belgium and demanded a reopening of the trial, which began July 10, 1824. MacGregor's lawyer presented a grossly inflated account of his client's career and depicted him as the victim of Lehuby's machinations. Mac-Gregor was acquitted and charges against his associates withdrawn, and Lehuby was sentenced to thirteen months in prison.

MacGregor Back in Britain

MacGregor was not yet done with trying to raise money from Poyais. He moved back to London, where he retained some creditability because of the conflicting reports about the disaster on the Mosquito Coast and his own indignant assertion that all problems were due to others. There was also a major financial crisis in Britain in 1825, which further distracted attention from MacGregor's earlier deeds. MacGregor began his new campaign by editing and adapting the book previously published under the name of Thomas Strangeways, reducing it to a forty-page booklet, supposedly written by a "Friend to Poyais" and titled *Some account of the Poyais country: shewing from undoubted authority the certain advantages to be derived from the establishment of colonial and commercial companies for trading with that country and working its gold mines with hints regarding the prejudices which have created by its opponents, &c.* (London: Effingham Wilson, 1825).

Soon after returning to England, MacGregor was arrested for failure to pay debts, but either he or one of his supporters must have resolved the problem because he was released after just a week. No charges were brought regarding the Poyais colonists or his earlier bond issue. MacGregor seems to have decided that royal pretentions were no longer in fashion and now styled himself "Cacique of the Republic of Poyais," abandoning the earlier spelling in favor of the Spanish and French usage. As England emerged from the financial crisis, MacGregor sought to sell £800,000 worth of new Poyais bonds at 3 percent annual interest. For the first three years, investors in bonds would receive their interest in the form of land certificates, and they could exchange their bonds for land certificates if they wished. Of course, MacGregor was also willing to sell land in Poyais directly. The bond and land sales did not do well. Too many in the financial community knew of the failure of the earlier Poyais bonds, and there was a new Mosquito king who was selling parcels of the land MacGregor claimed to lumber companies.

In 1831, MacGregor, who now called himself "President of the Poyaisian Republic," made another effort, attempting to sell "Poyaisian New Three per cent Consolidated Stock," with little success. As late as 1837, while living in Scotland, he managed to unload some Poyais land certificates, which, of course, had no value or validity.

Refuge in Venezuela

In 1838, MacGregor's wife, Josefa, died in Edinburgh. Shortly after he wrote to old friends in Venezuela, where his retreat to Barcelona had become one of the founding stories of the nation. The next year he traveled to Caracas, where he was awarded the pension due a retired general, which enabled him to live comfortably there. When he died in 1845, shortly before his fifty-ninth birthday, he was accorded a grand funeral with the president and other dignitaries in attendance, and he was interred in the city's cathedral.

Aftermath

The colony of Poyais was the fantasy of Gregor MacGregor. It had no chance of succeeding because it never really existed. It is seldom useful to attempt to understand the psychology of a historical figure; cultural norms vary greatly over time. It is nevertheless apparent that Gregor MacGregor exhibited many characteristics of psychopathy: grandiosity, narcissism, superficial charm, glibness, pathological disregard of the truth, exploitive manipulation of others, lack of empathy, and lack of remorse. His exploitation of fellow Scots constituted an affinity for fraud, similar in many ways to Bernie Madoff's exploitation of coreligionists.

The dream and fraud of Poyais has never really died. To this day, a site on the internet, https://www.youtube.com/channel/UCXdPCW41 WVjY9TDBYmS-cuA (accessed October 28, 2022) states, "The Republic of Poyais is a small independent nation situated between Honduras and Nicaragua in Central America" and offers citizenship along with a very official looking passport for only $240. Just as a century ago, the unwary might assume this to be real. Others see satire.

The Black Lagoon, now the Laguna de Bacalar, is the site of a small community. There is some farming, fishing, and some modest eco-tourism there, but the area remains largely underdeveloped. There are a few remnants to be seen of the Black Lagoon Settlement destroyed in 1800, but no trace remains of the unfortunate colonists sent by Gregor MacGregor.

Sources

The fullest and most critical account of MacGregor's early career to the time of publication is Michael Rafter, *Memoirs of Gregor M'Gregor: Comprising a Sketch of the Revolution in New Grenada and Venezuela, etc.* (London: J. J. Stockdale, 1820). Michael Rafter's brother William was among those abandoned by MacGregor at Portobelo and subsequently shot by the Spanish, and Michael Rafter was fortunate to have left Rio de la Hacha before the Spanish retook the town. Rafter was extremely critical of MacGregor, but where his account can be checked by other contemporary sources, such as survivors' accounts printed in newspapers, his facts are accurate.

W. D. Weatherhead was supposedly a military surgeon who took part in MacGregor's campaign against Portobelo, according to the title page of his published work, *An Account of the Late Expedition Against the Isthmus of Darien under the Command of Sir Gregor McGregor; together with the events subsequent to the recapture of Porto Bello, till the release of the prisoners from Panama; remarks on the present state of the patriot cause and on the climate and diseases of South America* (London: Longman, Hurst, Reese, Orme and Brown, 1821). Although Weatherhead also includes some mild criticism of MacGregor, he generally supports MacGregor's account of events, and the work seems to have been intended to counteract Michael Rafter's critical account of events. Weatherhead is otherwise an obscure figure and perhaps, like Thomas Strangeways, a pseudonym for MacGregor or one of his associates.

The title page of *Narrative of the Expedition Under General Mac-Gregor Against Porto Bello: Including an Account of the Voyage, and of the Causes which Led to its Final Overthrow* (London: C. and J. Ollier and R. and J Allman, 1820) indicates it was written by an "Officer who miraculously escaped." Internal evidence indicates he was Sir John Besant. The writer does not blame MacGregor for the disaster at Portobelo and barely mentions Rafter but attributes the disaster to drunken, disobedient soldiers. It is a shallow work; the author never questions why and how the discipline broke down. Rafter, *Memoirs*, maintains it was because of the troop's loss of respect for MacGregor, who spent his time drinking, designing new titles for himself, and supinely neglecting to exercise command.

Gregor MacGregor published his own self-serving account of events at Portobelo in the *Edinburgh Courant* magazine in September and October 1821. These letters are conveniently reprinted in David Sinclair, *Sir Gregor MacGregor and the Land That Never Was: The Extraordinary Story of the Most Audacious Fraud in History* (Boston: Da Capo Press, 2004), 331-343.

John Miller, *Narrative of a Voyage to the Spanish Main, in the Ship "Two Friends," The Occupation of Amelia Island, by M'gregor, &c.* (London: J. Miller, 1819) provides a general narrative of MacGregor's occupation of Amelia Island. Miller arrived at Amelia after MacGregor's departure and learned of events from others. His account is not detailed or insightful.

Thomas Strangeways, *Sketch of the Mosquito Shore, Including the Territory of Poyais, Descriptive of the Country; with Some Information as to its Productions, the Best Mode of Culture, &c. Chiefly Intended for the Use of Settlers.* (Edinburgh: William Blackwood, 1822) was probably written by MacGregor himself or one of his close associates. There is no indication that Thomas Strangeways was a real person. The work was designed solely to encourage migration. The material describing the flora and fauna of the area is copied from earlier published works and includes some information not relevant to the Mosquito Coast. The section projecting profits to be derived from agriculture is grossly exaggerated, and the description of the climate and conditions of the area is unrealistic.

James Hastie, a pit sawyer who cut lumber into boards, wrote a twenty-page account of the disaster at Poyais: *Narrative of a Voyage in the Ship* Kennersley Castle *from Leith Road to Poyais* (Edinburgh:

Printed for the author, 1823). Hastie was typical of those who could not admit they had been fooled and deceived, although conditions on the Mosquito Coast were nothing like they had been represented. Hastie simply could not imagine that the aristocratic, heroic MacGregor was capable of deception and attempted to absolve him of all blame.

Edward Codd, *Proceedings of an Inquiry and Investigation, Instituted by Major General Codd, His Majesty's Superintendent and Commander-in-chief at Belize, Honduras, Relative to Poyais*. (London: Lawler and Quick, 1824) is a factual account of the Poyais colonists' misfortunes and demonstrates MacGregor's responsibility for sending several hundred people to their deaths.

Gustavus Butler Hippisley was an English officer who had been deeply involved in the South American revolutionary movements, though he had grown discouraged and returned to England, where he fell under the spell of MacGregor. Honest and honorable, Hippisley unfortunately lacked critical judgment. He continued to believe in MacGregor even after the flight from England to France, and he was arrested along with MacGregor in France. French justice moved slowly, in part because a codefendant, managing director Lehuby of the Compagnie de Nouvelle Neustrie, had fled to Belgium, and the judicial process could not be completed until he was extradited. Hippisley spent eight months in a French jail before he was exonerated, and his account of the affair, depicting MacGregor as an honest man beset by enemies, was published as *Acts of Oppression Committed under the Administration of M. de Villèle, Prime Minister of Charles X, in the Years 1825–6* (London: Alfred Miller, 1831). The work was written several years before publication.

MacGregor continued to try to sell land in Poyais that he did not own and publish works designed to convince people that Poyais was a reality: Gregor MacGregor, *Plan of a Constitution for the Inhabitants of the Indian Coast, in Central America, Commonly Called the Mosquito Shore* (Edinburgh: Balfour and Jack, 1836) and Gregor MacGregor, *Proposed Colony, in the District of Black River, on the Northern Coast of Central America, Commonly Called Poyais* (London: W. Barnes, 1838).

In addition, newspaper articles, broadsides, government reports, court records, family papers, stock certificates, land deeds, Poyais banknotes, and even a Scots-dialect ballad, "We'll a' gang to Poyais thegither," written to promote migration, all contribute to elucidate Mac-Gregor's career and the imaginary colony of Poyais. These are scattered among the great libraries of Britain, the United States, and Venezuela. Of importance are the collections of the National Archives of Scotland, Archivo General de la Nación (Caracas), and the Public Record Office, London, Colonial Office Papers.

The chief modern account of Poyais and MacGregor is David Sinclair, *Sir Gregor MacGregor and the Land that Never Was: The Extraordinary Story of the Most Audacious Fraud in History* (London: Headline, 2004). The work, unsympathetic to MacGregor, is carefully researched, although it lacks footnotes, and the bibliography could have been fuller. Tulio Arends, *Sir Gregor MacGregor: Un escosés tras la aventura de América* (Caracas: Monte Ávila Editores, 1991) is less critical. Matthew Brown, "Inca, Sailor, Soldier, King: Gregor MacGregor and the Early Nineteenth-Century Caribbean," *Bulletin of Latin American Research* 24, no. 1 (January 2005): 44-70, attempts to rehabilitate MacGregor by placing him in his cultural context and referring to his "idealism." Brown barely admits that MacGregor was engaged in fraud regarding Poyais and totally ignores the hundreds of deaths that must be attributed to him at Portobelo, Rio de la Hacha, and on the Mosquito Coast. The reader is encouraged to decide whether Brown's article succeeds.

THIRTEEN

Southern Dreams:
Confederate Cultural Colonies
in Mexico, British Honduras,
Venezuela, *and* Brazil (1865–ca. 1875)

Introduction

During the nineteenth century, colonization essentially ceased in the familiar form of establishing communities in foreign lands unclaimed by European powers. By then nations had subdued and annexed large swarths of land, and there was little remaining unclaimed territory to colonize and most of that undesirable. A new form of colonization appeared: cultural colonization, groups establishing settlements often in foreign lands in the effort to preserve distinctive cultures. Such attempts were most often undertaken by religious groups but not always. The resettlement of former US Confederates in Latin America was at least in large part an attempt to preserve a disappearing way of life in a foreign context and escape from an unpalatable reality.

At the end of the Civil War, a debate arose in the American South whether to remain and attempt to create some sort of life amid the devastation or to leave and establish colonies where Southern culture and values could be preserved. Important Confederate leaders, including most prominently General Robert E. Lee, encouraged Southerners to remain and rebuild. Confederate President Jefferson Davis also advised Southerners to return to their homes, but at the end of the war he was captured while attempting to flee to Mexico, and that weakened the authority of his advice. A host of other Southerners also opposed migration, including important Confederate military figures and newspaper editors, some of whom accused those migrating of betraying the South. For most inhabitants in the South, leaving was quite impossible. They were too poor, or the resources remaining could not be readily converted to cash, or they were simply too tied emotionally to their relatives and friends. After a short period of Radical Reconstruction, the North greatly relaxed control over the Southern states. White Southerners then found life much less burdensome than they had anticipated. For recently freed African Americans, however, the situation became exactly the opposite as Northerners largely abandoned their earlier idealism and White Southerners reimposed control.

For some ex-Confederates, the memories of the dead, the widespread destruction, the end of their way of life, and the real or imaginary burdens of Yankee occupation were simply too great to endure, and they were eager to leave the South. Still others left in search of new and better economic opportunities than available to them in the ravaged Southern states. Some resolved to leave the defeated South even before the last shots were fired, and others departed in the months and years after the war.

Individuals established new lives in foreign lands, sometimes with remarkable success. Judah Benjamin, the talented Confederate secretary of state, fled to England, there to establish a successful law practice, even achieving the honorable title of queen's counsel and arguing cases before the House of Lords and the Privy Council. Others served in a wide variety of foreign armies, often holding high ranks and frequently serving beside Union officers against whom they had fought. Some remained in their new homes, and others returned to the South after a short time or after years abroad.

People left the South in groups to establish colonies where they hoped many more would join them in creating cultural enclaves where Southern expatriates could continue to live in an antebellum milieu without hated Yankee interference. The lands that offered by far the clearest opportunities for such colonies were Mexico and Brazil, although groups also migrated to British Honduras and Venezuela. Each presented different problems for the ex-Confederate cultural colonists.

Mexico

Mexico offered inducements and disincentives to potential colonists. It was underdeveloped, good land and labor were cheap, and Mexico was so close that immigrants could expect to maintain relations with those who remained behind in the South. Moreover, the royal government of Maximilian, who claimed the title emperor of Mexico, supported by France, actively sought to encourage ex-Confederate immigration. On the other hand, many Mexicans were hostile to all Norteamericanos, both Confederate and federal. Mexico had already lost over half of its territory to the United States, first by the cession of Texas and then as the result of the war with the United States. Mexican resentments remained as fresh and bitter as Confederate resentment of Yankees, and Mexicans particularly had reasons to remain distrustful of the ambitions of ex-Confederates. Before the Civil War, "filibusters," American military adventurers mostly from the Southern states, operated widely in Mexico, Central America, and the West Indies attempting to win territory for annexation to the United States as slave states or to create independent countries. The most notorious of all was William Walker, who, after a career of subverting and attacking Latin American governments, was captured in Honduras and executed by firing squad in 1860. Many who fought alongside Walker joined the Confederacy, and during the Civil War, prominent Confederates openly stated ambitions to carve new slave states out of northern Mexico, forcing Mexico to sell or simply conquering Baja California, Sonora, and Chihuahua. After the war, some of these same people took part in attempts to found colonies in Latin America.

Mexico was also torn by its own civil war. Encouraged by a few conservative Mexicans and dreams of a greater worldwide role for France, the French Emperor Napoleon III sought to impose a puppet government headed by Maximilian, an Austrian archduke, on the people of Mexico. The Mexican nationalistic Juaristas opposed the French-backed government of Maximilian, and the conflict reduced much of the country to a state of lawlessness. Both France and Maximilian's government favored the Confederate cause. After the Union capture of New Orleans, Matamoros in Mexico became the most important port for the Confederates to import war materials and export cotton.

France and Maximilian, however, did not feel sufficiently confident about Confederate prospects to recognize formally the rebel government and face an open breach with the United States. At the same time the Union government, under the guidance of the cautious Secretary of State William H. Seward, was equally reluctant to create an open breach with France and Mexico that would lead to their recognition of the Confederacy. Washington officially deplored the French breach of the Monroe Doctrine and protested the movement of goods through Matamoros to the South but would not go further while the Civil War was still being fought.

EX-CONFEDERATES MOVE TO MEXICO

As the fortunes of the South waned, Maximilian envisioned or allowed himself to be talked into believing that Confederate refugees could provide valuable aid to his cause and the development of Mexico. Even before the Civil War was over, William W. Gwin, once a senator from California and a Confederate sympathizer, attempted to launch a scheme of Confederate colonization in Mexico that Maximilian's government ultimately rejected. Gwin proposed settling the Confederates in northern Mexico, which would have been foolishly provocative toward the United States. The last influx of Norteamericanos into Mexican territory adjacent to the United States had led to an independent Texas and ultimately the war between Mexico and the United States. Moreover, Gwin was at best a dubious character who could provide little but rhetoric. In July 1865, just a few months after the end of the Civil War, Gwin abandoned his scheme and left Mexico.

Stronger plans were put forth by Matthew F. Maury. A distinguished oceanographer and geographer, Maury had briefly served as a naval officer for the Confederacy and then as an agent for the Confederacy in Britain, where he sold cotton for the Confederacy, arranged for blockade runners to carry cargoes to the South, and purchased and outfitted Southern commerce raiders. Anticipating that he would be imprisoned if he returned to the United States after the war, Maury became a leading advocate of colonization in Mexico. Internationally renowned as a scientist, Maury became a friend of Maximilian and his Belgian-born wife, Carlota (to use the Latina form of her name). Maximilian granted Mexican citizenship to Maury and appointed him honorary councilor of state.

In late June 1865, Maury presented an extensive plan for Southern colonization in central and southern Mexico. Maximilian's government accepted the plan with some modifications early in September and appointed Maury imperial commissioner of colonization. The immigrants were to be granted lands in the district of Cordoba in the department of Vera Cruz. Much of the land for the colonies had at one time been acquired by the Church from private owners by foreclosing mortgages and then confiscated from the Roman Catholic Church by Juarez's government before the French invasion. The church had hoped that Maximilian would return these lands, but he refused, although the land was to be appraised and the government was to pay the church to the extent of its mortgages, with any remaining sums going to the original landowners. The government purchased still more land from influential individuals but simply expelled Indians and peons from their small farms.

The government sold land to the Confederate immigrants under liberal terms. The best land, improved and under cultivation, was available for a dollar an acre, payable over five years at 6 percent interest. Unimproved lands were usually given to settlers for free. The colonists were guaranteed freedom of religion, immunity from taxes for one year, and exemption from military service for five years, and they were permitted to form their own militias for self-protection. Farming implements and animals could be imported without duties, and they might be accompanied by "servants," a euphemism for freed African American slaves. Other individuals put forth additional plans for other Confederate colonies, which Maury encouraged. He also hoped to induce discharged French soldiers to settle in Mexico and to encourage immigration from Europe.

Even before these plans were fully formulated, Confederates had begun to move to Mexico. As early as February 1, 1865, General E. Kirby Smith indicated in a letter that he was contemplating immigration to Mexico. Kirby Smith was the commander of the Confederate Trans-Mississippi Department, which had been virtually cut off from the rest of the South since 1863. Isolation from higher command seemed to suit Kirby Smith well. A man overly confident of his abilities, he commanded his department autocratically and was determined not to surrender until the last alternative was exhausted. His interest in immigration to Mexico grew stronger when the Confederate armies in the East surrendered, but at the same time he was determined to wait for Jefferson Davis, who had escaped the Confederate capital of Richmond and attempted to reach Texas. By the time word of Davis's capture reached Kirby Smith, most of his troops, realizing the war was over, had melted away, returning to their homes without waiting for formal discharge.

General Joseph O. Shelby, part of Kirby Smith's command, managed to hold together a portion of his cavalry command, often called the Iron Brigade, but when he began moving toward Mexico, he had only about one thousand men remaining out of what been a much larger unit. Shelby proceeded from Pittsburg, Texas, to San Antonio, where several other prominent Southern military men and politicians had converged on their way to Mexico. Some joined Shelby's troop while others journeyed in separate groups or as individuals. At the Rio Grande, Shelby's troops paused for a touching ceremony. As they left the United States behind, they weighted their Confederate battle flag with a boulder and sank it in the river.

Shelby and his men escaped the Yankees when they crossed the border, but they entered a host of new dangers. Four years of war had reduced many Mexicans to desperate poverty and destroyed any semblance of law and order in large areas of the country. Juaristas, who were well aware of the tacit alliance between the Confederacy and Maximilian's hated Imperialistas, ranged freely in areas of northern Mexico. In addition to some regular troops, there were also many Juarista irregulars, scattered, disunited, often undisciplined, and dangerous. Some were patriotic guerrilla nationalists who resented Norteamericanos intruding into Mexico, while others were no more than brutal bandits who claimed loyalty to the Juarista cause but looted and murdered indiscriminately. Nor could Shelby count on an enthusiastic reception from the French and Mexican commanders supporting Maximilian. They were uncomfortable with the sudden appearance of an armed, organized foreign military unit and conscious of the potential political consequences of alienating the United States by aiding the Confederate refugees.

As Shelby and his men were making their way through northern Mexico, they were also in danger of coming into conflict with the Kickapoo Indians who were making a similar migration. Originally from Illinois and the surrounding region, the Kickapoo had been driven west to Kansas. There they were harassed by Union and Confederate partisans during the Civil War until some four hundred warriors with their families moved first to Texas and then Mexico. Their legitimate grievances rendered them hostile to both Union and Confederate. Shelby and his men would have to be constantly on the defensive as they moved through the ravaged land.

Shelby had salvaged a considerable body of supplies from the wreck of the Confederacy. His men were mounted predominantly on mules and armed with breech-loading carbines and revolvers, and his commissary supplies filled nine large twelve-mule wagons. Shelby had also brought ten new French artillery pieces and several thousand British Enfield rifled muskets. Just south of the border, Shelby encountered an important official who offered to enlist him and his troops in the Juarista cause. After consultation with his men, Shelby declined. Confederate sympathies were with Maximilian, but for the time being, Shelby and his men attempted to appear neutral. Nevertheless, when Shelby encountered a Juarista force about fifty miles south of the border, he arranged to sell them his artillery and muskets. These were of no use to his cavalry, heavy and slow to transport, and Shelby and his troops needed the money. Their commissary wagons would be empty long before they reached Mexico City.

Shelby sought to avoid all conflicts in Mexico, camping outside of towns, buying supplies, and trading what he had in abundance, such as coffee and bacon, for fresh meat and vegetables. The territory was unfamiliar, dry, and devastated by war, and Shelby's small force had to move from available water source to water source, advancing indirectly to the south. About twenty miles north of Monterrey, a force of Juarista irregulars and Indians ambushed the Confederates while they were crossing the Salinas River. Shelby's men charged the attackers and routed them, killing many but also losing twenty-seven dead and thirty-seven wounded. A few days later they were attacked again but escaped without great loss.

When Shelby and his troops approached Monterrey, which was controlled by French troops, he called a meeting to vote on their future course of action. The majority decided to offer their services to the French as a unit, a decision Shelby found agreeable. Before they could enter the town, however, the French commander, General Pierre Jeanningros, confronted the Confederates with a force of several thousand French legionnaires and Mexican troops. He was highly suspicious of a foreign military unit moving into his district, and he knew of Shelby's sale of arms to the Juaristas. Shelby, who was relatively young, sent two of his older, dignified officers to parley with the French general, but the negotiations did not go well, and Jeanningros positioned his troops and artillery to attack Shelby's much smaller force. Shelby sent a proper but forceful memorandum to the French general, explaining that he and his men had been forced to sell their arms to survive and that his men wished to join Maximilian's army. If they were not allowed to proceed, they would, despite the number of sick and wounded in their ranks, forthwith attack with what weapons remained to them. With a rhetorical flourish, Shelby concluded the letter by asking Jeanningros, "Shall it be peace or war between us?" The memorandum won over the French general completely. The next morning he invited Shelby to a personal conference after which he arranged a banquet for the Confederate officers and gave leave for the Confederates to move on to Mexico City to offer their services to Maximilian.

As Shelby continued to move south, he encountered another French force, commanded by a Colonel Depreuil, who proved suspicious and insulting. The two leaders exchanged words that almost led to a duel, averted only by Jeanningros's timely arrival on the scene. Still farther south Shelby encountered yet another French force that had not received word of Jeanningros's authorization, but he was able to convince them of his bona fides. Finally, Shelby was able to get a message to Marshal François Bazaine, chief of staff of the French army in Mexico, who issued an order permitting Shelby to move with his troops to Mexico City and even provided some funds so they could purchase supplies on the way.

The Confederates reached Mexico City in the middle of August 1865, and Maximilian promptly and courteously received Shelby. The emperor indicated that he and his men were welcome in Mexico as individuals, but it was not acceptable that they continued to exist as an organized military unit, and they would not be incorporated into his army as such. The emperor invited them to settle in Mexico as farmers and indicated he would provide them with land, and he was even then planning where they might be best settled. Shelby left the meeting reconciled to disbanding his troops.

Other Confederates made their way to Mexico City either in small groups or as individuals, but the trip was neither easy nor safe. General Monroe M. Parsons of Missouri and two colonels and three privates were robbed and murdered by bandits nominally loyal to the Juarista cause. Some groups arrived in Mexico City well before Shelby, and others trickled in later. There had been wild talk of forty thousand or fifty thousand Confederate veterans seeking asylum in Mexico, but the real number was much less. No close approximation of their number is possible, though probably no more than several thousand made the trek.

Many of the wealthier migrants brought freed slaves with them, some of whom, lacking better opportunities, came voluntarily, while others had no choice. All knew or soon learned that slavery was illegal in Mexico, and after crossing the border most took their lives into their own hands and left their ex-masters. Some Southerners, deeply believing their own cultural mythology about slavery, were shocked, amazed, and distressed by such occurrences.

Forced to wait as Maximilian's government debated and modified Maury's plans, some Confederates behaved obnoxiously to Mexicans in the capital city. Others spent their time learning Spanish and cultivating friendships. A number slipped out of Mexico City and rode north, where they took service with Juarista forces against Maximilian. Others enlisted in the French army when Paris sent permission for such enrollments, provided no prominent figures were included. Still others left Mexico to return to the United States or go to a different country, while some found employment with the Mexican government or departed to go gold prospecting. For many, the hope of developing distinctively Southern enclaves in Mexico was shattered before anything substantial was accomplished.

THE ESTABLISHMENT OF EX-CONFEDERATE CULTURAL COLONIES
Finally, in September 1865, Maximilian issued the land decree, and a wagon train of ex-Confederates started toward their new homes in southern Mexico. The company included distinguished Southerners: General Shelby, General Sterling Price, five former governors, judges, politicians, professionals of various sorts, and army officers. Many of the most distinguished, however, lacked the humble skills required to turn bare plots of land into prospering farms and estates. The colony, called collectively New Virginia, was to consist of a main town, Carlota—named after Maximilian's queen, who had shown particular courtesy and friendship to the Confederates—and three satellite communities: Cordoba, Orizaba, and Omealco. Confederates also settled in about ten other small agricultural villages scattered through Mexico. Most notable of these colonies were Tumbadero and Zapotan, in the Tuxpan region on the Caribbean shore north of Vera Cruz, but even there the colonists numbered probably fewer than two hundred. Still other colonies were established on the Pacific coast. Little is known of them.

Initially, the colonists often wrote home glowing descriptions of their new lives, the magnificent scenery, and the fertility of the land, but all was not well. The area around Carlota was steaming low land, subject to frequent torrential downpours. The fields and unpaved streets were often a sea of deep, sticky mud. Carlota remained small and unattractive and boasted few facilities or amenities, and the other settlements were even less developed. The heavy rains made sanitation almost impossible, and the colonists began to fall victim to dysentery, typhoid, yellow fever, and malaria. Coffee was intended to be the chief cash crop, but coffee plants require three years to mature, and the colonists had to subsist with little income as they waited for the plants to grow. Some land had to be cleared of heavy jungle, which proved slow and difficult, and it was always laborious to keep the jungle from reclaiming the fields. The Confederates felt their farming techniques were greatly superior to the native ways, but the land and climate were different than that to which they were accustomed, and their farming techniques did not always succeed. Land speculators among the colonists quickly drove the price of farms to uneconomic levels, discouraging additional settlers. Mexicans who had been driven off the land to facilitate the Confederate colonization were understandably hostile. Some colonists hoped to create in Mexico an approximation of the plantation society they idealized in the Old South, but achieving it without slaves proved impossible, and attempts to adopt the Mexican system of peonage did little but further alienate the already hostile native population.

THE COLLAPSE OF THE CONFEDERATE COLONIES

As the Confederates were identified with the government of Maximilian, the dispossessed Mexicans threw their support behind the Juaristas. Bandits and irregular forces raided outlying farms and towns, killing and taking prisoners for ransom. Colonists had to rely on their own weapons and French garrisons for support. As the colonists grew discontent, bitter quarreling and factionalism divided them when they most needed to rely on one another. Individuals and families began to leave, some returning to the United States, others seeking better prospects in other lands, such as British Honduras or Brazil. Even General Shelby grew disappointed with the situation in Carlota and shifted his base of operations to the Tuxpan colonies north of Vera Cruz, but there the colonists faced attacks by the Toluca Indians, who had been driven off their land to make it available for colonization. Juarista irregulars cooperated along with the Indians to harass the colonists.

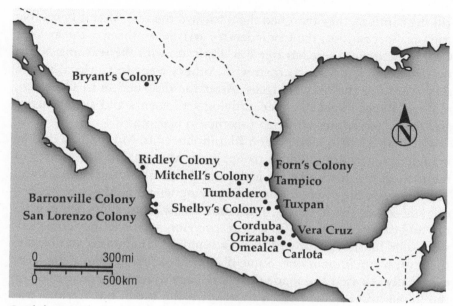

Confederate colonies in Mexico.

Perhaps the Confederate colonies in Mexico could have survived these challenges if they had enough time to develop and grow, but they did not. They were doomed by their association with Maximilian and by the rising tide of Mexican nationalism. Juarista forces gained strength daily as scattered bands of resistance fighters came together to form larger, better-coordinated units. Shelby and the colonists near Tuxpan also defended themselves against frequent attacks by the local Indians and managed to maintain their position until the nearby French garrison withdrew in February 1866. Within a few days, several thousand Indians besieged the colony, and Shelby and the Confederates made a fighting retreat to the beaches, where they hastily dug earthworks as the Indians looted and burned the homes they abandoned. The colonists attempted to escape in several old vessels. Some were successful, but other boats were set ablaze, and colonists died among the flames. The Tuxpan venture was finished.

On May 15, 1866, the satellite colony of Omealco, near Carlota, was attacked by a guerrilla force consisting mainly of dispossessed Indians led by Juarista officers. They rounded up the inhabitants, looted the town, and announced they were taking back the land. Rather than kill the captives, they marched them toward the sea. After a miserable trip on short rations, the Confederates arrived on the coast near Vera Cruz, where they were left free but destitute, with the warning not to return. Some left Mexico forthwith; others went to Carlota, where they were not the only refugees. After the destruction of Omealco, raiding parties attacked other outlying settlements and single farms, and the Confederates crowded together in Carlota.

On May 31, 1866, Napoleon III announced to Maximilian that he intended to withdraw French troops from Mexico. On the evening of the next day, a force of over a thousand Juaristas attacked Carlota. They overran the town, looting, destroying what could not be carried off, and setting fire to houses and shops. Many inhabitants fled in wagons and carriages toward Vera Cruz, carrying whatever they could salvage. The Juaristas captured about a hundred inhabitants and herded them off to the mountains. Some disappeared forever, but most were eventually released and made their way back to territory controlled by the Imperialistas. The French reoccupied the town, but Carlota was already dead. A few families held out a while longer, lacking the resources to leave immediately, but even they were gone by March 1867, when the French forces abandoned the town. The Indian farmers took back their fields and homes, and in a short time hardly a trace of the Confederate colony remained.

The collapse of the Imperialista cause was quick and complete. Maximilian refused to flee. He was captured and executed by firing squad on June 1, 1867, and the last Imperialista stronghold, Vera Cruz, fell on July 4, 1867, after the final contingent of French troops sailed for home. The great majority of the Confederates had left Mexico by that time, and almost all the rest departed as soon as they could, either returning to the United States or going to other foreign countries. A few with special skills remained in Mexico and built lives there, but they did so as individuals rather than as members of a Confederate colony.

AFTERMATH

Much has been written about the Confederate colonies in Mexico, but they were ultimately no more than a fleeting phenomenon. The Southerners hoped to recreate genteel cultural societies reproducing antebellum values and conditions, but even with aid from Maximilian's government, their small settlements failed to prosper. Conditions were inhospitable and their resources limited. More importantly, while escaping from the aftermath of one civil war, the ex-Confederates intruded into another, and by choosing to ally themselves with Maximilian's Imperialistas, they doomed their efforts. The Mexican people rid themselves of the French and those who had cast their lot with them.

SOURCES

The growth of general literacy in the nineteenth century expanded the amount and altered the character of sources. Far more letters, diaries, newspaper accounts, books, and general bureaucratic records survive than in previous eras, but that survival is far from uniform. In the case of the ex-Confederate attempts to found cultural colonies in Latin American countries, the records of intentions and early events are relatively abundant when compared to accounts of failure and abandonment of efforts. Enthusiasm for new ventures lends itself to expression, while depression following disillusionment and disaster does not. Sources are also far from uniform in the information they provide about the various settlements. Much is known about the largest and most prominent Confederate efforts in Mexico, but there are few sources concerning many of the smaller colonies beyond their names. They disappeared after a short time, leaving behind scarcely any written record of their existence.

In the years before the Civil War, aggressive Southern filibusters attempted to usurp control and annex territory of Mexico and other Latin American countries. Several leaders of Confederate colonial schemes took part in these expeditions, and such activities formed Latin American suspicions about the intent of Confederate immigrants. Charles H. Brown, *Agents of Manifest Destiny: The Life and Times of the Filibusters* (Chapel Hill: University of North Carolina Press, 1980); William O. Scroggs, *Filibusters and Financiers: The Story of William Walker and His Associates* (New York: Russell and Russell, 1969); and Robert E. May, *Manifest Destiny's Underworld: Filibustering in Antebellum America* (Chapel Hill: University of North Carolina Press, 2002) provide good introductions to the activities of the filibusters.

William M. Gwin was one of the first to promote Confederate colonization in Mexico, though he quickly abandoned the effort. See Hallie M. McPherson, "The Plan of William McKendree Gwin for a Colony in North Mexico, 1863–1865," *Pacific Historical Review* 2 (December 1933): 357-386. Matthew F. Maury played a much more important role, although he too abandoned the effort. See A. J. Hanna, "The Role of Matthew Fontaine Maury in the Mexican Empire," *Virginia Magazine of History and Biography* 55 (April 1947): 105-125; and Jacquelin Ambler Caskie, *Life and Letters of Matthew Fontaine Maury* (Richmond, VA: Richmond Press, 1928).

Major John N. Edwards was General Joseph O. Shelby's adjutant during the Civil War, and he took part in Shelby's march to Mexico City, which he recorded in *Shelby's Expedition to Mexico, An Unwritten Leaf of the War* (Kansas City, MO: Kansas City Times Steam Book and Job Printing House, 1872). That work forms a continuum with Edwards's earlier *Shelby and his Men, or the War in the West* (Cincinnati: Miami Printing, 1867), and additional material appears in Edwards's final work completed by Jennie Edwards, *Biography, Memoirs, Reminiscences and Recollections* (Kansas City, MO: Jennie Edwards, 1889). Edwards was an unreconstructed Confederate; his writing is notable for overblown prose, exaggerations, hyperbolic dramatic effects, and defense of all things Confederate, even guerrillas such as William Clarke Quantril and Jesse and Frank James. Edwards preserves a detailed record of events, but his interpretation of the chivalric General Shelby and his companions owes more to romantic writers such as Sir Walter Scott than to the gritty reality of war-torn Mexico. Edwards nevertheless remains the prime source for Shelby's expedition, as is apparent in Edwin Adams Davis, *Fallen Guidon: The Saga of Confederate General Jo Shelby's March to Mexico*, first published in 1962 and still in print (College Station: Texas A&M University Press, 1995). Davis is critical of Edwards's account and utilizes other sources, American and Mexican, wherever possible, but his account nevertheless constitutes a romantic retelling of Shelby's journey to Mexico City. Anthony Arthur, *General Jo Shelby's March* (New York: Random House, 2010) provides a more modern interpretation, although the influence of Edwards is still apparent.

Andrew Rolle, *Lost Cause: Confederate Exodus to Mexico* (Norman: University of Oklahoma Press, 1965) and Todd W. Wahlstrom, *The Southern Exodus to Mexico: Migration across the Borderlands after the American Civil War* (Lincoln: University of Nebraska Press, 2015) provide overviews of the Confederates in Mexico and excellent bibliographies. Samuel Basch, *Erinnerungen aus Mexico* (Leipzig: Duncker und Humbolt, 1868), now available in translation as Samuel Basch, *Recollections of Mexico: The Last Ten Months of Maximilian's*

Empire, trans. and ed. Fred D. Ullman (Wilmington, DE: Scholarly Resources, 2001) presents a vivid account of the circumstances that destroyed the Confederate colonies in Mexico. Carl Coke Rister, "Carlota, a Confederate Colony in Mexico," *Journal of Southern History* 11 (February 1945): 33-50, contains an overview of the most important Confederate colony and its demise.

British Honduras

Ex-Confederates encountered significantly different conditions in each of the countries where they sought to establish cultural colonies. In British Honduras they found a much more stable situation than in Mexico, though Indian raids did endanger those who settled near the border. The Spanish had not colonized the area that became British Honduras because it offered no quick wealth of gold, silver, pearls, or gems—local tribes were belligerent, and the Spanish had limited resources. British involvement began when privateers and pirates sought isolated anchorages where they could replenish water casks and maintain their ships. They traded for food with the Indians, who received them cordially since at least initially they did not seek to establish settlements and take land. The British also traded for a variety of dyewood that produced a desirable black or purple dye. In 1716, the British established their first permanent settlement in the area, today Belize City. The early British colonists imported African slaves who were put to work primarily to cut dyewood. Mahogany, reputed to be the finest in the world, also became a significant export, and over the years large areas were deforested, offering land that could be exploited for tropical crops.

British control of the area was formalized by the appointment of a superintendant in 1786. In 1833, the British abolished slavery, but a small White elite still controlled the land and economy. Individuals of African heritage and those of mixed heritage slowly improved their economic and educational situations, and escaped slaves from the Southern United States moved into the area during the first half of the nineteenth century. By the beginning of the American Civil War, the area was moving toward the status of a British colony, which it achieved in 1862 under the name British Honduras. Today, it is the independent nation of Belize.

The exportation of goods to the Confederacy provided the colony with a brief period of prosperity. The ruling elite made good profits supplying contraband material and military supplies to Southern blockade runners during the first two years of the Civil War, but during 1863, the effectiveness of the Union blockade eliminated British Honduras as a significant source of supply for the Confederacy. After 1863, the economic situation of British Honduras was grim. In the eighteenth century, mercantilism at least guaranteed colonies a market for their products in the homeland, but the growth of increasingly free trade in the nineteenth century subjected producers to international competition. British Honduras was seldom able to compete successfully. The abolition of slavery had led to a decline in agricultural productivity and a major increase in labor costs. Even its great resource, fine mahogany, suffered from declining prices as large quantities of Mexican mahogany came on the market. The citizens of British Honduras hoped that an influx of immigrants from the Southern states might contribute to a revival of the economy.

EX-CONFEDERATE MIGRATION

The first ex-Confederates to arrive generally came as individuals, while later immigrants often came in groups intending to settle together. Individuals sometimes joined such settlements in British Honduras or joined to form their own settlement after having arrived. The first prominent Southerner, the Episcopal Rev. R. Dawson of Mobile, Alabama, came to British Honduras in 1861. It is not apparent whether he was fleeing the violence of the Civil War, hoped to make converts among the Hondurans, or expected to work among other Southerners in British Honduras during the Civil War. As the fortunes of the Confederacy declined, increasing numbers of refugees came to British Honduras. The American consul to British Honduras reported in 1864 that many Texans, convinced that the Confederacy was destined for destruction, arrived in the colony. Later most ex-Confederates came to British Honduras from Louisiana and Mississippi, departing through New Orleans.

Shipping companies and land companies published broadsides and pamphlets and placed articles in Southern newspapers extolling the opportunities for immigrants in British Honduras, and colonists who had already arrived wrote home encouraging others to come so that distinctively Southern settlements might emerge. Efforts to establish regular shipping between the United States and British Honduras, however, faced problems. The first attempt to establish a scheduled steamship service ended after just two voyages. During the first, a

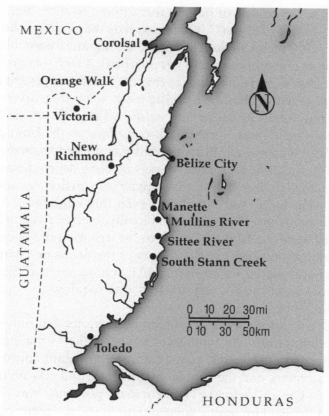

British Honduras with principal Confederate settlements.

storm delayed and badly damaged the ship, and during the second, weather drove the ship onto a coral reef and wrecked it. When regular steamship service was finally established, the trip to and from New Orleans took only four days, but freight rates and individual passage, forty dollars in gold per person, were too expensive for many Southerners whose resources had been damaged or destroyed in the war. Sailing ships, mainly sloops of no great size, were cheaper but often took two weeks to a month to make the voyage, and accommodations were often crowded and unhealthy.

There is no accurate count of the number of ex-Confederates who came to British Honduras. Estimates by the United States diplomatic personnel of 1,500 are certainly too low as they certainly failed to account for some groups of immigrants known to have arrived, but a modern estimate of about 7,000 far exceeds the evidence. An estimate of about 3,500 seems reasonable. Some immigrants, particularly those who came as individuals or families unaffiliated with any group movement, focused so exclusively on leaving the South and getting to British Honduras that they had no specific plans once they arrived. Many stayed a few weeks in Belize City before selling all they had brought to raise passage money to return, disconsolate, to the United States.

For those who stayed, British Honduras offered attractions to potential colonists, but each positive was in some degree balanced by a negative. English was the official language, a major advantage over Mexico, Venezuela, and Brazil, but even that came with a minor if laughable annoyance. The British habitually referred to all people from the United States as Yankees, much to the irritation of the ex-Confederates, who wrote letters to the editors of the Belize newspaper about what they considered a distasteful and insulting practice. Spanish was widely spoken in the countryside and was required to communicate with hired labor.

British citizenship was available to immigrants, but only with burdensome limitations. An immigrant had to make formal application, fill out bureaucratic forms, pay significant fees, gain approval of the colonial secretary and the lieutenant governor, and take an oath of allegiance to Queen Victoria. The lieutenant governor was the highest official in British Honduras, subordinate to the governor of Jamaica. Many migrants were distressed to learn that even then they did not have full British citizenship. An immigrant's citizenship was limited to British Honduras and did not extend beyond its borders. Moreover, immigrant citizens could not stand for election to the colonial assembly or even vote in elections. Ex-Confederate gentlemen, prominent in their own communities, had participated in government before and during the war. They found the new restrictions to their lives demeaning, made even more so because the lieutenant governor had the power to exempt immigrants from such restrictions, but that power was seldom exercised and then only for distinguished, wealthy, and particularly favored individuals.

Initially the British population of Honduras received the influx of ex-Confederates with enthusiasm, but ex-Confederates confronted unfamiliar race relations in British Honduras, and their attitudes were often maladaptive. Slavery had long been abolished, so the issue central to the Civil War was not a matter of concern in British Honduras. A White elite still dominated government and controlled most wealth and land, but after the abolition of slavery, those of African and mixed heritage were officially recognized as equal to Whites. Some of African and mixed heritage became moderately prosperous, owned land, took part in business, and filled responsible administrative posts, serving as policemen and customs officials. Southern migrants often refused to interact with people of African or mixed heritage, and the resentment was reciprocated. Many Blacks would not work for Southerners, who found themselves in the unaccustomed role of having to till their own fields or import workers from neighboring countries. Racial tensions and occasional incidents of Southern discourtesy and even violence undermined general respect for the ex-Confederates.

Fertile land was available to the immigrants, but it was expensive. Good land was priced at five dollars an acre, which contrasted to Brazil, where good land sold for twenty-two cents per acre, and Spanish Honduras, where land was generally given free to immigrants. A few parcels in British Honduras could be purchased for about thirty cents per acre, but that land was poor, recently logged, filled with stumps, and could not possibly soon sustain profitable agriculture. Land in British Honduras, like that in many other British colonies, had been awarded in large tracts to preferred friends of the government, many of whom became land speculators either individually or joining in corporations with other large land holders, and yet more land was held by the Crown and lay idle. Individuals and corporations agreed informally to maintain high prices for fertile farmland, particularly near the coast and along navigable rivers, and campaigned for the government not to undercut the value of their holdings. Many early immigrants left British Honduras in disgust when confronted with the land prices. Finally, the government announced a plan whereby buyers could purchase Crown land and farm it for five years before making any payment, after which they were obligated to pay a dollar per acre each year for five years. Thus, vacant land would be brought into production and the price of land for sale by private owners was maintained.

COLLAPSE OF THE CONFEDERATE SETTLEMENTS

The ex-Confederate settlers were at first delighted at the evident fertility of much of British Honduras and wrote home immediately extolling the virtues of the land, but their acquaintance was superficial, and they would soon learn all was not as it first appeared. Ship owners and land companies placed promotional materials in Southern news-papers claiming that the land would produce abundant cotton crops of the highest quality, but the promoters in typical fashion failed to mention some vital facts and perhaps did not know others. The warm climate and average rainfall of 160 inches a year that were largely re-sponsible for the lush vegetation also produced abundant biting and stinging flies, sand flies, mosquitoes, a wide variety of voracious ants, and other pests that feasted on man and crops, including insects that preyed on cotton plants. Those cotton bolls that survived the insects rotted in the frequent rain. Cotton failed as a chief crop in British Hon-duras, but planters eventually found that sugarcane grew well. The processing of cane to finished sugar, however, required mills, boilers, and other equipment that many could not afford. Planters might pay better-equipped neighbors to process their crop, but that consumed profits. Sugar producers also faced competition from the Caribbean islands, the Southern states, and the spread of sugar beet cultivation in Europe. In the interval between the failure of cotton as a cash crop and the development of sugarcane cultivation and processing, many settlers grew discouraged and returned to the United States. Others, more determined or with greater capital reserves, survived in the short term by exporting fruit such as bananas, pineapples, and coconuts, but the arrivals and departures of sailing schooners were irregular, and fresh fruit often rotted on the docks or in cargo bays when ships were delayed or becalmed. Steamship rates were so expensive that they sig-nificantly reduced or completely consumed profits from such exports.

The most famous Confederate colony in British Honduras was Toledo, established in the southern part of the country. The settlement was not named after the famous city in Spain but rather for Philip Toledo of the firm Young, Toledo and Company, who sold land and aided the settlers. Toledo was first settled by fourteen families, but the remote location, difficult economic situation, and constant labor prob-lems led ten families to abandon their farms and return to the United States during the first year and a half. More migrants came to Toledo, but not all stayed. Ex-Confederates had to import laborers from Guatemala and Spanish Honduras because most locals would not work for the Southerners. Imported labor was expensive, and the set-tlers quickly found that they could not impose dawn-to-dusk workdays and minimal living conditions on hired laborers, who, unlike slaves, could simply walk off the job and return home.

An unusual aspect of the Toledo settlement was its religious exclusivity. By 1870, nearly all the colony's inhabitants were Methodists, who, under the leadership of a severe and intolerant minister, imposed strict rules of behavior and decorum and prohibited the consumption of alcohol. The stringent religiosity alienated many Confederates, and most immigrants who came to Toledo soon left for other settlements or returned to the United States. Racial attitudes also segregated the ex-Confederates from the broader community in the area, which was composed mainly of African and Latino heritage. The population of the Toledo settlement at its height in the early 1870s was less than a hundred. The village survived but never prospered, and it certainly never constituted the enclave of gracious Southern culture once envisioned. A few families still in the area can trace their descent from Confederate immigrants.

To the north of Toledo lay a group of large plantations established by wealthy ex-Confederates around South Stann Creek, Mullins River, and Manette, and one corporate farm at Sittee River owned by Young, Toledo and Company. These were generally large, well-equipped estates that grew fruit for export and produced sugar. They were initially successful although beset by a shortage of reliable labor. Yet by 1872, most of the plantations lay abandoned. No matter how prosperous, the plantations were far apart, and the lack of community and separation from relatives and friends who remained in the United States weighed heavily on plantation families. Children were customarily sent back to the United States for education, adding further to the sense of isolation. Almost all ex-Confederates who settled in this area soon returned to their previous homes in the United States.

Confederate settlements were also established inland, most notably at New Richmond near the center of the country and Corosal, Orange Walk, and Victoria near the Mexican border. New Richmond was the dream of Rev. B. R. Duval of Virginia, begun with great hope but ended in disaster. Duval and his family had first gone to Mexico, where they settled with General Sterling Price. When the Mexican venture collapsed, they moved to British Honduras, where Duval purchased a large tract at a good price, and Lieutenant Governor Austin granted Duval exclusive navigation rights on the Belize River, a valuable prerogative. Duval recruited about two hundred people from Louisiana who intended to move to British Honduras as soon as the 1867 cotton crop was harvested, but the crop failed, and people could not afford to migrate. Then the British home government revoked Austin's navigation grant, a significant financial blow.

Nevertheless, Duval persisted and received some comfort when General Colin J. McRae bought a large tract of land nearby. McRae had been the Confederate financial agent in Europe and as such had sold US government property. At the end of the war he was not included in the general pardon. In addition to developing his land, McRae went into business with Joseph Benjamin, the younger brother of Judah P. Benjamin, who served at various times as the Confederate attorney general, secretary of war, and secretary of state. McRae and Benjamin sold cattle, mahogany, and general merchandise, but Joseph Benjamin proved a poor businessman and intemperate. He lost $25,000 lent by his older brother and repeatedly came to the attention of the law for assaults.

In late 1869, Duval recognized that New Richmond was a failure and resolved to return to Virginia. He had to sell the family possessions, including furniture he had brought from Virginia, and even then, Duval only had enough to pay for his own passage. He traveled alone to Virginia, where he had to raise money to bring back the rest of the family. McRae never dared to return to the United States but remained in British Honduras until his death in 1876, after which his family left the colony.

In spring 1868, the younger brother of General P. G. T. Beauregard, Captain Armand T. Beauregard, purchased an estate of 640 acres near Corosal in the northwest of British Honduras. There he grew sugarcane, distilled rum, and raised livestock. Several other Southern families settled in the area during the same year, but the Icaiche Indians frequently raided from Mexico. The ex-Confederates and their families began to abandon the region in 1869. A militia initially defended the colony, but the British government withdrew it in 1870, and Indian raiders soon overran the town of Corosal itself. Before the end of 1870, the Confederate settlement by Corosal was no more.

Confederates also settled near the town of Orange Walk, establishing sugar plantations that prospered initially. The area suffered a cholera epidemic in 1868, and, like at Corosal, Indians raided from across the border. Ironically, the ex-Confederates' homes and plantations were defended by the African-Honduran soldiers of the Queen's West Indian Regiment. Residents also organized a cavalry militia that on one occasion rode to the rescue of the regiment when it was attacked by a large force of Indians. The Indians were severely defeated, soon made peace, and ended raiding. Nevertheless, the Confederate community did not survive as such. One by one, the families sold out and returned to the United States until only two plantations owned by ex-Confederates remained. Again, loneliness and disappointment with the realities of Honduras played major roles in the decision to return to the South. A group of Southerners also settled at Victoria, but virtually nothing is known of the community other than that it soon failed. It is likely that again the combination of Indian raids and home sickness combined to destroy the endeavor.

AFTERMATH

Confederate attempts to establish cultural colonies and preserve the essence of antebellum Southern life in British Honduras failed for a variety of reasons. Conditions were less salubrious than advertised, British citizenship was restrictive and disappointing, race relations proved difficult, cotton failed as a primary crop, and sugar required expensive equipment to process. Land was expensive, despite government efforts to spread payment out over years, and many immigrants came with insufficient resources to establish a new life. Most importantly, all efforts failed to achieve the fundamental goal of creating communities that reflected antebellum Southern culture. There were some men of wealth among the immigrants who built or bought large plantations, but lonely plantations did not constitute communities, and no matter how prosperous, such seclusion produced a sense of ennui and homesickness. The great majority of even the wealthy and successful soon returned to the South, where even Reconstruction was preferable to isolation. The sole Confederate community that lasted for a considerable time was Toledo, but even at its height the population was less than a hundred, and its grim religiosity, intolerance, and hectoring morality seems more like Puritan New England than gracious Southern living.

SOURCES

The Confederate settlements in British Honduras have been less studied than those in Mexico and Brazil. Donald C. Simmons Jr. has written the sole monograph devoted to the subject, *Confederate Settlements in British Honduras* (Jefferson, NC: McFarland, 2001). It provides an excellent comprehensive survey and bibliography, including newspapers in the South and British Honduras, the Public Archives of Belize, and dispatches from US consuls in Belize. B. R. Duval, who created the New Richmond colony, published an account of his colonizing efforts, *A Narrative of Life and Travels in Mexico and British Honduras* (Boston: W. F. Brown, 1881). General Colin J. McRae, who settled near Durval, is the subject of Charles Davis, *Colin J. McRae: Confederate Financial Agent* (Tuscaloosa, AL: Confederate Publishing, 1961).

Narda Dobson, *A History of Belize* (London: Butler and Tanner, 1973); O. Nigel Bolland, *The Formation of a Colonial Society: Belize, from Conquest to Crown Colony* (Baltimore: Johns Hopkins University Press, 1977); and Wayne M. Clegern, *British Honduras: Colonial Dead End, 1859–1900* (Baton Rouge: Louisiana State University Press, 1967) provide the essential background of the Confederate efforts in British Honduras from different perspectives.

Venezuela

Henry Manore Price was the central figure in the attempt to establish a Confederate colony in Venezuela. He was born in Virginia about 1821 and became a doctor, receiving his medical training at Randolph-Macon Medical School, near Farmville in Prince Edward County, Virginia. He served in the Confederate army, initially in the infantry and later in the artillery, and at one point he was wounded. It is not known when he began to formulate plans for a Confederate colony in Venezuela, but his grand vision of the Venezuela Land Company that would preserve Southern life and culture in the underpopulated lands of southern Venezuela was well advanced by September 1865. Price sometimes referred to his business as the Venezuelan Emigration Company. The two names are an indication of Price's loose organizational abilities.

Venezuela was and remains a complex country. After the dissolution of the Spanish empire in South America, Venezuela was part of the state of Gran Colombia that included much of northern South America. Gran Colombia was inherently unstable and came apart in 1830–1831, at which time Venezuela became independent. Venezuela has never experienced a lengthy period of political stability, and throughout the nineteenth century, rebellions and coups were frequent; the so-called Federal War wracked the country from 1858 to 1863. In 1865, Venezuela, still recovering from the war, was poor, underpopulated, and ready to encourage migrants who could improve the economy.

Even the borders of Venezuela were and remain a matter of dispute. In the nineteenth century, Venezuela claimed the northern half of what had been Dutch Guyana, then British Guyana, and now is independent Guyana. The United States intervened in the dispute between Venezuela and Britain, resulting in a resolution in 1899 awarding the great bulk of the territory to British Guyana. Although the settlement was declared "full, perfect and final," Venezuelans felt the decision was unfair and forced on them. In 1962, as British Guyana moved toward independence as Guyana, Venezuela reopened the issue, charging that it had been "robbed" in 1899, and pressed its claim for over half the territory of the new nation. Predictably, the case has found no quick resolution, and in 2018 the United Nations referred it to the International Court of Justice, where the matter remains unresolved. Most of the territory that was available for the Confederates lay within the borders of modern Venezuela, but some lay in the disputed zone, and a few seem to have moved into that area.

On September 13, 1865, the Venezuelan government issued a resolution setting forth conditions under which foreign settlers might take up vacant lands in the southern part of the nation and the rights they would enjoy. The resolution specified that any such project should commence within the next eighteen months and bring initially at least fifty settlers. The resolution stipulated that the lands available to settlers were agricultural and not previously granted to others. Henry M. Price proposed to take advantage of the offer, which was not restricted to immigrants organized by Price but open to all who might also come to settle.

The Venezuelan government resolution was not itself a concession or grant. The government never issued a formal grant to Price, and Price seems not to have ever signed any agreement with the government. Negotiations were supposed to take place between Price and the Venezuelan minister to Washington, but Price dealt with just the secretary of the Venezuela legation to the United States. Nevertheless, Price claimed he had received a substantial grant from the Venezuelan government, and at times representatives of the Venezuelan government acted as if he had, although conceptions of the grant were vague and often contradictory.

PRICE'S CLAIMS

The Venezuelan government apparently planned to make awards consisting of individual farms of 1,280 acres on which the immigrants, including ex-Confederates, would settle with their families. The Venezuelan government made no mention of a total amount of territory that they would grant as no one could anticipate how many Confederates and others might migrate to the country. In contrast, Price at his most grandiose maintained that the Venezuelan Emigration Company owned the "absolute title and control . . . embracing two hundred and forty thousand square miles." The total land area of Venezuela is 340,560 square miles, so Price seemed to be claiming over two-thirds of the country, though on closer examination it becomes apparent that Price's calculations were wrong. Price also claimed that the holdings would be divided into 80,000 shares, each entitling a holder to 1,280 acres, the total of which equaled half the grant, 120,000 square miles. But the actual area of 80,000 shares of 1,280 acres each is 160,000 square miles. If that were half the grant, Price and the Venezuela Land Company would have been claiming 320,000 square miles, or nearly all of Venezuela. Certificates for 1,280 acres were printed and some sold to would-be colonists in the South, Confederates who had moved to England after the war, and any British citizens who might want to join the effort. Price even proposed awarding shares free to poor ex-Confederates. The company appointed agents to encourage and recruit colonists, but most of them seemed to lack all direction and did nothing.

EFFORTS TO ESTABLISH COLONIES

The most effective of Price's associates was Frederick A. Johnson. He had served briefly during the Civil War as the adjutant of the Fifth Louisiana Battalion with the rank of captain. Price chose Johnson to lead the first party of colonists to Venezuela and conferred on him the grand title of director of the Venezuela Emigration Company. The group, meeting the Venezuelan government requirement of fifty colonists, gathered at New Orleans, where one person, an eager teenager, also joined the expedition. Problems immediately arose as the schooner that was supposed to transport them required time-consuming repairs. Johnson decided to charter another ship, but problems with finance and a reluctant ship owner delayed departure. Johnson contributed to the final resolution by giving the ship owner his personal note. The ship finally sailed at the end of January 1867 and took six weeks to reach Venezuela, where it sailed up the broad Orinoco River and disembarked the passengers at Ciudad Bolivar. The town was founded in 1764 and renamed in honor of Simon Bolivar in 1846.

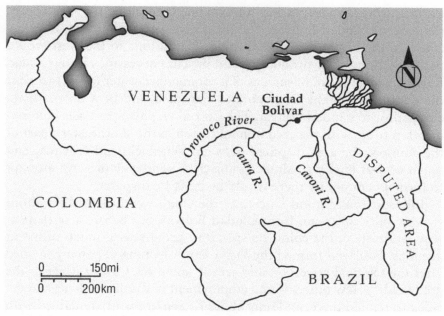

Confederate settlements in Venezuela.

Venezuelan officials greeted the settlers cordially and presented them with official certificates recognizing their legitimate status as immigrants to the Price Grant. The Venezuela authorities also released 1,250 pesos to Johnson, an eighth of the sum pledged by the government to aid the settlers. The money was subsequently distributed among the colonists. In contrast to the Venezuelans' convivial reception, Price and his company had done nothing to provide for the settlers on their arrival or to indicate where they might settle. Price and company promised that supplies would be sent, that sympathizers in England were collecting a library of five thousand books for the colonists, and that more colonists and Price himself would soon come to Venezuela. For the present, however, the first settlers were simply left to fend for themselves.

Although Price's broadsides indicated he intended to found a commercial settlement on the Caroni River, a tributary flowing into the Orinoco from the south, Johnson and many of the initial group were more concerned with settling on good farmland that they could develop into plantations. Johnson consulted with the local Venezuelan leaders, who encouraged him to examine land along the Orinoco to the west of Ciudad Bolivar. The officials gave good advice, but they also had their own interests in mind. Plantations to the west would naturally bring their produce to and procure necessities from Ciudad Bolivar, while the establishment of a commercial center to the east near the confluence of the Orinoco and Caroni would be a downstream competitor to Ciudad Bolivar. The Caroni was also the basic communication route with the gold mining region in the southeastern part of the country, the area disputed between Venezuela and Guyana, and much of that land was already subject to mining claims. An attempt to form a community there would be beset by disputes.

Johnson found good land near the small town of Borbon about twenty miles upstream from Ciudad Bolivar, but before a settlement was established, the colonists split into groups with much different agendas. Fourteen formed the Dalla Costa Mining Company, named after the regional governor, and set off down the Caroni River to the gold fields. A few others found employment in Ciudad Bolivar and decided to remain there, and only about fifteen or twenty remained with Johnson. They settled a few miles farther upstream beyond Borbon on vacant land and named their tiny community Oronoco City. The land was good, but they needed money and supplies if they were to build cattle herds, plant orange groves, and grow acres of sugarcane. Price had promised that more colonists would soon arrive along with the necessary equipment and financial support, but nothing came. On April 21, 1867, Johnson set sail for America, where he hoped to hasten the dispatch of necessities. From the time the colonists gathered in New Orleans until the day he left Venezuela, Johnson had guided the colonists and provided for them out of his own pocket. He ruined himself financially doing so, and, lacking even the fare to get back to the United States, he had to give the ship's captain a promissory note. Johnson retained faith in the great potential of a settlement in Venezuela, but he never returned. At the same time Johnson was at sea returning to America, Price was sailing to Venezuela with a second contingent of settlers.

Price first attempted to organize the second expedition in New Orleans, but, making little progress there, he moved to Wilmington, North Carolina. He advertised for fifty immigrants to accompany him, but when the schooner sailed in early April, he was accompanied by only about fifteen. He brought no financial support or significant supplies for the those already in Venezuela. The voyage to Venezuela was relatively rapid and trouble free, and as the schooner sailed up the Orinoco River, Price paused at Las Tablas, a largely depopulated town on the southeastern side of the confluence of the Orinoco and Caroni Rivers, today part of Ciudad Guyana. There he decided to establish his commercial colony, but first he had to continue to Ciudad Bolivar to confer with the provincial governor.

Juan Bautista Dalla Costa, the provincial governor and principal businessmen of Ciudad Bolivar, received Price extravagantly, but when Price expressed his determination to establish a commercial center at Las Tablas, the governor and others encouraged him to consider rather the excellent agricultural prospects of land along the Caura River, a tributary flowing into the Orinoco to the west of Ciudad Bolivar. Price toured the area with a few companions and thought the land seemed good, but he remained intent on founding a commercial center to the east. Price seems to have misunderstood the elaborate courtesy of his Latino hosts and the nature of their suggestions. Had he better understood the cultural context, he would have realized they sought to support his colonization endeavor and retain his friendship, but they would not permit him to destroy the economy of Ciudad Bolivar by establishing a business center downstream.

When Price failed to respond to Dalla Costa's friendly persuasion and persisted in previous plans, Dalla Costa ordered him and one close associate to board a small river boat. Dalla Costa had them dumped by the mouth of the Caroni River and kept them under surveillance. With little in the way of resources, Price and his companion subsisted in villages in the region for a few weeks, where they both contracted malaria. Dalla Costa was finally able to deport them to New York on a Dutch freighter carrying a load of stinking hides. Price's companion died soon after they returned to the United States, and Price remained ill and confined to bed for weeks, but his apparent enthusiasm for his Venezuela project remained unimpeded.

Fifty-one immigrants came with Frederick Johnson and about fifteen more with Price. By the time Price was expelled from Venezuela, four had died of unspecified fevers, others had gone to prospect for gold, and, according to best evidence, nineteen had grown discouraged and returned to the United States. The company had failed to produce fifty permanent settlers. During summer 1867, another group recruited by Price's company consisting of twenty-nine eager immigrants sailed from New Orleans to Venezuela. Price's company sold certificates for $100 each to some of the immigrants, entitling the purchasers to 1,280 acres, and at least one individual bought several certificates. Upon arrival the new colonists found that again the company had done nothing to prepare for them, and the great majority knew no Spanish. Many soon grew discouraged and found their way back to the United States. A subsequent voyage in 1868 was even less successful. The vessel put into a northern Venezuelan port, where the leader of the group died, and the ship was sold to cover debts. A couple of the passengers settled in northern Venezuela as individuals, but the majority returned to the United States with difficulty.

THE PATTISONS IN CONTROL

Price's disorderly approach to the Venezuela venture is typified by the Venezuela Land Company, which also operated under the name Venezuela Emigrant Company. Price never incorporated the company, and throughout its existence it remained informal and extemporary. After returning to Virginia, Price was still in poor health, and associates used the opportunity to impose a formal structure on the Venezuelan effort. The Venezuela Land Company and Venezuela Emigrant Company disappeared to be replaced by the legally incorporated American, English and Venezuelan Trading and Commercial Company. The incorporation papers state that the company was based on the grant made to Price but nowhere mentioned ex-Confederates or colonization. Price later claimed that was implicit. Price was no longer president of the company but rather just one among a long list of directors that included James F. Pattison, who had been hired by Price. Virtually nothing is known about Pattison's background. His wife, Margaret Amanda, claimed to be from Baltimore County, Maryland, but in 1867, they were living in England.

In 1868, a power struggle took place within the newly incorporated company. Pattison emerged as president, and Price was given the meaningless title of honorary president. In 1868, Margaret Pattison, probably with the aid of her husband and nephew, J. Leslie Clark, wrote and published *The Emigrant's Vade-Mecum, or Guide to the "Price Grant" in Venezuelan Guyana*. Although filled with rhetoric extolling Southern culture and values, the 150 pages contain enough hypocrisy and deceptions to embarrass the most avaricious Yankee carpetbagger. Testimonies to the wonderful opportunities in Venezuela consist of reports taken out of context, grossly altered accounts, and outright lies. Whatever Price's original intentions may have been, in the hands of the Pattisons, the Venezuelan scheme was nothing more than a scam designed to defraud potential settlers. The Pattisons even shifted their target audience from ex-Confederates to potential British settlers, and Margaret Pattison assumed the position of chief swindler in England. She sold grant allotments at grossly exaggerated prices far more than the real price of land in the area near the proposed settlement of Pattisonville on the Caura River. She also misrepresented the real costs of passage to Venezuela and even peddled fake "luggage passes," which she claimed exempted personal belongings from Venezuelan customs duties.

The able and insightful V. K. Mathison, British vice consul at Ciudad Bolivar, alerted the British home government that the *Vade-Mecum* was filled with lies, and the government tried to discourage potential immigrants, but in the age before mass communication that was not an easy task. The Pattisons shifted some of their activities to Germany, beyond British jurisdiction, and in October 1869, sixty-nine enthusiastic British settlers sailed from Hamburg for Venezuela.

On arrival, the immigrants found a sad repetition of previous settlers' experiences. There was no agent of the company to guide them; none of the promised provisions, supplies, and tools awaited them; no arrangements had been made to move them to the area where they were supposed to settle; and no preparations had been made at the proposed site. The colonists were truly fortunate in that Governor Dalla Costa took pity. He informed them that the Venezuelan government declared that Price and associates had failed to fulfill the conditions requisite to establishing settlements. Although the government considered the Price Grant terminated, Dalla Costa granted them the land they thought they had purchased to settle on the Caura River and provided them with provisions for three months and a store of basic medicines. Nevertheless, the settlement failed. The area was overgrown jungle, subject to frequent flooding, and unhealthy. Even after the settlers laboriously cleared the ground, it was apparent that the site offered only poor potential for agriculture, and the colonists still lacked even basic agricultural implements to cultivate crops. Tropical fevers and dysentery spread through the colonists, some died, and the rest sought to return to Britain.

As word of the situation reached England, the government placed notices in newspapers warning about the Venezuela emigration fraud.

In 1870, Charles Dickens Jr., son of the famous writer, penned an article titled "The Last New Eden," in the journal *All the Year Round*, founded by his father. Dickens Jr. noted that for decades "swindling of emigrants has been a lucrative profession" and vividly described the Pattisons and the Venezuela scheme as typical of the genre.

The Pattisons returned to the United States, where they again targeted ex-Confederates. They and their associates, some apparently sincere and honorable men, attempted to recruit a hundred colonists, but reports from England and from earlier Southern colonists circulated widely. When the final Price Grant expedition sailed from New York in May 1870, there were only fifteen passengers, among whom were a number going to investigate the situation in Venezuela rather than to settle there. The Pattisons also took part in the group, and Margaret Pattison's dominant personality was apparent. The group was cordially received in mid-June at Ciudad Bolivar by Governor Dalla Costa, who arranged for them to settle on the northern Caroni River. His earlier objection to Price's settling in the region was no longer relevant as the current group had no intention of creating a commercial center; they merely sought agricultural land that they could develop into plantations.

Thomas S. Waring, an honest man, kept a diary and wrote home about events, presenting a vivid picture. The group did not settle on vacant land but rather acquired acreage along the Caroni from an inhabitant of the region. They did not form a compact settlement but rather scattered to find housing wherever they could, traveling to cultivate their fields. Conditions were primitive, and by early July, Waring had determined that he would not remain in Venezuela. The Pattisons also decided quickly to abandon Venezuela and returned to the United States, where they faded into well-deserved obscurity. A few members of the party seem to have endured longer, and a couple may have stayed in Venezuela permanently, but they did so as individuals and not as part of anything to do with the Price Grant or a unified cultural colony.

AFTERMATH

Price spent the next thirty years petitioning the US and Venezuelan governments for recompence for his exaggerated claims. He had clearly become an obsessed crank, and finally, in 1901, the US government refused to continue corresponding with him. The last notice of the man was in that year. He was then eighty and living with his son in Tennessee.

The Price Grant Confederate colonies in Venezuela failed before they were really established. Price had a vision, but he provided no leadership. Neither Price nor any of his early associates had ever been to Venezuela before the first colonizing expedition, and despite their lurid promotional material, they had no real understanding of the conditions into which they were sending people. Price's companies consistently failed to fulfill promises to aid and provide for colonists, who were simply dumped at Ciudad Bolivar. Left to their own devices, the colonists lacked the resources to develop holdings in remote Venezuela on their own.

The question remains whether the Venezuelan colony was ever anything more than a money-making scheme, and whether during the earliest efforts, Price was simply inept or criminally corrupt. The most charitable explanation is that Price assumed that others would deal with pragmatic concerns and details would just somehow resolve themselves, but he must have realized that the Venezuela Land Company lacked the financial resources to fulfill promises made to colonists. Later, in the hands of the Pattisons, the scheme was clearly a fraud. Price, ill after his trip to Venezuela and never an effective personality, remained passive as they cheated and swindled.

SOURCES

The attempt to establish Confederate colonies in Venezuela is known primarily through official records of the US National Archives, Washington, DC; the Venezuela Foreign Office Archives, Caracas; and the British Foreign Office, London. Frederick A. Johnson wrote an extensive report of the first colonization attempt, which he led. The original copy is apparently lost, but a reliable copy survives. Thomas S. Waring's papers in the University of South Carolina Library at Columbia provide important evidence of the last effort. Many newspaper articles provide information about the promises made by Price's companies and the experiences of the colonists. All these are noted in the one monograph on the subject, Alfred Jackson Hanna and Kathryn Abbey Hanna, *Confederate Exiles in Venezuela.* Confederate Centennial Studies, no. 15 (Tuscaloosa, AL: Confederate Publishing, 1960). This is an excellent work, although the authors seem reluctant to question Price's fundamental honesty.

Charles Dickens Jr., "The Last New Eden," *All the Year Round*, o.s., 8, n.s., 4 (June 11, 1870): 37-41, forthrightly labels the activities of the Pattisons, who succeeded Price, as typical emigration scams.

The Emigrant's Vade-Mecum, or Guide to the "Price Grant" in Venezuelan Guyana (London: Trubner, 1868) was published anonymously, although Margaret Amanda Pattison signed the short preface. Evidence indicates the Pattisons and a nephew wrote the work. It is filled with glowing accounts of Venezuela and testimonies by settlers, but the quotations are not reliable, often taken out of context, and sometimes altered and falsified. In addition, the company also printed a much shorter but equally unreliable abridgement by Pattison's nephew: J. Leslie Clark, coll. and arr., *Emigration to Venezuelan Guayana*, (n.p: n.p., 1868).

Brazil

Confederate migration to Brazil was more organized than elsewhere. Potential colonists combined funds to send agents charged to investigate conditions and scout favorable locations for colonies. There were over a dozen of these scouting expeditions, and the scouts frequently met and cooperated in Brazil. The first ex-Confederate agent to write about the possibilities of migration to Brazil was William Wallace Wood. In 1860, Wood was a major general in the Mississippi militia, and in 1861 he organized a company from Natchez but soon resigned. Shortly after the war, he traveled to Brazil, and by summer 1866, he returned to the United States, where he published a short booklet, *Ho! for Brazil* (Natchez: n.p., 1866). He had no other role in migration to Brazil as his health failed, and he died after a prolonged illness in September 1867.

Three other books played fundamental roles in organizing the Confederate migration to Brazil. Rev. Ballard S. Dunn, a Confederate veteran and Episcopal minister, was among the early agents who traveled to Brazil. He published his findings as *Brazil, the Home for Southerners: or, A Practical Account of What the Author, and Others, who Visited that Country, for the Same Objects, Saw and Did while in that Empire* (New York: G. B. Richardson, 1866). Dr. James McFadden Gaston also traveled to Brazil to investigate the advisability of Confederate settlement. His book, *Hunting a Home in Brazil* (Philadelphia: King and Baird, 1867), written in diary format, provided an examination of Brazilian culture and recounted discussions with Brazilians and recent migrants to Brazil. Lansford Warren Hastings, a lawyer, was interested in emigration long before the Civil War. His book *The Emigrants' Guide to Oregon and California* (Cincinnati: G. Conclin, 1845) reflected his hope to establish a Republic of California as an independent country. In 1864, Hastings submitted a plan to Jefferson Davis to conquer California and annex it to the Confederacy. Davis conferred the rank of major in the Confederate army on Hastings, but, of course, the plan came to nothing. After the war, Hastings traveled for six months in Brazil scouting locations for a colony and published *The Emigrant's Guide to Brazil* (Mobile, AL: n.p., 1867). Inspired by these books, by newspaper articles, and by reports from other agents, groups formed to move to Brazil.

Unlike Confederate migrants to other destinations, those who set out for Brazil usually had definite destinations and generally arrived with better resources. Individual Confederate migrants also came to Brazil, but they tended to arrive later than the initial groups, in contrast to British Honduras, where migration by individuals generally preceded the arrival of groups. Individual immigrants to Brazil often joined existing colonies.

The Brazilian government actively supported Confederate immigration and contracted with the United States and Brazil Mail Steamship Company to transport colonists. Apparently respectable immigrants who could not afford to pay the fare could apply to Brazilian government officials in the United States for a certificate entitling them to passage. The fee would eventually be added to the modest price of government land in Brazil, payable over the course of several years. Migrants could, of course, also arrange their own passages. On arrival, high officials and sometimes Emperor Dom Pedro II himself welcomed the Confederados, as the Brazilians called the migrants. Those arriving in Rio de Janeiro could stay for up to a month for free in a well-appointed government hotel, where they were given nourishing meals before departing to their new settlements, and the government provided steamships to carry migrants from Rio to the port nearest their proposed colonies.

Of course, there were problems as well. Some Southerners eagerly learned Portuguese and became fluent in a relatively short time, while others learned little of the language or persisted in relying entirely on English. Those who failed to learn Portuguese remained isolated from the culture and daily life of their new country. Brazilian government bureaucracy was often nearly incomprehensible even for those who learned Portuguese. It was difficult to establish who had the responsibility to deal with issues, and the government was generally slow to act. For instance, the Brazilian government initially required immigrants who utilized official government transportation to depart through the port of New York, which placed an unnecessary burden on Southerners. For ex-Confederates, departure through New Orleans, Galveston, or another Southern port would have been less expensive and more convenient, required less travel, and eliminated the necessity to interact with Yankees. This was eventually permitted, but only after long, frustrating delays.

EX-CONFEDERATES' REACTIONS TO BRAZIL

Slavery was legal in Brazil at the time of the Confederado immigration and would remain so for about twenty more years, but an abolitionist movement was already growing. Some of the Southerners purchased slaves and attempted to recreate the plantation culture of the old South, while others hired free labor. Many could afford neither and for the first time in their lives labored in the fields. All found themselves in a society with different attitudes toward race than they had ever experienced. In the American South, any African heritage classified an individual as Black, and the distinction between White and Black was felt to be absolute. Racial discrimination certainly existed in Brazil as well, but there every free person was legally equal, and people of color, particularly those of mixed heritage, achieved respectable positions in society and in some cases wealth and power. Some ex-Confederates recognized and adapted to these new circumstances, but others retained their imported prejudices and were unable to accommodate fully to their new environment.

The Southern immigrants were only a small portion of a larger Brazilian phenomenon. The government encouraged not only ex-Confederate migration but also migration from Europe, seeking settlers who could bring farming technology and new skills to Brazil. Large numbers of Germans and Irish and lesser numbers from other countries flocked to Brazil at the same time the Southerners were arriving.

It is impossible to arrive at an exact or even close approximation of the number of ex-Confederates who migrated to Brazil. Probably more Southerners migrated to Brazil than to other Latin American destinations, but the suggestion of a few overly enthusiastic commentators that twenty thousand Southerners migrated to Brazil is a fantasy. The total population of all the colonies and a generous allowance for individuals who remained in Brazilian cities rather than joining colonies still does not approach that figure. An estimate of a little more than five thousand agrees best with the evidence.

The groups that left the South for Brazil had similar ambitions as those who went to other Latin American countries to create cultural colonies where they could live in some approximation of the antebellum South. Their experiences in Brazil varied initially, but the fate of almost all the settlements were strangely similar.

THE SANTARÉM COLONY

Lansford W. Hastings, author of *The Emigrant's Guide to Brazil*, focused his effort on the area around the town of Santarém on the Amazon River, far to the north of other Confederate colonies. Returning to the United States after an initial scouting trip, he recruited a group of colonists who left from New Orleans for Brazil, but their ship was wrecked on the coast of Cuba. Some of the colonists went to Mexico, though others found another ship to carry them to Brazil. Hastings's second effort terminated when smallpox broke out, killing forty-six of the passengers, and the ship returned to harbor. When Hastings's third attempt paused at St. Thomas, creditors seized the ship, and the passengers had to wait for a month to find new passage to Brazil. During that month, Hastings fell ill with yellow fever and died.

The rest of the group proceeded to Brazil, where families built successful plantations near Santarém. Hastings's father-in-law, a man named Judge Medenhall, took control of his tract of land and made it into a prosperous farm. The Confederates grew a variety of crops for domestic use and cash crops, primarily rubber trees and sugarcane. Sugar crops were additionally processed to molasses, distilled to the Brazilian spirit *cachaça*, and occasionally to American-style moonshine. Others built sawmills, and Confederados made wagon construction a specialty. Not everyone succeeded, however. Some complained farming in the Amazon jungle was enervating, provisions were expensive, the local cuisine was unfamiliar and not to their liking, and the Brazilian government did not provide adequate roads. At best, Santarém was little like the antebellum South, a disappointment to some immigrants who would not or could not adapt. According to an official Brazilian government report, 192 Confederados arrived at Santarém by 1869, but after a few months only 87 remained. Several dozen colonists took advantage of a generous offer to return to the United States on US Navy ships. By 1872, only 77 Southerners remained in the area, although a few more came to Santarém as late as 1874. Brazilians always formed the dominant cultural bloc in the area, and English migrants arrived in the early 1870s. All got along well with the Confederados, but they diluted the Southern character of the settlement. As time passed, more Southern colonists grew nostalgic for friends and family, sold their holdings, and returned to the United States. Still others moved away from Santarém, attracted by easier life in urban centers. A few remained in the area for the rest of their lives, but their children were largely absorbed into Brazilian culture. Today Santarém is a prosperous city of around three hundred thousand people, but the only traces of the Confederado colony are an occasional Confederate flag hung in a bar, the persistence of a few Southern family names, and tombstones in a local cemetery.

RIO DOCE COLONY

Charles Grandioson Gunter sponsored a settlement far to the south of Santarém but still north of the major group of Confederate colonies. About two hundred men, women, and children settled at a beautiful site near the town of Linhares on the bank of the Rio Doce and the shore of the Juparanã Lagoon, a substantial freshwater lake framed by distant mountains. The soil was rich, but malaria was endemic throughout the region, and the river proved too shallow for even small paddlewheel steamboats except during the wet season, making it difficult to get crops to markets.

Dr. John Washington Keyes and his family took part in the Rio Doce colony. During the Civil War, he served initially with a Confederate cavalry unit and ultimately as the surgeon of the 17th Alabama Infantry Regiment. His daughter, Julia (Jennie) Rutledge Keyes, kept a diary from the family's departure from Montgomery, Alabama, in 1867, until their return to the United States in 1870, providing a unique insight into the Confederado experience. Jennie, who was about fifteen when she began her diary, was well educated and wrote clear and expressive prose, painting an optimistic and positive view of her new home.

Many of the Rio Doce colonists were professional men, doctors, lawyers, and dentists, and a number had managed plantations in the South. The members of the colony set to work with will and energy, clearing ground, planting crops, and replacing the huts they had initially constructed with larger and better housing. Men who had been part of the elite in the South, however, soon tired of working like field hands, and women who never before had to cook, sew, wash, and clean found their days were now filled with those activities. Even improved housing was primitive: thatched roofs, walls of mud daubed

Confederado settlements in Brazil. The shaded area was the site of the Confederate settlements of Juquiá, New Texas, Xiririca, and Paranaguá.

over lattices of twigs, and floors of pounded clay. Then malaria swept through the colony, and drought destroyed the crops. Families began to return to the United States, including the Keyeses, and others abandoned the Rio Duce colony to move to the vicinity of Santa Barbara, where Confederados were congregating. A few remained in the area, including Charles Gunter, who continued to cultivate sugarcane and coffee until his death in 1873. His son, Basil Manley Gunter, remained in the area and grew rich investing in railroad building in Brazil, and, although a Brazilian citizen, he served as US consular representative in Victória, Brazil.

THE CONFEDERADO COLONIES IN SOUTHERN BRAZIL

A group of four Confederado colonies were founded in southern Brazil: Juquiá, New Texas, and Xiririca in close proximity, and Paranaguá about a hundred miles south. None succeeded in establishing enduring Southern cultural enclaves. Each faced problems and crises individual to that colony, but one factor influenced all and worked against the establishment of cohesive communities. The colonists grew cotton, a crop with which they were familiar in the South, but cotton there and in Brazil quickly exhausted the soil, forcing them to move on to new lands. This tended to scatter the Southern colonists and destroy community cohesion.

JUQUIÁ, OR "LIZZIELAND" COLONY

Rev. Ballard S. Dunn, author of *Brazil, the Home for Southerners*, acquired a large tract of land in southern Brazil by the town of Juquiá. He named his property "Lizzieland" after his recently deceased wife, Elizabeth, and recruited about four hundred Southern immigrants to settle on and around his land. Dunn seems to have been a troublesome personality. His decision to migrate to Brazil was at least partly motivated by quarrels with ecclesiastical superiors about financial matters. After only three months in Brazil, Dunn mortgaged this property and borrowed substantially before returning to the United States, where he said he would recruit more colonists. He never returned to Brazil. Soon after Dunn's desertion, a flood destroyed colonists' crops and buildings, and malaria swept through the area.. The settlers scattered, some returning to the United States and others moving to the vicinity of Santa Barbara with other Confederados. In 1896, a traveler reported that only six Southern families remained in the area.

NEW TEXAS COLONY

Frank McMullan and Willian Bowen were the guiding forces behind the New Texas colony. In 1857, McMullan took part in an abortive filibustering expedition led by the notorious William Walker. While on this voyage, a sailor told McMullan the story of João Aranzel, who supposedly found a lake in the mountains of southern Brazil, the shores of which were rich in gold. When Aranzel returned to civilization, he brought enough gold to make him wealthy for life. He never returned to the lake and only revealed the secret location on his deathbed. The sailor, of course, had Aranzel's directions to the golden lake, which he shared with McMullan, who was apparently of a trusting and credulous nature. He believed this all-too-typical tale, perhaps the last manifestation of the El Dorado story much mutated, and he never seems to have considered why the sailor had not followed the directions himself. McMullan's subsequent decision to move to Brazil seems to have been motivated in part by the desire to go treasure hunting.

In the late 1850s, McMullan contracted tuberculosis, and during the Civil War he resided in Mexico hoping the dry air would benefit his condition. His condition improved somewhat, but the tuberculosis remained active. Early in December 1865, McMullan and William Bowen traveled to Brazil on a scouting expedition. They were well received and chose an area in southern Brazil from which, not coincidentally, a search for the golden lake could easily be initiated. McMullen did not share the information about the gold with Bowen, who remained behind to prepare the area for settlers while McMullan returned to Texas to lead them to Brazil. While McMullan was determined to search for Aranzel's gold, he was equally determined to create a distinctively Southern cultural colony, requiring potential participants to "give satisfactory references that they are Southern in feeling, pro-slavery in sentiments and that they have maintained the reputation of honorable men." According to a few of the colonists, these ideals were not always achieved, and among the 154 settlers who eventually departed for Brazil there were characters described as "very rough in their ways."

McMullan traveled to New Orleans to arrange passage, but he first had to get permission from the Brazilian government for the immigrants to depart from a Southern port rather than New York, a frustrating and lengthy process. Then McMullan had to find a ship; because the colonists' resources were limited, he sought to arrange the cheapest transportation possible. He found a ship owner who was in financial distress and made what seemed to be a good bargain, but it proved to be an expensive misstep. The ship was in poor condition and needed extensive refitting that the owner could not afford, and it was also encumbered by financial liens. McMullan drew on money from the colonists to ready the ship for the voyage and settle outstanding debts, but matters were not quickly or cheaply resolved. All took a toll on McMullan's health. A photograph taken of him in New Orleans reveals a feverish-looking individual with hollow eyes and sunken cheeks.

McMullan signed the lease on the ship on November 6, 1866, and the initial plan was to depart from New Orleans on the first of December for Galveston and there embark the waiting immigrants. Most colonists camped on the beach there, while a few wealthier families found temporary accommodations in town. Finally, after many delays, the colonists departed on January 25, 1867. The voyage did not go well. Before dawn on February 10, a storm drove the ship ashore, wrecking it on the coast of Cuba. The colonists all survived and were able to salvage much of their goods, but the expenses in preparing the ship and the delay in sailing left many short of funds. The Cubans were extremely generous to the stranded travelers while McMullan went to New York to arrange transportation with Brazilian officials.

After inevitable bureaucratic delays, a ship was dispatched from New Orleans to Cuba, and from there it carried the Texans to New York, where a larger ship would bring them to Brazil. The trip to New York was galling. Not only were the colonists moving in the wrong direction, but a storm forced their ship to take refuge at Norfolk, Virginia, where they were stranded for about a week. They finally arrived in New York on March 26, 1867, where they remained until April 22, when they departed for Brazil on a filthy ship with a disagreeable crew. The voyage took twenty-eight days to reach Rio de Janeiro, where a few of the colonists elected to remain. Five days later, the majority departed for the town of Iguape at the mouth of the Ribeira de Iguape. From there they had to travel upriver, but the steamer to transport them would not depart for nearly a month, and again the colonists had to find temporary shelter and rely on the kindness of strangers. The New Texas colony was to be located beyond the coastal plain and high enough to be immune to flooding. During the wait, McMullan's health deteriorated, and he revealed the secret of Aranzel's gold to his uncle, Judge James Harrison Dyer, and Dr. George Barnsley, a close friend. Neither expressed skepticism, and both became avid treasure hunters.

Finally, in early June, an advance group traveled up the Iguape River for two days by steamer and then transferred to dugout canoes before finally arriving at the Juquiá, São Lourenço, and Itariri Rivers and the territory between the towns of Peruibe and Conceição, where McMullan and Bowen had chosen land for their new homes. The main body of colonists followed in late June. Bowen met them where he had built basic shelter for the colonists until they could establish their own housing on their chosen farms, and the Brazilian government initially provided food for the colonists. Even as the colonists sought to establish themselves, McMullan grew weaker, and he died on September 29.

A power struggle soon divided the colonists. William Bowen had been McMullan's partner from the beginning of the project and his obvious successor. He was cordial, polite, and sought consensus, but he was not a strong leader. Bowen was opposed by an alliance of Judge Dyer and Dr. Barnsley, who kept the story of Aranzel's gold secret. Dyer, described as forceful but hard and overbearing, often alienated rather than attracted support among the colonists, most of whom supported Bowen. Dyer and Barnsley petitioned the Brazilian government to place Barnsley in command of the colony, but the government refused to intervene in the dispute and discontinued food support for the divided, failing colony.

The colonists' first crops grew well, but they now faced the problem of getting them to market. There was no regular steamboat service that might carry the crops, and it was impractical to use dugout canoes for transport. The colonists hoped to build a road to the town of Santos over which they could carry their crops, but such a road required causeways across swamps, bridges over rivers, and grading in hilly country. The colonists lacked sufficient resources for the task, and the state government aid was inadequate. The road was not built, and crops brought no profit.

The colony began to disintegrate; besides the continuing dispute over leadership and the failure to find a market for crops, other factors contributed: isolation, primitive conditions, lack of social life, and longing for friends and family in the United States. Letters from relatives and friends back home indicated that Yankee occupation was not as oppressive as anticipated, and conditions in the South were becoming more acceptable, at least to the White population. Many individuals and families returned to Iguape and then journeyed on to Santa Barbara, or to Rio de Janeiro, where some remained, or to the United States, if they could afford the passage. A few remained in the region near the headwaters of the São Lourenço River, including Dyer and Barnsley. Barnsley's fate was sad. Though a skilled doctor, he could never settle down and develop a substantial practice. After a short interval, he inevitably set out on another futile quest to find Aranzel's gold. At one point he returned briefly to the South, where he quarreled with his family and soon returned to Brazil and treasure hunting.

Barnsley died in 1918 at age eighty-one, still believing a wealth of gold remained to be discovered but without having found anything.

Judge Dyer and his son-in-law, Columbus Wasson, also sought Aranzel's gold, but they had a practical nature. They built a sawmill and began to harvest fine hardwoods, which found a ready market. They built a second mill and borrowed substantially to purchase a steam riverboat to carry their wood to market, but the heavily mortgaged steamer was soon wrecked on a sand bar, and Dyer was also distressed by the death of his wife about the same time. Dyer and Wasson sold one of the sawmills and returned to Texas in 1871. Before leaving, Dyer gave the second sawmill to Steve Watson, a slave he had brought to Brazil. Watson had ably managed the sawmill for Dyer, and after Dyer's departure, Watson prospered, grew wealthy, and married a Brazilian woman. He was ultimately the only successful resident of the New Texas colony, and his descendants bearing the name Vassão, the Brazilian Portuguese pronunciation of Watson, still live in the area.

XIRIRICA COLONY

Dr. James M. Gaston, author of *Hunting a Home in Brazil*, began his colony in a strangely disorganized manner for one who scouted the country. Gaston recruited about a hundred colonists who sailed to Brazil from New York on the same overcrowded ship that carried McMullan's New Texas colonists, but Gaston arrived without any particular Brazilian destination in mind. He first thought to colonize in the region of Paranaguá Bay but changed his mind before even traveling there and decided on land near the town of Xiririca, in the vicinity of the Juquiá and New Texas colonies. The colonists began by building shelters and clearing ground, but matters soon deteriorated. The colony was located even farther upstream than McMullan's New Texas and faced the same difficulty in moving crops to market. Moreover, land titles to the area proved faulty and would require extensive and expensive legal procedures to clarify, with no guarantees of success. Colonists soon drifted away, a number going to the vicinity of Santa Barbara.

PARANAGUÁ COLONY

Colonel M. S. McSwain and Horace Manly Lane led a small initial group of about thirty-five Confederados to the area near the city of Paranaguá to the south of Juquiá, New Texas, and Xiririca. The situation was beautiful, the climate more temperate than locations to the north, and the soil good. The founders of the colony wrote back to the South encouraging more immigrants and the population of Confederados grew to about two hundred. Many of the immigrants did well, especially those with sufficient financial resources to purchase a sufficient quality of good land. For $5,600, Dr. John H. Blue purchased 8,000 acres, 5,000 covered with good timber; 150 acres in cultivation; two water-powered mills for processing sugarcane and cassava (the root of which is used to make flour and tapioca); and two distilleries. Yet nothing like a distinctive Southern community emerged at the Paranaguá colony. The Confederado holdings were too scattered, many German immigrants moved into the area, and there was also a considerable Brazilian population. As elsewhere, some grew nostalgic and returned to the United States, but most seem to have been absorbed into the general German-Brazilian cultural mix.

SANTA BÁRBARA D'OESTE/AMERICANA COLONY

The settlement near Santa Barbara, eventually named Americana, was the closest to success of all the Confederado efforts to build a distinctively Southern cultural colony in Brazil. William Hutchinson Norris, who was a colonel in the militia during the Mexican-American War, was the first Southerner to settle in the region. He was a lawyer and state senator in Alabama, and he took part in the Mexican War, but he was sixty at the beginning of the Civil War and judged too old to serve. At the end of the war he still had considerable wealth and moved to Brazil, settling near Santa Bárbara d'Oeste in 1866, slightly to the north and inland of the main group of Confederado colonies in southern Brazil. His family joined him there during the next year.

Unlike with most other colonies, Norris and the others who settled near Santa Barbara did not have a governmental land grant but rather purchased holdings from individuals. It was more expensive to acquire land from private owners, and land became increasingly expensive as more Confederados moved to the area, but most of the land they purchased was developed agricultural and pasture land. The settlers could begin to grow food and cash crops immediately and did not have to go through the exhausting process of clearing fields of trees and brush. The area was also higher, dryer, and healthier than the Confederado settlements to the south. The Santa Barbara community also benefitted from gradual growth. Rather than a mass of colonists descending at once, all needing shelter and support, Confederados trickled into the Santa Barbara area over time from other, failing colonies, and there they found established settlers who could provide aid and advice. The

Confederate immigrants did not settle in a single compact community at Santa Barbara but rather lived on individual holdings in the vicinity and at four communities nearby: Funil to the north, Retiro to the southwest, Campo to the south, and Estação to the east. All were less than fifteen miles from Santa Barbara, sufficiently close to maintain a sense of community.

Estação (Station) became the most important settlement. The area was originally known as the Fazenda do Machadinho (Machadinho Estate). There William Norris, the first Confederado settler, purchased about four hundred acres and established a successful farm. By 1870, railroads were beginning to spread across Brazil. It was impractical to establish a line directly to Santa Barbara, but the area to the east near the Norris farm was suitable. The coming of the railroad was of greatest importance to the Confederado community, as crops could be brought rapidly and cheaply to markets, and goods could be similarly imported. The railroad did not reach the area until 1875, when the São Paulo Railways Company railroad established Estação de Santa Bárbara (Santa Barbara Station), but progress into the area gave hope and reason to persevere in the years before its arrival. The community that grew up around the railroad station was officially known as Villa da Estação de Santa Bárbara, but as the Confederados established their farms, residences, and businesses in and around the rapidly growing community, the settlement became known commonly as Villa dos Americanos (American Town) or simply Americana. The name Americana was officially recognized in 1904.

The Confederados around Americana grew cotton productively, but the crop was subject to diseases and insect attack, and many soon shifted to growing sugarcane, coffee, and Georgia "rattlesnake" watermelons. This variety of watermelon exhibits a green and yellowish pattern thought to resemble a rattlesnake's skin. Watermelons were previously unknown in Brazil, and rattlesnake melons are sweet and large and have a tough protective rind, ideal for shipping and wide distribution. The melons became popular throughout Brazil, and Americana farmers were soon selling as many as one hundred railroad boxcars of melons each year. Confederados also built businesses and shops in Americana. They introduced the wheelbarrow and the kerosene lantern and, much more importantly, the moldboard plow, which improved the efficiency of agriculture and even enabled the opening of new lands.

Not all found contentment in Americana. Some grew nostalgic for family and friends and returned to the United States, while others, particularly doctors and dentists, sold their farms and businesses at Americana and the neighboring towns and moved to the Brazilian cities, where many integrated themselves fully into Brazilian culture. Even at their greatest number, the Confederados of Americana were a minority among the Brazilians, and additional migration by Germans and Latvians further diluted the Southern character of the area.

Campo became the site of the community Protestant chapel and graveyard, and it remains the center of Confederado community consciousness. The graveyard is now the site of fewer internments than previously, and as years pass, more Portuguese and less English is heard at gatherings there. But it is still a unifying factor, the site of quarterly and annual pilgrimages and celebrations by descendants of the Confederados—those who remain in the area and those who return for these activities. Some regard Americana and Campo as the exceptional successful Confederado colony among failed colonies, a romantic, sentimental, and amusing survival of Southern culture in the foreign, exotic context of Brazil, but modern accounts usually ignore problematic aspects of Americana culture. It can be equally argued that it is just a persistent remnant of a colony that has failed in its own particular manner.

Americana maintains no authentic cultural continuity from the old South, not even memory of antebellum dance or costume. Old Southern dances, hoop skirts, and Confederate uniforms that characterize the Confederado Festa at Campo have all been introduced from the outside, chiefly by journalists to improve the story and the visual impression. The result is a highly artificial tradition that owes much to sources other than authentic continuity and promulgates an artificial and incomplete vision of the antebellum South. Americana is much like *Gone with the Wind* but in some respects even less authentic, such as women dancing in hoop skirts decorated with the Confederate battle flag.

While many descendants have moved to cities and fully integrated into Brazilian society, other Confederados remain isolated from the prevailing Brazilian culture, failing to confront hard questions about Southern culture and the Confederacy. They embrace the Lost Cause interpretation of the Civil War, maintaining that protection of states' rights was the principal cause of the war, while minimizing the role of slavery. In reality, the chief states' right in question was obviously the right to own slaves. Racist attitudes remain common among Confederado descendants living in the vicinity of Americana, where association and interaction with Brazilians are largely restricted to necessity. Marriage within the community and with neighbors of German and Latvian heritage is accepted, but whole families have been ostracized because one member married a Brazilian not regarded as purely "White." Such attitudes leave these Confederado descendants outside the dominant culture of Brazil, clinging to a superficial and inaccurate image of the antebellum South, and irrelevant except as a curiosity.

SOURCES

In addition to the three important books mentioned above that promoted migration, letters from Brazil, newspaper articles, and personal accounts illuminate the experiences of the Confederados. The fullest and most famous is the diary of Julia (Jenny) Rutledge Keyes, the daughter of Dr. John Washington Keyes. His family accompanied him to Brazil, where they took part in the Rio Doce colony. Jennie's diary was first partially published in Peter A. Brannon, ed., "Southern Emigration to Brazil: Embodying the Diary of Jennie R. Keyes, Montgomery, Alabama," *Alabama Historical Quarterly* 1, no. 2 (Summer 1930): 74-95, no. 3 (Fall 1930): 280-305, and no. 4 (Winter 1930): 467-488, but the death of the editor and the Depression curtailed plans to publish it fully. That was finally achieved in Julia L. Keyes, "Our Life, in Brazil," *Alabama Historical Quarterly* 28, nos. 3-4 (Fall and Winter 1966): 127-339. Few personal accounts are as expansive and informative.

Most secondary articles and books about the Confederados in Brazil focused primarily on the Americana colony, the one surviving settlement with a connection to the Confederate past, and most interpret Americana in a quaint, romantic light. Eugene C. Harter, *The Lost Colony of the Confederacy* (College Station: Texas A&M University Press, 2000; Jackson: University Press of Mississippi, 1985) is more scholarly than most but otherwise typical of the genre. Harter, a descendant of Confederados, became US consul in Brazil in 1971. His book is an account of the Southern migration to Brazil and a sentimental tribute to the settlers and their descendants, tinged with a bit of Lost Cause ideology.

Alcides Fernando Gussi, *Os norte-americanos (confederados) do Brasil: Identidades no contexto transnacional* (Americana: Prefeitura

Municipal de Americana, SP, 1997) is an excellent and more objective treatment but only available in Portuguese. Cyrus B. Dawsey and James M. Dawsey, eds., *The Confederados: Old South Immigrants in Brazil* (Tuscaloosa: University of Alabama Press, 1995) contains eleven essays by specialists covering every aspect of the Confederado experience in Brazil, as well as a thoughtful introduction, conclusions, and postscript, and an excellent annotated bibliography. Blanche Henry Clark Weaver, "Confederate Emigration to Brazil," *Journal of Southern History* 27, no. 1 (February 1961): 33-53, presents an overview with excellent insights.

William Clark Griggs, *The Elusive Eden: Frank McMullan's Confederate Colony in Brazil* (Austin: University of Texas Press, 1987) provides an overview of the Confederate experience while presenting a detailed account of the failed New Texas colony. The author admires McMullan for his determination and fortitude but never questions the wisdom of a man profoundly ill with tuberculosis presuming to lead people to settle in a distant land among poorly understood conditions. Griggs is hardly critical of the belief of McMullan and others in the fanciful story of the lost lake of gold and of the colony's failure to secure a way to bring crops to market, both of which demonstrate a similar baseless optimism and lack of critical thinking that contributed to the failure of the colony. Griggs nevertheless presents an original, important, and detailed examination of a Brazilian Confederate colonial effort. Norma de Azevedo Guilhon, *Confederados em Santarém: Saga americana na amazónia*, 2nd ed. (Rio de Janeiro: Presença, 1987) similarly treats the Santarem colony. In addition to providing a narrative history of the colony, the work traces the family histories of the colonists and reproduces many photographs.

Riccardo Orizio, *Lost White Tribes: The End of Privilege and the Last Colonials in Sri Lanka, Jamaica, Brazil, Haiti, Namibia, and Guadeloupe*, trans. Avril Bardoni (New York: Free Press, 2000) provides a sober overview of European communities left isolated by the retreat of colonial powers or, in the case of the Confederados, by their own decision to remove themselves to a foreign environ. This is a rare treatment of the Americana colony that is not entirely and uncritically positive.

Auburn University in Alabama maintains a special collection of material related to the Confederado immigration, including correspondence, memoirs, genealogies, and newspaper clippings, especially related to Colonel Norris, the primary settler of what became the Americana colony.

A Final Note

COLONIES THAT FAILED DID SO IN MANY WAYS, none because of just a single cause. Yet some causes played particularly large roles in the failures. The quest to take a share of the riches of the New World led to unreasoning optimism and rash decisions. Colonists were ignorant of the conditions into which they hastened and so were ill prepared. Poor location, forced by necessity or chosen with too little consideration, doomed more than one colony. Disastrous leadership ruined others. Many failed because resources available to support them were simply inadequate. National and religious conflicts destroyed still more. Fraud played a role as early as the seventeenth century and became a common component of failure in the nineteenth century.

Many colonists died in failed colonies and those that survived, but their numbers pale in comparison to the deaths they caused. Colonists destroyed Native American cultures and brought about the deaths of literally millions of indigenous habitants, some reduced to slavery, others killed in warfare, and still more who perished from European diseases. The European demand for Black slaves devastated African societies and caused untold deaths during the sea passage, and still more among the slaves who labored under the lash in the New World. These disasters are often acknowledged, but their magnitude is seldom fully appreciated. Colonists created the modern nations of the Americas, but the cost was high.

Further Reading

Chapter 1

Columbus's Failures: La Navidad and La Isabela (1492–1497)
The literature on Columbus is enormous, and best consulted in the bibliographies of Samuel Eliot Morison, *Admiral of the Ocean Sea, a Life of Christopher Columbus*, 2 vols. (Boston: Little, Brown, 1942); Laurence Bergreen, *Columbus: Four Voyages 1492–1504* (New York: Penguin, 2011), and Foster Provost, *Columbus: An Annotated Guide to the Study on His Life and Writings, 1750–1988* (Detroit: Published for the John Carter Brown Library, 1991). Additionally, the following on the Native peoples are particularly to be noted:

Keegan, William. *The People Who Met Columbus: The Lucayan Taino*. Gainesville: University Press of Florida, 1992.

Moya Pons, Frank. "The Politics of Forced Indian Labor in La Espanola 1492–1520." *Antiquity* 66, no. 250 (1992): 130-139.

Rouse, Irving. *The Tainos: Rise and Decline of the People Who Greeted Columbus*. New Haven, CT: Yale University Press, 1992.

Stannard, David E. *American Holocaust: The Conquest of the New World*. New York: Oxford University Press, 1993.

Wilson, Samuel, ed. *The Indigenous People of the Caribbean*. Gainesville: University Press of Florida, 1997.

Chapter 2

The Follies of Alonso de Ojeda and Diego de Nicuesa:
San Sebastian de Uraba (1510) and
Santa María la Antigua del Darién (1510-1524)

Bulmer-Thomas, Victor. *Thirty Years of Latin American Studies in the United Kingdom 1965–1995*. London: Institute of Latin American Studies, 1997.

Crosby, Alfred W. *The Columbian Exchange: Biological and Cultural Consequences of 1492*. Westport, CT: Greenwood, 1972.

Floyd, Troy S. *The Columbus Dynasty in the Caribbean, 1492–1526*. Albuquerque: University of New Mexico Press, 1973.

Friede, Juan, and Benjamin Keen, eds. *Bartolomé de las Casas in History: Toward an Understanding of the Man and His Work*. DeKalb: Northern Illinois University Press, 1971.

Gibson, Charles, ed. *The Black Legend: Anti-Spanish Attitudes in the Old World and the New*. New York: Alfred A. Knopf, 1971.

Keen, Benjamin. "The Black Legend Revisited: Assumptions and Realities." *Hispanic American Historical Review* 49, no. 4 (1969): 703-719.

Mann, Charles C. *1491: New Revelations of the Americas Before Columbus*. New York: Alfred A. Knopf, 2005.

———. *1493: Uncovering the New World Columbus Created*. New York: Alfred A. Knopf, 2012.

Morison, Samuel Eliot. *The European Discovery of America: The Southern Voyages*. New York: Oxford University Press, 1974.

Sauer, Carl Ortwin. *The Early Spanish Main*. Berkeley and Los Angeles: University of California Press, 1966.

Thomas, Hugh. *Rivers of Gold: The Rise of the Spanish Empire, from Columbus to Magellan*. New York: Random House, 2003.

Chapter 3

German Bankers in the Jungles: Venezuela (1528–1556)

Friede, Juan. "Geographical Ideas and the Conquest of Venezuela." *The Americas* 16, no. 2 (Oct. 1959): 145-159.

Haebler, Konrad. *Die überseeischen Unternehmungen der Welser und ihrer Gesellschafter*. Leipzig, Germany: Hirschfeld, 1903.

Hugh, Thomas. *The Golden Empire: Spain, Charles V, and the Creation of America*. New York: Random House, 2010.

Humbert, Jules. *La première occupation allemande du Vénézuéla au*

XVIe siècle: période dite des Welser, 1528-1556. Paris: Société des Américanistes de Paris, 1904.

Johnson, Christine R. *The German Discovery of the World: Renaissance Encounters with the Strange and Marvelous.* Charlottesville: University of Virginia Press, 2009.

Lang, Stefan. "Problems of a Credit Colony: The Welser in Sixteenth Century Venezuela." History's Shadow. Accessed May 10, 2020. historysshadow.wordpress.com/2015/06/04/problems-of-a-credit-colony-the-welser-in-sixteenth-century-venezuela/.

McAlister, Lyle N. *Spain and Portugal in the New World, 1492–1700.* Minneapolis: University of Minnesota Press, 1984.

Morón, Guillermo. *A History of Venezuela.* London: G. Allen & Unwin, 1964.

Moses, Bernard. *The Spanish Dependencies in South America: An Introduction to the History of Their Civilization,* 2 vols. London: Smith Elder, 1914.

Quintero, Gilberto. *El Teniente Justicia Mayor en la administración colonial venezolana. Aproximación a su estudio histórico jurídico.* Caracas: Academia Nacional de la Historia, 1996.

Roth, Julia. "Sugar and Slaves: The Augsburg Welser as Conquerors of America and Colonial Foundation Myths." *Atlantic Studies* 14, no. 4 (2017): 436-456.

Thomas, Hugh. *The Golden Empire: Spain, Charles V, and the Creation of America.* New York: Random House, 2010.

Wagner, Henry Raup, and Helen Rand Parish. *The Life and Writings of Bartolomé de Las Casas.* Albuquerque: University of New Mexico Press, 1967.

Waszkis, Helmut. *Mining in the Americas: Stories and History.* Cambridge, England: Woodhead, 1993.

Chapter 4

Quarrelsome French in Brazil: France Antarctique (1555–1567)

Arciniegas, German. *Amerigo and the New World: The Life and Times of Amerigo Vespucci.* Translated by Harriet de Onís. New York: Alfred A. Knopf, 1955.

Bourquelot, Félix, ed. *Mémoires de Claude Haton, contenant le récit des événements accomplis de 1553 à 1582, principalement dans la Champagne et la Brie,* 2 vols. Paris: imprimerie impériale, 1857.

Bourquin, Laurent, ed. *Mémoires de Claude Haton,* 4 vols. Paris : éditions du CTHS, 2001–2007.

Fernández-Armesto, Felipe. *Amerigo: The Man Who Gave His Name to America.* New York: Random House, 2007.

Gannon, P. S. *Huguenot Refugees in the Settling of Colonial America.* New York: Huguenot Society of America,1987.

Roukema, E. "The Mythical 'First Voyage' of the 'Solderini Letter.'" *Imago Mundi* 16 (1962): 70-75.

Chapter 5

Spanish Hidalgos and Covert Jews: Jamaica (1509–1655)

Andrade, Jacob. *A Record of the Jews in Jamaica.* Kingston: Jamaica Times, 1941.

Black, Clinton Vane de Brosse. *A New History of Jamaica.* [Kingston?] Jamaica: W. Collins and Sangster, 1975.

———. *The Story of Jamaica: From Prehistory to the Present.* London: Collins, 1973.

Bloom, H. I. *The Economic Activities of the Jews in Amsterdam in the 17th and 18th Centuries.* Williamsport, PA: Baynard Press, 1937.

Bodian, Mariam. *Hebrews of the Portuguese Nation, Conversos and Community in Early Modern Amsterdam.* Bloomington: Indiana University Press, 1997.

Bridges, George Wilson. *The Annals of Jamaica.* London: J. Murray, 1827–1828.

Coulton, Barbara. "Cromwell and the 'Readmission' of the Jews to England, 1656." *Cromwelliana* (2001): 1-21.

Edwards, Bryan. *History of the British Colonies in the Western Indies.* Vol. 2. London: John Stockdale Piccadilly, 1801.

Gardner, W. J. *The History of Jamaica: From Its Discovery by Christopher Columbus to the Year 1872.* London: Unwin, 1909; reprint London: Routledge, 2014.

Goodwin, William B. *Spanish and English Ruins in Jamaica.* Boston: Meador, 1938.

Harlow, V. T. "The Voyages of Captain William Jackson 1642–1645." *Camden Miscellany* 13 (1923): 1-39.

[Leslie, Charles]. *A New History of Jamaica: From the Earliest Accounts to the Taking of Porto Bello by Vice-Admiral Vernon. In thirteen letters from a Gentleman to his friend.* London: printed for J. Hodges, 1740. Published anonymously, the author has been identified as Charles Leslie, whose family was prominent in Jamaica. The work has often been reprinted, recently by Cambridge University Press, 2015.

Long, Edward. *The History of Jamaica*. 3 vols. (n.p.: n.p., 1774). This is the first comprehensive description of Jamaica by an Englishman long resident on the island. It has frequently been reprinted, recently in Montreal by McGill-Queen's University Press, 2002.

Sherlock, Sir Philip Manderson, and Hazel Bennett. *The Story of the Jamaican People*. Kingston: I. Randle, 1998; Princeton, NJ: M. Wiener, 1998.

Wolf, Lucien. "Crypto Jews Under the Commonwealth." *Transactions of the Jewish Historical Society of England* 2 (1893–1894): 55-88.

Chapter 6
Courlanders on Tobago: Troubled Isle (1638–1654)

No additional readings.

Chapter 7
The Graveyard of Colonists: The Wild Coast (1576–1830)

Amussen, Susan Dwyer. *Caribbean Exchanges: Slavery and the Transformation of English Society, 1640–1700*. Chapel Hill: University of North Carolina Press, 2007.

Barber, Sarah. "Power in the Caribbean: The Proprietorship of Lord Willoughby of Parham." In *Constructing Early Modern Empires: Proprietary Ventures in the Atlantic World, 1500–1750*, edited by L. H. Roper and B. Van Ruymbeke. Leiden, Netherlands: Brill, 2007.

Bennett, George W. *A History of British Guiana. Compiled from Various Authorities*. Georgetown, Demerara: L. M'Dermott, 1875.

———. *An Illustrated History of British Guiana*. Georgetown, Demerara: L. M'Dermott, 1866.

Bridenbaugh, Carl, and Roberta Bridenbaugh. *No Peace beyond the Line: The English in the Caribbean, 1624–1690*. New York: Oxford University Press, 1972.

Brown, Enid. *Suriname and the Netherlands Antilles: An Annotated English-Language Bibliography*. London: Scarecrow Press, 1992.

Dalton, Henry G. *The History of British Guiana: Comprising a General Description of the Colony; a Narrative of Some of the Principal Events from the Earliest Period (and) Its Climate, Geology, Staple Products*. London: Longman, Brown, Green and Longmans, 1855.

Daly, Vere T. *A Short History of the Guyanese People*. Oxford: Macmillan, 1975.

Edmundson, George. "The Dutch in Western Guiana." *English Historical Review* 16 (1901): 640-675.

Fey, Toon. *Suriname Discovered*. Schiedam: Scriptum, 2007.

Gimlette, John. *Wild Coast: Travels on South America's Untamed Edge*. New York: Alfred A. Knopf, 2011. Gimlette's work is a modern travelogue but excellent for understanding the climate and background of the area.

Goslinga, Cornelius C. *The Dutch in the Caribbean and on the Wild Coast, 1580–1680*. Gainesville: University of Florida Press, 1971.

———. *A Short History of Netherlands Antilles and Surinam*. The Hague: Nijhoff, 1879.

Chapter 8
Puritans and Pirates in the Caribbean: Providence Island (1630–1641)
No additional readings.

Chapter 9
Burghers in the Tropics: Dutch West India Company in Brazil (1624–1654)

Boogaart, Ernst Van den, et al. *Johan Maurits van Nassau-Siegen, 1604–1679: A Humanistic Prince in Europe and Brazil*. The Hague: Johan Maurits van Nassau Stichting, 1979.

Canny, Nicholas P., and Philip P. Morgan. *The Oxford Handbook of the Atlantic World, c. 1450–c. 1850*. Oxford: Oxford University Press, 2013.

Groesen, Michiel van, ed. *The Legacy of Dutch Brazil*. New York: Cambridge University Press, 2014.

Kritzler, Edward. *Jewish Pirates of the Caribbean*. New York: Anchor Books, 2008.

Moraes, Ruben Borba. *Bibliographia Brasiliana: Rare Books about Brazil Published from 1504 to 1900 and Works by Brazilian Authors of the Colonial Period*. Los Angeles: University of California, Los Angeles Latin American Center Publications, 1983.

Nellis, Eric Guest. *Shaping the New World: African Slavery in the Americas, 1500–1888*. Ontario: University of Toronto Press, 2013.

Schwartz, Stuart B. *Early Brazil: A Documentary Collection to 1700*. New York: Cambridge University Press, 2010.

Chapter 10

Phillippe de Longvilliers de Poincy: A Rogue Knight of Malta in the Caribbean (1651–1665)

Attard, Joseph. *The Knights of Malta*. San Gwann, Malta: BDL, 2010.

Bridenbaugh, Carl, and Roberta Bridenbaugh. *No Peace beyond the Line: The English in the Caribbean 1624–1690*. New York: Oxford University Press, 1972.

Buttigieg, Emanuel. *Nobility, Faith and Masculinity: The Hospitaller Knights of Malta, c.1580–c.1700*. London: Continuum, 2011.

Crouse, Nellis. *French Pioneers in the West Indies, 1624–1664*. New York: Columbia University Press, 1940.

———. *The French Struggle for the West Indies, 1666–1713*. New York: Columbia University Press, 1943.

Dubé, Jean-Claude. *The Chevalier de Montmagny: First Governor of New France*. Translated by Elizabeth Rapley. Ottawa: University of Ottawa Press, 2005.

Emmer, P. C., and Germán Carrera Damas. *General History of the Caribbean*. Vol. 2, *New Societies—the Caribbean in the Long Sixteenth Century*. New York: Palgrave Macmillan, 2007.

Haring, Clare Henry. *The Buccaneers in the West Indies in the XVII Century*. London: Methuen 1910.

Highfield, Arnold R. *A Brief History of St. Croix*. Christiansted, St. Croix: Carib Things, 1973.

———. *Sainte Croix 1650–1733: A Plantation Society in the French West Indies*. Christiansted, St. Croix: Antilles Press, 2013.

Hubbard, Vincent K. *A History of St Kitts*. Oxford: Macmillan Caribbean, 2002.

———. *Swords, Ships & Sugar*. Corvallis, OR: Premiere Editions International, 2002.

Joines, Stanford. *The Eighth Flag: Cannibals, Conquistadors, Buccaneers, Pirates; The Untold Story of the Caribbean and the Mystery of St. Croix's Pirate Legacy, 1493–1750*. United States: Amazon Digital Services LLC–KDP Print US, 2018.

Knight, Franklin W. *General History of the Caribbean*. Vol. 3, *The Slave Societies of the Caribbean*. London: Macmillan, 1997.

Kozlesski, Lisa. *Leeward Islands: Anguilla, St. Martin, St. Barts, St. Eustatius, Guadeloupe, St. Kitts & Nevis, Antigua & Barbuda, and Montserrat*. Discovering the Caribbean: History, Politics, and Culture. Broomall, PA: Mason Crest, 2009

Lawaetz, Erik J. *St. Croix: 500 Years pre-Columbus to 1990*. Herning, Denmark: P. Kristensen, 1991.

Lewisohn, Florence. *Divers Information on the Romantic History of St. Croix from the Time of Columbus until Today*. [Christiansted, US Virgin Islands]: St. Croix Landmarks Society, 1964.

———. "Highlights of Cruzan History." St. Croix Landmarks Society, 1963.

Mandelblatt, Bertie. "Atlantic Consumption of French Rum and Brandy and Economic Growth in the Seventeenth- and Eighteenth-Century Caribbean." *French History* 25, no. 1 (2011): 9-27.

Peyrefitte, Roger. *The Knights of Malta*. London: Panther, 1971.

Porter, Whitworth. *A History of the Knights of Malta*, 2 vols. Cambridge: Cambridge University Press, 1858 and 1883.

Roberts, W. Adolphe. *The French in the West Indies*. Indianapolis: Bobbs-Merrill, 1942.

Roux, Benoît. "Pastor Charles de Rochefort and the Natural and Moral History of the Caribbean Islands of America." In *The Lesser Antilles: From the First Amerindian Settlements to the Beginnings of European Colonization*. Colonial American History Papers, no. 5. Edited by Bernard Grunberg, 175-216. Paris: Harmattan, 2011.

Sire, H. J. A. *The Knights of Malta*. New Haven, CT: Yale University Press, 2005.

Southey, Thomas. *Chronological History of the West Indies*, 3 vols. London: Longman, Rees, Orme, Brown, and Green, 1827.

Tertre, Jean Baptiste du. *Histoire générale des antilles habitées par les Francois*, 4 vols. in 3 parts. Paris: Chez Thomas Jolly, 1667[–1671]. An expanded edition of his 1654 book (see next) incorporating material from his second voyage to the Caribbean in 1656–1657.

———. *Histoire générale des isles de Christophe, de la Guadeloupe, et le Martinique et autres dans l'Amerique*. Paris: Chez Iacques Langlois, 1654.

Williamson, James A. *The Caribee Islands under the Proprietary Patents*. London: Oxford University Press, 1926.

Chapter 11

The Fate of a Nation: Scots in Panama (1698–1700)

Barbour, James Samuel. *A History of William Paterson and the Darien Company, with Illustrations and Appendices*. London: Blackwood and Sons, 1907.

Bingham, H. S. "The Early History of the Darien Company." *Scottish Historical Review* 3 (1906): 210-217, 316-326, 437-448.

Cullen, E. *Isthmus of Darien Ship Canal; with a Full History of the Scotch Colony of Darien, Several Maps, Views of the Country, and Original Documents.* London: E. Wilson, 1853.

Cundall, F. *The Darien Venture.* New York: Hispanic Society of America, 1926.

Hart, Francis Russell. *The Disaster of Darien* (Boston: n.p., 1929).

Hidalgo, Dennis R. "To Get Rich for Our Homeland: The Company of Scotland and the Colonization of the Darien." *Colonial Latin American Historical Review* 10, no. 3 (Summer 2001): 311-350.

Insh, George Pratt. "The Founders of the Company of Scotland." *Scottish Historical Review* 25, no. 100 (1928): 241-254.

———. *Papers Related to the Ships and Voyages of the Company of Scotland Trading to Africa and the Indies, 1696–1707.* Edinburgh: University Press by T. and A. Constable, for the Scottish History Society, 1924.

———. *Some Notes on the Literature of Scots Colonisation.* Glasgow: n.p., 1928.

———. *Some Notes on the Scottish Settlement in Darien.* Edinburgh: n.p., 1946. Reprinted from *The Scottish Geographical Magazine.*

Magnusson, Magnus. *Scotland: The Story of a Nation.* New York: Grove Press, 2000.

McKendrick, John. *Darien: A Journey in Search of Empire.* Edinburgh: Birlinn, 2018.

Orr, Julie. *Scotland, Darien and the Atlantic World, 1698–1700.* Edinburgh: Edinburgh University Press, 2018.

Prebble, John. *The Darien Disaster: A Scots Colony in the New World, 1698–1700.* New York: Holt, Rinehart and Winston, 1969.

Storrs, C. D. "Disaster at Darien (1698–1700)? The Persistence of Spanish Imperial Power on the Eve of the Demise of the Spanish Habsburgs." *European History Quarterly* 29 (1999): 5-38.

Whatley, C. A. *Bought and Sold for English Gold? Explaining the Union of 1707.* Glasgow: Economic and Social History Society of Scotland, 1994.

Chapter 12

Sir Gregor MacGregor: Cacique of the Never-Never Land of Poyais (1820–1838)

Bennett, Charles E. *General MacGregor: Hero or Rogue?* Jacksonville, FL: River City Press, 2001.

Brooke-Hitching, Edward. "Gregor MacGregor: Clansman, Conquistador and Coloniser on the Fringes of the British Empire," In *Colonial Lives across the British Empire: Imperial Careering in the Long Nineteenth Century*. Edited by David Lambert and Alan Lester, 32–57. Cambridge: Cambridge University Press, 2006.

———. *The Phantom Atlas: The Greatest Myths, Lies and Blunders on Maps*. San Francisco: Chronicle Books, 2018.

Bushnell, David. "The Florida Republic: An Overview." In *La República de las Floridas: Texts and Documents*. Edited by David Bushnell, 8-18. Mexico City: Pan American Institute of Geography and History, 1986.

Calvo, Alfredo Castillero. "La invasion de Gregor MacGregor y la independencia de Panamá." *Tempus: Revista Historia General Medellin* (Colombia), número 3 (April–May 2016): 135-160.

Davis, T. Frederick. "MacGregor's Invasion of Florida, 1817; Together with an Account of His Successors Hubbard and Aury on Amelia Island, East Florida." *Florida Historical Society Quarterly* 7, no. 1 (July 1928): 2-71.

Dawson, Frank Griffith. "William Pitt's Settlement at Black River on the Mosquito Shore: A Challenge to Spain in Central America, 1732–87." *Hispanic American Historical Review* 63, no. 4 (Nov. 1983): 677-706.

Gregg, Richard T. *Gregor MacGregor, Cazique of Poyais, 1786–1845.* London: International Bond and Share Society, 1999.

Gresham, Carling. *General Gregor MacGregor and the 1817 Amelia Island Medal*. Pomona Park, FL: Carling Gresham, 1992.

Griffith, Dawson F. *The First Latin American Debt Crisis: The City of London and the 1822–25 Loan Bubble*. New Haven, CT: Yale University Press, 1990.

Hasbrouck, A. "Gregor MacGregor and the Colonization of Poyais, between 1820 and 1824." *Hispanic American Historical Review* 7 (1927): 438-459.

McGinlay, Paul. *The MacGregor Prince: The Amazing Life of Gregor MacGregor, Prince, Warrior, Hero, Villain, Fraudster*. [Scotland?]: Trossachs Publications, [2004?].

Naylor, Robert A. *Penny Ante Imperialism: The Mosquito Shore and the Bay of Honduras, 1600–1914: A Case Study in British Informal Empire*. Teaneck, NJ: Fairleigh Dickinson University Press, 1989.

Norris, L. David. "Failure Unfolds: The Loss of Amelia Island." In *La República de las Floridas: Texts and Documents*. Edited by David Bushnell, 19–33. Mexico City: Pan American Institute of Geography and History, 1986.

Olien, Michael. "The Miskito Kings and the Line of Succession." *Journal of Anthropological Research* 39 (1983): 211–214.

Owsley Jr., Frank Lawrence, and Gene A. Smith. *Filibusters and Expansionists: Jeffersonian Manifest Destiny, 1800–1821*. Tuscaloosa: University of Alabama Press, 1997.

Rodríguez, Moises Enrique. *Freedom's Mercenaries: British Volunteers in the Wars of Independence of Latin America*, 2 vols. Lanham, MD: Hamilton Books, 2006.

Yeates, F. Willson. "MacGregor's Florida Medal." *Numismatic Chronicle and Journal of the Royal Numismatic Society*, 4th ser., vol. 16 (1916): 196-197.

Chapter 13

Southern Dreams: Confederate Cultural Colonies in Mexico, British Honduras, Venezuela, and Brazil (1865–ca. 1875)

No additional readings.

Index